THORSTEIN VEBLEN

AND HIS CRITICS, 1891–1963

THORSTEIN VEBLEN AND HIS CRITICS, 1891–1963

CONSERVATIVE, LIBERAL, AND RADICAL PERSPECTIVES

RICK TILMAN

PRINCETON UNIVERSITY PRESS

PRINCETON, NEW JERSEY

Copyright © 1992 by Princeton University Press
Published by Princeton University Press, 41 William Street,
Princeton, New Jersey 08540
In the United Kingdom: Princeton University Press, Oxford

Library of Congress Cataloging-in-Publication Data

Tilman, Rick.
Thorstein Veblen and his critics, 1891–1963 / conservative,
liberal, and radical perspectives / Rick Tilman.
p.   cm.
Includes bibliographical references and index.
ISBN 0-691-04286-1
1. Veblen, Thorstein, 1857–1929.
2. Economics—United States—History.   I. Title.
HB119.V4T55   1991   330′.092—dc20   91-21134   CIP

This book has been composed in Linotron Primer

Princeton University Press books are
printed on acid-free paper and meet the guidelines
for permanence and durability of the Committee
on Production Guidelines for Book Longevity
of the Council on Library Resources

Printed in the United States of America

10 9 8 7 6 5 4 3 2 1

To my grandfather,
the late Arthur Yelland (1892–1971),
and my father and mother,
Lee R. and Noma J. Tilman.
Nevadans all.

CONTENTS

T
HORSTEIN VEBLEN (1857–1929) was arguably the most original and penetrating economist and social critic that the United States has produced. His analyses dealt with fundamental social mores; fundamental social, economic, and political processes; and the fundamental belief system that underlies individual behavior, public policy, and social science analysis. A critic of the market economy as he found it developing at the end of the nineteenth and the beginning of the twentieth centuries and of the ideas of economic orthodoxy in the form and with the content then characteristic of the discipline, Veblen was one of the first to identify and emphasize the emergence of the modern corporation, and thereby the corporate system, as a principal mode of economic organization and control. He was one of the principal prehermeneutic analysts of the preconceptions that lay behind all thought and analysis, he identified status emulation as a driving force in economic affairs, provided the language with such terms as *conspicuous consumption, pecuniary versus industrial employment,* and *status emulation,* and was an intellectual ally of the philosopher John Dewey. He was a founder of institutional economics, the leading non-Marxian school of economic heterodoxy in the United States.

As an institutionalist, for many *the* institutionalist, Veblen emphasized that the economy could be, and in fact is most meaningfully, comprehended in holistic terms and as an evolving process. The economy is a nonteleological process of unfolding sequence exhibiting ongoing cumulative causation. It is a complex of institutions, understood as habits of thought and as neither sacrosanct nor ontologically given. It is an arena of conflict. Above all, it is something that could be studied adequately only if one could somehow transcend the self-perceptions and self-rationalizations that, ensconced in culture, come to dominate the mind-sets of individuals and whole populations.

The centerpiece of the neoclassical conception of how the economy works was orthodox value theory. Veblen's critique centered on his denial of the rationality assumption. He argued that people were not "lightning calculators of pleasures or pains, who [oscillate] like a homogeneous globule of desire of happiness under the impulse of stimuli that shift [them] about the area, but leave [them] intact." He believed that people were driven by habits and custom and by whatever constituted achievement in the currently reigning system of status emulation. Veblen believed that marginal utility analysis, indeed the entire apparatus of neoclassical marginalism, was static. It therefore could not capture the important evolutionary, processual elements of the economy, including the changing institutional and power structures of society. Because mainstream economics was not an evolutionary science, Veblen argued in a famous essay, it had become little more than a sophisticated and subtle defense, albeit selectively, of existing institutions, the existing power structure, and the systemic and ideological status quo.

Veblen's critique of capitalism centered on the dominance therein of a nonproductive ruling class, a leisure class practicing conspicuous consumption and thereby setting the stage for status emulation and waste.

Veblen's critique also centered on a distinction he drew between industrial and pecuniary considerations. He argued that business often, indeed conventionally, sabotaged production through its dedication to profit making—its interest in making money rather than in making goods. Conventional economic theory, and indeed the general set of preconceptions of our culture, affirmed that the incentive to produce more goods, and especially more of the goods desired by consumers, and to do so efficiently, operated through the quest for profits. Veblen believed that financial manipulation and decisions and plans made for purposes of pecuniary advantage alone—for example, mergers utilized for the purposes of capturing cash flows in order to finance the debt payments generated by the takeovers themselves for the purpose of financial empire building—subverted and sacrificed the production of goods.

Veblen also stressed the existence of the business cycle—during a period when the phenomenon was largely anathema to formal economic theorists—which he attributed, in part, to the overexpansion of bank credit by pecuniarily oriented financial misanthropes. (Some of Veblen's critique centered on the system *qua* system, and some on the behavior of individuals.)

Veblen elevated an idealized conception of the engineers as a group professionally interested in making goods and juxtaposed to them the businessmen who interfered with making goods in the interests of making money.

Veblen also drew a distinction between technology, which he considered the driving, progressive force in human society and economy, and institutions, which he thought of as ceremonially legitimized arrangements useful at any time for perpetuating the power of the *vested interests*, another distinctive Veblenian term. Indeed, Veblen established a model in which social process was marked, and also marred, by the contest between technology—including the process of industrialization—and the retarding influences of established institutions. It is a curious paradox that the founder of institutionalism had in his analysis a rather negative role for institutions.

The key to both Veblen's analyses of the economic system and his criticisms of orthodox economics resides in his affirmation of methodological collectivism (or holism), in his correlative demotion of methodological individualism, in his affirmation of the reality of social control and social change, and in his correlative denigration of the conventional imagery of laissez-faire and noninterventionism. It resides also in his emphasis on technology as a driving force and his rejection of economic statics as both uninteresting and ideological sedative. Above all, Veblen believed, in the words of one of his chief disciples, Clarence Ayres, that

> the object of dissent is the conception of the market as the guiding mechanism of the economy or, more broadly, the conception of the economy as organized and guided by the market. It simply is not true that scarce resources are allocated among alternative uses by the market. The real determination of whatever allocation occurs in any society is the organizational structure of the society—in short, its institutions. At most, the market only gives effect to prevailing institutions. By focusing attention on the market mechanism, economists have ignored the real allocational mechanism.

Veblen also believed that there exists a valuational process in society that transcends the market. He believed that the basic criterion is whether something enhances the life process ultimately of all people and that an evolutionary theory of value must be constructed out of the habits and customs of social life. Operative in this valuational process, of course, is the process of industrialization, in which technology is constantly at war with established institutions.

The meaning and the status of a body of ideas such as Veblen's are not a function of their creator(s) alone. Consider the situation in which there are several schools of economic thought, A, B, C, and D. There exists A's view of itself, B's view of itself, and so on. There also exists A's view of B, of C, and of D; B's view of A, of C, and of D; and so on. Each views its own ideas and the ideas of the others from the perspective of its own system of thought. There is, therefore, a matrix formed of each school's views of its own and of the other schools' ideas. Which is correct, A's view of A or, say, C's view of A, and so on? Why should any one of these be given a privileged position? It would seem that great insight is potentially to be derived from the matrix comprised of all positions, rather than one. At the very least, it is important to appreciate that the meaning of a body of ideas is dependent on the perspective from which it is viewed. But one can go beyond that, without privileging any particular standpoint, and comprehend the relevant body of ideas from a number of standpoints simultaneously.

There is also the correlative problem that even among those within a particular school, say A, there likely exists differences in formulation of what A is "really all about." So in addition to the total set comprising each school's general view of itself and of the other schools, there also are varied particularistic formulations of each school's view of itself, and by extension of the others.

The foregoing is important in one respect because institutional economics eventually developed several different forms or traditions, only one centering on Veblen, and even that one has had a variety of formulations. But it is important in another, presently relevant, respect: Veblen set forth his own ideas, and they were interpreted and critiqued by other writers. These other writers contemplated and interpreted Veblen's ideas in terms of, and in relation to, their own systems of thought. The status of Veblen, therefore, was very much a matter of the reception and use of his ideas by critics who approached him from variegated standpoints.

Rick Tilman's study of Thorstein Veblen and his critics between 1891 and 1963 is a significant contribution to such an approach to the history of economic thought as I have just outlined. Tilman's study tells us a great deal about the differential reception and use of Veblen's ideas, about how Veblen's ideas were interpreted and critiqued differently depending upon the perspective of the critic, some of whom were friendly and others not. It tells us much about the direct and indirect fecundity of Veblen's ideas, and about the different perspectives on the basis of which Veblen's ideas were interpreted and critiqued. It also informs us that determining "what Veblen really meant or may be understood to mean or signify" is no simple one-dimensional matter. Finally, it helps us to appreciate the roles of ideas and of the further reinterpretation of ideas in the social reconstruction of socioeconomic reality. The latter is of particular significance in regard to Veblen's analyses, in part because he stressed that human institutions were artifacts (that is, social products), and not given by nature; in part because human institutions were neither teleological nor established once and for all time, but were products of processes of working things out; and in part because in those processes of working things out, ideas laden with preconceptions were very important.

Tilman has had to use some taxonomic schema in order to provide some ready order to the enormous diversity of perspectives of those who felt compelled to react in writing to Veblen. He classifies the critics as conservative, liberal, and radical, with three or four varieties within each category. The important thing, it seems to me, is not so much the particular structure of this taxonomic division but both the substance of the variety of larger systems of social thought and Tilman's sensitive perception and subtle appreciation of what Veblen was saying and what his critics understood him to be saying, the latter in the context of their own ideas. Beyond that, of course, the volume is a wonderful introduction to both the ideas of Veblen and the enormous diversity of the social theory of the first half of the twentieth century.

In all the foregoing, and still other respects, this volume will both expand one's intellect in general and further cement one's understanding of the intellect of Thorstein Veblen and its place in the history of economic and social thought.

Warren J. Samuels
Michigan State University

PREFACE

THIS is the first of a trilogy of monographs on the American economist Thorstein Veblen (1857–1929). It focuses on his radical, liberal, and conservative critics since 1891, when analysis of his work began. It assesses the weight of their criticisms, both positive and negative, as well as their sometimes mistaken interpretations of Veblen's work. Veblen was a broad-gauged thinker whose writings cut across disciplinary lines that included history, sociology, government, psychology, anthropology, economics, philosophy and aesthetics. His work has attracted attention from specialists in all these fields. However, a monographic appraisal of Veblen and his critics requires that the scope of the project be narrowed to manageable proportions. My focus is thus restricted to the doctrinal and theoretical aspects of his political economy and social thought and the reaction of critics to them.

The second study, *Thorstein Veblen and His Contemporaries, 1880–1940*, will evaluate his intellectual relationship with his European contemporaries and place him in the context of European social thought from 1880 to 1940. It will focus on the relationship between his ideas and those of such eminent European thinkers as Emil Durkheim, Max Weber, Antonio Labriola, Achille Loria, Knut Wicksell, Arthur Pigou, Georg Simmel, John Hobson, Alfred Marshall, Georges Sorel, Roberto Michels, Vilfredo Pareto, Gaetano Mosca, Ferdinand Tönnies, and Werner Sombart. In short, it will relate his ideas to the late nineteenth and early twentieth century intellectual milieu of Western Europe and Britain.

The third volume in the trilogy *Thorstein Veblen and Current Social Theory* will deal with sociological theories and methods in vogue in the West since 1945. It will analyze Veblen's work in relation to Marxism and critical theory, symbolic interactionism, structural-functionalism, ethnomethodology, exchange theory, and other theoretical trends. Veblen's relationship and contribution to contemporary social theory and methodology will be explicated and clarified and the theoretical potential of his work more fully exploited.

The first published criticism of Thorstein Veblen's work appeared in 1891. The author, George Gunton, found Veblen's views on socialism to be vague and idealistic. He defended status emulation against Veblen's attacks on it by arguing that otherwise human idleness would result. Ideological opposition to Veblen thus emerged some years before the publication of *The Theory of the Leisure Class*. Since 1891, a large volume of writing has appeared on Veblen's life and work. Given the great variety of opinion concerning the nature and significance of his contribution, it is important that this body of scholarship be placed in perspective. Equally important is analysis of the doctrinal underpinning of his opponents' thought, as this is manifest in their criticism of him. This is a study, then, not merely of Veblen but of the ideological structure of his critics' thought, be they radicals, liberals, or conservatives.

It has been necessary both to briefly survey the critics' backgrounds and to engage in textual exegesis of their work on Veblen. If the coherence of the text seems broken at times on account of the many vignettes of American social scientists, the reader will recognize the necessity of providing basic biographical information and placing it in an appropriate historical and political framework.

Little use is made of the reviews of Veblen's books that appeared at the time of their publication. The reason for this is that Joseph Dorfman, in his two major works on Veblen, devoted large sections of both to an elucidation of the reviews. Readers who are interested in the initial reaction of critics to Veblen's books are thus referred to Dorfman's *Thorstein Veblen and His America* and his "New Light on Veblen" in *Essays, Reviews and Reports.* Whatever Dorfman's shortcomings in his approach to Veblen's personal life and family background, he sheds massive illumination on both the development and the cultural and institutional environment of his thought. However, Dorfman's work on Veblen is not "critical" in the sense of expressing ideological opposition to him. Consequently, Dorfman, who is the single most important Veblen scholar, plays but a small role in this study, although I have occasionally used *Thorstein Veblen and His America* as a source of information about Veblen's life and work.

Three important realms of cultural discourse are deliberately neglected, although not ignored, in this book. The first is aesthetics, the second is linguistics, and the third is the communication arts. Veblen's work in all three areas is important and has received considerable attention. His ideas about aesthetics, especially leisure-class aesthetics, have challenged three generations of aestheticians and humanists ranging from classicists and art historians to sculptors, architects, literary critics, novelists, and philosophers. His use and, perhaps, abuse of the English language has attracted the attention of philologists, linguists, semanticists, rhetors, and communication specialists. Any book that claims to deal with Veblen and his critics must focus at times on these facets of his work. Nevertheless, candor compels the author to acknowledge that these aspects of Veblen's thought are not dealt with except when they impinge directly on his political economy and social theory. Those writers whose primary orientation is not political, economic, or sociological are excluded because to do otherwise would require another book.

Many social scientists have analyzed Veblen's work without engaging in the patterned systematic criticism that facilitates ideological comparison or contrast. Since they do not confront the doctrinal structure of his thought or offer alternatives to it, they do not play a significant role in this study. Instead, the focus is on critics who perceived fundamental weaknesses in Veblen's work and attacked significant portions of it.

For two reasons this study is primarily about English-speaking critics of Veblen. First, because the foreign-language literature on Veblen is so large that it would require a separate book to evaluate it, and second, because it would take extraordinary proficiency in foreign tongues to translate from the dozen or so languages essential to such a project. Perhaps only Veblen, himself among American social scientists possessed the requisite knowledge to understand most of the writing about himself in other languages.

Although the emphasis in this study is on ideologically structured criticisms of Veblen that emphasize the deficiencies in his work, most of his critics admitted that his work had its virtues. Obviously, if Veblen were lacking in influence and stature, there would be no reason to evaluate his work or criticism of it. Even the most negatively inclined of his critics, such as Paul Baran, Irving Fisher, and Talcott Parsons, tacitly acknowledge his eminence and impact just by writing about him. Probably few would claim he is comparable to Marx or Weber as a general theorist or seminal thinker. But, perhaps, he approaches their stature when treated in a specifically American context as a theorist and critic of our culture and institutions.

ACKNOWLEDGMENTS

I WOULD LIKE to thank the following individuals for reading and commenting on the manuscript as a whole or in part when it was in draft form: Warren Samuels, John P. Diggins, Bill Dugger, Malcolm Rutherford, Stephen Edgell, and Paul Goldstene. The usual disclaimers hold. I also thank my colleagues Colin Loader, Jeff Waddoups, Keith Schwer, Nasser Daneshvary, Djeto Assane, Andy Fontana, and John Brown for their interest in and support of the Veblen project. I would like to thank Baldwin Ranson for his help with the chapter on Irving Fisher and Edyth Miller for her critique of the part on Frank Knight.

Cultural and intellectual stimulation of a high and sometimes low order and many coarse jests in bad taste about Veblen came from my friends Chuck Rasmussen, Vern Mattson, Pat Goodall, Jeff Halverson, and Scott Locicero. Frank Dempster, Lauri Hahn, Mike Sheehan, Jim Frey, Andy Fry, Terry Knapp, Gene Moehring, Jay and Jamie Coughtrey all listened with good humor to my interminable commentary on the state of Veblen studies. Over the years Bill Marion helped me immeasurably with my writing style and I thank him for it.

My friends at the University of Nevada, Reno, Mike Reed, Glenn Atkinson, and Elmer Rusco often acted as sounding boards when I wanted to discuss Veblen or related topics in institutional economics. My cousin Pete Tilman and his wife, Susan, offered friendship and hospitality during trips to Reno to do research in the University library.

John Kohl, Phillip Lowry, and Lew Karstensson were instrumental in obtaining release time for me from teaching and deserve thanks for their aid.

The University Sabbatical Leave Committee, the University Research Council, and the Research Committee of the College of Business and Economics all provided support during the last ten years or so while I did the basic research on Veblen and his critics.

I would like to thank Paul Sweezy, Daniel Bell, David Riesman, Lev Dobriansky, Arthur Davis, A. W. Coats, and Robert Merton for commenting on those parts of the manuscript that dealt with their own interpretations of Veblen. The usual disclaimers hold. Jay Weinstein and Jo Schneider provided valuable commentary and lent me an as yet unpublished manuscript by the late Louis Schneider, part of which deals with Veblen. Harold Orbach helped me with research on George H. Mead and read a draft of the section that deals with Mead's views on Veblen. William Buxton provided me with insights and information on Talcott Parsons that I would otherwise have overlooked. Ruthemary

Penick, long-time archivist and Veblen devotee at Carleton College, Northfield, Minnesota, was kind enough to give me copies of taped interviews with Veblen's stepdaughters.

My fellow institutional economists in the United States and Western Europe have been a constant source of encouragement and support. I would particularly like to thank Paul Dale Bush, Greg Hayden, Anne Mayhew, Walter Neale, Ron Phillips, Laurence Shute, Marc Tool, Milton Lower, Ingve Ramstead, Larry Reynolds, Charles Leathers, Charles Whalen, Mark Evans, Meb Bolin, Andrew Larkin, Doug Brown, Jim Swaney, Carol Peterson, Ron Stanfield, Bill Waller, Janice Peterson, Lewis Hill, and Harry Trebing.

Bill and Barbara Elkins offered me their friendship and hospitality on many occasion during my stays in London; Stephen, Val, Mathew, and Ben Edgell did the same during my visits to Manchester.

Finally, I would like to thank Janet Banker, Ann Tipton, Pat Hudson, Sherrie Brown, Donna Evans, and Elaine Caravelli for typing drafts of the manuscript and Annette Irwin and Cathy Marion for their support of interlibrary loans at Dickinson Library, University of Nevada, Las Vegas.

. . . . .

The State Historical Society of Wisconsin for permission to quote from materials in the Thorstein Veblen, E. A. Ross, Richard Ely, and John Commons collections.

The Western Historical Manuscript Collection-Columbia, Missouri for permission to quote from the Jacob Warshaw Papers, 1910–1944.

The Columbia University Libraries for permission to quote from the Wesley C. Mitchell Papers, Rare Book and Manuscript Library, Columbia University.

The Yale University Library for permission to quote from the Underhill Moore Papers, Manuscripts and Archives, Yale University Library.

Dr. Gunzelin Schmid Noerr for permission to quote from the letters of Max Horkheimer to Theodor Adorno, Max-Horkheimer-Archiv, Stadtundt Universitats-bibliothek, Frankfurt Am Main, Federal Republic of Germany.

The Trustees of the National Library of Scotland, Edinburgh, Scotland for permission to quote from the letters of Victor Branford to Patrick Geddes.

The Minnesota Historical Society for permission to quote from the letters of Andrew A. Veblen in the Andrew A. Veblen Papers.

The Harvard University Archives for permission to quote from unpublished materials in the Talcott Parsons Papers, Pusey Library.

Wallace W. Atwood, Jr. for permission to quote from the Wallace Atwood, Sr. Papers, Clark University Library, Worcester, Massachusetts.

The Barker Texas History Center, The University of Texas at Austin, for permission to quote from the correspondence of C. E. Ayres in Clarence E. Ayres Papers.

THORSTEIN VEBLEN

AND HIS CRITICS, 1891–1963

Chapter One

VEBLEN: THE MAN AND HIS CRITICS

BIOGRAPHY

T HE CRITICAL writing on Thorstein Veblen (1857–1929) that began to appear around the turn of the twentieth century continues unabated up to the present time. Although critics and commentators disagree about the significance of his work, interest in Veblen has not declined. Mostly reared in Scandinavian-Lutheran communities in the Midwest, he was the fourth son of Norwegian immigrant farmers who raised a large family, most of whom received higher education. Several of the Veblen children went to Carleton College in Minnesota; there Thorstein obtained his training in economics and philosophy under John Bates Clark, who later became a prominent American economist. After receiving his bachelor's degree at Carleton, Veblen went to Johns Hopkins for graduate study. After a short stay, he transferred to Yale, where he obtained his doctorate in philosophy and economics in 1884 while studying under such eminent academics as Noah Porter and William Graham Sumner.

He was then unemployed for seven years, most of which was spent on the farms of relatives or in-laws in the Midwest. Veblen's agnosticism made him unacceptable to schools with religious affiliations and he had not yet established a reputation in economics. Finally, in 1891 he obtained a graduate position at Cornell University, where he once again became a Ph.D. candidate. The economist A. Laurence Laughlin was impressed by him and in 1892, when Laughlin moved to the newly founded University of Chicago, took Veblen with him. Veblen soon became managing editor of the *Journal of Political Economy* and began publishing in the field of economics. In 1899 his book, *The Theory of the Leisure Class*, appeared and achieved a fame all its own. But Veblen's personal idiosyncrasies and his failure to properly "advertise" the university angered the administration at Chicago and he had to leave. His next job was at Stanford where he encountered similar difficulties that were exacerbated by his "womanizing." He was forced to move again, this time to the University of Missouri.

World War I found Veblen briefly in Washington as an employee of the Food Administration. At the end of the war, he served for a short time as one of the editors of the *Dial*, a journal of literary and political opinion, and on the faculty of the recently founded New School for Social Research in New York City. By then, even though his reputation as an original thinker had reached its peak, his academic career was at an end. Veblen retired and moved to California, near Stanford, where he lived an isolated existence in an old house in the hills. He died in August 1929, shortly before the start of the depression.

VEBLEN THE MAN

Thorstein Veblen's reputation as a seminal thinker in economics and sociology is well established thanks in part to the massive study of him by Joseph Dorfman. Dorfman gave an able analysis of Veblen's economics and sociology even if he failed to offer a clear or consistent portrayal of him as a human being. Veblen scholars owe Dorfman a serious debt, but the lacunae left by him as regards Veblen's personal traits and temperament can be filled in part by using materials not available between 1926 and 1934 when he wrote *Thorstein Veblen and His America*.[1] Future biographers of Veblen may want to revise Dorfman's conclusions regarding Veblen's acquisition of English, the cultural and social isolation of the Veblen family, and its material circumstances when he was young. In any case, readers interested in Veblen's biography are referred to Dorfman's writings on him even though Dorfman is not always a reliable source of information as regards his childhood and adolescence.

Perhaps the most authoritative criticism of Dorfman's *Thorstein Veblen and His America* came from Andrew Veblen (1848–1933), Thorstein's older brother, professor of mathematics, and father of Oswald Veblen, the eminent American mathematician. The older Veblen had corresponded with Dorfman while he was writing his magnus opus and read drafts of it before it was published. He could see little virtue in them and believed that they included several fundamental misinterpretations of his brother's life. Andrew was particularly incensed at Dorfman's claims that Thorstein only learned English well when he was an adult. In a letter to Dorfman written in 1930, Veblen commented that

> Thorstein had English-speaking playmates as early as he could toddle 1/8 of a mile to the nearest neighbor; and before that the neighbor's children were daily at our house or in the yard. His four older brothers and sisters knew and spoke English, with these other children, and more and more between themselves. Thorstein was sent to school before he filled five years. He had a bilingual training in speech, from the start. When he came to Carleton he spoke as correct and idiomatic English as any of the young people he en-

countered, and his rhetoricals, (not oratoricals) at once attracted attention for his facility in the use of idiomatic English.[2]

However, Andrew Veblen told Dorfman that the myth that he knew no English until he was an adult may have been cultivated by Thorstein for reasons of his own. But he concluded that

if you still believe these stories of his ignorance of English, all I can say is that you do not lack company in your willing credulity. If he actually succeeded in carrying off such a process of deceit and delusion it is another tribute to his cleverness. I do not know why I should waste any more words on this myth about his ignorance of English, when as a matter of fact he was better equipped than any of his schoolmates and even some of the instructors.[3]

Veblen's older brother also believed that Dorfman greatly exaggerated the cultural isolation of the Norwegian settlement in which the Veblen family lived and pointed to the fact that many of their neighbors and acquaintances were of Yankee origin and still others were Catholics. It is also interesting to note that many of the Veblen siblings married individuals of British ethnic origin. It appears, then, that Veblen's idiosyncratic personality and ideas had sources other than the social marginality induced by living in an ethnic Norwegian environment.

Both of Veblen's marriages were to women who either were or became mentally or emotionally ill. Of course, much is made of Veblen's "womanizing," but insufficient attention is paid to the mental state of his wives as a plausible explanation of this. Andrew Veblen wrote of his first wife that

she was interested in a theosophical establishment, the headquarters of which I understood was situated at Halcyon. This was a branch of the cult of theosophy, which consisted of followers of Madame Blavatsky. . . . she was much absorbed in spiritual-religious matters and problems.[4]

Although Veblen divorced Ellen Rolfe Veblen in 1911, they apparently corresponded for many years thereafter. Only one letter has survived, but it is quite revealing of her state of mind:

Think of all that has happened in our lifetime! The Bahai Movement, Spiritualism, Theosophy, Christian Science, Darwin, Spencer, Shaw, Mills, James, Edmund Carpenter, Ghandi, Blavatsky, Healers of all sorts, the upheaval of the nation, Bolshevism, Karl Marx, the world war in progress [unintelligible], radio, art, and, as I hear, a new ray which renders metal permanently hot. Then, also, the oscilloscope.[5]

History does not record Veblen's reaction to this bizarre juxtaposition of ideas, thinkers, religious movements, and inventions, but the quotation, from a letter written in 1920, does provide insight into his former wife's mind-set and emotional state.

Veblen's second wife, Ann Fessenden Bradley, a former student whom he married in 1914, had to be committed to Maclean Hospital, a mental asylum, in 1919. Her brother-in-law, Wallace Atwood, president of Clark University in Worcester, Massachusetts, told Veblen after a visit with Mrs. Veblen that

> her mind of course wanders far afield, but the fact that it doesn't linger long on any one particular illusion, but flits about from one to another, is to me quite encouraging. She is quite conscious of her own behavior, and that also is encouraging to me. She knows that she gets overexcited and knows what she does at those times.[6]

That university administrators used Veblen's dalliances with women as a reason for firing him is beyond doubt. Evidence of this is provided in a sanctimonious message written by the president of Stanford to the president of the University of Chicago. In a letter marked "confidential," David Starr Jordan told Henry Pratt Judson that

> I have been able, with the help of Mrs. Veblen, to find out the truth in detail as to Professor Veblen's relations. He seems unable to resist the "femme mecomprise." It is fair to say, that in my final talk with him, he [indecipherable] behaved in manly fashion, with no attempt at denial or evasion. He has tendered his resignation to later effect at my discretion. This will probably mean with July of next year. For the University cannot condone these matters, much as its officials may feel compassion for the individual.[7]

Clearly, Veblen's philandering was offensive to academic administrators. Yet the truth about his several dismissals from academic posts is more complex, for his ideological leanings also influenced administrators against him. Interestingly, however, President Jordan's later correspondence with Veblen indicates that he still read and admired Veblen's work and bore him no personal ill will.[8]

Perhaps the most focused analysis of Veblen the man came from Jacob Warshaw, professor of romance languages at the University of Missouri, who came to know him well during his seven-year stay in Columbia. Warshaw read Dorfman's *Thorstein Veblen and His America* when it was published in 1934. He believed that while it mostly did justice to Veblen's sociology and economics, it failed to adequately capture some of his basic personality traits. The following reflections are based on his acquaintance with Veblen when the latter was in his mid- to late fifties.

> Though I always felt sorry for Veblen as a misunderstood man and a man of sorrows—if he had known of my compassion he would have withered me

with a look—I never thought of him as, in his heart, the suave, imperturbable, sphinx-like character who stands out in Dorfman. He struck me rather as a man of spontaneous passions who had found it not the easiest task in the world to keep smiling and to say nothing.[9]

The only scholarly portrait of Veblen based on primary sources available to us is the Dorfman book. All commentaries on his personality made by other Veblen scholars are from this source and are thus derivative. Obviously, Warshaw knew Veblen far better than Dorfman, so his commentaries on the man and on Dorfman's study of him are an invaluable source of information. Up to this time, the thirteen-page Warshaw sketch has rarely been used, but it is likely that some future revisionist biographer of Veblen will systematically exploit it. However, the significant point is that at least one of Veblen's contemporaries saw him differently than he is portrayed in Dorfman.

The general impression that I get from Dorfman is that Veblen was a quiet, suave, passionless person who broke loose only once or twice in his life and never laughed. Had I not known Veblen pretty well that would have been my picture of him out of Dorfman. My recollections, however, are different. Veblen could get as irritated as the next man and gave signs of his irritation. . . . He once gave me a dirty look when I declined one of his Russian cigarettes on the ground that my stomach was out of whack and that I thought I was losing weight through smoking too much. . . . If you didn't appreciate a joke of his, a frown would form on his face or his eyes would take on a somber look.[10]

For those who remain convinced of the value of psychobiography in explaining the relationship between personality and theory, Warshaw's analysis of Dorfman's Veblen is more penetrating than either Dorfman's or David Riesman's study, although the latter relied heavily on Dorfman for information regarding Veblen. In perhaps Warshaw's most discerning comments he wrote

The point that I would make is that, under the surface, Veblen was highly emotional. His philanderings with women are one indication. His constant, bitter irony and sarcasm—which are good exhaust valves when you are inhibited from doing bodily damage—may be regarded as another. To realize this emotional quality in Veblen is, it seems to me, to get another light on his ideas and projects, to forgive him most of his cynicism, and to find him a more sympathetic and human individual than he is usually credited with being. He was never a cold-blooded, calculating radical—at least, so it appears to me.[11]

Veblen's sense of humor and the emotional structure it provides evidence of were not adequately expressed in his sardonic scholarly posture. The bitter cynicism and sarcasm noted by Dorfman that found its outlet in his theories was only one part of his temperament. Warshaw pointed to another aspect of it:

> As for his ability to smile and laugh, I can say that I never found him mark-edly lacking in it. At 911 Lowry Street, where he was to a certain extent in the public gaze, his smile was somewhat pinched and guarded, but in our rambles over the golf links it was frequent, natural, and infectious. In fact, his smile is one of the features that I best remember him by. It was a kindly, amused, rather Olympian smile, and thoroughly genuine. I have also heard him laugh—not once, but a number of times.[12]

Dorfman treated Veblen essentially as a social scientist and sati-rist whose main interests were the social order, the government, and the economy. But Warshaw discerningly portrayed the humanist in him that might be expected of a scholar of Romance languages and literature.

> Few of the readers of Dorfman will realize after they have finished the book that they have been reviewing the life of one of the most learned and most curious of latter-day humanists. By "humanist" I mean in this case "a lover of learning" and not merely "a lover of polite learning or the humanities," as was true during the Renaissance. . . . It is this insatiable curiosity and this accumulation of all kinds of knowledge that I should call Veblen's hu-manism. There was probably a limit to the stock of knowledge that he could hold and manipulate, but I never saw it reached. He would have been in his glory among the Renaissance humanists or the eighteenth-century encyclopedists.[13]

Since Warshaw was an accomplished linguist in his own right, his comments on Veblen are significant and provide still another link with his humanism.

> As a linguist alone, Veblen was unusual. Among students the legend ran that he knew twenty-six languages. The combination of languages that he could handle was somewhat uncommon, It included, along with the classics and the more widely known modern languages, Spanish, Dutch, and the Scandinavian tongues, including Icelandic. I do not doubt that Veblen had a working knowledge of other languages not usually studied and that he was capable, in an incredibly short time, of "getting up" in any language that he was interested in or had need of. His accomplishments in French, Spanish, and Italian I can vouch for. Whether or not he could speak them I can't be sure. But he surprised me frequently with his familiarity with minutiae of the Romance literatures and once or twice with his shrewd analyses of the history of Romance words. I did not know at the time that he had once had ambitions of becoming a philologist.[14]

Warshaw was also an observer of Veblen's personal idiosyncracies and these oddities shed light not only on his personal tastes, but on his capacity for absorbing and assimilating knowledge. Warshaw interpreted them this way:

> He preferred not to have anybody read his newspaper over his shoulder. That may have been due either to his abnormal personal sensitiveness or to his faculty, mentioned several times to me by one of his close friends, of being able to read two columns of print simultaneously—a circumstance that would keep him and the onlooker woefully out of step.[15]

The last claim, that Veblen could read two columns of print simultaneously, if true, may shed light on how it was that he was able to master such an extraordinary amount of printed material.

Warshaw also knew the personal side of Veblen from the perspective of one who had enjoyed the hospitality of the Veblen home, an opportunity of which few could boast.

> He could be whole-heartedly congenial, as the few persons who visited him in his home can testify. Lounging about in his loose dressing-gown and looking not nearly as anemic and fragile as in his street clothes, he reminded one, with his drooping mustaches and Nordic features, of nothing so much as a hospitable Viking taking his ease at his own fireside. At such times, he was at his best, pouring out curious information, throwing off a little malicious gossip which, in view of his seclusiveness, he must have picked miraculously out of the air, mixing picturesque slang with brilliant phrases of his own coinage, solicitously watching out for his guests' comfort, and in general, behaving like a "regular guy." An evening with him—when you were fortunate enough to get one—was as good as a French salon or an eighteenth century London coffee-house. When it was over you wished that you had had a Boswellian memory and eye.[16]

Warshaw tellingly concluded that "the fact is that Veblen the friendly companion was quite a different person from Veblen the ponderous, pontifical writer and dangerous iconoclast."[17]

An amusing account of a New York bookstore trying to sell a customer a copy of *The Theory of the Leisure Class* shortly after the end of World War I also provides insight into the character of our central figure. Madge Jenison, a bookseller, recalled that

> a man used to appear every six or eight weeks quite regularly, an ascetic, mysterious person with keys to unlock things, I took him to be, and with a gentle air. He wore his hair long and looked Scandinavian. I do not know just why or when I made him a Swedenborgian minister. . . . I used to try to interest him in economics. . . . I even once tried to get him to begin with *The Theory of the Leisure Class*. I explained to him what a brilliant port of entry

it is to social consciousness. But it became clear that if he was ever to be interested in sociology and economics, he would not be interested in them by me. He listened attentively to all I said and melted like a snow drop through the door. One day he ordered a volume of Latin hymns. "I shall have to take your name because we will order this expressly for you," I told him. "We shall not have an audience for such a book as this again in a long time, I am afraid." "My name is Thorstein Veblen," he breathed rather than said.[18]

Why did Veblen not explain in his numerous visits to the bookstore who he was, particularly after the store tried to sell him a copy of a famous book he wrote? No doubt his droll sense of humor needed some outlet at times, and as he grew older perhaps there were fewer opportunities to express it. Nevertheless, the episode recounted by Jenison reveals an unusual detachment from self or, perhaps, unusual qualities of self-deprecation.

Andrew Veblen, in a letter to economist Edward Bemis, who had once been Veblen's colleague at Chicago, described his brother's death in 1929 in these words:

My youngest daughter with her husband and two children, near, and at times with, whom he had lived in Chicago, made him a visit in July; and they, as well as Becky [his stepdaughter], were there with him when he was taken ill and died. It seemed he had been anticipating, lately, that the end might come though this only became evident afterward. He was taken with a fainting attack, and lived only an hour, or a little more, part of the time he was conscious, but did not seem to have much pain. This was the afternoon of August 3.[19]

Thus ended the life of the American iconoclast and satirist and, perhaps, unwitting founder of institutional economics. Most important, his thought had achieved considerable notoriety and several identifiable critical attitudes toward it were already crystallizing.

Veblen's Critics

However, with the exception of the attacks of George Gunton and John Cummings on Veblen in 1891 and 1899 respectively, there were no systematic critical analyses of Veblen of any length until 1924. In that year, in addition to the study published by William Jaffe in French, a number of eminent American economists contributed to a set of essays edited by Rexford G. Tugwell. The title of the book was *The Trend of Economics* and it surveyed recent developments in American economics from various ideological perspectives. Such luminaries of the economics profession as Morris Copeland, Sumner Schlichter, Frank Knight, Wesley Mitchell, Paul Douglas, and John M. Clark contributed original essays, most of which mentioned Veblen, although he was not the central figure in the book. Nevertheless, he was subjected to praise and criticism from liberals and conservatives alike that was to establish patterns of considerable durability. Ideological opponents already felt obliged to read him if only to refute him. For example, Frank Knight was indignant with Veblen's views on the subject of causation in history and culture,[20] John M. Clark was skeptical about Veblen's half-truths about business enterprise,[21] Wesley Mitchell wondered whether he had grasped the whole truth regarding the impact of the machine process on human nature,[22] and Paul Douglas felt Veblen's work was marred "by excessive theorizing upon scanty biological and psychological evidence."[23] At this point in the development of Veblen studies, critics portrayed him as either a utopian visionary or a proponent of liberal experimentalism, although the view also surfaced that he might even be a radical conservative who thought progressive change impossible. A few years later, Max Lerner, at the time a radical apologist for Veblen, shrewdly commented that

> Veblen's was perhaps the most considerable and creative body of social thought that America has produced. While his thinking does not fall easily into the accepted categories of liberalism and radicalism, he has affected both traditions powerfully. His intellectual attitudes and methods are those of liberalism, especially in his appearance of disinterestedness and his lack of a program of real direction; but his criticism of capitalist society is drastic and, at least in its implications, revolutionary. . . . his most powerful effect was not on academic theory but on economic opinion and policy. He was in no small measure responsible for the trend toward social control in an age dominated by business enterprise.[24]

That Veblen himself was no reformist liberal will be argued throughout this study. But the questions that Veblen's role in the New Deal raise concern both the identification and measurement of intellectual influences on public policies. No thinker will appear to exert any influence if all that counts as influence is uncritical subscription to the minute details of his doctrine. Yet tracing lines of influence becomes an exercise in naïveté if every policymaker's claims about the systematic theoretical structure and ideational origins of his policies are accepted.

The view that Veblen presented a single, unambiguous set of theories or ideas will seem implausible to many. It would be hard to find a writer who indulged himself more in wit, irony, paradox, dialectical rhetoric, and convoluted language. Clearly, the ambiguity of his legacy does not derive just from its being filtered through the ideological lenses of various political persuasions. But it is no mere rhetorical ploy to point out that these lenses have played an important part in the distortion of American intellectual history and of Veblen's role in it. Social scientists and journalists writing in the 1930s and 1940s were particularly prone, often with inadequate justification, to portray Veblen as a main source of influence in the creation of the social welfare and regulatory policies of the New and Fair Deals.

By the late 1950s, so much scholarship was devoted to Veblen that he had been scrutinized from almost every conceivable political and ideological angle. Indeed, in 1957 Arnold Rogow was able to make these penetrating comments:

> Those who stand to the left of events, as do Mills, Rosenberg, Davis and a minority of social scientists, are apt to take from Veblen substance and sensitivity. Those who stand in the middle of events, as do Riesman and a majority of social scientists, are apt to respond, perhaps nostalgically, to the sensitivity alone. And if one stands to the right of events (or properly speaking not in the stream at all), as do most of the students, he will see in Veblen neither substance nor sensitivity.[25]

At the same time, however, the economist Kenneth Boulding wrote that

> in Veblen we see a rather grandiose but at the same time ramshackle attempt to draw widely on psychology, sociology, and anthropology in the search for interpolations of economic life—but he draws on an instinct psychology, a racist anthropology, a mechanistic biology, and an analogical sociology, and the result while an admirable medium for preaching (disguised as objective science) is hardly a durable system.[26]

But neoinstitutionalist Allan Gruchy wrote in rebuttal that

> a careful reading of Veblen will not show that he used an "instinct psychology" or "racist anthropology." He was concerned not with instinctive or racist behavior, but institutionally shaped behavior. His analysis after all, stressed the evolution and functioning of economic institutions. He used the "instinct of workmanship" and "parental bent" to analyze and evaluate institutions, not ultimate motivation.[27]

As long ago as 1954, A. W. Coats complained that Gruchy's *Modern Economic Thought: The American Contribution* (1947) was too "eulogistic" of Veblen and that this was not uncommon among early writings on Veblen. He intriguingly commented, however, that the road was "now being prepared for a definitive reappraisal of Veblen's entire system of thought."[28] Although Coats wrote these words a generation and a half ago, it does not appear that this goal is much closer now that it was in 1954. The reasons for this are evident. Veblen was a political economist; political economy is an inherently value-laden enterprise and "value-laden" is not to be understood in any trivial sense. The "definitive reappraisal" that Coats prescribed is only possible if the discipline of economics is politically and ideologically unified. That it is not now and unlikely to be in what Veblen called the "calculable future" is evident judging from the ideological fragmentation that has produced many different groupings of economists and journals with conflicting political and methodological orientations. In short, the definitive reappraisal recommended by Coats is impossible both in the politically fragmented discipline of economics and in sociology, the other discipline to which Veblen made a notable contribution.

No consensus now exists on the value or even the meaning of Veblen's work. This can easily be illustrated by pointing to divergent interpretations of both that have persisted for a long time. For example, in 1928 the American economist Clair Wilcox sardonically wrote that

in Veblen we have the radical philosopher, the prejudiced critic, the satirist who, behind his scientific pose, does not scruple to handle facts with violence that he may the more vehemently condemn the competitive order.[29]

Veblen's friend and admirer Leon Ardzrooni described him in 1934 as "a keen analyst of current economic forces and as a man endowed with something of a prophetic insight into things."[30] More recently, Donald Walker described him as someone "primarily animated by normative convictions," who "wrote as a publicist,"and was "a shaper of attitudes, a social philosopher and ideologist";[31] while H. F. Cruise commented on his capacity for "disturbing these habits of vested compliance" through the "distorting mirror of satire and the Veblenian way of calculated disrespect."[32]

Perhaps the least flattering estimate of Veblen in recent years comes from the black economist Thomas Sowell, himself a Veblen scholar. This is not unexpected in view of Sowell's political conservatism and his affiliation with the strongly procorporate and anticommunist Hoover Institution. In an "authoritative" entry in *The New Palgrave, A Dictionary of Economics*, Sowell found no real merit or validity in Veblen's work and concluded that "it is difficult to see how economics as it exists today is any different from what it would have been had there been no Thorstein Veblen."[33] Were this statement applied to the discipline of economics as a whole, its inaccuracy would be evident. However, it is likely from the context in which Sowell wrote that he did not regard heterodox forms of economics such as neo-Marxism, neoinstitutionalism, social economics, and perhaps post-Keynesianism as legitimate kinds of economic inquiry. Sowell's statement was apparently intended to apply to an economics profession that is so entirely neoclassical in orientation that dissenters such as Veblen are banished to the hinterlands of sociology and social philosophy. Although Sowell's statement rests on paradigmatic assumptions that fundamentally distort what actually exists in the politically fragmented discipline of economics, it is important in that it exemplifies a mind-set that has long existed in American neoclassical economics. Indeed, it shows that the doctrinal biases Veblen fought against in his own time are still both tenacious and influential. Their pervasiveness can only lend legitimacy to an enterprise such as this that seeks to account for the persistence of such interpretations of the corpus Vebleniana. In 1973 Joseph Dorfman wrote in summation of the controversy over Veblen that

> as to the merits of his work, opinions differ more widely and more fervently than on any other writer of equal prominence. He is rated among the great economists of history, or as no economist at all; as a great original pioneer or as a critic and satirist without constructive talent or achievement. And he was, one might almost say, all of these things; from different standpoints and by different criteria, each of which it is possible to understand and even to appreciate. One thing at least can be said. If he chose to paint after a futurist technique of his own devising, it was not for lack of capacity to master the academic canons.[34]

Veblen, a man of massive erudition, had few peers when it came to a knowledge of the social sciences, philosophy, and languages; mostly his mastery of the academic canons is thus not in doubt. It is his utilization of them to achieve political and moral ends not shared by his critics that is the focal point of the controversy.

So much has been written about the nature and role of ideology in recent years that it would be difficult to contribute to this discourse conceptually. Veblen himself provided much useful commentary on this subject. But he also often unintentionally provided the means of ideological legitimation for his own doctrinal manipulation; that is, he unwittingly aided those wishing to use his work for their own professional purposes, political programs, and public policies.

However, ideologies also serve either to sustain or erode social relations of domination and exploitation. Veblen was a political intellectual who tried to undermine the latter through his own writing. Many of his most serious critics realized this, which may account for the volatile and inflammatory nature of their response to him. After all, who wants to be accused of working intellectually to sustain structures of domination and exploitation, not to mention waste and war?

Veblen was ultimately interpreted by many of his conservative critics and by more than a few of the liberals as believing that whatever is, is wrong. But what left-liberal or radical worth his or her salt could ignore the intellectual sustenance Veblen made available for erosion of existing structures? The Nobel laureate Kenneth J. Arrow commented in this respect that "the world is indeed full of injustices, and the writings of economists full of attempts to disguise them but these propositions [for Veblen] are causes for laughter and scorn not for agitation."[35]

Veblen understood that a critique of ideology that simply reduced ideological and theoretical developments to the mere expression of social relations would ignore the fact that they were attempts to solve problems of pressing importance. It was evident, however, that he also believed that the main ideological function of neoclassical economics was to obfuscate structures of domination and exploitation and, it might be added, waste.

THE IDEOLOGIES OF CONSERVATISM, LIBERALISM, AND RADICALISM

Do the ideological traits and doctrinal assumptions of liberalism, conservatism, and radicalism have a coherence and continuity that make them a generic type-form? Do the three leading Western political creeds lend themselves to the construction of ideal types with visible domain and paradigmatic assumptions? If so, this should be evident in liberal, conservative, and radical critiques of a broad-gauged thinker like Veblen who managed to offend important figures in every major ideological camp at some point in his career. As examples of each critique are analyzed, the degree to which the conventional ideological sterotypes are adequate as well as deficient will become more apparent. This book is thus a comparative study of generically Western but specifically American political ideologies and social philosophies as well as an appraisal of appraisals of the ideological structure of Veblen's thought.

An unanswered question is whether the terms *conservative, liberal,* and *radical* possess a continuity and coherence of meaning in twentieth-century America. One way to determine this is to show that the same assumptions and criticisms that informed Veblen's critics at the turn of the century are still current today. If this is so, the generic traits of conservatism, for example, should repeatedly exhibit themselves in conservative analyses of Veblen's work. By the same token, the generic traits of liberalism and radicalism should also be evident in liberal and radical critiques of him. Or, if they are not, doctrinal discontinuities and inconsistencies in the body of literature that interprets him can be located and exposed.

The generic traits of an ideological position should be evident in the particular writings of an ideologue. Only those not consciously aware of their own values and the parts of whose creed that are not logically consistent with each other will fail to qualify as ideologues. It would be surprising to discover that such people have written about Veblen; indeed, practically none did. Veblen was in his own way such a politically, morally, and aesthetically volatile thinker that those who systematically confronted his thought developed a more crystallized and formal ideological position as a result. Of course, this is an important claim that there is no satisfactory way of proving, short of in-depth interviews with people, most of whom are long dead. Consequently, I will do what is second best, which is to rely on textual exegesis of their writings on Veblen. It is apparent, however, that mere textual exegesis of his writings and interpretation of biographical data about his life, important as these are, will not adequately explain the use and abuse of Veblen's ideas by his interpreters. The key to understanding the latter lies in analyzing the ideological content of these interpreters' thinking on Veblen and related topics; in short, in laying bare the *Weltanschauung* of conservative, liberal, and radical Veblen scholars.

The different receptions that Veblen's critics gave to his work have varied greatly, depending upon their domain or paradigmatic assumptions. These assumptions involve the underpinnings of the human sciences as these have been understood since the Victorian Era. They include (1) views of human nature, (2) social value theories, that is, criteria of choice, (3) attitudes toward property and property rights and, closely related to these, theories of economic exploitation, (4) theories of ethics by which to measure both individual and social behavior or, at least, sets of moral attitudes, (5) theories of the state and its "proper" role in society, (6) views both of how the modern economy *is* organized and functions as well as prescriptive analyses of how it *should* be organized and function, and (7) views of what the social order consists of, of what holds it together, and of how best to study it. Although it is not possible in each instance to delineate in any detail these assumptions made by Veblen scholars, important aspects of them can be articulated. Consequently, the paradigmatic and domain assumptions of each doctrinal position, based on textual exegesis of the writings of Veblen's critics, are summarized. This summation amplifies the difficulty that interpreters of ideology encounter when they analyze doctrinal structures that cut across the political spectrum from far left to extreme right and converge with three generations of scholarship on one of the most inflammatory thinkers America has produced.

Chapter Two

CONSERVATIVE CRITICS: THE EARLY PERIOD

ONSERVATIVE economists have occasionally praised Thorstein Veblen for his brilliance and encyclopedic learning. John Cummings (1899), Irving Fisher (1909), and Richard Teggart (1932), mostly conceded his massive, if iconoclastic, intellect and his enormous erudition. Yet they ultimately found little of substantive value in his work in economics or the other social studies. Considered as a study in comparative ideology, the sharp contrast between Veblen and his conservative critics suggests the unlikelihood of reaching agreement on fundamental issues in political economy. The reader is thus forewarned that the points that separate Veblen from his conservative opponents are perennial areas of conflict in the history of economic and social theory. But it is also worth noting that the political conservatism of his critics is ultimately rooted in the premises of classical liberalism not in the organic-aristocratic tradition of conservatism. It is Adam Smith, Jeremy Bentham, and David Ricardo upon whom they draw, not late medieval or early modern organicism.

JOHN CUMMINGS ON VEBLEN

John Cummings (1868–1936) was the only conservative critic of Veblen who was well acquainted with him personally. For many years, he was Veblen's colleague at Chicago and edited the *Journal of Political Economy* after Veblen left Chicago for Stanford. Cummings's professional career also included a long stint at Harvard, as well as service with the Federal Reserve Board. Politically, he was quite conservative at the time he wrote about Veblen's thought.[1] However, according to Joseph Dorfman, Cummings later had a fundamental change of heart regarding the value of Veblen's work. Indeed, Cummings heaped lavish praise on Veblen and in 1931 wrote, "I have often wondered how I could have been so blind."[2]

But given Cummings's ideological position in 1899, the year he wrote a lengthy review of *The Theory of the Leisure Class*, he could not have reacted to Veblen's ideas differently than he did; for Cummings clearly worked within the narrow parameters of the paradigm of neoclassical economics. He exemplified what was, from Veblen's perspective, deficient about conventional economics, namely, that it was an expression of classical liberal ideology. Believing as he did that the role of the regime of competition was to defend rights of property and vested interests, Veblen could only view the evolution of neoclassical economics as an adaptive ideological rationalization of laissez-faire and as a vehicle for maintaining a constitution of perpetual privilege.

On the only known occasion in which he answered a critic, Veblen responded to "Mr. Cummings' Strictures."[3] His satirical abilities were probably never surpassed in his own work and certainly never put in more subtle form than when he rebutted his former colleague's defense of the "idols of the tribe." The impression he conveys to his readers is that while Cummings is sincere in his allegations, he does not understand the book on which he has written a thirty-page review. It requires careful scrutiny of the text, however, to appreciate the subtlety of Veblen's jibes. For example, Veblen wrote that "the paper is notable for its earnestness,"[4] but "earnestness" here seems to mean sincere but stupid. As usual, Veblen, tongue in cheek, claimed that he was not making value judgments but rather was involved in detached scientific observation that Cummings did not understand. He complained that "the argument of the book deals with the causal, not with the moral competence of the phenomena which it takes up. The former is a question for the economist, the latter for the moralist."[5] Veblen slyly commented that the scientist's "inability to keep the cultural value and the moral content of these categories apart may reflect credit upon the state of such a person's sentiments, but it detracts from his scientific competence."[6] Obviously he was referring here to Cummings and those who make similar epistemological errors. However, Veblen readily admitted that many of Cummings's criticisms could have been avoided had he [Veblen] been more precise. Veblen complained that although Cummings made his points clearly, his use of the logical principle of the excluded middle led him to view the subject matter of *The Theory of the Leisure Class* in terms of "exclusive alternative."

Cummings linked Veblen's choice and use of words with his lack of "objectivity" as a social scientist. Veblen was accused of claiming that he did not make moral and aesthetic judgments, while doing so at every available opportunity. Indeed, Cummings complained that Veblen's "use of obviously ethical terms without any declared ethical significance suggests a sophistry which amounts almost to duplicity. . . . The consistency characterizing the selection of the epithets argues a conscious purpose on the part of the author to convey exactly those judgments which are so perfunctorily denied."[7] However, Cummings conceded that Veblen was damnably clever in his use and choice of words. Nevertheless, the evidence indicates that he was making ethical judgments regarding social institutions while pretending not to do so. Veblen was "clearly a master of sophistical dialectic."[8]

Individual Ends versus Generic Ends

Perhaps the main difference between Veblen and Cummings as regards individual tastes and preferences was over what economists were later to call "interpersonal utility functions." Cummings believed that, in the final analysis, all tastes and preferences are individual in nature and that what Veblen called the "generically human" can only be expressed subjectively through individual choice. But Veblen believed that certain ends are generic and he pointed to the fact that a coherent set of values

> is to be found in a community of descent, traditions, and circumstances, past and present, among men living in any given community, and in a less degree among men in all communities. It is because men's notions of the generically human, of what is the legitimate end of life, does not differ incalculably from man to man that men are able to live in communities and to hold common interests.[9]

Cummings believed that Veblen's use of such terms as *generically human* and *impersonal usefulness* were inappropriate, for the former is an "imaginary and fictitious phantom" and the latter has no meaning apart from the individuals who conceive it.[10] Clearly, Cummings, like many other neoclassicists of the time, subscribed to a methodological individualism that atomizes the social order to the point at which it is no longer possible to assert the collective nature of mankind. Indeed, he wrote indignantly

> that is "useful" which ministers to our wants individually and severally, and an impersonal serving of the "generically human" is utterly inconceivable. That which any individual sets up to be the "generically human" proves on analysis to be so only on the assumption that all other human beings exactly resemble the one who undertakes to declare what the "generically human" is. This assumption is obviously unwarranted, but even if it were true, it would still be true that the "generically human" was an individual conception; and the declaration of one individual would carry no *ex cathedra* weight of authority over other similar declarations, since the coincidence of the individual conception with the truly generic would be in any event a most phenomenally accidental occurrence, susceptible of no verification whatever.[11]

Cummings believed that economic values are based only on the subjective preference of individuals and have no meaning apart from the person who prefers them; interpersonal comparisons of utility are thus meaningless. If all value is purely subjective in nature and all preferences are ultimately expressed through individuals, it is incorrect to speak of the "generically human" and of "impersonal usefulness." To illustrate, Cummings complained of Veblen's claim that the erection of expensive church edifices amounts to sheer waste. This is an objectionable example of Veblen's bias because he failed to recognize "that devotional sense is just as generically human as the sense of cold, and the desire for warmth and nourishment!"[12] Cummings did not believe that judgments should be made regarding the tastes or preferences of either the community or individuals. Rather, these are given and their origins and development are of no concern to the professional economist. Since Veblen used a critical-genetic method to explain their evolution and relevance and focused on those values that are emulatory in nature, he assumed a role unbecoming to an economist.

The Business versus Industry Dichotomy

Cummings believed the Veblenian distinction between industrial and business pursuits was "unreal."[13] Contrary to Veblen, he argued that both the laborer and the capitalist are worthy of their hire. "Society" needs both their services and pays them according to their contribution. Indeed, Cummings claimed that "every quality having an economic bearing has its economic value as accurately determined as may be in its economic efficiency." Cummings took issue with Veblen's claim that the pecuniary attitudes are invidious and self-regarding while the industrial attitudes are "non-invidious and economical."[14] Even though his distinctions and analyses are untrue, they are not "any the less dangerous for propagandic purposes."[15]

Clearly, a fundamental difference between the author and the critic was the latter's repudiation of the distinction between industrial and pecuniary employments. Cummings believed that both the financier and the manual laborer are productive and that the productivity and income of both are due to the ability exercised. But Veblen, in opposition, claimed that it is

> bootless to contend that there is no difference between the "pecuniary" and the "industrial" employments in respect of their disciplinary and selective effect upon the character of the persons employed. Neither should it be necessary to point out that the pecuniary employments, with the aptitudes and inclinations that give success in them, are, in their immediate bearing, in no degree serviceable to the community, since their aim is a competitive one. Whereas the latter commonly are serviceable in their immediate effects, except in so far as they are, commonly under the guidance of the pecuniary interest, led into work that is wasteful or disserviceable to the community.[16]

Veblen conceded that marginal cases exist in which lines of employment "cross and blend," that is, that partake of both pecuniary and industrial traits with no clear line of demarcation between them. This observation is followed by Veblen's listing of several examples includ-

ing "retail shopkeeping, in newspaper work, in popular art, in preach-
ing, in sleight-of-hand" which have both industrial and pecuniary
value.[17] Despite his satirical jibes, Veblen never wavered from his
claim that industrial employments differ in kind, not degree, from business pursuits, the marginal cases mentioned being exceptions to the
rule. In short, as Veblen saw it, the distinction between industrial and
pecuniary employments aims at showing "the different economic value
of the aptitudes and habits of thought fostered by the one and the other
class of employments."[18]

Leisure Class Incomes: Rationalizing Unearned Gain

Cummings contended that *The Theory of Leisure Class* asserts "that a
'confiscation' of the products of the 'productive laborers' takes place."
However, Veblen claimed, tongue in cheek of course, that the book
does not deal with whether or not capitalists and workers "earn" their
incomes.[19] In any case Veblen said that such analyses rest on "incon-
clusive" grounds, so he complained that Cummings "assumes the validity of the natural rights dogma that property rests on production.
This relation between production and property rights is a moral, not a
causal relation, if it is assumed to subsist at all."[20] But Cummings
claimed that a living could not be obtained except by providing a good
or service that was deemed valuable in the exchange mechanism of the
market. Consequently, he was forced to conclude that Veblen believed
in miracles as the source of income, a conclusion that the latter attempted to rebut by pointing to the "miraculous" element in the nut-
shell game!

Veblen's emphasis on the social nature of the stock of industrial
knowledge and tools, his stress on the organic character of all economies, and his focus on the collective process by which goods and services are produced led him to egalitarian conclusions regarding the distribution of wealth and income. He did not believe it was possible to
trace the origin of the value of a commodity to a particular input of
land, labor, or capital. This perspective did not set well with Cummings, who reasoned from diametrically opposite assumptions.

> On the contrary, the rise in wages during the last quarter century is to a very
> considerable extent, if not altogether, due to the confiscation by the commu-
> nity in general of the increment to production and labor efficiency which has
> resulted from improvements, inventions and the industrial genius of a few;
> and, it may be added, that the efficiency of labor in all times—more particu-
> larly its efficiency today—depends entirely upon the efficiency and genius of
> the industrial captain, who comes to be in the natural course of events asso-
> ciated with the wealth holders in the community.[21]

Like many conservatives, Cummings stressed not only the dominating contribution of the elite to the economy as a whole, but the significant role of individual volition as well. Consequently, if as he claimed, the wealthy are responsible for their own economic success, the poor must take responsibility for their own failure. He thus satirized Veblen's claim that accumulation of wealth at the upper end of the pecuniary scale implies privation at the lower end of the scale.

> There is, of course, a sense in which it is true that accumulation at one end of the scale implies privation at the other; this is in the very simple sense that, if the wealth accumulated at the one end were distributed at the other end, there would be less privation there—at least immediately after the distribution. In this sense the industrious man deprives the lazy man of his livelihood, since the lazy man would have more, and suffer less, if he could pool his earnings with the earnings of the industrious man and share equally; in the same way the temperate man deprives the intemperate, the efficient the inefficient. (P. 439)

Veblen stressed that the concentration of ownership and control placed the corporate elite in a position where as predators and exploiters they could obtain "something for nothing" at the expense of the underlying population. Their function was parasitic and they were obsolete manifestations of the predatory culture, that is, living, but archaic examples of cultural lag. But Cummings gives a different interpretation of their function.

> Those adopting the new culture have benefited by its greater efficiency, and have worsted those clinging to less efficient methods, who are bound to lose prestige and position as industrial leaders. The possession of wealth has become an evidence of economic efficiency and facility in apprehension and adoption of more productive exploitation of labor and environment. Such considerations as these are directly counter to much of the philosophy elaborated in the *Theory of the Leisure Class*. (P. 443)

The income of the industrialist is thus the result of his greater efficiency and not the consequence of his prowess as a predator.

The Captains of Industry

Much of Cummings' essay is written in tones that indicate a barely concealed astonishment and naive indignation that any economist should hold such outlandish views as those expressed in *The Theory of the Leisure Class*. Veblen seemed to be denigrating all those values, processes, and institutions that Cummings held sacred. Take, for example, the role of the executive. Cummings believed that Veblen thought that the exercise of executive ability is merely a game of chance. To be sure the financier, the captain of industry, and the man of wealth do participate in a contest in which they "take risks, venture stakes, and compete with one another, in the effort to win" (p. 451). The victors in this game, however, are not mere risk-takers who win on the basis of luck. Rather those who are successful possess foresight, which is the ability to relate present action to future events, and it is a matter of skill and calculation, not blind chance as Veblen implies. Furthermore, making the right choices or the wrong choices greatly affects society at large, not just the executive. Cummings thus believed it is wrong to view the ordinary laborer as "productive" and the executive as "unproductive" because the latter is "economically more productive in the sense that it results in more tangible commodities being turned out than does the labor of the ordinary workman" (p. 450). As Cummings also put it, "The possession of wealth is the possession of power—not always to consume the wealth, but always to direct the investment of labor. Upon the wise exercise of this power depends the material prosperity of the community, and the penalty for inefficient misdirection is loss of all economic power whatever" (p. 450). Thus, it appears that Cummings had not considered any alternative way to direct the investment of labor, so Veblen's implied alternative role for the community and the labor force passed him by unnoticed.

In the neoclassical paradigm, economic growth requires investment and the source of investment funds are savings. Savings in turn are the result of abstinence, an explanation that Veblen found both unconvincing and incomplete. Cummings insisted, however, that

> the "inertia" of the wealth holders is inertia against the multifarious means of wealth dissipation, and it is largely because of their capacity for resisting schemes for wealth dissipation that society enjoys any accumulation of wealth whatever. The ability to conserve wealth is less common than the ability to earn it. (Pp. 438–39)

From Veblen's perspective, the wealthy save by abstaining only in the absolute sense of spending less than they earn. Relatively speaking, middle- and lower-income groups abstain more in the sense of actually consuming less. Abstinence is imposed on these groups in order to permit saving by upper-income groups upon whom the process of abstaining is no real burden, or so Veblen's line of reasoning suggests.

Status Emulation and Invidious Distinction

Cummings commented that "in Dr. Veblen's philosophy . . . all our judgments are based on invidiousness" (p. 432). In perhaps the most indignant part of his review of *The Theory of the Leisure Class*, Cummings went to considerable lengths to discredit Veblen's claims about the invidious nature of consumption (p. 430). Cummings, in fact, saw emulation not as destructive or wasteful, but as an integral part of the pursuit of excellence. Indeed, it is an important force in the progress of civilization. Turning Veblen upside down, he commented that "the more universal and dominant the spirit of emulation is, the more essentially generic it is in its character" (p. 430). Cummings plainly failed to understand that, for example, in Veblen's eyes the display of finery in dress is a wasteful process not an exercise in the pursuit of excellence.

To Cummings, wealth was earned, not ill-gotten, and the invidious distinctions it enables the upper class to make are "a just award of honor" (p. 453). The ownership of wealth is an emblem of genuine economic efficiency and service, not a result of predatory exploits as Veblen claims. Cummings conceded, however, that Veblen makes his readers realize "that men living in society to a much greater extent than they can possibly realize, are conventional in their conceptions, and substitute for their own naive judgments, the judgments of society" (p. 434).

Cummings believed that Veblen attributed sordid moral traits to the wealthy leisure class, and to it alone, while exempting other classes from such charges. As he put it, "the unscrupulous man is not, by virtue of his unscrupulousness, a member of any class" (p. 449). Veblen claimed Cummings misunderstood him and that once again the latter was guilty of exclusion of the middle. Veblen then reworded his earlier writing to meet Cummings's objection. "Individual members of the wealthy leisure class resort to chicanery and fraud, *as do also many other persons. . . .* the unscrupulous man is not, by virtue of his unscrupulousness, *a member of any class.*"[22] At this point, however, Veblen conceded too much, for he could simply have argued that, on the average, the institutional effects of individual moral dereliction are more far-reaching when practiced by upper-class miscreants than by representatives of the lower classes.

In summation, Cummings and Veblen engaged in an ideologically vitriolic dialogue, for their disagreements involved fundamental issues in economics and moral philosophy. Although at times they talked past each other, on the whole, their discourse juxtaposed neoclassical and institutionalist domain assumptions at a time when the latter were still fermenting in Veblen's mind.

THE EXCHANGE BETWEEN IRVING FISHER AND VEBLEN

Irving Fisher (1867–1947), the eminent American neoclassical economist, spent his entire academic career at Yale University, first as mathematician and later as an economist.[23] Like Veblen, Fisher was a student of William Graham Sumner.[24] Unlike Veblen, however, he did not invert Sumner's Social Darwinism into a radical attack on the existing order, nor did he engage in the wholesale repudiation of laissez-faire.[25] Indeed, while he recognized the need for a larger role for government to restrain the excesses of economic individualism, Fisher was not fundamentally critical of capitalist property or power relations. Instead, much of his reformist impulse focused on individual hygiene and diet, rather than on reconstruction of the economy. He waged war, so to speak, against alcohol, bad posture, gambling, pornography, and bad eating habits and thus belonged to that group of gentile reformers whom Veblen never ceased to satirize.[26]

The origins of Veblen's exchange with Fisher can be traced to the summer of 1906, when E. R. A. Seligman, the managing editor of the *Political Science Quarterly*, asked Veblen to write a brief review of Fisher's *The Nature of Capital and Income*.[27] Veblen wrote a longer review than Seligman requested and was asked to shorten it. In the meantime, Fisher also published *The Rate of Interest*, so Seligman asked Veblen to deal with both of his books in the review. In his reply to Seligman, Veblen suggested that the second work have a short review of its own, to which Seligman agreed. Veblen then attacked Fisher's work in two review articles in 1908 and 1909 and, in a highly esoteric exchange, the latter attempted shortly thereafter to rebut his assault.[28]

The Issue of Hedonism

Those familiar with Veblen's earlier attacks on neoclassicism will recognize most of the familiar themes as well as some new ones. According to Veblen, Fisher's economics were deficient because his psychology was hedonistic, his explanation of distribution was based on marginal productivity theory, his method was excessively taxonomic, and his assumptions lacked "realism." Perhaps worst of all, he violated the logic of a pecuniary system and analysis by injecting considerations of a nonpecuniary kind. However, Fisher could not accept such criticisms and at the outset of his rebuttal complained that

> the impression which Professor Veblen's two reviews have made on my mind is that he . . . is influenced by a kind of phobia against certain school's methods. Having classified (or misclassified) me in a particular "school," he seems to make his attack almost indiscriminately. His criticisms are almost all generalities on methodology and concepts, and for the most part they disregard the special conclusions which differentiate my books from others on his *index expurgatorius*.[29]

Fisher did not agree with Veblen's claim that he was guilty of using psychological hedonism in his economics. For Fisher denied that he gave undue attention to utility, enjoyable income, livelihood and the "calculus of pleasure and pain."[30] He continued his complaint by arguing that

> Veblen has apparently overlooked the fact that I had expressly disclaimed being either an advocate of classification (Professor Veblen's "taxonomy") or an advocate of classification measuring utility in terms of pleasure and pain (Professor Veblen's hedonistic calculus).[31]

So there will be no further misunderstanding, he then made a fundamental distinction between *pleasure* and *desire*. He believed this distinction was the key to whether or not Veblen's allegations of "hedonism" are valid. The question, however, was whether Fisher had managed to jettison the ideological baggage of utilitarianism as completely as he claimed. In explanation of this point he wrote,

> I agree with him [Veblen] on the general thesis that the "calculus of pleasure and pain" has been terribly misused by theoretical economists. Economists have burdened themselves with a crude psychology. It is unnecessary for economists to enter within the field of psychology, but it is necessary to acknowledge contact with that field. The point of contact is human *desire*. It is quite impossible for any economic theory to be completely worked out without some place in the analysis for human desires. Many economists have confused pleasure and pain with desire and aversion. If Professor Veblen has not made this confusion, he has at any rate been greatly mistaken in the views he has ascribed to me.[32]

Veblen agreed that some neoclassical economists had lessened their dependence on hedonism, not to the extent of severing their ties with it, but through recognition that economic conduct must no longer be read solely in terms of the hedonistic calculus. As he put it,

> This gain in serviceability has been won—in so far as the achievement may be spoken [of] in the past tense—at some cost to the hedonistic point of view. Such serviceability as the newly achieved interpretation of the capital concept has, it has because, and only so far as, it substitutes a pecuniary for a hedonistic construction of the phenomena of capitalization. Among those who speak for the new (pecuniary) construction is Mr. Fisher, although he is not by any means the freest of those who are breaking away. . . . His . . . is an equivocal or perhaps greater an irresolute position at the best.[33]

So there will be no misunderstanding of what Veblen and Fisher understand by *hedonism*, let us examine what Veblen actually said and interpret Fisher's reaction to it. In Veblen's own words:

> The normal end of capital, as of all the multifarious phenomena of economic life, is the production of pleasure and the prevention of pain; and in the Benthamite system of theory—which includes the classical-Austrian economics—the normal end of the life of man in society, economic and otherwise, is the greatest happiness of the greatest number. . . . Under the rule of normal serviceability nothing can be included in the theoretically right "capital summation" which does not go to swell the aggregate of hedonistic "services" to mean nothing which is not "productive," in the sense of increasing the well-being of mankind at large.[34]

Veblen then explained that in the *Weltanschauung* of the hedonist, the center and boundaries of economic existence involve "pleasant feeling" that is produced only by tangible, physical objects acting upon the senses.

The extent to which Fisher was successful in stripping utility of its hedonistic connotations and uses is certainly debatable. Veblen did not believe Fisher had succeeded in this quest. In fact, he thought that Fisher's work was almost as contaminated with hedonism as classical economics.[35] But Fisher himself must have the last words:

> It is difficult to see why so many theorists endeavor to obliterate the distinction between pleasure and desire. Whether the necessary antecedent of desire is "pleasure" or whether independently of pleasure it may sometimes be "duty" or "fear" concerns a phenomenon in the second remove from the economic act of choice and is completely within the realm of psychology.[36]

Fisher believed that hedonism had made the work of the neoclassical economist unnecessarily difficult to interpret. He thought, however, that by substituting terms like *satisfaction* and *desire* for *pleasure* he had overcome its deficiencies.

Veblen's and Fisher's academic careers lasted from the apex of the dominance of hedonism in the late nineteenth century to what John R. Commons prematurely referred to as its "collective suppression" in the post–World War I era.[37] Efforts like Veblen's to free economics from the smothering grasp of hedonistic and utilitarian doctrines rested upon the belief that their residues remained potent in marginalism although at times camouflaged. Indeed, Paul Homan wrote in 1928 that "in their origin and in their nature, the majority of formal economic doctrines partake of a hedonistic hue. . . . More recent disavowals are merely the protective gestures of men guarding their worthless treasure of economic generalization, because it is the only treasure they possess."[38] This harsh indictment, appropriate for many of Homan's contemporaries, when applied to Fisher needed modification. Nevertheless, Veblen was essentially correct in his claim that Fisher failed to jettison the ideological baggage of Jeremy Bentham and his band of Philosophic Radicals.

Fisher versus Veblen on the Issue of Taxonomy

Although the core of Veblen's critique of neoclassicism was his attack on hedonism, his repudiation of hedonism was closely tied to his assault on taxonomic economics. Indeed, it is evident that his disagreement with the Fisherian system was so great that his criticism of selected parts of it was closely linked with a repudiation of the rest. To illustrate, Veblen wrote tongue in cheek that

> there is no intention here to decry taxonomy, of course. Definition and classification are as much needed in economics as they are in those other sciences which have already left the exclusively taxonomic standpoint behind. The point of criticism, on this head, is that this class of economic theory differs from the modern sciences in being substantially nothing but definition and classification. Taxonomy for taxonomy's sake, definition and classification for the sake of definition and classification, meets no need of modern science. Work of this class has no value and no claims to consideration except so far as it is of use to the science in its endeavor to know and explain the processes of life. . . . It is on this head, as regards the serviceability of his taxonomic results, that Mr. Fisher's work falls short.[39]

Fisher's answers to Veblen's charges were both theoretically interesting and polemically intriguing. As to Veblen's claims that his work is primarily taxonomic, Fisher wittily argued that Veblen "made a mistake in his own scheme of classification when he attempts to classify me as a classifier."[40] To this he added that

> from this definition [of wealth] Professor Veblen dissents; but I took pains to state that the term wealth could also be well defined in a restricted sense as "material objects owned by man and external to the owner." What breadth of classification we employ in defining wealth is of little consequence and is not worth the attention which has been devoted to it. The important point is the relation between a stock of wealth (whatever is included) and the flow of its service.[41]

Interestingly, Fisher claimed not only that he was not a taxonomist, but that he and Veblen "substantially agree on the futility of mere classification."[42] Nevertheless, Fisher accused Veblen of confusing classification and analysis. Fisher believed classification meant labeling and inventorying, while analysis meant evaluating the relations between things. Fisher also complained that the literature on "methodology" is full of misconceptions of analysis similar to that of which Professor Veblen seems to be guilty. . . . One of the best examples of Professor Veblen's confusion between classification and analysis appears when he accuses me of distinguishing "savings" and "income" simply in order to have two mutually exclusive classes.[43]

Fisher concluded that the questions involved were not terminological but, instead, were relational in nature; the terminology could be altered, but the relations would reappear under new labels.[44]

Veblen's exposure of Fisher's strong taxonomic tendencies was also evident in his critique of the latter's treatment of capital. But again Fisher charged him with failing to understand that he was dealing with relationships, not with terminological absolutes. He complained that

these general relations are entirely independent of particular valuations or applications. . . . Veblen here as elsewhere falls into the error which . . . has so often been committed by those who object to mathematical treatment because they imagine it assumes that economic magnitudes must be exactly measurable. . . . The laws of capital summation, like the laws of arithmetic, evidently refer to relations between assets and liabilities, and they are entirely independent of the question as to the value which those assets and liabilities may or may not possess.[45]

Veblen repeatedly emphasized the lack of explanatory power of taxonomic economics, a charge that Fisher attempted to rebut. Fisher's "hedonistic taxonomy" was, in Veblen's view, an example of cultural lag in the sense that even his new definitions and classifications lag behind changes in the economic situation and, in any case, fail to explain the circumstances that they were developed to explain.[46] Veblen claimed that Fisher's concept of capital and, worse yet, his concept of income, were the "perfect flower of economic taxonomy, and it shows, as no previous exposition of the kind has shown, the inherent futility of this class of work for other than purely taxonomic ends."[47] Despite his protestations, Fisher's work continued to have a taxonomic stigma attached to it, at least in Veblen's eyes.

Marginal Utility

Veblen argued that the intellectual pedigree of marginal utility lies in hedonism and that both are ideological mainstays of English and Austrian economics. He complained that

according to the hedonistic postulates the end and incentive is necessarily the pleasurable sensations to be derived from the consumption of goods, what Mr. Fisher calls "enjoyable income" or "psychic income" . . . and for reasons set forth in his analysis . . . it is held that, on the whole, men prefer present to future consumption. This is the beginning of economic (marginal-utility) wisdom; but it is also the end of the wisdom of marginal utility. To these elemental terms it has been incumbent on all marginal-utility theorists to reduce their formulations of economic phenomena.[48]

The marginal utility system is basically a theory of distribution that is nonetheless tied to the problem of value. As Veblen put it:

Interest and the rate of interest is a matter of value, therefore to be explained in terms of valuation, and so in terms of marginal utility. Within the scheme of value theory for which Mr. Fisher and Bohm-Bawerk are spokesmen no analysis of a value phenomenon can be brought to a conclusion until it is stated in terms of marginal utility. All fundamental propositions, all theorems of the first order in this theoretical scheme must be stated in these terms.[49]

Those familiar with the corpus of Veblen's work will recognize the relevance here of his belief that there is no objective way to measure individual contributions to product. Due to his claim that the organic nature of the economy make technology the collective legacy of society, and to his view that existing rights to property and income have a basis primarily in make-believe, Veblen concluded that doctrines that assigned rights to individuals based on their alleged economic "contribution" were indefensible.[50] Consequently, the Marxian labor theory of value and the neoclassical marginalist doctrine thus both erred, if in different ways, by claiming that absolute rights existed to the income stream of the community. Since these rights could not be assigned objectively anyway, they ignored what Veblen believed most important, namely, the right of the community to use its industrial arts to ensure its own adaptability and thus survival.

Value, Choice, and Emulatory Consumption

Unlike many neoclassical economists, Fisher qua economist was not a consistent moral agnostic for, at times, he claimed that some tastes and values were to be preferred over others. Also, he endorsed Pareto's distinction between the desires of men as they are and as they should be, that is, between what is actually desired and what is intrinsically desirable. Interestingly, he argued that

a whole range of problems of social betterment is opened up through the distinction. Economists have received with derision the suggestions of reform of Ruskin. But, however impracticable his specific proposals, his point of view is certainly saner than that of most economists; for, as Ruskin has pointed out, it is absurd to regard as equivalent a million dollars of capital invested in opium culture, and a million dollars invested in schools.[51]

Fisher made some mildly critical comments on emulatory consumption at about the same time he and Veblen engaged in their exchange. Indeed, in 1907 he wrote that

> it is hard to overestimate the tax which is laid upon society through social racing [emulatory consumption]. Many ingenious arguments have been made to justify luxury and in some of them there may lie truth. The fact that luxurious expenditure can be so readily cut down in hard times provides a sort of buffer against want and famine. The relations of luxury to the growth of population deserve careful study. But whatever the indirect benefits of luxury, certain it is that it forms a tax upon society, and a heavy one.[52]

In view of Fisher's own life-style and that of his contemporaries at Yale, the critic may be skeptical of his expressed attitudes toward status emulation as theory, collective behavior, or personal life-style.[53] In any case, the way in which he assured his readers that he shared Veblen's attitudes toward emulatory consumption made it evident that Fisher did not adequately appreciate the radical nature of Veblen's attack on it in *The Theory of the Leisure Class*.

Business as a Pecuniary Phenomena

Veblen's analysis of Fisher's *The Nature of Capital and Income* began with high praise when he stated that it "is of the best-thoughtful, painstaking, sagacious, exhaustive, lucid, and tenaciously logical."[54] But immediately he qualified this by commenting that "what it lacks is the breath of life" (p. 148). Perhaps the most damning of all Veblen's indictments of Fisher was his neglect of "intangible assets." The reason that the latter must exclude "immaterial wealth" or "intangible assets" from "capital" become obvious when viewed from the logic of the hedonistic calculus. "Intangibles" cannot produce pleasure or pain because they cannot bear directly on the senses (p. 163). Fisher's error is compounded by the fact that while his work is infected with hedonism, he can neither live with hedonism or without it. It is clear that Veblen believed Fisher confused business accountancy with hedonistic gratification. As Veblen put it, "The resulting confusion marks a taxonomic infirmity in the proposed capital concept, due to an endeavor to reach a definition from a metaphysical postulate (of hedonism) not comprised among the postulates on which business traffic proceeds" (pp. 171–72). It was Veblen's view that "the logic of economic life in a modern community runs in terms of pecuniary, not of hedonistic magnitudes" (p. 160), and further, that the scheme of accountancy of economic theory is not that of the modern business community (p. 160). Fisher complained, however, that

> as another example of my critic's desire to narrow many economic concepts to their money manifestation may be mentioned his attitude toward the concept of income. He maintains that, "As a business proposition, nothing that cannot be rated in terms of money income is to be accounted income at all; which is the same as saying that no definition which goes beyond or behind the pecuniary concept can be a serviceable definition of income for modern use." My own statement would be that no definition which does *not* go beyond or behind the pecuniary concept (or concepts) can be a serviceable definition for modern use, especially use in economic analysis. Would Professor Veblen wipe out of the economic literature all study—analysis and statistics alike—of, for instance, "real" in contradistinction of "pecuniary?"[55]

Evidently, Fisher had not grasped Veblen's meaning or seen the illogic in his own position. For Veblen had shown that modern business is a pecuniary not a hedonistic or a production phenomena. It measures success and failure in terms of a pecuniary calculus characterized by profit and loss. It does not employ criteria that maximize pleasure over pain or standards that utilize the yardstick of physical quantification. Veblen believed that Fisher had not adequately understood this basic essential of capitalism because he often substituted nonpecuniary phenomena. Veblen commented that "it is therefore an inversion of the logical sequence when Mr. Fisher, with others of the school, explains pecuniary interest and its rate by appeal to non-pecuniary factors."[56] Veblen summarized this portion of his case against Fisher when he wrote that "the logic of economic life in a modern community runs in terms of pecuniary, not hedonistic magnitudes."[57] But, as though in direct rebuttal, Fisher complained that "Veblen repeats his faith in the adequacy of pecuniary concepts."[58] This statement shows a misunderstanding of Veblen's analysis on Fisher's part. For it is certainly not he who had faith in pecuniary concepts. Rather, it is businessmen and the logic they bring to bear in exchange transactions that are based on the pecuniary calculus.

Fisher's response to Veblen's two review articles quickly recognized that Veblen's critique was of fundamentals: "All other reviews I have yet encountered are favorable to the extent of granting the validity of my main contention, but Professor Veblen finds evidences of error everywhere" (p. 505). He then quoted a sentence in which Veblen criticized him for dissolving interest—a pecuniary concept—into the elements out of which it is derived, to which Fisher responded: "Such statements will, I believe, to most readers carry their own refutation. Without such analysis, we should revert to the superficial mercantilism with which economics began" (p. 505).

This last sentence was where Fisher diverted his attention from the main issue between himself and Veblen to a nonissue. By stating "without such analysis," he permitted himself to think that Veblen is opposed to *analysis per se*, rather than opposed to *such* analysis. So Fisher defended himself against the accusation that he focused on analysis rather than on history (p. 506) and that he was a classifier rather than a analyst (p. 509). But he did not defend his kind of analysis against Veblen's kind. Instead, he complained that

> if Professor Veblen's criticisms are directed against *analysis* as well as classi-
> fication, I am ready to join issue. He himself draws no such distinction; yet
> the distinction is vital. It separates definitions, which are based on classifica-
> tion from those which are based on analysis. These are, respectively, defini-
> tions of *things* and definitions of *relations* between things. The former relate
> to the concrete; the latter to the abstract. The former are useful to the user
> of language; the latter to the student of science. Examples of the first cate-
> gory (concrete or classificatory) are definitions of a house, a chair, land,
> money; of the second category (abstract or analytical) are definitions of an
> average, a circle momentum, coefficient of correlation, velocity of circulation
> of money, balance of trade, in economic analysis, as in any other branch of
> science, the leading role must be played by such concepts of relation. (P.
> 509)

Rather than rejecting analysis per se, as Fisher thought, Veblen was simply rejecting the *kind* of analysis in which Fisher engaged. One sentence from Veblen's 1909 review shows explicitly that this was his intent. "It is therefore an inversion of the logical sequence when Mr. Fisher . . . explains pecuniary interest and its rate by appeal to non-pecuniary factors."[59] Had Fisher juxtaposed this sentence next to his own, he might have recognized the central difference between them. Fisher's assertion was that "nothing has led to more errors than fixing attention on the money surface of things and neglecting psychologic forces beneath."[60] Here are identified two kinds of analysis between which economists must choose: Is economic behavior to be explained by psychological forces inherent in human nature, or is it to be explained by institutions such as socially enforced pecuniary obligations? In order to make this choice, the evidence each man presented for his position must be examined.

Veblen presented his evidence for an alternative form of analysis immediately after explaining how Fisher and other marginal-utility economists invert the logical sequence. Even granting that psychological forces provide the motive for economic life, it is impossible to convert business behavior into terms of primordial livelihood or desire for pleasure.

The reason why these terms [business and livelihood] are not convertible, and therefore the reason why an argument proceeding on their convertibility or equivalence must reach a fallacious outcome, is that a growth of institutions intervenes between the two—granting that the hedonistic calculus is the primary incentive and guide of economic activity. . . . If the contrary were true, if men universally acted not on the conventional grounds and values afforded by the fabric of institutions, but solely and directly on the grounds and values afforded by the unconventionalised propensities and aptitudes of hereditary human nature, then there would be no institutions and no culture.[61]

Since human communities pattern their behavior in distinctive ways, Veblen concluded that observed behavior can only be understood by explaining those distinctive institutions, not by appeal to universal psychological traits. He sought to make his point concrete by commenting on an example Fisher took from the American farm community. Farmers borrow at harvest time, and thus bid up interest rates, because, said Fisher, their preference for present over future income rises. Veblen argued, on the contrary, that farmers' real income is greatest at that time, and thus their psychological preference for present income should logically be at its lowest. Veblen thus rejected Fisher's psychological analysis and replaced it with institutional analysis of farmers' borrowing:

There is also no doubt that the farmer is willing to bid high for funds at this period; and the reason seems to be that then the fresh access of income enables him to bid high, at the same time that he needs the funds to meet pecuniary obligations. His need to borrow is due to the necessity of marketing his crops . . . , it is a business or pecuniary need, not a matter of smoothing out the income stream. . . . The cycle of business enterprise closes with a sale, a conversion of "income" into money values, not conversely, and the farmer is under more or less pecuniary pressure to bring this pecuniary cycle to a close.[62]

While Veblen both argued against and presented an alternative to Fisher's kind of analysis, Fisher did neither in return. He did not refute Veblen's arguments against psychological explanations of cultural behavior, nor Veblen's alternative institutional explanations. By seeing in Veblen only "my critic's desire to narrow many economic concepts to their money manifestation,"[63] Fisher revealed his failure to recognize the nature of Veblen's challenge as well as Veblen's alternative method.

Fisher's deficient understanding is nowhere more evident that in his response to Veblen's comment on borrowing by farmers at harvest time. Fisher insisted that the money transactions are merely measures of real income, made up of goods that provide psychic income when consumed.

> The money of itself has no force except as it represents other things, and these other things in the last analysis have no force except as representing enjoyable income. If they represent capital, this is itself the representative of future enjoyable income. What can Professor Veblen mean by "pecuniary pressure" except the psychological preference for present over future satisfaction to which he would shut his eyes?[64]

To assert that the pecuniary pressure felt by farmers must mean their psychological preference reveals that, for Fisher, his taxonomy was so real that no inquiry into the (superficial) facts of the case is relevant. There is no need to talk to farmers or bankers or analyze business institutions because economists already know that the behavior has a psychological cause and explanation. Mistaking this assertion for an empirical fact, Fisher could only feel grieved that Veblen accused him of being a Benthamite hedonist and a pre-Darwinian taxonomist. He would have been comforted by Friedrich Von Hayek's 1939 observation, in reference to capital theory, that economists cannot expect ordinary mortals to understand the profound reality of economic taxonomy:

> This phenomenon of a scarcity of capital making it impossible to use the existing capital equipment appears to me the central point of the true explanation of crises; . . . That a scarcity of capital should lead to the existing capital goods remaining partly unused, that the abundance of capital goods should be a symptom of a shortage of capital, and that the cause of this should be not an insufficient but an excessive demand for consumers' goods, is apparently more than a theoretically untrained mind is readily persuaded to accept.[65]

In his debate with Veblen, Fisher recognized neither Veblen's challenge nor his alternative, and thus lost the debate. The power of Veblen's institutional analysis and the flaws in Fisher's psychological analysis, although at times subtle, have rarely been so squarely juxtaposed as in this exchange.[66]

Conclusion

Although Fisher was no advocate of strict laissez-faire, his portrayal as an ideological conservative whose views were not far from the political center is revealing. He was an independent who could boast that during his first three decades of voting "every presidential candidate for whom he had voted had also been elected."[67] Interestingly, like his mentor William Graham Sumner, he was an anti-imperialist of sorts.[68] By the 1930s, Fisher found himself voting for Herbert Hoover and opposing many of the most important New Deal regulatory and social welfare measures, although Fisher was on good terms with Roosevelt and may have influenced his thinking on monetary matters.

However, it was evident in their exchange that Fisher did not understand his political and philosophic differences with Veblen. Indeed, he concluded his rebuttal by providing evidence of his own ideological insensitivity: "Again, Professor Veblen seems to misconceive my attitude toward the older school of laissez-faire. My views on this subject . . . are not unlike those of Professor Veblen."[69]

Various examples of Fisher's inability to come to grips with Veblen's critique have been analyzed. Considered as a study in comparative ideology, the sharp contrast between the two shows the improbability of reaching agreement in the calculable future on the divisive issues of political economy.[70] The fact that Veblen found chinks in Fisher's intellectual armor and fired his penetrating shafts through them may not detract from the latter's contribution to monetary theory, for example, but it facilitates the study of ideology by baring part of the skeletal framework of Veblenian and Fisherian doctrine. Indeed, the ideological freight exchanged during the controversy is illuminating as regards the nature of assumptions made by institutionalists and neoclassicists alike.

The suspicion remains, however, that Veblen opposed Fisher's hedonistic utilitarianism for reasons in addition to those he articulated. It is likely that he thought it an ideological pillar of political conservatism and thus an obstacle in the way of solving pressing socioeconomic problems. He also believed that utilitarianism was a doctrine that mystified the nature of emulatory consumption, and that it was at best irrelevant to an adequate understanding of human growth and development. In Veblen's view, there were more important values than those the hedonistic calculus could express and among them were the pursuit of idle curiosity, proficiency of workmanship, and altruism. In the final analysis, it was his commitment to these values that formed the basis of his assault on his neoclassical opponent.

THE CONSERVATIVE CRITICS: RICHARD V. TEGGART

Richard V. Teggart (1903–1979), author of an important study published in 1932, shared most of the ideological predilections of the other conservatives and made similar criticisms of Veblen.[71] But his study of

Veblen is significant for two reasons: first, because of its early date of publication, only three years after Veblen's death; and second, because ideologically and politically, it clearly exemplifies the tenets of the conservative position. Evidence of this is found in the fact that Teggart praised Cummings "most exhaustive and devastating criticism" of *The Theory of the Leisure Class*[72] (p. 29). Teggart correctly believed that Veblen was an opponent of both the theory and the theorists of economic individualism. As he put it:

> his writings are devoted to showing how the competitive system has broken down, and how fully the present form of political and economic organization in America succeeds in shackling the natural creative impulses of men. There runs throughout his thought the notion of the real advances which could be scored in the absence of just the type of institutional life which the economic theorist and the American legislator attempt to maintain to restore to life—a competitive regime. (P. 12)

As is so often the case among Veblen's conservative and liberal critics, Teggart attempted to explain away his ideas by reducing them to a function of his social environment and personal idiosyncrasies. The conservative Teggart's reductionism is similar to that articulated by the liberal David Riesman's twenty years later. He claimed, for example, that Veblen's ideas regarding trade and business were drawn from his early memories of the farmer's relations with the business community in the upper midwest. As Teggart put it:

> Frequently he wrote of the "chicane" of the "business traffic" in the small town. . . . Veblen always retained this conception of "business." He rarely considered at any length the role which trading has played in the development of Western life: and his ideas of capitalism do not often rise above the picture of the disservice done to the small farmer by the small-town business man. (P. 22)

Like many of Veblen's other conservative critics, Teggart did not seriously or systematically analyze Veblen's claim that classes have exploited each other since the beginning of history. He did not even bother to use marginal productivity theory to explain or rationalize existing inequalities. Instead, he used Veblen's idiosyncratic personal characteristics and what he perceived as the main environmental influences on him in an attempt to discredit his attack on inequality and predation. For example, Teggart complained that Veblen's views are the result of "a life of economic vicissitudes and the malaise produced by his cultural maladjustment" (p. 43). He also claimed that

> when he became a social investigator, he gave heed to these promptings and turned away from the prevailing philosophy of economic and political liberal-

ism. Impressed with what appeared to be social injustices, and informed with the idea of the importance of economic factors in this condition of society, Veblen set himself the task of formulating a theory of economic society which would expose the bootless rewards and vain glories of the leisure class. (P. 43)

Still another example of this is found in Teggart's claim that "individualistic to an extreme, self-contained, if not self-sufficient, peculiarly devoid of the vestiges of common sociability which might have afforded a leaven for his own thoughts, Veblen seemingly turned to the past for a model of social life" (p. 16). Since Veblen was constantly at odds with his environment, he was forced to look to the past for escape—according to Teggart he found it in the "archaic anarchism" of old Scandinavia where the prevailing mode of life was once based on a philosophy of "live and let live." But Teggart also complained of an "ever present, rasping bitterness in his judgments which seems to pass far beyond the puzzled curiosity of the "farm-lad" (p. 21). Interestingly, Teggart commented on the difficulty of interpreting the author's meaning, which is due primarily to the "deeply subjective swagger peculiar to Veblen's character" (p. 38). At times Teggart rose above the level of sociological and psychological reductionism to a more detached and analytical perspective, but, in the final analysis, he could not avoid accusing Veblen of sordid motives: "Veblen supposed himself to be the champion of the Common Man against the blind habituation of the acquisitive interest. The tone of his exacerbations, however, was determined 'less from love of the many than from hatred of the few'—as Bentham said of James Mills" (p. 63). By proclaiming his own belief that Veblen's harsh criticism of capitalism is rooted in antisocial motives, Teggart thus revealed his own cynicism.

Veblen and the Betrayal of Objectivity in the Social Sciences

Teggart, like many of Veblen's critics, found fault with his use of the English language and his writing style. He commented that "his stylistic mannerisms make him akin to such masters of obscure circumlocution as Immanuel Kant and Karl Marx" (p. 40). His main objection, however, was that Veblen "did not heed the rule of common acceptation in determining where they [words] should be used" (p. 40). Consequently, "he would proceed with a settled routine of admonishment to his readers that no moral valuations were really intended, but that his abiding purpose was description from a detached scientific viewpoint" (p. 41). Teggart thus believed that Veblen successfully manipulated his readers by continuously garbing his own ideas in pseudoscientific dress. At times, Teggart conceded Veblen's brilliance, but just when his reader anticipates an elucidation of his contribution, Teggart again turned to denigration of Veblen's motives. Now he compared his accomplishments with the "heavy locutions of Karl Marx, the vociferous broadsides of Upton Sinclair, and the capitalistic witchhunt led by the militant Ida M. Tarbell" (p. 15). If positive value exists in Veblen's work, Teggart failed to identify it.

However, it is primarily Veblen's invocation of science and scientific method and its preeminent status in Western life that Teggart objected to in his detractions. His essay is laden with derogatory comments, for example: "He employs ideas with singular and unusual promiscuity as to their source or logical capability. . . . He was primarily attentive to the effect of his work rather than to the disinterested pursuit of balanced interpretation. . . . Veblen thought himself to be 'scientific' while philosophizing ex capita about human history without meticulous empirical verifications" (p. 38). Teggart also argued that both Marx and Veblen "stretch ideas to match their last largely by the device of abstracting a given detail or aspect of a theory and treating that part which meets their purpose as possessing the validity of the whole" (p. 74). However, the most negative comment Teggart can muster takes the form of an interrogative:

> Where, within the range of modern science, could Veblen have found his "generic" method of interpretation vindicated? Except in a meta-physical sense, in which "teleological" enjoyed a vogue with Karl Marx and writers in the entourage of Positivism, the idea must be traced to the theory of animism first advanced by Edward B. Tylor. (P. 53)

In this passage, Teggart attempted to turn the tables on Veblen. In much of the latter's critical writing on classical and neoclassical economics, he accused writers in these schools of teleological and animistic tendencies—but now Teggart suggested that just such traits are to be found in his own employment of the critical genetic method. Unfortunately, Teggart did not develop this argument any further by offering specific examples of these faults.

Veblen did leave himself open to criticism by using the terms *animism* and *teleological* interchangeably, whereas, in fact, in common usage as well as in scholarly discourse, they do not have the same meaning. *Animism* is the idea that natural objects have souls or that inanimate objects are inhabited or infested with spirits while *teleological* signifies evidence of design or purpose in nature and is a doctrine of final causes or purpose. It is at least worth a footnote to explain why the two are not the same. Veblen knew the difference between the two but for reasons of his own assigned them the same general meaning hoping to convince his readers that there is no real difference between the superstitutions of primitives who practice animism, Catholics who believe in natural law with its teleological underpinnings, and neoclassicals with their focus on equilibria as a norm.

Also, much of Teggart's attack on Veblen's "pseudo-science" was based on his belief that Veblen's intellectual position was badly infected with the influence of Kant, Marx, and Darwin. Kant's influence was particularly evident in that

> first . . . he is reconciled to a horizon of intensely subjective human knowledge; second . . . "induction" means to him almost exactly the qualities which are usually associated with deductive reasoning. "Induction" is not the act of simple inference, of reasoning from the particular to the general, but is, on the contrary, the process of subsuming the particular under the terms and reach of an a priori category. (P. 38)

Veblen, under Kant's influence, was thus guilty of relativizing and personalizing knowledge and of engaging in deductive reasoning while suffering from the illusion that he was an inductivist.

Teggart also commented on Veblen's use and abuse of Charles Darwin. Veblen claimed that economics was a pre-Darwinian discipline because of its taxonomic, teleological, and static bias. Teggart complained, however, that "indeed, Veblen was at no pains to work out the implications of Darwinism except as he made Darwin the hallmark of the scientific. Yet, while making the use of the idea of 'evolution,' or 'process,' the criterion of a scientific approach to economics, Veblen did not reveal his own theory in unequivocal fashion" (p. 75). It is, of course, true that Veblen did not "reveal his own theory in unequivocal fashion." But Teggart missed the point at issue, which is whether economics at the time Veblen wrote was taxonomic, teleological, and static and could be improved by adopting an evolutionary perspective. Teggart went to even greater extremes when he claimed that "Veblen seemed to hold that 'Darwinism' forbids the recognition of intelligent observations as a scientific fact. Only self-moving process is a scientific category" (p. 71). Apparently, Teggart was now making the assertion that ideas have no efficacy in the Veblenian system. Men are moved only by habit, convention, and material force, not by reflective intelligence. Among other things, Teggart had lost sight of the important role of idle curiosity in Veblen's social theory.

Specifically, he charged Veblen with the pursuit of particular social ends under the guise of scientific impartiality. In one respect, he preferred the later Veblen to the early one because in his last years Veblen, freed from the restraints of the academic community, "divested himself of some of his scientific pretensions and became more pointedly the radical reformist" (p. 108). While Veblen criticized conventional

economic theory for its unscientific pre-Darwinism, what he was actually doing was pleading for his own social doctrines (pp. 63–64).
Teggart pushed his claim still further when he argued that "Veblen's
primary concern with economic theory was to introduce a different
philosophy rather than a distinctive method into economic thought in
America" (p. 64).

Teggart then claimed that Veblen was not objective for two reasons.
First, his analysis is dialectical in that he divides economic activity into
two categories: industrial and business, which he believed are polar
opposites. Teggart argued that this division is too simplistic, for it excludes types of work and economic processes that may have the qualities of both or neither. Second, he claimed that Veblen tried to generalize about human behavior at all times and placed with insufficient data
to support his claims (p. 37). He believes that Veblen, instead, should
have been historically and culturally more specific.

However, the main differences separating the two men were different social values and political goals. This becomes evident early in Teggart's study when he claimed that Veblen subsumed the evidence he
had marshaled "under the totality of a 'process' research from 'the very
origin of things' to a prophetic vision of that which is to follow" (p. 37).
Veblen's "industrial republic" was not the material from which Teggart's dreams were made.

Teggart placed great emphasis on Veblen's invocation of the prestige and methods of science, while in reality substituting his own social
values and goals for genuine scientific analysis. For example, a main
conclusion of Veblen's critique of conventional theoretical economics
is that, if Veblen's own "logic of process" were grasped, "a different
theory of distribution would supersede that now currently accepted"
(p. 57). Or, even more explicitly, Teggart wrote that

> this oblique attack of Veblen, the "scientist," produces an optical illusion.
> Seemingly the movement of his thought was directed toward the solution of
> the theoretical difficulties of economic science. In effect, however, it was a
> storming attack directed against the citadel of the theory of distribution.
> Lulled to a sense of security, the warders discover themselves overpowered.
> (P. 63)

Teggart also believed that Veblen's misuse of both the prestige and
methods of science was aimed at promoting the social control of industry through a policy of deliberate government intervention. By pretending to be able to project the path of social development, the ground-
work is laid for a program of collectivist control at the appropriate time
and place (p. vii). Most sarcastically, but with prescience, since he was
writing before the New Deal, Teggart claimed that "Veblen's dialecti-

cal subleties have contributed toward a current tendency of thought which pretentiously links the name of science with suggestions and demands for the social control of economic activity" (p. vii).

To Teggart, even Veblen's internationalism was suspect because it represented unavowed political aims pursued under the guise of scientific objectivity. In an interesting passage, Veblen was accused of promoting racial egalitarianism and internationalism in a pseudoscientific manner.

> Veblen assumes all Europeans to be racial hybrids, and, as such, to possess a common heredity. The characteristics of people living within national boundaries are simulated racial traits. This interpretation seems to have been important in Veblen's mind as a phase of a general thesis that one "common man" is everywhere the same, his seeming differences being due to institutional habituation. Possibly his efforts to enforce these concepts were directed to vindicating scientifically the internationalism of Kant and Marx. (P. 101)

Teggart's own patriotic animus and his intellectual hostility toward Veblen surfaced in a related context when he charged that Veblen was also anti-American. For *Imperial Germany and the Industrial Revolution* "is written from the point of view of a German apologist during the early years of the war" (p. 104). A more discerning analysis of this book, however, will show it to be even more critical of German than British institutions, about which, at times, it is scathing.

Veblen's Misuse of Anthropology

Teggart analyzed Veblen's use of anthropological literature and data and, not surprisingly, discovered that he used it to grind his own ideological axes. Veblen had read widely in the discipline of anthropology and was familiar with the work of Franz Boas, Edward Tylor, James Frazer, and Lewis Henry Morgan. He found in this body of work support for his own vision of the good society; a society composed of communities where equality and good will, peaceful intent and human solidarity flourished. Veblen anticipated a possible resurgence of such traits and values in modern industrial societies. What stood in the way of such a social order were the predatory instincts, that is, the atavistic survivals that underpin cultural lag. Teggart complained, however, of Veblen's scholarly lapse, for Veblen claimed the data utilized were derived from "everyday life," either by "direct observation" or through "common notoriety" when, in reality, they came from the writings of anthropologists Veblen often failed to cite (p. 81). In any case, Veblen simply illustrated his theses by reference to anthropological literature of "dubious authenticity" (pp. 105–6). Teggart also complained that

> as is the case with economic literature generally, the author of this probing diatribe makes use of anthropological material as a conveniently vague hinterland from which to draw forth illustrations to fit his aprioristic theories. The technique is not different from that of the age which made the Noble Savage either a brute or symbolical of Man's station in life before the Fall from Grace. (P. 85)

Teggart believed that Veblen derived much of his anthropology from the evolutionary school, particularly Edward Tylor. Consequently, his writings were "susceptible to the well understood objections of practically every representative group of anthropologists writing today"(p. 105). Because Veblen used an evolutionary explanation of material culture and human invention in which social development had gone through three stages—savagery, barbarism, and modernity—he could be attacked by antievolutionists, that is, by those with extreme historical attitudes, as well as by geographical diffusionists and functionalists.

Veblen had argued that leisure classes generally, and the American leisure class in particular, were conservative in the sense of being more change-resistant than other classes, particularly industrial workers, whose psyches were being reconditioned by the machine process. But Teggart complained that "it is far-fetched to suppose that only the subjugation of the worker prevents him from eagerly embracing innovation. Cultural conservatism is as much a part of the lives of those carrying on any well defined task in a social group as are the ulterior motives of a leisure class" (p. 86). Teggart thus raised an important question as to why different social strata react the way they do to change. This was a question that Veblen never satisfactorily answered, but was among the first to ask. Hence he contributed to the research agenda in this area for many years to come, a contribution readily conceded by several of his critics.

Veblen's Attack on Hedonism

Teggart believed that Veblen attacked the hedonistic psychology of conventional economics not simply because he disagreed with it, but because he had other ideological axes to grind. He thought that for Veblen, hedonism was the linchpin of neoclassicism. If it could be undermined, then the rest of the structure would crumble. Thus his attack on hedonism could also be interpreted as an assault, for example, on the "marginal theory of distribution as a mere apologetic for business and preposterous abstraction from the productive activities of men which look to the 'generically human ends of life'—that is, their industrial employments" (p. 58). In short, the marginal-hedonistic theory of distribution relies for its basic validity "upon the uncritical acceptance of the hedonistic calculus" (p. 58). In Teggart's view, hedonism provides intellectual support for all theories of distribution developed since the eighteenth century. Unfortunately, in Veblen's eyes, it diverted the study and theory of distribution from a science of productive force to a theory of ownership and expenditure. It asserts the priority of ownership over production and satisfaction of wants, thereby violating the first principle of Veblen's "'science of causal sequence,' which enforces the priority of human effort over expenditure" (p. 60). Teggart believed that Veblen himself was inconsistent when he used hedonistic assumptions to explain the conduct of businessmen, for he assumed they act selfishly from the "incentives of a single capacity" (p. 96). This is an interesting allegation in view of Veblen's attack on economists for making the same assumptions regarding human behavior in general. Teggart thus believed that his attack on hedonistic psychology and ethics was directed toward showing its inadequacy in fulfilling his demand for a universal human psychology (p. 53). This places Veblen

> himself in the position of denying autonomy to the several human interests and to the values which arise in conjunction with them. He is prone to belittle and disparage values which do not coincide with his philosophy of an absolutistic, deterministic monism; values which do not accord with his opinion of the purpose and end of human development. (P. 35)

What were the values that Veblen sought through his intolerance and single-mindedness to impose on mankind? In Veblen's view, the generically human was "an inclusive measure of human serviceability . . . the 'good' was always equivalent to immediate usefulness" (p. 21). Strangely, Teggart's comments did not account for Veblen's use of the instinct of idle curiosity, which fosters ideas of no immediate value or utility. Also, and he shifts ground, Teggart claimed that the

> real basis of his criticism of hedonism is at last apparent. Were economics to become "scientific" in the many senses that are peculiar to Veblen, it would be compelled by the logical priority of labor to product, "genetically," by "the sequence of cause and effect," and by the scientific interpretation of conduct, to emerge as a science of labor value. (P. 60)

This comment seems consistent with Teggart's earlier claim that Veblen's theory of value "means an approach to the estimation of men's acquisitive activity or interest by way of some extra economic standard of reference. It is, briefly, an attempt to evaluate economic life critically from the standpoint of values which are not themselves an integral part of economic life" (p. 3). However, Teggart was vague about what constitutes "economic" and "extra-economic" standards of reference, though he appeared to believe that only pecuniary motives and acquisitive activity are "economic" in nature. If this is his position, then Veblen's alleged view that economics should become a "science of labor value" can only be seen as wrongheaded.

Teggart rejected Veblen's attitudes toward the price system and the pecuniary economy because he could not visualize an economy functioning with equity or efficiency that is organized otherwise. Veblen was simply wrong in making the institution of the money economy a self-sustained entity when it must more properly be understood as evidence of the economic life and activities of individuals. He was wrong again in pushing to the background "any conception of the need for a pecuniary economy" (p. 114). Thus Teggart confused Veblen's criticisms of the price system under capitalism with support for abolishing the price system itself.

It is not surprising to discover that Teggart rejected Veblen's distinction between business and industrial pursuits; that is, between making money and making socially useful goods. The key reason for this is that the dichotomy severs the tie between productivity and remuneration. If the Veblenian distinction is accepted as valid, it raises serious questions regarding the receipt of gain by those engaged in essentially pecuniary occupations. Teggart, of course, believed that these occupations are of immense value to society, while Veblen viewed them as largely wasteful and parasitical. In sum, the former was a consistent supporter of capitalism while the latter was a consistent critic who believed that neoclassical economics cannot be ideologically disaggregated as a support mechanism from the economic system it claimed to scientifically explain.[72]

Chapter Three

CONSERVATIVE CRITICS: THE CHICAGOITES

TWO CONSERVATIVE economists who were critical of Veblen were also colleagues at the University of Chicago. They were Frank Knight (1885–1972) and Abram Harris (1899–1963). Knight was an ideological opponent of institutional economics, and his critique of it exemplifies the doctrinal structure of his own brand of political conservatism and neoclassical economics. Unfortunately, he never systematically treated Veblen's ideas as such in an article or book, and his scattered comments about him were written over a period of nearly sixty years. In order to present a coherent analysis of Knight's critique of Veblen, his thoughts must be collected from his sporadic published comments on him and from his unpublished papers, particularly his correspondence with other economists. It is also necessary to extrapolate from the ideological structure of his thought when it focuses on thinkers such as Karl Marx and John Hobson, who were doctrinally similar in certain respects to Veblen.

Although Knight supported Veblen for president of the American Economic Association, a position Veblen refused, and occasionally praised his work, what is most striking about their intellectual relationship is their political differences. Indeed, the writings of Knight and Veblen provide doctrinal mirrors in which to image their contrasting ideological positions.

KNIGHT'S ATTACK ON VEBLEN AND THE INSTITUTIONALISTS

Ideologically and politically, Knight was a conservative, but early in his career he was neither a doctrinaire advocate of laissez-faire nor a collectivist liberal.[1] Indeed, much of his work clearly indicates his skepticism toward both the night-watchman state and state collectivism. However, after the New Deal began in 1933, Knight attacked its philosophy and policies and their expansion in the post-1945 era.[2] In retrospect, it is evident that while Knight was not a dogmatic supporter of laissez-faire before the New Deal, the bulk of his criticism after 1933 was directed against interventionist policy rather than against laissez-faire.

Most of the time, Knight left little doubt in the mind of his reader as to where he stood—the sympathetic critic who called him a "gentle cynic" presumably had not read some of his more polemical writings. Nevertheless, the forceful way in which he identified and defended his own ideological ground made it easy to contrast his doctrinal position with Veblen's. Knight's critique of Veblen is so closely aligned with his attack on institutional economics that it is difficult to separate the two. Indeed, no effort will be made to disaggregate them, which is probably what Knight himself intended.

Knight believed, however, that there were three distinguishable schools of thought among the institutionalists, each with its own leader but with minor differences among the followers. The common theme in the thinking of the three leaders—Thorstein Veblen, John R. Commons, and Wesley Mitchell—was their demand for (a) greater realism and concreteness in the scientific treatment of the subject matter, and (b) more relevance for social policy and more direct application to problems of social action. But the actual content under both these heads was somewhat vague, and variously conceived.[3] Of course, Knight himself was an institutional economist, in the generic sense of recognizing the impact of social and political forces on the market, but not in the more specific sense of being an evolutionary economist. Indeed, it was from this perspective that he launched his attack on the institutionalists.

Methodological Issues and the Problem of Objectivity

Although Knight was more inclined than Veblen to sanction deductive method and to employ it in his own work, he sensed the need for a methodological eclecticism in a discipline and an economy that were rapidly changing. Nevertheless, he believed that the institutionalists had failed to cooperate in the development of methodological innovations that would facilitate more fruitful lines of inquiry.[4] His own eclecticism regarding methodological issues as well as his antipathy toward institutionalism are summarized in his comment,

> When I am talking with an orthodox economist who expounds all these economic principles as gospel, I am a rip-roaring institutionalist, and when I am talking to an institutionalist who claims the principles don't make any sense at all, I defend the system, the "orthodoxy" that is treated with so much contempt by followers of Veblen and others who wear the institutionalist label.[5]

That Knight's and Veblen's ideological differences were irreconcilable is evident on the basis of their methodological differences alone. Knight wrote long after Veblen's death that the concept of a Crusoe economy seems to me almost indispensable. This has come to be another cuss-word to people who crave realism and are contemptuous of theory, largely because they uncritically dislike the individualistic economy. I do not see how we can talk sense about economics without considering the economic behavior of an isolated individual. Only in that way can we expect to get rid by abstraction of all the social relations, mutual persuasion, personal antipathies, and consciously competitive or cooperative relationships which keep the behavior of an individual in society from being, in any closely literal sense, economically rational. Crusoe would be in this position: he would actually use given means to achieve given ends, his purely individualistic wants.[6]

Contrary to Knight, Veblen did not believe that the atomized individual à la Robinson Crusoe was even a useful methodological device. His reasoning was that consumption is essentially an emulatory process, and emulation signifies that individuals are members of some larger social aggregate, parts of which they are attempting to imitate. It is thus nonsensical, assuming the validity of Veblen's theory of status emulation, to believe that individual behavior can be understood in isolation from the social environment. What economists like Knight would have achieved, at least in Veblen's eyes, was to impute to individuals both autonomy of motives and degrees of rationality that they did not really possess.

In a 1959 review of Lev Dobriansky's study of Veblen, Knight complained, "The crux of Veblenism is perhaps the pretense to 'colorless objectivity' when describing cultural history in terms of 'cumulative change'; ridiculing 'orthodox' economists for holding a 'static' view of human nature; and denouncing or satirizing nearly everything."[7]

On another occasion, Knight complained that "the labor of interpreting Veblen's inextricable mixture of satire that is more or less amusing with 'science' that ranges from inspired insight to dogmatic assertion of generalizations impossible to take seriously, has not always seemed remunerative."[8] This is evidence that Knight, like other Veblen critics left, right, and center, was both puzzled by, and in disagreement with Veblen's values as expressed in his own work and in his critique of the work of others. Indeed, it is difficult to tell how serious Veblen was in his attacks on other economists for embedding their own values in analyses that they claimed to be "scientific," that is, value-free.

Spontaneous versus Coerced Social Action

Knight believed there were three "great principles of human social order—custom, authority and free association."[9] It is clear that of the three, he preferred "free association," and part of his critique of Veblen and the institutionalists rested on his conviction that they intended to interfere with it on a massive scale. Indeed, he argued,

> The later institutionalists . . . slurred over the contrast between two kinds or meanings of institution, i.e., patterns of action moving in predestined grooves under the influence of relatively unconscious social forces, versus those embodying deliberate organization and control, such as the political organs of the state.[10]

Knight thus drew an important distinction between unconscious social forces that produce "patterns of action moving in predestined grooves" and those that take the form of "deliberate organization and control," that is, the state. The later institutionalists stand accused of failing to adequately distinguish between the two.[11] Implicit parallels were then drawn by Knight between the followers of Veblen and Dewey to the effect that

> in the field of social policy, the pernicious notion of instrumentalism, resting on the claim or assumption of a parallelism between social and natural science, is actually one of the most serious of the sources of danger which threaten destruction to the values of what we have called civilization. Any such conception as social engineering or social technology has meaning only in relation to the activities of a superdictatorship, a government which would own as well as rule society at large, and would use it for the purposes of the governors.[12]

Thus according to Knight, "instrumentalism" of the Dewey-Veblen variety aims not at human liberation, but at subjugation of the species. In what is apparently a reference to the same school of thought, he commented that "still more absurd, and vicious as well, is the theory that practical problems of personal relations and social policy are to be solved by utilitarian application of positive science. An effort of men to manipulate and use each other (however intelligently) would literally realize the war of each against all."[13]

Yet Knight also commented in a similar vein that "if the formulation and clarification of social patterns or systems of organization are to be fruitful in the same way, we must be able to assume that society also is in some sense, as a unit, a free agent in molding itself."[14] Apparently what Knight meant here was that society must be free to change itself, but should not rely primarily on the state to do this. Knight's distrust of institutional economists, Veblen in particular, was thus rooted in his belief that their theory aims at the creation and use of instrumental knowledge for purposes of social control. In Knight's eyes, the lodging of such power in government threatens personal freedom and civil liberties. Early on, Knight saw clearly that Veblen and institutional economists, in their strong support for social control of economic life, represented a path of development away from neoclassical economics. Interestingly, Knight found important parallels in this respect between German "socialism of the chair," English Fabianism, and American institutionalism.[15] However, since the institutionalists were American, they became the focal point of Knight's attack until the home-grown collectivist menace dwindled into insignificance next to the foreign totalitarianisms of Hitler and Stalin.

As a classical liberal, Knight reasoned on the basis of assumptions foreign to Veblen when he wrote that "the ideal of active individual freedom gives a highly distinctive form to the problem of political order and political life."[16] Veblen's own ideals, no doubt, included individual liberty of various sorts but this was not stressed in his writing. Rather, his ideals supported enhancement of certain human qualities that, while they might require some degree of "active individual freedom" for their fulfillment, could not be conflated with it; for idle curiosity, altruism, and proficiency of workmanship are not reducible to the core value of classical liberalism, namely, liberty understood in the negative sense as absence of restraint.

Differential Access to the Means of Production

Knight believed that Veblen perceived the ownership of capital as similar to the possession of landed property in that both give the owner superior access to the means of production. But Knight objected to the view that ownership of "capital is equivalent to property, which is to be regarded as mere power over the economic activities of others due to the strategic position of ownership over the implements of labor. It is analogous to a robber baron's crag, a tollgate on a natural highway, or a political franchise to exploit."[17] And in the footnote he added, "Veblen's conceptions of capital and profit show strong leanings toward the same views."[18] The view that Knight is attacking, insofar as it stresses the superior power position of the owners of capital and property, is a truism to radical social scientists. To Knight, however, it was evidence that Veblen gave inadequate consideration to the role of risk and uncertainty. For, in his view, superior bargaining power explains little under normal circumstances about the profitability of capital. Rather, it is possession of superior foresight and willingness to engage in risk-taking activities that is the source of such income. Knight did not accept Veblen's contention that capitalists usurped the community's social legacy of technology and technical skills through the present system of ownership and control over industrial assets, nor did he accept the claims that followed. This is evident in his comment that thus . . . confusions are involved in Veblen's contention that the world's stock of knowledge is its most important "capital," which is without value merely because not privately exploited. It could be exploited only by having its use restricted, i.e., by monopoly. The notion that capital is significant as limiting access to the world fund of technical knowledge is absurd, for the reason, already noted, the production is joint, and the productivity of anything may be viewed as a productivity conferred on only things.[19]

Knight could not accept the other ideologically corrosive point Veblen made, namely, that the existing system places control over the stock of technological knowledge and skill in the hands of individuals who are often technologically incompetent. In Knight's eyes, only the price system and market mechanism are capable of objectively measuring the efficient allocation of resources, and the captains of industry and finance understand its operations best. Their technological incapacity, if such it be, apparently does not matter.

Industrial versus Pecuniary Employments

Knight's attack on the Veblenian dichotomy between business and industry, that is, pecuniary and industrial employments, was based on his view that it means transferring power from financiers to technicians, a change that he described as "grotesque."[20] He wrote indignantly that

> the quantity of goods, if there is more than one kind, must so obviously be measured in value units. . . . There is no more important function of a first course in economics than to make the student see that the whole problem of social management is a value problem; that mechanical or technical efficiency is a meaningless combination of words.[21]

Knight interpreted Veblen as advocating a complete and total displacement of the price system itself and a substitution of technological or mechanical value for value as measured by market price. Once more, a leading conservative critic of Veblen attempts to discredit him by focusing on *The Engineers and the Price System* as though this were typical of his work as a whole or, at least, exemplified important tendencies in it.[22] As usual, it aimed at demonstrating the utopian, and thus impractical, nature of Veblen's proposal.

Knight believed that "the most serious defect of the Veblenian philosophy comes out in the contrast between pecuniary and industrial employments," although he thought Veblen's use of these terms was not very clear.[23] Knight claimed, however, that Veblen's meaning is idiosyncratic and personal—"the simplest and apparently the correct view is that pecuniary values mean those of which he disapproves."[24] Then he pressed his point home with little heed for Veblen's cultural anthropology and social value theory:

> As to the reasons, grounds, or standards of this approval and disapproval, he does not find it pertinent to make a statement. . . . He doubtless means to disapprove only of keeping up appearances in "improper" ways, which is to say, in ways of which he disapproves. If he has an objective test for distinguishing between valid and false aesthetic values (and equating the innumerable kinds) he does the world grievous wrong in withholding it from publication.[25]

The stress placed by Veblen on both continuity and fullness of life, that is, the generic ends of life impersonally considered, escaped Knight's attention; as if Veblen had never written about the pursuit of idle curiosity, the parental bent, and the proclivity of workmanship.

Industrial Sabotage and Predatory Business Enterprise

At this point the doctrinal assumptions of both conservative and radical become paramount. The conservative Knight stressed the willingness to take risk and the entrepreneurial skills of the capitalist as the sources of gain, while the radical Veblen focused on private ownership and control of the means of production, exchange, and distribution as a source of unearned income. But Knight's own ideologizing of Veblen's perspective reached its apex in his claim that

> matters become still worse when the managers of productive property begin to manipulate their industrial and financial policies with a view of *producing* changes in capital values, of which they inevitably know in advance of outsiders and of which they take advantage with corresponding ease. . . . Perhaps it had been neglected unduly by economists, but Veblen's allegation that such stealing through the production of disturbance in business arrangements is the usual or characteristic activity of modern economic life is of course merely humorous.[26]

Although Veblen did at times emphasize the manipulative and predatory behavior of industrial statesmen who engage in sabotage, a more characteristic way by which he explained it was systemic and institutional. He claimed that unearned incomes were seized not "through the production of disturbance in business arrangements," but through absentee ownership of the corporate sector of the economy. It is a matter of power and ownership, not an aberrant conspiratorial manipulation, that is the "usual or characteristic activity of modern economic life" in Veblen's view.

In any case, Knight made a three-point indictment of Veblen. The first was that he was unable to properly distinguish between legitimate and illegitimate business undertakings, the second was that he wanted to impose his own values on others, and the third was that he was unable to articulate any standard other than his own tastes by which to do this. It was the third criticism he made of Veblen that was most unwarranted, namely, that Veblen had no standards except personal bias by which to make judgments regarding value.[27]

The Problem of Value and the Practice of Status Emulation

Veblen's repudiation of utility theory made it necessary for him to develop a different approach to the problem of value, although he did not explicitly claim that he had provided an alternative. Nevertheless, while the idle curiosity, proficiency of workmanship, and parental bent he prized could not be transformed directly into goods or services, each with a discrete price tag, they still provided criteria to measure social progress. Of course, in his role as a conventional economist, Knight only had available a price system by which to measure progress toward fullness of life and its "generic ends." This is not to suggest, however, that he believed that exchange value was the only valid measure of value, for he thought that both ethical and aesthetic standards were largely independent from market values. Nevertheless, the inadequacies of price alone as a measure of the quality of life are apparent and Knight qua economist could not escape the closure of the neoclassical paradigm.

Veblen's attitude toward value can be labeled "objective" because he believed that external standards existed by which to measure consumer tastes and preferences. On the other hand, Knight's attitude was "subjective" since he believed that "consumption is strictly the subjective enjoyment of products."[28] However, Knight was not consistently a radical value relativist who believed there was no disputing about tastes. Indeed, he laid down ground rules for the discussion of value.

> Value will be used exclusively to denote exchange value or money value practically speaking as measured by price. Price and value will be distinguished, if at all, only in the case where some temporary and accidental circumstance causes goods to be sold at a price notably different from that which would be established by the ordinary working of economic tendencies.[29]

However, despite his distinction between exchange value and other value, Knight did not lose sight of the fact that "money incomes do not correctly measure human values."[30] Indeed, his sensitivity on this issue manifested itself in one provocative set of examples:

> No one contends that a bottle of old wine is ethically worth as much as a barrel of flour, or a fantastic evening wrap for some potentate's mistress as much as a substantial dwelling-house, though such relative prices are not unusual. Ethically, the whole process of valuation is literally a "vicious" circle, since price flows from demand and demand from prices.[31]

Although Knight attacked Veblen's radical critique of emulatory consumption on several grounds, he clearly shared Veblen's position that consumer tastes and preferences are socially induced. Nevertheless, unlike Veblen, he was willing qua economist to accept these values as given without attempting to explain either their origin or the consequences of their satisfaction. But, unlike many neoclassicists, he was more aware of the need for inquiry into both knowledge of means and satisfaction of ends even if this work was to be left to other social scientists to accomplish.[32] As he put it, "In the science of economics the wants are largely taken for granted as facts of the time and place, and the discussion of their origin and formation is left for the most part to the distinct studies of social psychology and cultural anthropology."[33]

The parallels between Knight and Veblen are intriguing even if, in the final analysis, Knight qua economist was more willing to acquiesce in whatever choices were expressed by the individual in the marketplace. For while he was aware of the social processes by which values were formed, as a classical liberal he, nevertheless, believed that tastes were expressions of subjective preference and individuals were, in any case, the best judge of their own self-interest. Despite this, however, he acknowledged that "the satisfaction derived from consumption itself is seen to be derived largely from the social situation rather than from the intrinsic qualities of the goods. . . . Higher up, consumption becomes less and less a matter of physiology and more a matter of aesthetics or the social amenities."[34] On occasion, without actually endorsing Veblen's theory of status emulation, Knight went further in his direction, commenting that

> the content of the wants for the goods and services for which people strive as producers and consumers is predominantly social, conventional, cultural, and aesthetic; the urge or animus is very largely emulation and rivalry—to "keep up with the Joneses" or to get ahead of them. To this end people will endure much discomfort, including the consumption of costly goods for which they have a positive distaste.[35]

The problem of how to evaluate the tastes and preferences of consumers has always perplexed economists, and Knight was no exception. He put it this way:

> In a more or less obscure and indirect way, the treatment of wants as data from which and with which to reason has already been challenged more than once. . . . Hitherto the chief emphasis has been placed on the factual instability of wants and their liability to be changed as well as satisfied by business activity. This is usually coupled with a depreciating attitude, a tendency to regard the growth of wants as unfortunate and the manufacture of new ones as an evil; what have not advertising and salesmanship to answer for at the hands of Veblen, for example.[36]

However, unlike many neoclassicists, Knight was not really a consistent moral agnostic or radical value relativist who believed there is no disputing about tastes.[37]

> A sounder culture leads away from this view, to be sure, but it leads to a form of tolerance very different from the notion that one taste or judgment is as good as another. . . . The consideration of wants by the person who is comparing them for the guidance of his conduct and hence, of course, for the scientific student thus inevitably gravitates into a *criticism of standards*, which seems to be a very different thing from the comparison of given magnitudes.[38]

Perhaps at this point Knight failed to realize the relationship between his own position and that of Veblen. Clearly, Veblen believed that standards or criteria existed by which to ascertain whether some tastes and wants were preferable to others. Like Knight, he thought that rational disputation about tastes was a significant enterprise worthy of the economist's time and effort. Unlike Knight, however, he believed that emulatory consumption based on invidious distinctions was not conducive to "fullness of life" and achievement of the generic ends of human existence—ends that Knight believed were not only ill-defined, but perhaps nonexistent.

It is interesting to note that Knight, after criticizing Veblen for using individual value judgments of his own, freely substituted judgments of an equally subjective nature; yet he warned of the danger of the process in which he was engaged.

> The activity of business in the way of manufacturing wants has received much attention in the literature of late, again under the leadership of Veblen. It is a serious fallacy to condemn this sort of activity without discrimination. Whether it is good or bad to create wants depends altogether on the character of the wants created. One cannot condemn advertising and salesmanship out of hand, unless one is prepared to repudiate most of education, and of civilization in general; for most of the desires which distinguish man from

the brutes are artificially created. Ethically, the creation of the right wants is more important than want-satisfaction.[39]

Obviously, Knight believed that some tastes or preferences were preferable to others. But unlike Veblen, he made no real attempt to establish any criteria or standards that would demonstrate why some judgments about consumption are superior or inferior to others. Veblen's attacks on consumer sovereignty were unconvincing to Knight, for he believed that "all such distinctions ultimately resolve into value judgments, and at that point, argument must cease."[40]

Evidently, Veblen used the degree to which the economy enhances idle curiosity, proficiency of workmanship, and altruism as a measuring rod by which to determine the quality of its performance. But for reasons that are unclear, Knight paid little heed to what is clearly the locus of value in Veblen's work. This may be because these sources of value are impossible to analyze within the neoclassical paradigm, for despite Knight's criticisms of utility theory, he was ultimately unable to break with it. In any case, Knight's inability to come to grips with Veblen's value system is often evident in his scattered writings on him.[41]

Darwinism and the Veblenian View of History

While he never ceased to be critical of them, Knight did not lose interest in Veblen or institutional economics as he grew older.[42] Indeed, a generation after Veblen's death, he faulted him for failing to develop an adequate theory of history that coherently encompassed the Darwinian perspective. Veblen's utilization of concepts drawn from evolutionary biology, which he used to belabor neoclassical economics as "pre-Darwinian," was now turned against him. Also, he was castigated for letting his own values color his explanation of future institutional trends. Knight's point is that the Darwinian paradigm is based on evolutionary drift and, to inveigh for or against aspects of it, is to inject purpose into what is essentially a purposeless process.[43]

Like many other critics of Veblen, Knight was more bewildered than enlightened by his use of Darwinian concepts. Interestingly, however, in spite of his uncertainty, he linked Darwinism with the economic interpretation of history and then commented on the ambiguous relationship of Veblen to both:

> The best meaning for the expression "economic interpretation of history" is surely to take it . . . as the application to human history of the Darwinian principle of selective survival on the basis of biological efficiency. This gives in effect a technological interpretation which . . . has much truth in it. It also has limitations, among them its incapacity to explain decadence, which is a historical fact as real and as important as progress. The important but puz-

zling pretentions of Veblen to be the apostle of the Darwinian method in economics come to mind in this connection.[44]

Veblen's satirical qualities are at both their best and worst in his use of the Darwinian concepts and legacy, and for this reason it is difficult to tell how seriously to take his comments. Although it is evident that by claiming neoclassical economics is "pre-Darwinian" he meant "taxonomic," "teleological," and "static," it is less clear as to how Darwinism is actually interwoven in the texture of his own work. Knight was not the only critic of Veblen puzzled by his use of evolutionary biology.

Conclusion

Despite their fundamentally different philosophies, there are, nevertheless, points of convergence between Knight and Veblen.[45] Interestingly, these convergences are rooted in their criticisms of neoclassical economics and its ideological baggage, such as utility theory.[46] To illustrate, they were both critics of psychological hedonism and ethical utilitarianism, the first because it was tautological and led to circular reasoning, the second because it confused the good with the pleasurable. They were both critics of extreme value relativism and its corollaries, moral agnosticism and subjective preference, although Knight could find no convincing alternatives to them and criticized Veblen for believing that he had. Finally, both were critical of the neoclassical assumption that treated man as a rational economic actor, although Knight, despite his recognition of the unrealistic nature of the assumption, believed it had considerable analytic and heuristic value.

Veblen thought that there were no such phenomena as "non-ordered," that is, spontaneous or natural institutions, because market processes and the cultural and social forces underlying them were coercive human contrivances. Their emergence and behavior were no more natural or spontaneous than were the origins and activities of political and governmental agencies. As a consequence, Knight never agreed with Veblen and the institutionalists, because in his view they sanctioned the deliberately contrived rather than the spontaneous or natural institutions. Thus Veblen was essentially a reformer of the stripe that Knight disliked on account of his willingness to use governmental coercion to impose his values on others. But Myron Watkins critically summarized Knight's case against Veblen in these words:

> At bottom Knight is following in Veblen's footsteps in contending . . . that wants are not only ineluctably changeable but also indefeasibly subject to valuation by standards which are neither absolute nor, from the standpoint

of the community as a whole, arbitrary. I would deny that Veblen, any more than Knight, was intent on promoting (securing acceptance of) *his* "values." His basic objective was to "unhinge" valuation from tradition and convention, to bring it "out in the open," to make it a deliberate, and so far as possible rational, process—both individually and collectively.[47]

Much of Knight's animus against Veblen undoubtedly stemmed from his perception of him as the source of interventionist and collectivist schemes for the restructuring of society. This is not to suggest, however, that Knight held him directly responsible for the policies implemented during and after the New Deal. Rather, he believed that in a broader sense, Veblen was the author of a doctrinal critique of laissez-faire and capitalism that opened the floodgates for the social control of industry. Lawrence Nabers perceptively commented in this respect that

> Knight among others has objected that any system of analysis which rejects as a point of departure consumer sovereignty has dangerous political implications. Specifically in his review of *The Place of Science*, . . . he says: "It goes without saying that there is a great deal in this distinction between real value and trumpery, but we wish to remark that it is a canon very difficult to apply in a democracy." . . . Veblen would have replied: (1) consumer sovereignty is myth derived from an acceptance of the hedonistic calculus; (2) in any event the gains to be made from the application of the canons of serviceability for society as a whole would outweigh any other possible loss; and (3) to the implied question of who is to make the decisions for individuals he would ask, "Who makes them now?"[48]

Nabers's summation of the differences between Knight and Veblen is valuable in understanding both men's perceptions of the main sources of power in American society. Knight, particularly after the New Deal, found the locus of power in a federal government acting under pressure from organized labor and the farm bloc with vote-hungry politicians fronting for them and irresponsible intellectuals proposing and rationalizing policy. But Veblen, prior to his death in 1929, clearly saw American society as a business-dominated culture with commercial interests exercising ideological hegemony and extending their tentacles of control through the legal and political system. Although focused at different points in time, there is a yawning chasm between these two fundamentally different perceptions of the locus of power in American society.

Knight's candid acknowledgment of the role of political and ideological ax-grinding in the discipline of economics is not unique but it is unusually forceful. He wrote that it is no marvel that the classical economists were accused of being apologists. I suppose three quarters of the economists writing today accuse each other of being special pleaders for one interest or another—and this is more or less true with the possible exception of the mathematical economists. Such things keep economics from being very strictly scientific.[49]

Knight suggested that technocrats, collectivist liberals, and radicals drew intellectual sustenance from Veblen's theories. Ultimately he approached, if he did not arrive at the view, that groups who obtain significant income from other than market processes are the beneficiaries of Veblen's doctrinal legacy. Thus even after Knight's penchant for aesthetics and his multifaceted cultural interests are acknowledged, Veblen was on target when he criticized economists like Knight for making "exchange value the central feature of their theories rather than the conduciveness of industry to the community's material welfare."[50]

The Ideological Transformation of Abram L. Harris

Abram Lincoln Harris (1899–1963), one of American's few black economists, wrote extensively about Veblen on numerous occasions between 1932 and 1958.[51] However, during the 1920s and 1930s when he was on the faculty at Howard University, he espoused a different political position than he did later, when he joined the economics department at Chicago. He clearly underwent an intellectual transformation from Left to Right that was reflected in his scholarly work, particularly his writings on thinkers such as Marx and Veblen.[52] As his Chicago colleague Frank Knight sanctimoniously put it:

> His personal background . . . which presented quite unusual obstacles to intellectual and academic advancement, [had] caused him to grow up inclined to radically "leftist" notions. He has overcome the handicaps and achieved a distinguished academic position. He has also outgrown his adherence to radical reformism, but without at all losing interest in social betterment. In becoming intelligently critical of easy solutions for hard problems, he has not ceased to favor measures of progressive reform not impossible to carry out and which offer a reasonable prospect of doing more good than harm.[53]

Knight also commented with regard to Harris's book *Economics and Social Reform* that "the standpoint of the critique is economic common sense rather than a closely knit theoretical system of the author's own."[54] It remains to be seen, however, as to what Knight, and presumably Harris, meant by "progressive reform" and "economic common sense."

Harris's Attack on Veblen

Harris was an authority on heterodox economics during his time and labeled all these approaches as "institutionalist." Institutionalists were those economists whose interest had shifted from what was conceived by classical and neoclassical theorists to be the central problem of economics. Harris viewed traditional economic theory as a system of supply-and-demand equations in which value and the distributive shares between productive factors were found to be determinate by means of abstract logic utilizing the concept of normal equilibrium developed by the classical and reformulated in the marginal-utility school. In contrast, the institutionalists attacked equilibrium and the marginal theory of value and distribution, and assigned a comprehensive role to industrial fluctuations in the analysis of economic behavior and organization.

Harris also constructed a typology of institutionalists that included (1) the "quantitative-statistical" group of whom Wesley Mitchell was the main representative, (2) the "critical-genetic" category of whom Veblen in the United States and Sombart in Germany were the premier exponents, and (3) the class-struggle variety of whom Marx was the prototype. But beyond these, Harris could not detect any other basic similarities except that Veblen's institutionalism was closely allied with Marxian class-struggle theory rather than with Mitchell's quantitative economics or business-cycle analysis; he concluded, probably correctly, that though Mitchell's quantitative analysis could be considered a variant of Veblen's institutionalism, from a doctrinal viewpoint it was more closely allied with classical theory.

Harris held that in the past, scholars were either too enthusiastic or too negative in their appraisals of Veblen. Of course, this suggests that his appraisal will be more objective.[55] Nevertheless, in spite of his early praise of Veblen, by the late 1950s, Harris found little of value in Veblenian economics. Also, like many other liberals and conservatives, he resorted at time to reductionist explanations of Veblen.[56] However, more than any other of Veblen's conservative critics except Lev Dobriansky, he engaged in a concerted effort to deal with Veblenian economics.

The common theme unifying Harris's later work is a rejection of all statist and collectivist schemes for the large-scale reconstruction of the economy. This includes the corporatism of Social Catholicism exemplified in the writings of Heinrich Pesch, the conservative institutionalism of John R. Commons, the radical institutionalism of Veblen, the "German" socialism of Werner Sombart, the "utopianism" of Karl Marx, and even the cooperativist schemes of John Stuart Mill. As Harris put it in 1958:

I came to believe that while Marx and Veblen had made some important contributions as critics and historians of capitalism, their conception of the basic defects of the system was mistaken and that their programs of economic reorganization, designed to increase industrial efficiency, lessen economic inequality, and obtain greater "effective" freedom for the masses of men, would achieve none of these things, but would probably create greater "evils" than those attributed by them to capitalism.[57]

Like other conservatives, Harris complained of Veblen's evasive concealment of his own value judgments and ideological bias behind a facade of scientific objectivity. Interestingly, he was not impressed by claims that Veblen's social marginality equipped him with a novel impartiality and detachment (p. 423). Harris also intriguingly commented that Veblen "is a curious dualism between a sort of scientific positivism and ideal principles or values that are hidden in the background of his thinking" (p. 211). Yet, two years earlier, in a review of Bernard Rosenburg's study of Veblen, he commented to the effect that "Veblen's positivism was hardly skin deep" (p. 424). Harris's analysis of Veblen's epistemological commitments and his claims of "scientific objectivity" was not sufficiently developed or consistent enough to be further analyzed here. Nevertheless, it exuded skepticism regarding Veblen's role and status as an economic "scientist."

The Engineers and the Price System

Veblen's perhaps tongue-in-cheek proposal for a soviet of engineers and technicians takes up little more than a short chapter in *The Engineers and the Price System*. Yet liberals and conservatives alike have placed great stress on it in their interpretations of his work. Harris was no exception to the rule. He wrote that "in a sense the whole of Veblen's work might be considered as intended to supply 'scientific' arguments in support of a program of industrial reorganization and reequipment under the guidance of technicians" (p. 157). Harris believed that such a scheme, if implemented, would threaten fundamental freedoms because the mass of the workers would suffer from "managerial despotism" in the new society. Veblen may have been aware of this possibility, but he failed to articulate "the means of checking the power of his technician managers and preventing the tyrannical exercise of it over the subordinate worker" (p. 160). There is little recognition in Veblen's work of the extent to which his proposals might reduce individual freedom. As Harris put it in another context:

One may of course contend that Veblen, being the incorrigible individualist that he was, necessarily considered individual freedom to be a value in itself.

But there is nothing in his criticisms of hedonism to indicate that this was his view. One is greatly perplexed by his failure to consider how individual freedom is to be preserved and extended in his technocracy. (P. 201)

Harris raised questions that he believed Veblen left unanswered regarding the proper division of labor between the technocrats who were to run the economy and the political state, however the latter was to be constituted. Was the state going to wither away, leaving an anarcho-syndicalist social and economic organization, or did Veblen have some other set of institutional devices in mind? Harris also claims that Veblen failed to indicate how the right of absentee ownership would be disallowed. If the state were to do this, the result would be state socialism, which would be in conflict with Veblen's anarcho-syndicalist ideals. It did not occur to Harris that the state might disallow absentee ownership and then turn industry back to the employees, which is, perhaps, what Veblen had in mind. But Veblen's vagueness certainly leaves his prescriptions on ownership an open question. His Darwinian view of the economy as an evolving set of institutions and processes perhaps made him reluctant to endorse the crystallization of property into particular forms of ownership or control.

However, Harris's main criticisms of Veblen were those that an economist influenced primarily by Chicago-style free market economics would advance. As Harris put it:

In judging the presumed superiority of Veblen's technocratic organization over capitalism, one would certainly want to know on what basis the technicians would make their decisions about the things to be produced, the relative amounts of these things, and the order in which they would be produced. If these and other important decisions are to be made in the absence of the market mechanism whereby consumers freely express their choices, they are bound to be arbitrary, if not authoritarian. Veblen is silent about the matter. (P. 160)

Harris ignored one main point of Veblen's writing, which is that consumers do not "freely express their choices." Rather, their "freedom" is constrained by their emulatory aspirations, the illusory nature of which is concealed from them by the mystification of social relations. In short, they confuse achievement of status aspirations with fulfillment of their own needs as consumers.

Harris believed that the role of markets and the price system are not well-defined by Veblen in *The Engineers and the Price System*. He indignantly commented that in capitalism, businessmen organize and guide production, and that in another system of economic organization, technicians, like businessmen, would determine the amount of different goods it would be profitable to make:

To arrive at this decision, they would necessarily have to have some scale or value standard by which to gauge the relative importance of the physical quantities of different goods, measured by the costs of producing them and the prices paid for them. They would soon find out, if they did not already know, that sheer physical output can never serve as a criterion of economic efficiency, that this efficiency is always a matter of the ratio between total useful (valuable) output and different amounts of useful (valuable) input in the form of human productive capacity and natural resources. (P. 161)

In short, Veblen stands accused of failing to recognize that economics can only be the study of the most efficient way to allocate scarce resources through a price system and market mechanism. He is thus indicted for mistakenly believing that there are equitable and efficient alternatives to this system.

Risk, Abstinence, and Entrepreneurship

Harris claimed that the assumption of risk, the social value of abstaining from consumption in order to save, and the expertise invested in the organizing and directing functions of entrepreneurship are not appreciated by the anticapitalist. He thus believed critics of capitalism like Veblen do not understand the role played by risk-bearers, abstainers, and entrepreneurs. He also claimed that the latter's mastery or not of technological processes and mechanical efficiency is irrelevant. In fact, Harris argued that it is necessary to separate entrepreneurial decisions from technological decisions and he claimed that Veblen's analysis "utterly confuses the nature of entrepreneurial decisions and the 'know-how' necessary for making them with the type of decisions the engineering expert must make on the basis of 'exact' knowledge of the physical and chemical sciences" (p. 188). One of Veblen's main points was that entrepreneurs were technologically and scientifically incompetent. One implication of this is that if entrepreneurs had more technical knowledge and expertise they could function more effectively. Harris claimed, however, that "in production . . . the technological best may not be generally the economically best" (p. 161). He added to this "the fact that the persons responsible for deciding the question do or do not possess a knowledge of scientific technology is an utterly irrelevant consideration" (p. 187). Indeed, according to Harris, Veblen's fixation on technology was a major source of his sins. Harris complained that "since the nineteenth century, innovation and, accordingly, entrepreneurship have increasingly become the function of the engineers and technicians. The entrepreneurial function is thus connected by Veblen with mechanical performance and not with business uncertainty, as it should be."[58] Harris's view shows the probable influence of his Chicago colleague Knight, whose stress on uncertainty as the essence of the entrepreneurial function is too well-known to need repeating here. Nevertheless, his claim that the entrepreneurial function bears no relationship to mechanical and technical knowledge and expertise is extreme. Entrepreneurs could reduce their own, and what is ultimately society's, risk, if they had a better understanding of the technological aspects of their own enterprises. It is difficult to believe that technical ignorance is as irrelevant as Harris indicates.

The Business versus Industry Dichotomy

Next to his work on emulatory consumption and display, Veblen is perhaps best known for his distinction between business and industrial pursuits. This distinction and its implications for economic analyses were objectionable to Harris because they delegitimized income derived from purely business as opposed to industrial work. He refused to accept the Veblenian distinction because he believed that all owners of the factors of production, including land, labor, capital, and entrepreneurship, are entitled to the value of their marginal productivity. It is the dictates of the market that should determine the value of each factor, not Veblen's arbitrary distinction between business and industrial pursuits; for capitalists are as entitled to their gain as laborers are to their wages.[59] Harris believed Veblen claims that intangible property is essentially "hold-up" value, for he associated tangible productive equipment with technological efficiency, and he contrasted material output with pecuniary acquisition (p. 256). But he complained that Veblen did not understand that

> from the standpoint of economic theory, all production is the creation of utilities, or saleable values. This being the case, to identify productive efficiency with sheer physical quantity, or output, per se, is meaningless. It is not the rate of output per unit of input that matters in the organization of productive resources. The important fact is the value of the given units of output relative to that of the useful input. (P. 256)

Apparently, Harris did not regard unused industrial capacity as a problem so long as firms are able to operate at a profit. He thus rejected the claim that microeconomic efficiency is directly related to macroeconomic efficiency. For similar reasons, Harris could not accept Veblen's distinction between pecuniary and capital goods. As he put it,

> Capital is pecuniary in magnitude and indistinguishable from credit. It consists of "intangible" or business assets. Capital goods are of a different order.

They are the tangible equipment. Capital goods are the embodiment of the immaterial wealth of society, in other words, of knowledge of ways and means resulting from education, discovery, and invention. If this conception of the nature of capital goods is consistently adhered to, it will be seen that Veblen's differentiation of capital goods from pecuniary capital cannot be accepted. (P. 256)

Harris thought the attempt made by Marx and later by Veblen to "explain the business cycle phenomenon in terms of a conflict between "technical efficiency" and "pecuniary values" contributed little to an understanding of the phenomenon (pp. 130–131). Harris's analysis was, of course, expressed through the doctrinal channels of neoclassicism when he claimed that Veblen

does not take into account: (1) that however economic life is organized, a determination must be made by the value of the contribution of the various resources to production (2) that such a determination can never be made in terms of physical units, either of human energy or mechanical power; and (3) that values will in any case be assigned to the productive contribution of these sources, either on the basis of market competition, by political authority, by the pressure of organized bargaining groups, or by some combination of these three. (Pp. 130–31)

Again, Harris relied almost entirely on *The Engineers and the Price System* and ignored Veblen's other more serious and better-known books. Why conservative and liberal critics emphasize so unrelentingly the deficiencies of a book, probably written tongue in cheek, that is not representative of his thought, is an intriguing question. Perhaps it is because they are primarily interested in discrediting his other ideas and find *The Engineers and the Price System* an easy target because of its utopian and visionary nature. Also, despite the book's satiric qualities, Veblen's programmatics and policy prescriptions are more visible in it than elsewhere. His conservative critics as a whole have readily located those facets of his work that best lend themselves to undermining his theoretical system and, consequently, like Harris, produce an unbalanced portrayal of his work.

Competition and Monopoly

Although Harris believed Veblen's economics are mischievous as well as erroneous, he did credit him with being an innovator of sorts (p. 211). More important, however, he attempted to summarize Veblen's teaching on competition and monopoly, which is not easy to do. He complained that

Veblen thinks of competition in a highly personalized sense and equates it to emulation or rivalry between economic units. But this is not what economists since the days of Jevons and Marshall have understood the term to mean. Emulation and rivalry do occur in economic life, but these personalized relationships are not essential content of behavior in a competitive pricing system. The more competitive the relations between economic units, the more impersonal these relations are. (Pp. 202–3)

Harris also criticized Veblen for attempting "no serious evaluation of the real limitations of competition or of its utility as method and policy" (p. 203). He stressed the propagandistic nature of Veblen's claim that the corporation is usually "a monopolist in the sale of products and a monopsonist in the hire of labor . . . the individual businessman possesses a large amount of discretion in fixing his prices and wage rates" (p. 203). However, Harris believed that there is far less monopoly in the 1950s than in the period around the turn of the century when Veblen first analyzed the American economy. Thus, what was most disturbing to Harris about Veblen's economics was his tendency to ignore the role of competition, of markets, and of the price system, and to greatly overstress the function and importance of technological and mechanical efficiency. To illustrate, Harris complained that Veblen did not analyze the problem of return in relation to scale of plant or that of increasing and decreasing cost. As he put it,

His argument concerning the "excessive productivity" of machines leaves one with the impression that he thinks that in industries making use of scientific technology on a large scale the cost curve slopes downward indefinitely. This of course is not true. It is because he failed to consider these problems of cost and of returns relative to scale that his discussion of the methods and pricing principles of corporate business is loose and inaccurate. (P. 186)

Harris undoubtedly achieved some measure of ideological gratification in stating that Veblen believed cost curves slope downward indefinitely, which, of course, strongly suggests that he was an incompetent microeconomist. However, since Veblen never wrote a systematic treatise on industrial organization, it is difficult to understand the stress Harris placed on this facet of his work, or the authoritative tone in which he indicted him.

Social Value and Individual Consumer Preference

Veblen's conservative critics believed that preferences or tastes are subjective rather than objective. Although there is some discussion of the problem of interpersonal comparisons of value in their work on Veblen, they placed little credence in the evaluation of interpersonal utility functions. Value is thus essentially individual and subjective. As Harris put it,

> It is undoubtedly true that exchange value is in some remote manner influenced by general esteem, into which aesthetic and moral considerations enter. Still it is difficult to conceive of exchange value except . . . in terms of individual choices or utility preferences, of which price is a function. And while the choices made or preferences expressed have undoubtedly been influenced by a variety of social influences, past and present, an investigation of these influences would handicap rather than facilitate an explanation of a market determination of price or value. (P. 319)

Thus, according to Harris, a determination of exchange value on the basis of individual choice would run counter to Veblen's ideological tenets, for his thinking was controlled by the notion of a socially determined exchange value to which individual value judgments must adjust themselves. Hence, even in the early 1930s, while he was still under the influence of radicalism, Harris found Veblen's attitude toward value to be inadequate. As he put it in a letter to Frank Knight,

> Veblen is rather consistent in maintaining that the "fitness" of institutions to survive depends upon the degree that they promote "facility of life." His notion of "mechanical efficiency" must certainly be admitted an inadequate gauge of human self. . . . And it seems to me that he finally falls back upon wants as his ultimate criteria. These are cultural and physical, but mainly the former. . . . Veblen's theory of change, like Marx, becomes involved with a larger problem, the theory of value. But unlike Marx, Veblen never attempted consistently to work out a comprehensive value theory although it is possible to piece together something that might pass for one.[60]

Many years later, Harris succeeded in synthesizing what he took to be Veblen's theory of value, but was thoroughly dissatisfied with it then, too, in part because he mistakenly believed that it was primarily mechanical and technological.

Anthropology

Veblen's critics found his anthropology deficient both in its use of literature and data. Harris was no exception to the rule, and he alleged that in Veblen's early work racial types have psychological characteristics that are transmissible in the same way as biological or physical traits. Harris based this assertion on Veblen's claim that the racial mixture of the communities in which there is a large admixture of the dolicho-blond is more efficient in the machine industries, more likely to think in materialistic terms, and more given to iconoclastic behavior. In rebuttal of this view, Harris commented that

> there is today no scientific theory which supports Veblen's view that "the pervasive difference in technology and workmanship" between Western culture and the Far East is due to "a specific difference in the genius of the people." The anthropology from which Veblen derived his racial theories has long since been discarded.[61]

Harris thus concluded that Veblen's anthropology was obsolescent; however, he failed to note the changes in his use of anthropology in his later works. Once more Harris attempted to discredit Veblen through selective reading of his works, for Veblen denied any significant connection between race and psychological characteristics in *Imperial Germany and the Industrial Revolution* and *The Instinct of Workmanship*.[62]

Utopia or Antiutopia

Harris, like other conservatives, attacked radical schemes as "utopian" and strongly distrusts visionary programs of social reconstruction. Clearly, he had thinkers like Veblen in mind when he rejected such schemes as syndicalism, guild socialism, and cooperative production as "utopian" rather than as grounded idealism, and claimed that they would sacrifice personal and political freedom for permanently unattainable goals.[63] However, Harris prescribed a particular institutional apparatus and sanctioned a system of power relations that neither disperses nor fragments power at the enterprise level. Like other conservatives, he willingly endorsed organizationally authoritarian arrangements when they protect existing power and property relations.

Obviously, Harris believed there are no equitable or efficient alternatives to a capitalist economy. However, he devoted considerable attention in his *Economics and Social Reform* to the major radical alternative to bureaucratic state socialism which, at present, is commonly referred to as "self-management," or "autogestion." Harris opposed not only bureaucratic state socialism but all other schemes that demand change in the system of power or property relations. His conservatism was evident in his claim that workers' control of industry would only change the form in which the problems of power and freedom manifest themselves in human institutions.[64] Harris clearly believed that any type of democratic control of industry would prove illusory and that efforts to achieve it would only result in the usurpation of power now exercised by capitalist managers by trade-union officials and working-class politicians. Even with "the focus of power thus shifted"[65] the masses of the workers would not be able to participate in any meaningful way in the decision-making process in industry. In any case, Harris claimed that there was "little evidence to show that the overwhelming mass of workers are greatly concerned over the question of who actually runs industry."[66] Since there are no viable alternatives to the existing pattern of power and authority in industry, the proposed changes would only make the situation worse by jeopardizing the personal and political freedoms now enjoyed.

Harris fundamentally differed with Veblen in his analysis of human motivation and value. He did not believe that altruism plays or can play a large role in motivating the common man. But he is sensitive to the fact that various creeds "reject" gain "as a motivation or as an end worthy of human striving," and that they project "dignity or respect for human personality as the value of highest rank in the order of ends to be achieved by a social transformation."[67] To Harris, however, people are and must remain instruments of one another's pleasure. They cannot be treated as ends as proposed, for example, by both Kant and Christ; instead, their role, insofar as it is economic, must be instrumental.[68] Clearly, Harris did not share a commitment to either the ends or the means supported by heterodox economists and typified American conservatism in believing that any major changes not due to market forces but induced by governmental or political action will produce not utopia but an authoritarian dystopia.

While at Howard University, Harris had been a social activist involved in the civil rights movement. His retreat from social activism and his disengagement from the civil rights movement began in the late 1930s and was far advanced by the time he joined the University of Chicago faculty in 1945. Perhaps his silence after 1940 on racial issues would not have been so pronounced and his gravitation toward classical liberalism less abrupt had he remained at Howard. In any case, he became consistently skeptical about all programs for progressive change, which, of course, was well in keeping with the political and ideological tenor of the economics department at Chicago after the Second World War. Indeed, like many of his colleagues, he developed a strong fear of the possibilities of totalitarianism and professed to see its seeds in any type of economic planning, whether democratic or not. The implications of both his ideological shift from Left to Right and his disengagement from civil rights activism for understanding his treatment of Veblen are too obvious to need further examination.[69]

Chapter Four

CONSERVATIVE CRITICS:
THE RELIGIOUS ASSAULT

L EV D OBRIANSKY

T HE MOST detailed study of Veblen's work is by Lev Dobriansky.[1] It is also the only significant analysis of him in English
that systematically displays the doctrinal bias of Roman Catholicism.[2] For that reason alone, it is of concern to Veblen scholars who
are also interested in the study of comparative ideology. Dobriansky
(b. 1918), once a professor of economics at Georgetown and U.S. Am-
bassador to the Bahamas from 1982 to 1986, may be regarded as one of
Veblen's conservative critics not because he was a perfect specimen of
that ideological type but because he shared much of the doctrinal and
programmatic bias of conservative economists toward the Veblenian
system. In a sense, he was a classical rather than a modern liberal, but
his faith in the efficacy of laissez-faire was tempered by the needs of
society, which require that the government play a positive role in con-
cert with the private sector. It is again the "via media" approach of the
"perennial philosophy," adaptable to change, but conserving of values
and institutions of the post–New Deal era, which means acceptance of
those of its welfare and regulatory policies that will allow for the broad
expansion of the private sector.

Dobriansky's study of Veblen was originally done as a doctoral dissertation at New York University; its metaphysics were Thomistic and
Augustinian, its politics mainstream but colored with doctrinaire anti-
communism, and its economics mainly neoclassical although tempered by Catholic social economics.[3] That Dobriansky's ethics were
also Thomistic rather than secular in origin is evident in his critique
of the Veblenian system. For he believed that Veblen's moralism was
just another form of sentimentalism that was not an adequate substitute for the "moral certainty and the general certitudinal outlook that
result from a sound metaphysics."[4] Dobriansky's social and political
conservatism are also evident in his repudiation of Veblen's abstract
categories and antithetical thought because, in his view, they precluded consideration of more realistic conceptual and policy alternatives. However, he also laid claim to an "undoctrinaire liberalism" that

could accommodate both the old and the new while repudiating the doctrinaire radicalism of Veblen that would destroy all in order to build anew.[5] Dobriansky thus believed his middle way avoids both "totalitarian bound socialism: as well as the "socially disintegrative tendencies of laissez-faire capitalism."[6] His political philosophy is evident in his criticism of Veblen for his exaggerated stress on "pecuniary coercion, irresponsible profit-seeking and wealth amassing," which Dobriansky believed were curbed or eliminated by the controls and regulations of the Roosevelt and Truman administrations.[7] Dobriansky claimed that only "political demagogues" take Veblen's line against the corporate structure. Dobriansky did not say who these "political demagogues" were, but he believed Veblen was indirectly responsible for their behavior since he was a main source of their ideas. Apparently, Dobriansky, like many post–New Deal conservatives, thought that corporate enterprise changed its ways because the reforms of the 1930s directed its energies into more socially constructive channels. Consequently, the newly created welfare and regulatory system and improved macroeconomic policies invalidated radical criticism of American capitalism of the kind Veblen articulated in his own day.

Methodological Criticisms

There were serious deficiencies, according to Dobriansky, both in Veblen's own methodological approach to the social sciences and his critique of other methodologies, particularly in his use of ideal types or "type forms" as Veblen called them. These "abstractive elements"[8] include such devices as the dichotomy between business and industry, the peaceful and predatory types of humanity, and the stages of savagery and barbarism. This highly simplified schematic approach both distorts reality and misdirects the process of inquiry. Despite his strictures on Veblen's methodology, however, Dobriansky offered sound advice to those who are engaged in exegesis of his work. He pointed out that

> [Veblen] displays a dialectical continuity in his thought which tends to make any piecemeal analysis of his works necessarily somewhat misrepresentative of the totality of his thought. Actually it is only through a pattern of understanding the whole of Veblen's thought that accurate and proper meaning can be assigned to its various essential parts. (P. viii)

Dobriansky emphasized the organic nature of Veblen's thought and his stress on its systematic structure and its interrelatedness was a valuable antidote to criticisms that ignore these facets of it. He also commented on Veblen's relationship to Western cultural history and its various doctrinal influences on him, pointing to the complexity of his intellectual pedigree (pp. 4–13). The ideological and professional ax grinding of several Veblen scholars caused them to stress the influence on Veblen of thinkers who probably had little impact on him. It also ignored more significant influences on him because these fail to provide the doctrinal weaponry necessary for the implementation of a political agenda or the satisfaction of professional ambitions. It is to Dobriansky's credit that such misinterpretations played an insignificant role in his analysis.

Metaphysical Issues

Dobriansky made no effort to conceal the ideological structure of his own thought. Indeed, because he explicated its philosophical underpinnings as he developed arguments against Veblenism, the contrast between the two is glaring. One of his most damning criticisms thus provided a valuable source of doctrinal contrast between himself and Veblen:

> Culture in essence springs from spirituality, is sustained fundamentally by the moral requisites of harmonious social life, and can flower only insofar as the organized community is maintained by the responsible acts of men sharing common values. Briefly, in what is purported to be a Veblenian cultural theory, these characteristics of cultural entity receive little or no consideration. Judged on the basis of Veblen's philosophical tenets, which deny the reality of permanent values, this neglect should not surprise the reader. . . . Veblenism spurns the realm of "imponderables." (P. 222)

Dobriansky believed that Thomism, or the "perennial philosophy" as he called it, is the source of "a certitudinal understanding of basic human and social values" when it is properly combined with the otherwise "uncoordinated mass of social scientific knowledge" (p. viii). It is clear that these immutable truths are swallowed up by "the errors in Veblen's use of the genetical technique and his historicist interpretations which today masquerade under the absolute form of historical relativism" (p. 384). Veblen's use of the evolutionary method of analysis had some merit, but ultimately led to a grossly deficient view of the relationship between theory and action, since it ignored the "perennialist distinction between speculative and practical intellect" (p. 276). Once more Aquinas, Augustine, and Aristotle had triumphed over the American pragmatists who influenced Veblen, at least in Dobriansky's eyes.

Habit, Volition, and Anti-Intellectualism

Many critics, including Dobriansky, commented on Veblen's emphasis on the constraining impact of habit, and the very limited role that volition and reason thus play in his explanation of adjustment to social change. Dobriansky also claimed that Veblen ignored the values of habits, customs, and institutions in channeling individual and social adjustment to new circumstances. Dobriansky criticized Veblen for misunderstanding their utility in these respects and complained that "the whole tendency of his works is one of rebellion against their conservative and ostensibly obstructive features" (p. 256). In a sense, Veblen belonged to the anti-intellectualist or irrationalist camp of the late nineteenth and early twentieth centuries and was thus a participant in the "revolt against reason." His doctrinal compatriots were, of course, Freud, Nietszche, Pareto, and Sorel, among others, for all stressed the limited role that reason plays in human affairs.[9] To these thinkers, reason is ultimately submerged by emotion, habit, or subconscious factors of which the individual is hardly aware. Dobriansky also faulted the neoinstitutional economist Allan Gruchy for failing to recognize the irrationalist tenor of Veblenian doctrine; for nowhere did the latter show awareness of Veblen's anti-intellectualism, by force of which habits become more determinative of behavior than reason.[10] Dobriansky criticized the inconsistency of Veblen's indictment of human irrationalism when he commented that "is it not odd for a confirmed skeptic of rational conduct to attach such determining importance to the calculated manipulations of corporate and financial interests?" (p. 323). However, in Veblen's eyes, such behavior was no more or less ceremonial in nature than the Kwakiutl chief engaged in potlatch, and for that reason should not be labeled "rational." But much depends on what the term *rational* is assumed to mean and Dobriansky used it to mean "the calculated pursuit of self-interest."

Individualism

Dobriansky stressed the paradoxical nature of Veblenian thought. This is particularly true in his interpretation of Veblen's attitudes toward individualism. Of course, much of Veblen's work can be construed as critical of any kind of individualism, whether it be economic, social, or methodological. With the possible exception of J. K. Galbraith, no more comic writer than Veblen existed in the social sciences and much of his humor was directed at the demystifying or unveiling of individualist claims with regard to social relations. However, Dobriansky commented that "one of the many paradoxes in Veblen is his adherence to an individualistic epistemology in the face of his furtherance of a social theory assuming organismic proportions" (p. 384). Dobriansky mistook Veblen's desire for a flattened or leveled society devoid of inequalities for an inconsistent classical liberal stance that separates individual and society. At this point, Dobriansky also overlooked Veblen's preference for an "ungraded commonwealth of masterless men" in which atomistic individualism is absent. However, if Veblen was interpreted in this respect as an egalitarian radical rather than as an ambivalent classical liberal, then the paradox disappears.

Also of interest in this regard was Dobriansky's rejection of Veblen's "elimination" of the personal factor in human affairs. The latter made so negative an impression with his stress on impersonality of relationships that

> it is clearly naive of Veblen to suggest that in his industrial republic—where science, technology and material prosperity would reign supreme—the "personal equation" and "personal discrepancies of judgment," phenomena which are permanently inherent in the reality of human relation, would count for little. (P. 278)

Dobriansky believed that idiosyncratic behavior based on whim and fancy or on personal feelings about other individuals is an inescapable part of social relationships. He thus prescribed individualistic behavior alien to the norms of Veblen's industrial republic. This provides a contrast for his readers between a radical egalitarianism which immerses the individual in the collective as opposed to his own liberal sanction of individualist eccentricities. In the case of Veblen and Dobriansky, such a contrast facilitated the comparison of their social epistemologies at the risk of losing sight of Veblen's own personal iconoclasm and his admiration for "marginal" men. But the latter should not lead to confusion with a generic individualist epistemological stance on the part of Veblen, which is the impression conveyed by Dobriansky.

Instincts

Veblen's use of the term *instincts* and his failure to consistently distinguish between tropismatic and learned behavior is evidence of a vocabulary in transition and at a point where precise meaning can be assigned to either. Dobriansky recognized this, but in addition to charges of conceptual vagueness, he added allegations of the biological usurpation of ethical norms. By this latter claim, he meant that Veblen was guilty of deriving ethical standards from instinctual forms of behavior, instead of recognizing the essentially spiritual origin and significance of moral values. As Dobriansky put it,

> he imbues these elements with a normativeness and natural law authorita-
> tiveness. They are supposed to be "scientifically accepted" as substitutes for
> the dictates of old natural law founded on metaphysical reasoning. In the
> evolutionary analysis above, time and again Veblen is seen seeking authori-
> tative justification for his generalizations in these ostensible, biological
> norms. Actually, however, their very authenticity in the form he advances
> them is subject to fatal doubt; we need not elaborate on their inability to
> resolve problems on determining issues of social authority, punishment and
> rewards, just distribution, and rightful property. (P. 249)

Dobriansky also believed that Veblen's understanding of "instincts" was biologically untenable (p. 251). This was evident in his claim that much of what Veblen believed is instinctual is actually learned behav-ior. However, Dobriansky recognized that Veblen's later work mani-fested the "progressive disuse of instincts in the biological and psycho-logical sciences" (p. 256). Yet he erred in failing to completely jettison outmoded concepts of instinct. Consequently, Dobriansky could still claim that

> if it can be demonstrated that this theory is basically groundless and untena-
> ble, then it will be readily conceded that the entire structure of Veblen's
> system of thought suffers serious impairment. His calculated attempt to
> substitute biologically oriented norms for the established principles of moral
> philosophy would become a vain and hollow endeavor. (P. 256)

Probably, an ideologically committed Thomist like Dobriansky could not logically reach any other conclusions; at this point, he was merely stating what his position compelled him to say, since textual exegesis of Veblen's work would not support his claims. However, he also thought that Veblen believed "contemporary behavior is in its many aspects the result of some earlier reaction grafted into the human ma-terial by centuries of experience" (p. 258). Dobriansky then explained that

> a choice example of this is cited with reference to the writing of the instinc-
> tivist Patrick who "derives the love of baseball from the activities of prehis-
> toric savages who had to run, throw, and strike." In Veblen's biting satire,
> *The Theory of the Leisure Class*, similar examples abound; witness the attri-
> bution of such contemporary features as occupational distinctions, owner-
> ship, and dress to earlier primitive reactions of invidious comparison, forcible
> seizure, and conspicuous display, all respectively depicted in the context of
> ostensibly concrete, primitive experiences and events. (P. 258)

Dobriansky believed that in Veblen's explanation of behavior, past experience of the race becomes a permanent graft on the human raw material. However, a more perceptive reading of *The Theory of the Leisure Class* will show that the graft is embedded in institutions and must be transplanted from them to the individual psyche.

The Forms and Rights of Property Ownership

Dobriansky with his Aristotelian-Thomist attitudes toward the right of property ownership was sensitive to the fact that Veblen did not share his attitudes toward property. Indeed, he complained that "the rational basis upon which the doctrine of natural law rests its argument for private ownership is rejected by him [Veblen] as anthropomorphical" (p. 274). Dobriansky then developed at greater length the rationale underlying the natural law tradition, but his are not just traditional conservative arguments for various forms of private property—rather they overlapped with Catholic arguments rooted in a spiritual conception of man and his social relationships. In fact, when conservative doctrine was used by Dobriansky in this respect, it was employed in a secondary capacity to reinforce arguments already legitimated by Catholic theology:

> Whether in its individual or more organic form—where many individuals are concretely and functionally related, as in a particular firm—the basis of private ownership is, according to natural law doctrine, the human personality which in itself does not belong to society. Arguments from expediency, such as the incentive provided, the enforced responsible care for one's own, or the dispersion of power entailed by private property holdings, contain some measure of truth, but themselves do not furnish the foundation of this right. The foundation rests in the fundamental fact that man as a material being is intimately dependent on society and, so to speak, is an individual unit in the herd; but as a person with a immaterial soul, he transcends and is independent of society by cultivating the non-social elements constituting his personality, notably the intellectual.[11]

Dobriansky's analysis of Veblen's attitude toward property was a skilled, although brief, exposition of the ambiguity of the latter's doctrinal position, which never fully crystallized in support of a particular property form. Although Veblen probably favored the socialization of large-scale enterprises, it was never clear what this meant by way of a new mechanism of ownership in industry.[12] He did not unequivocally support state ownership and operation of the means of production perhaps because he objected to the separation of ownership from function. If, early in his career, he was sympathetic to state socialism, later his rhetoric took on an anarcho-syndicalist or guild socialist cast. Yet, in the final analysis, "Veblen is insisting upon a strict material relation to the property employed as the determining criterion for legitimate ownership"[13] which excludes absentee ownership by either individuals or the state. Strangely, Dobriansky then claimed that the Veblenian attitude toward property is not to redistribute wealth and income nor does it lead to "socialism," for his use of this term is ambiguous and imprecise. Dobriansky concluded that Veblen was an advocate of a "technocratic managerialism" in that particular property forms are a matter of indifference so long as they do not obstruct managerial prerogatives that aim at maximum production.[14]

Patriotism, War, and Business

Like many conservatives, Dobriansky could not accept Veblen's explanation of the linkage between patriotism, war, and capitalism. In words reminiscent of George H. Mead, he criticized Veblen's definition of patriotism because the latter failed to realize that patriotism need not take the form of "a chauvinist nationalism obstructing international amity and fanning the flames of ever threatening warfare."[15] By this he meant that Veblen's doctrines point to war as the logical outcome of national pride and ambition on the part of the dynastic states such as Imperial Germany, Austria, Russia, and Japan, while the fusion of patriotic sentiment with business enterprise was its cause in the democratic commonwealths such as Great Britain, France, and the United States. Veblen doubted the institutional adequacy of both dynastic monarchy and business enterprise for the achievement of permanent peace, but his explanation of the cause of international conflict, to Dobriansky, closely resembled the devil theory of war.[16]

Technology, Culture, and Economic Change

Dobriansky believed that Veblen exaggerated the role of technology in social change as well as the persistence of cultural lag. It is difficult to avoid the conclusion, however, that Dobriansky was implicitly defending the Roman Catholic church against Veblen's view of it as an "imbecile institution" that epitomizes cultural lag and atavistic continuities. Nevertheless, despite Dobriansky's doctrinal rationalizations, some provocative comments emerge regarding Veblen's emphasis on technology as a fulcrum of social change. For example, he claimed that

> the technological dynamism in Veblen's thought predetermines an omnipresent cultural archaism and lag, extending itself in perpetuity and conditioning an indefinite disequilibrium. . . . Any survival of institutional form

appears to imply a cultural lag for him, instead of signifying an element with definite functions in the social system. The root cause of this excess in Veblen is undoubtedly his unwarranted magnification of technology as a transforming social agent. (Pp. 287–88)

Connected to Dobriansky's criticisms of overemphasis on technology are his repeated complaints against Veblen's "economic determinism," for Veblen's materialist orientation led to an exaggerated stress on the material determinants of social change (pp. 287–88). Because of its materialist nature, Veblen's social philosophy could not adequately accommodate the unique creativeness of the religious mystic with his potency for transforming social structures and rearranging institutions for the "perpetuation of social growth" (pp. 287–88). Strictly speaking, Veblen might not have been an economic determinist, but he placed too much emphasis on the conditioning effects of economic factors in history (p. 227), and, in Dobriansky's eyes, this diminishes man's stature as a spiritual being and autonomous moral agent.

The discipline of the machine process on the human psyche is one major reason for movement toward a better society in the Veblenian analysis (p. 298). This is not an irreversible process, for as Dobriansky put it, "there is no element of necessity in this sequence inasmuch as a different outcome is possible" (p. 298). Yet he complained of Veblen's "strong imputation of almost absolute social corrosive powers into the discipline of the machine" which would "discredit all the animistic thought embodied in our laws, customs, religious observances and the like" (p. 298). This would even lead to a skepticism regarding the rights of property owners. A climate might be produced in which a classless society is possible, but, added Dobriansky, "this logical possibility is not pursued by Veblen. He views the psychological roots of man as too deeply entrenched for this to happen. Indeed, he is even skeptical about the solidifying effects of the machine process on the habitual behavior of the productive elements" (p. 285). Dobriansky was thus critical of the motives of those who failed to grasp the technocratic roots and thrust of Veblen's work, for his supporters wanted "to erase the technocratic stigmata from the name of the master" (p. 370).

The Dichotomy between Business and Industry

Veblen's dichotomy between business and industry, that is, making money versus making socially useful goods, needs no reiteration here. But it drew criticism from Dobriansky for several reasons. He believed that Veblen's imprecise grouping of pecuniary professions under the rubric of "business" was itself false. For Veblen ignored the real value of the work done by realtors, speculators, and militarists. Also, his Darwinian materialism had a heavy overlay of ungrounded idealism that assumed the abolition of risk and war. To make matters worse,

> Veblen's passion for efficiency in no way exceeds that of any economist whose eyes are fixed on the real economic relations and are not blinded by monetary and fiscal magic. If this passion were given unbridled expression,, as marks Veblenism, it would inevitably create greater inefficiencies. John M. Clark rightly observes, no one has ever shown "how social efficiency can be organized on a technical basis alone"—and this includes Veblen![17]

Dobriansky indicted Veblen for his designation of certain occupations as parasitical or wasteful and his belief that the income derived from rent, interest, and profit is largely unearned. The pecuniary occupations, of course, include realtors, attorneys, brokers, bankers, advertising, and salesmen. Dobriansky could not agree that, on the whole, they are unproductive or exploitive and thus undeserving of their income shares. As he put it, "his early statement of them signalized the need for some theoretic readjustments in economic expositions on distribution," and in this sense Veblen made a positive contribution to economics (p. 303). But, in the final analysis, Veblen's attack on conventional economics was like that of his contemporary and friend John Hobson, which was based on

> notions of class power, conventional predation, and arbitrary acquisition. In a sense, all of his criticisms are negative since he offers no criteria of distribution in line with his own narrow conception of productiveness. But, then, that would amount to an involvement in the general problem of economic organization, and, as frequently seen, no such problem apparently exists or would exist for Veblen. (P. 303)

Because Veblen did not accept the legitimacy of profit making, he "evinces no appreciative understanding of the function of profits in the modern economy" (p. 309). However, Dobriansky believed that Veblen's view of profit was inconsistent, for at times he seemed to object only to gains over and above normal returns necessary to justify continuation of a given line of production. At other times, he appeared to oppose profit in principle. Whatever his real views may have been, his criticism misrepresented the functional role of profit and, in this sense, he performed a public disservice (p. 310).

Related to this deficiency in Veblen's thought were his teachings on credit, which are relevant to an understanding of his theory of the business cycle, in that unwarranted borrowing is the device used to produce overcapitalization. Ultimately, the widened discrepancy between industrial equipment and business capital with no addition to material output of product is what produces the difference between aggregate nominal capital and actual earning capacity. The consequence is another business crisis. Dobriansky admitted the partial validity of Veblen's insight into the use of modern loan credit as a control device of absentee ownership, but he believed that

> the activistic and control properties of loan credit which Veblen uniquely emphasizes are of considerable importance. But they certainly do not justify his mischaracterization of the essential nature of credit, its unquestionably productive role in the economic process, and the beneficial effects of its employment provided it is not misused both in its distribution and application. (P. 315)

Dobriansky also believed that Veblen wildly exaggerated the burden placed by salesmanship and sales cost on the underlying population when he suggested that its elimination would reduce the load by 50 percent (p. 330). In the final analysis, the Veblenian dichotomy between business and industry fails because it rests on the "fallacious production-for-use and production-for-profit distinction" (p. 335). But Dobriansky did not effectively argue the case against the Veblenian dichotomy; he simply assumed that any reasonable economist would understand its inadequacies, thus exhibiting once more his own neoclassical biases.

Veblen's interpretation of consumer motivation and behavior attracted more attention than any other facet of his work. Dobriansky conceded there is some merit in his claims about emulatory consumption, but his concession is well within the doctrinal parameters of political conservatism. To illustrate, Veblen failed to recognize the high degree of personal freedom that exists in advanced capitalist systems by ignoring "the general prevalence of a wide range of individual choice unguided by arbitrary dictation" (p. 312). Of course, to Veblen much of this alleged "freedom" was fundamentally illusory and could only lead to the defeat of the generic ends of human life. But Dobriansky would have no truck with such claims. Instead, he articulated both the ideology of the modern welfare and regulatory system and the ideal of consumer sovereignty, which meant that

> consumers may not abide religiously by the recommendations of consumer research reports as possibly they should. However, they certainly are not haplessly exposed to the economic discrepancies between pecuniary and material serviceability as excessively portrayed by Veblen. Moreover, surely they are not expected to sacrifice freely the many aesthetic values reflected in the presumed superfluities of goods for his drab brand of "materialist puritanism." The strong implication of consumer education in Veblen's conception of material serviceability is well taken, but his valuation of consumers' wants is unwarrantedly austere. (P. 305)

Apparently, Dobriansky believed that "consumer education" adequately described Veblen's prescription for change, as though the main thrust of his indictment was the ignorance of consumers rather than the emulatory bent of their behavior. Dobriansky failed to ask what would be accomplished by helping them shop more intelligently if the net result was simply to integrate them more completely into the processes of conspicuous consumption and ostentatious display. Dobriansky also believed that Veblen's "valuation of consumer wants is unwarrantedly austere." But surely Veblen's point was not austerity or its opposite, but whether consumption is life-enhancing, that is, "serves the generic ends of life impersonally considered" as he put it. Because Dobriansky was a Catholic who perceived man as a spiritual being seeking the hereafter, he largely stripped himself of any criterion except the religious one for evaluating the purely secular ends Veblen sought.

Like many conservatives, Dobriansky misinterpreted the actual proposals Veblen made for restructuring the economy. Nowhere was this more evident than in his claim that "possibly no more absurd feature can be found in Veblen's thought than his literal proposal for the elimination of the price system or the market apparatus" (p. 378), which, in Dobriansky's eyes, were an "undesigned achievement of man." This last statement indicates his belief that the price system and market mechanism are "spontaneous" rather than deliberately contrived phenomena. Dobriansky added that "through this the complexity of our social division of labor is maintained without the coercive intervention of authority" (p. 378). Unlike Veblen, he did not believe that the price system and market mechanism possess a coercive authority of their own. Dobriansky complained that "what is real progress in productivity for the engineer is not always so for the businessman and economist. His comprehension of cost and want phenomena is further marred by his reliance on the fallacious theory of war performance" (p. 328). Dobriansky was referring to Veblen's "misunderstanding" of the performance of the American economy during World War I, evident in his exaggerated emphasis on the great increase in gross industrial output and food production that resulted from temporary removal of institutional restraints on productive capacity.

Dobriansky appreciated part of Veblen's attack on the promotion of vested interests through the granting of copyrights and patents. He pointed out, however, that "it can be easily deduced that the existence of a patent system symbolizes nothing more than legalized business engrossment of the technological stock of the community" (p. 331). This interpretation of a fundamental Veblenian claim was then followed by Dobriansky's assertion that this, of course, does not settle the problem of sufficient incentive. As one of the basic arguments in support of the patent system, without the security of a patent no enterprise would be undertaken in a new development if rivals, by sheer waiting and no sustaining of costs, would merely adopt the developed technique. There is, too, a subsequent threat of economically undercutting the original bearer of cost. Veblen simply does not face this problem. (P. 331)

Dobriansky endorsed John Common's observation that "Veblen, like Marx is theoretically inept in regard to the distinction between flow of time and lapse of time. . . . He fails miserably in any balanced recognition of the distinction between moving points of time and intervals between points of time" (p. 320). Dobriansky then elaborated on this criticism, commenting that "the distinction is the basis for the difference between change and waiting, process and valuing, profits and interest. . . . His unsatisfactory explanation of interest and risk-taking as simply business propositions emerges from this common source of error" (pp. 320–21). Apparently, Dobriansky thought that the lender and the investor are entitled to their take because their ability or willingness to wait makes possible capital accumulation and investment. Such claims have a long pedigree in American economic thought, stretching back at least to Irving Fisher's popularization of them among economists in the early twentieth century. Probably from Veblen's perspective, however, they only mystified the accumulation and investment processes by ignoring the claims of the community upon its own stock of technique and technology. By defending the parceling out to individuals of what is actually the collective legacy of the community, and by failing to acknowledge that it is easier for people with money to wait than it is for those without it, Dobriansky reached conclusions similar to Fisher's.

Critics have often been puzzled by Veblen's attitudes toward monopoly and competition. Since he never wrote a formal treatise on industrial organization, his views must be pieced together from a variety of sources, including the speculations of various economists. Although Dobriansky found important insights in Veblen's analysis, he commented that

serious doubts arise as to Veblen's reasoned perspective on the limits of competition, on the all-important element of time, and the empirical character of competitive practice. His dynamism again blinds his insight into the excesses that unrestricted competition would produce if necessary time allowance were not made for short-run economic adjustments. He fails, whereas Professor Schumpeter evidently succeeds in demonstrating the long-run meaning of certain restrictive practices by firms. In a dynamic economy marked by the undercutting sweep of technologic advances, these practices are aimed at monetary security rather than exorbitant profits. (P. 333)

Dobriansky's own views on the virtues or merits of reform capitalism were fully evident in other comments that he made regarding the changed nature of the economic system. It is clear that he believed New Deal and post–New Deal reforms had succeeded in harnessing corporate power to the common good and that countervailing power was now exercised by several social forces. As Dobriansky put it,

> Veblen's prosaic formula of monopolistic elements, higher prices, extortion-
> ate profits, and restricted output becomes almost puerile when one considers
> the many counteracting phenomena in the economic situation. The elastic-
> ity of demand, improved techniques, trade union surveillance, and other
> powerful elements are surely real phenomena that no sound analysis can
> afford to overlook. (P. 333)

Critics have often commented about Veblen's emphasis on large in-dustrial technologies and economies of scale. Dobriansky believed he overemphasized the economic gains from huge plant size and claimed that "he is even obsessed with megalolatry and wholly oblivious to the economic law of optimum size" (p. 307). Dobriansky believed that in-stead of maximum economies of scale being reaped by great size, "sav-ings effected are in large measure those of management and competi-tive marketing costs than in prime costs of production" (p. 308). Of course, during much of Veblen's active career as a scholar, such claims were irrelevant, since he wrote during an era of consolidation in which horizontal mergers facilitated achievement of greater economies of scale. The era to which Dobriansky was referring, in which manage-ment and competitive marketing costs were the prime areas of effected savings, did not become significant until the early to mid-1920s, which is when Veblen ceased writing.

Dobriansky believed that far too much of Veblen's analysis of cor-porate mergers was based on the creation of the United States Steel Corporation, the gigantic merger underwritten by J. P. Morgan and Company in 1900. Veblen's penetrating analysis of this episode unfor-tunately served as the basis of much of his theorizing about corporate mergers and, because he was generalizing on the basis of one impor-tant but very atypical example, caused him to err. His depiction of the captains of industry and finance attributed the sins of Andrew Carne-gie and the House of Morgan to other consolidations and, according to Dobriansky, it was inaccurate and unfair. Dobriansky claimed that Veblen's charges of excessive operating costs, overcapitalization, delay of necessary technological renovation, and the ascendancy of pecuni-ary capital leading to financial control over industry were all greatly exaggerated (pp. 317–24). Dobriansky apparently preferred to think of the great capitalists of Veblen's day as "industrial statesmen" rather than as "robber barons."

Politics and the State

Dobriansky also took Veblen to task for his denigration of constitutional government. He believed Veblen's view of constitutional government was flawed because it grossly exaggerated the political power of the business community. This was reflected in Veblen's overemphasis on the effects of business contributions to political parties and the subsequent weakening of the regulatory process. Veblen was thus wrong in claiming that representative government meant only the representation of corporate interests (pp. 347–48).

It is true that Veblen made uncomplimentary comments regarding the republican form of government and Dobriansky accurately described certain aspects of his analysis. Dobriansky did not, however, give adequate stress to Veblen's belief that the dynastic and autocratic states were considerably worse than the republics. Even a casual reading of *The Nature of Peace* illustrates Veblen's awareness of the differences between America and Great Britain on the one hand and Imperial Germany and Russia on the other and his preference for the former over the latter. Dobriansky preferred, however, at times to stress Veblen's basic utopian anarchism, which he objected to because he believed "the political element is well nigh uneliminable" (p. 345). Dobriansky also claimed that

> unless one is blinded by a chronic and often misdirected iconoclasm, the truth is that the modern democracies are fundamentally sustained by sentiments, habits, and convictions founded on personal rights, equitable law, and sound justice. These bases have no active meaning in the philosophical context of Veblenism and are consequently ignored as functional political elements. (P. 350)

Dobriansky made such claims in part because he could not accept ideological systems such as Veblen's that were not ultimately grounded in the Thomistic version of natural law that views man as a spiritual being. Evidence for this assertion lies in his criticism of Veblen's system of thought to the effect that "it is a striking paradox that a presumably hard, objective, evolutionist materialist is so deeply steeped in naive social idealism" (p. 345). Between the two men lay an unbridgeable ideological chasm bounded on one side by a Catholic perspective of social relationships and ontology and on the other by atheistic materialism and secular humanism.[18]

Dobriansky was convinced that there is no room for the progressive improvement of either business enterprise or constitutional government in the Veblenian system.[19] These claims, of course, raise larger questions regarding the doctrinal relationship between Veblen and the reform of capitalism during the New Deal—questions dealt with elsewhere.[20] It suffices here to point to the fact that Veblen's writings appeared between 1884 and 1925. The only period of reform during this period was the Progressive era and by almost any applicable standard, the changes induced by government during it were modest indeed. It is not difficult to justify Veblen's disdain of them for they produced only small gains for the "underlying population," as he liked to call it. If government and business enterprise were capable of reform, it was during the New Deal era that this was to occur, which was after Veblen's death. Dobriansky might better have complained, instead, that he failed to anticipate such changes as occurred in the 1930s, although even that is a debatable assertion.

Conclusion

Veblen believed that life has certain generic ends—those of "impersonal usefulness" as he put it. But Dobriansky argued that "his conception of the common good as comprising, first, the satisfaction of the three dominant instincts and, second, the plentitude of material goods is plainly defective and even ethically naive."[21] The bases of Dobriansky's judgments were the natural law philosophy of Aquinas and Catholic social economics. However, Dobriansky shifted grounds for standards of judgment and at times used utility theory as employed by mainline neoclassicists. It was no longer the absolute, immutable, and eternal verities of the "perennial philosophy" that informed his position, but rather the highly relativistic idea of subjective preference and, at times, this inconsistency marred his analysis of Veblen.

Dobriansky did not believe that Veblen articulated "any constructive scheme of organization that will insure economic order, the efficient realization of freely determined choice, and a safe dispersion of power."[22] Unfortunately, Veblen did not understand "that conditions of economic order and progress necessitate the continued existence of pecuniary expedients. The issue boils down again to one of difference in degree rather than in kind."[23]

In any case, Dobriansky's claim provided evidence of the doctrinal constraints imposed on him by neoclassicism that caused him to confuse Veblen's ambiguous satirical efforts with utopian proposals for reconstruction of the economy. Dobriansky believed that Veblen's "most basic revulsion against the modern system of business enterprise is of moral character,"[24] which is true in that the latter believed it thwarted achievement of the generic ends of life. Dobriansky had already indicated that Veblen's ends were not his ends, nor were they compatible with the "perennial philosophy" of Aquinas or the social teachings of the Roman Catholic church. Yet at times his attitudes toward Veblen were equivocal, for he also claimed that Veblen's conception of the good society was compatible with the Catholic vocational movement.[25] But in the final analysis, Dobriansky was caught between Christian moral imperatives that demand altruism and neoclassical economists who, in Veblen's words, make "the theory of exchange value the central and controlling doctrine in their theoretical systems."[26]

Chapter Five

LIBERAL CRITICS: THE PROGRESSIVES

AMERICAN progressivism, at least as a coherent domestic political reform movement, largely ended with the declaration of war
in April 1917 on the Central Powers, and most domestic intellectuals supported the Wilson administration's policies. In this respect,
they were like European intellectuals, writers, artists, and scientists,
even those with left-wing views, who displayed an "almost manic belli-
cosity" at the beginning of the First World War.[1] Overwhelming and
uncritical support to the governments and armies of their own nations
was forthcoming and little effort was made to be objective about the
origins of the hurricane of war blowing from the Balkan Peninsula.

Nevertheless, there was small-scale resistance to the contagion,
even in war countries. However, it was in neutrals like the United
States that it was easiest for intellectuals to achieve a degree of detachment from the war aims and claims of the Entente and Central Powers.
Indeed, the outbreak of the conflagration led many radical and liberal
American intellectuals to consider, or reconsider, the whole idea of patriotism, as well as its relationship to war and peace. On the far left,
writers for the *Masses*, such as its editor, Max Eastman, viewed patriotism as a device for manipulating the common man to act contrary to
his own interests. They called upon both intellectuals and the American working class to declare a plague on both sides in the new war and
pushed for a policy of noninvolvement on the part of the United
States.[2] The liberal editors of *The New Republic*, Herbert Croly, Walter
Weyl, and Walter Lippmann, while they sanctioned a policy of American neutrality in its editorial pages, privately advocated an early intervention on the side of the Allies. Other liberals, like John Dewey,
sympathized with the Allied cause but waited until later in the war to
endorse intervention on the side of the Entente.[3] Still others, such as
Randolph Bourne, broke ranks with Dewey and advocated a policy of
nonintervention and noninvolvement.[4] The impact of William James's
famous essay "The Moral Equivalent of War" was felt anew and some
of his disciples began to look for a practical moral equivalent of war that
would divert the bellicose energies of the young into more constructive
channels.[5]

A "SCIENTIFIC" REFORMER

Two other Americans, Thorstein Veblen and George H. Mead (1863–1931), were too sophisticated in affairs of state to swallow the propaganda of either side with their allegations of primal innocence versus brute aggression.[6] However, their political and ideological positions were different in fundamental ways. Although Mead once occupied a position on the left wing of the existing political spectrum, in maturity he turned to what he perceived as "scientific" social reform as opposed to socialism, which in his view was a form of utopian hope without a realizable program. Like Veblen he identified Marxism as a purposive philosophy of history and opposed it because of its teleological implications. However, unlike Veblen he did not share with Marxists a belief in the efficacy of large-scale structural change.[7] Mead was not a radical like Veblen, but neither was he a complacent middle-of-the-roader satisfied with the modest reforms of the Wilson era and the bread-and-butter aims of the craft unions in the American Federation of Labor.[8]

In his mind's eye, Veblen, perhaps, envisioned establishment of a cooperative commonwealth in which absentee ownership would be abolished, institutional religious belief and practice discarded, and perpetual peace and prosperity achieved through disallowance of vested interests. The liberal Mead, with his experimentalist, pragmatic, ameliorist outlook and his advocacy of reform capitalism, was distrustful of such dreams of general social reconstruction. Had Veblen and Mead engaged in a full-scale political debate, an unlikely occurrence given their noncombative dispositions, Veblen's anarcho-socialism as opposed to Mead's liberalism would be evident. It is to be expected that their different ideological positions would also be reflected in their views on patriotism, war, and peace. Unlike many European intellectuals, Veblen did not think the war would lead to resurrection of community; indeed, he saw it as the result of a kind of false consciousness, while Mead, on the contrary, viewed it as a genuine force for cohesion and unity.

The Subject of Patriotism

Few are aware of either the existence or the significance of Mead's evaluation of Veblen's *An Inquiry into the Nature of Peace and the Terms of Its Perpetuation.*[9] Veblen, in his justly famed but little-read work of 1917, and Mead, in a lengthy review of it written in 1918 for

the *Journal of Political Economy*, which Veblen once edited, were concerned with the role of patriotism in peace and war. Veblen defined
patriotism as a "sense of partisan solidarity in respect of prestige" and
"a sense of undivided joint interest in a collective body of prestige."[10]
However, according to Mead, when it is so defined it becomes "the only
important common social trait of the common man in the community
and the member of the wealthy class, so that when appealed to it unified the community for the time being."[11] Mead chided Veblen for believing that the material interests of the possessing class on the one
hand and of the common man of the other are so diverse that "no patriotic enterprise can be of common interest to both." Worse yet, Veblen
believed that no "patriotic enterprise can possibly be of benefit to the
community at large in a material sense."[12] Thus Mead was unhappy
with Veblen's completely negative attitude toward patriotism.

Patriotism for Mead was not simply jingoism under the self-seeking
manipulative control of the vested interests. Indeed, while patriotism
may be construed negatively, he thought it provided the social cement
that binds the social order together, for it gives society a set of common
goals and shared mission and makes it possible to undertake tasks for
the common good, that is, the collective benefit of the community.
Mead believed Veblen wrong for claiming that the use of patriotism is
for illicit purposes only, that is, power aggrandizement and exploitation; for Veblen unfortunately shared the characteristic radical view of
power as controlled by the vested interests and exercised primarily in
zero-sum games where conflict leads only to winners or losers. Mead
believed, instead, that power is more likely to be exercised for the benefit of all, at least in industrial societies with political systems akin to
the American one. Consequently, he could not accept Veblen's view
that the interest of the privileged classes in the common welfare is one
"of the same kind as the interest which a parasite has in the well-being
of his host."[13]

Veblen believed that a lasting peace would only be possible if the
dynastic states involved in World War I, such as Germany, Austria,
Turkey, Japan, and Czarist Russia, were dispossessed of their autocra-
cies and if structural changes also occurred in the liberal democracies.
He argued that "the emulative spirit that come under the head of patriotism"[14] must be subjugated through disallowing the property claims
of citizens abroad, eliminating protective tariffs, and ending imperialist
control of weaker communities by the stronger in the supposed interest of domestic industry and commerce. Otherwise there would be an
inevitable resurgence of militarism, war, and aggression. But Mead
wrote that

there seems to be an inherent tendency in social groups to advance from the hostile attitudes of individuals and groups toward each other through rivalries, competitions and cooperations toward a functional self-assertion which recognizes and utilizes other selves and groups of selves in the activities in which social human nature expresses itself.[15]

Mead was critical of Veblen for contemplating

a situation in which national consciousness would largely if not entirely disappear, and with it any citizenship which would have to be protected when the individual found himself in foreign parts. . . . The author [Veblen] finds nothing in a national consciousness which has any function than that of providing possible causes for hostilities between different communities."[16]

To Mead, the solidarity that is induced in groups by their hostility toward others ultimately is a "progressive" process that in the long run would unite mankind more than divide it. But Mead was not naive about the nature of war in general or trench warfare on the Western Front in particular. He was well aware of the butchery taking place long before American entry into the war in April 1917. For example, he wrote to his son Henry regarding the German offensive in the spring of 1916 that "the murderous-most murderous phase of this war is well on now on the West front. Its hideousness is beyond belief."[17] Henry was shortly to join the American army and serve in the European theater of the war. Although his father made some effort before this to temper his pro-Ally sentiments, he made little pretense afterward at concealing his contempt for the Central Powers.

Despite his general pacifist bias, Veblen's attitude toward American entry into the war has not been easy to decipher. His biographer, Joseph Dorfman, ambiguously stated that "on the basis of his books alone, Veblen's position regarding the war might seem rather difficult to determine, but the entrance of the United States on the Entente side seems to have pleased him."[18] Veblen worked for government agencies during the war and even drew up a proposal for an antisubmarine defense system. Yet he was extremely critical of government persecution of the Industrial Workers of the World and of the postwar settlement.

Veblen's thinking during the war may seem ambiguous due to the promotion of his book on *Imperial Germany and the Industrial Revolution* as effective anti-German propaganda at the same time the post office was banning it from the mails as pro-German! However, this ambiguity is more illusory than real when the book is placed within the corpus of Veblen's writings and situated in the context of the development of his thought. Veblen liked to distinguish between republics such as the United States, Great Britain, and France and the dynastic systems of Hohenzollern Germany, Hapsburg Austria, and Romanov Russia. Clearly he preferred the republics to the dynasties, which, no doubt, helps explain his support for the Allies after America entered the war. However, his analysis differed both from revolutionary socialists like Lenin, who conflated both kinds of political systems and called for their revolutionary overthrow and liberals like Mead who asked their fellow citizens to close ranks and make the world safe for democracy. For Veblen perceived the war itself as caused by the larger system of imperialism of which the republics and dynasties were an integral part; yet he remained cognizant of the important differences between the two. It was evident that he believed the long-term chances for peace depended on dismantling the entire system that brought on the war, not simply on an Allied defeat of the Central Powers.

Shortly before Mead wrote his critical review of Veblen's *An Inquiry Into the Nature of Peace*, he wrote a tract for the National Security League that was published as part of its Patriotism Through Education series. In *The Conscientious Objector*, Mead gave a fundamentally different account of the origins of the war and its probable effects on American society than that offered by Veblen. In this propagandistic piece written to sway public opinion, Mead claimed that

> America finally entered this world war, because its issue was that of democracy, democracy defined as the right of peoples to self-government, the right of a people to determine the foreign policy of its government, the right of the small nations to existence because they are nations, and the right of the whole western world to be free from the threat of imperialistic militarism. We are fighting for the larger world society which democratic attitudes and principles make possible.[19]

Mead advanced such claims in part because he believed that America was a democratic community in which the conscientious objector might "arouse a public sentiment which condemns and leads to the repeal of the law."[20] Veblen, of course, had no such illusions about the nature of American society including both its democratic nature and the right of dissenters to criticize the involvement in war. Indeed, while Mead proclaimed the achievement of democracy in America and the right of dissenters within limits to criticize the war, Veblen critically observed the persecution of the Industrial Workers of the World and the beginnings of the anticommunist hysteria that was shortly to engulf the country. Nothing could match Veblen's biting indictments of the American mass mind. The war had shocked Americans into a "dementia praecox." The power of organized religion, the "puerile credulities," the persecutions and deportations of advocates of "constructive sedition," the baiting of wobblies and conscientious objectors and pacifists for "excessive sanity," all signified mental derangement.[21]

Although Mead lacked Veblen's detachment regarding the Allied war aims, he did not endorse the persecution of opponents of the war. Also, he well recognized the dangers of militarism and its incompatibility with certain American ideals. In referring to the impact of army life on his son Henry and the other young men in his company, he felt fortunate that "militarism has set no evil stamp upon them yet."[22] However, much of Mead's work was colored with efforts to achieve a politically neutral posture. He did this by using illustrations that showed him to be a "dispassionate" observer. For example, in showing how social unity is threatened by imaginary forces, he used the hobgoblins of conservatism, radicalism, and classical liberalism as though all at one time or other were equally the result of irrationality and paranoia.

> Today we dread the Bolsheviki. At another time it has been the "interests," at times the mob, and at other times the arbitrary power of a monarch.[23]

Mead's thinking epitomized the liberal *Weltanschauung* in which political truths are relative to circumstance. Thus no classes or interests can make permanently binding claims on the community or represent anything more than a passing threat to it. Unlike the radical Veblen who focused on the vested interests, his array of antisocial agents was diffuse and astructural, for Mead could not locate the "enemy" except in a transient, fleeting manner.[24]

Nationalism, Ameliorism, and the Welfare State

Mead chastised Veblen because the latter "ignores positive social forces which in the midst of imperialistic, political and economic movements tend toward democratic control."[25] Mead thus detected an ameliorative trend in human affairs that Veblen had overlooked. He complained that "Veblen isolates the forces of national and class self-assertion in dynastic and capitalistic control and insists that they inevitably work out in social exploitation alone."[26] But, he continued, "self-assertion in groups and individuals has led through rivalries, competitions, and finally cooperations to new types of individuals."[27] Again, it is apparent that Mead believed in the likelihood of human progress, whereas Veblen failed to see what is to Mead an obvious ameliorative tendency. As Henry Steele Commager once put it, "Where others saw progress, Veblen saw merely change."[28]

Mead repeatedly criticized Veblen for failing to recognize the "positive" attributes of patriotism. Mead disagreed with Veblen's definition of patriotism as a "sense of solidarity in respect of collective prestige" since this could not adequately explain the "attitude of members of the community toward other communities in their cooperation and arbitrations and satisfactions of mutual claims, or even in their rivalries and competition which are conducted in other ways than fighting."[29] The Veblenian categories were too "rigid" and Veblen's formulas too "abstract" to explain how an imperialistic, militaristic, and dynastic state like Hohenzollern Germany was nevertheless able to implement a large-scale program of progressive social legislation. Given Veblen's basic assumptions, Mead thought such a welfare state could never have emerged. Nor could Veblen explain the leftward swing of the English Labour party at the end of the war, for he saw "only the tendency of wealth to gravitate into the hands of the few and their tendency to spend it for purposes of conspicuous waste or to use his other formula 'pecuniary waste and personal futility.'"[30] Contrary to Veblen, Mead thought that patriotic values, the nationalistic state, and social reform could coexist and prosper together, and he sanctioned the emergence of such a symbiotic relationship. This is evidence once more of the political cleavage between the two men that was rooted in their radical and liberal reform ideologies respectively.

Patriotism, War, and Peace

Patriotism, in Mead's view, was the only source of social cement adhesive enough for purposes of communal bonding. Indeed, at times Mead became so ardent in his quest for social unification that he even sanctioned the kind of patriotism that in the past had led to war. He wrote that

> while war was still a possible national adventure, there was a certain rough psychological justification for that test, that at least one war in a generation was essential for the spiritual hygiene of the nation. The toleration of secret diplomacy, the cherishing of national honor and peculiar interests as lying outside the field of negotiation had behind it an obscure but profound feeling that in national honor and in these peculiar interests were symbolized a national unity which could be made precious by the arbitrament of war.[31]

Obviously, Veblen could not acquiesce in Mead's rationalization of war as an essential part of the process of social unification were he confronted with it. To Veblen, war was ordinarily the result of the atavistic thrust of "imbecile institutions." Thus he attributed the militarization of industrial society not simply to the inherent nature of capitalist institutions as such, but also to the survival of archaic feudal attitudes, structures, and ideologies. Such anachronisms remained in Imperial Germany and Japan and in the social structure of England.

The effectiveness with which these advanced industrial societies adapted themselves to war was due, he thought, to the continuing habit of deference to and emulation of a military ruling class. Indeed, Veblen sharply contrasted the parochial politico-military dissension of the age with its cosmopolitan technological knowledge when he wrote that, "into this cultural and technological system of the modern world the patriotic spirit fits like dust in the eyes and sand in the bearings."[32]

By contrast, at times, in Mead's discussion of war and patriotism, it is difficult to tell whether he was aware of the implications of his own words. For example, Mead wrote in 1929 that "War on occasions makes the good of the community the supreme good of the individual. What has the pacifist who would abolish war to put in its place?"[33] Apparently Veblen's earlier answer of "peace" was insufficient!

In his analysis of Veblen's writings on patriotism, war, and peace, John Diggins criticized Veblen for equating nationalism and patriotism that "led him to dismiss almost contemptuously one of humankind's healthiest sentiments."[34] Patriotism, Diggins argued, in terms reminiscent of Mead himself, is "essentially an emotional bond fired by a sense of community,"[35] and is quite different from nationalism, which is "an ideological abstraction, a bastardized form of patriotism that one attempts to expand as a universal export, by military force, if necessary."[36] Diggins's distinction thus suggested some of the complexities of Mead's view, as well as some of the difficulties of Veblen's own perception of patriotism.

C. T. Gillen argued that Mead's theory "ideally fitted the progressive consciousness of the Teddy Roosevelt era. . . . he was caught up in the 19th century notion of progress and its reification in the historical form of imperialism."[37] This is an exaggeration of Mead's position, yet Mead, like his former colleague and friend John Dewey, did support American entrance into the Great War. On the other hand, Veblen remained an unreconstructed opponent of the system of imperialism that he believed caused the war, although, unlike many revolutionary socialists, he preferred an Allied victory over the Central Powers. Mead looked upon men as brothers who were serving a common purpose which ordered priorities and spurred cooperative effect, even though this meant death or mutilation in war. But Veblen interpreted war as an archaic manifestation of prowess and institutional imbecility.

For Mead, as nations maintained their own sense of solidarity and self-respect by animosity toward other nations, so groups lesser than nations maintained their self-respect in and by a hostile attitude toward other groups. Patriotism and even war provide a bonding agent that holds society together and holds great promise for the future cooperative effort. However, for Veblen, war only epitomizes the failure of the national community to overcome its self-regarding and destructive "instincts," which are "sport" and "predation." War thus means that the other-regarding "instincts" of parenthood, idle curiosity, and workmanship have become temporarily "contaminated" or at least submerged. Veblen could never forget the primitive tribes that played so prominent a role in his historical anthropology with their ethic of "live and let live." It was this peaceful type-form of humanity and communities constructed in the pacifist image that international relations now lacked.

Conclusion

Veblen often criticized neoclassical economists for believing that the price system and the market mechanism perform neutral functions without recognizing the way they serve underlying cultural norms and the system of power and property relations. He was as bold in asserting that the price system and the market mechanism are not value-neutral as Mead was in claiming that patriotism is value-neutral and can be used for good or bad purposes. Patriotism may be separated from the social structures that channel it and from the social consequences that ensue from its working, but Veblen emphasized more than Mead the unreality of mere analytics divorced from both social underpinnings and long-term effects. Veblen was thus a stronger opponent of formalism in the social sciences than Mead. However, his views tended to be both more critical and more absolutist than Mead in that he stressed alternatives that might require establishment of an entirely different order. Thus in Veblen's analysis we find such contrasts as peace *or* the price system, international disarmament *or* intensified conflict.[38] Once more this is indicative of Veblen's radicalism, while the liberal Mead usually focused on partial solutions and on shorter-range alternatives.

Mead believed that future wars might be avoided between the major powers by skillful diplomacy, the encouragement of a more wholesome patriotism, the prudent use, or threat of the use, of force, and the implementation of international conflict resolution mechanisms. Such beliefs, of course, were the stock in trade of early twentieth century liberals, and Mead held views that were no exception to the rule. Veblen did not think peace could be so easily achieved, for he believed that war was the logical outcome of the capitalist and imperialist systems. Thus, his main focus was on the need for disallowing vested interests, for it was in the fundamental transformation of the existing system of property and power relations that any realistic hope for peace lay. Without a renovation of the existing class structure and price system in the capitalist nations and the disallowance, or at least limitation of, corporation property holding in the developing world, peace had little chance. Veblen's analysis was more far-reaching in its explanatory claims and in its historical prognosis than Mead's, because he traced the psychological and moral impetus for war to its roots in economic institutions and the class system, instead of letting them remain structurally unanchored as was so often the case with Mead.

Veblen's social theory is ultimately rooted in a dichotomous view of class while for Mead considerations of class, power, and authority were assimilated into or submerged under "role." Veblen's view of international politics was thus class-based and his social psychology of the common man, including patriotism, linked with the class structure. Veblen's social theory thus forced him to the conclusion that diplomats and statesmen are greatly constrained by the class structure and the dominant ideology which, no doubt, explained his pessimism regarding the future of mankind and the likelihood of perpetual peace. As he once put it, "history records more frequent and more spectacular instances of the triumph of imbecile institutions than those whose insight saved themselves alive out of a desperately precarious institutional situation, such, for instance as now faces the people of Christendom."[39]

Mead's conception of freedom, on the other hand, was based on his theory of taking the role of the other. The organization of perspectives leading to the integration and coordination of the behavior of individual role performers does not lessen the freedom of the individual. Rather, it increases human freedom and, in fact, is essential to it. In Mead's view, organizations, institutions, and government do not restrict one's freedom but make it possible.[40] His social theory, by contrast with Veblen's, enabled him to be more optimistic about the future because there is more latitude for policymakers, including diplomats, to maneuver and more freedom for them to devise policies of their own choosing. Mead, who largely detached political actors from the class system with his astructural focus on role, thus reached different conclusions regarding the reconstructive potential of international relations.

Veblen held that the problems of power in international politics could be more rapidly ameliorated were it not for the vested interests of the governing classes that created them; for weapons systems were not created to serve real security needs, but to satisfy the interests of militarists and their industrial and financial supporters. Nevertheless, he believed that massive pressure from below might eliminate the whole tangled web of international suspicion and rivalry. This last scenario was made problematic, however, by the hold that the vested interests had on the underlying population in terms of shared values coagulated with patriotic gore. Veblen's view of the darker side of human institutions made it impossible for him to ignore the likelihood of the persistence of atavistic continuities such as war.

However, Veblen's views on the subject were more complex than this because there was also a strong vein of pacifism in his thought, often expressed in his admiration for the practice of "live-and-let-live" among primitive peoples. Consequently, in order to obtain a balanced view of Veblen's attitudes toward force as a method of conflict resolution, his occasional praise of pacifism must be weighed against his sympathy for the Russian Revolution. In this last respect, Veblen's outlook bore at least a family resemblance to neo-Marxist theories of the social dynamics of international relations. In fact, in viewing imperialistic capitalism and its ideology, Veblen wrote that

> the quest of profits leads to a predatory national policy. The resulting large fortunes call for a massive government apparatus to secure the accumulations, on the one hand, and for large and conspicuous opportunities to spend the resulting income, on the other hand; which means a militant, coercive home administration and something in the way of imperial court life—a dynastic fountain of honor and courtly bureau of ceremonial amenities. Such an ideal is not simply a moralist's daydream; it is a sound business proposition, in that it lies on the line of policy along which the business interests are moving in their behalf.[41]

Thus, as early as 1904, Veblen rejected his Chicago colleague Mead's liberalism by implicitly denying the efficacy of any conflict resolution mechanism or policy that fails to recognize a primary source of modern warfare in capitalist property institutions and the cultural values they induce.

Mead perceptively argued in the aftermath of the Bolshevik Revolution that "the danger of the spread of revolutionary spirit from one country to others might well lead those countries that viewed with alarm a revolution elsewhere to come to the assistance of the propertied classes with their military power."[42] Thus even if Imperial Germany were vanquished, the existence of class struggle and the spread of revolutionary doctrine might provoke still further international strife. This part of Mead's analysis is prescient not only of the Allied intervention in Russia in 1918 but, indeed, of the course of American foreign policy during the post-1945 era.

However, Mead was not as skeptical as Veblen of the pervasive American belief that the United States had a mission in the world. For the latter well understood the social dynamics of the interventionist policies this messianic outlook reflected. In any case, the burden of the intellectual was not to inflame the missionary spirit but to defuse it.

Throughout this analysis, the ideological, theoretical, and issue orientations of the two men have been juxtaposed so as to facilitate a choice between them.[43] The critic may ultimately decide in favor of Veblen or Mead, but in either case the decision can be rationalized by pointing to an important, but hitherto neglected, chapter in the history of American political thought.

RICHARD ELY, THE JAFFES, AND VEBLEN

In the early 1880s, while he was a young professor at the newly founded Johns Hopkins University, Richard Ely (1854–1943), began work on "The Story of Economics in the United States." In this study he intended to trace the evolution of American economic doctrines from their earliest formalization in theoretical form up to the present. During this same period, a young Norwegian-American graduate student by the name of Thorstein Veblen spent a semester at the new university in Baltimore and took a course in economics from Ely.[44] Little did Ely realize that Veblen would ultimately become the focal point of a chapter in his study, which was never published, although Ely and his coauthors wrote several drafts of it during the next sixty years. It is also interesting to note that Ely had selected two graduate students at Johns Hopkins to coauthor the book with him, and the three worked together for a time on the project. One of these students was Woodrow Wilson, and although Wilson ultimately withdrew from the project to pursue other aims, Ely dedicated the never-to-be-published manuscript to him in drafts written in the early 1930s.[45]

Ely left Johns Hopkins for the University of Wisconsin in 1892.[46] At Madison, Ely chaired the Department of Social Sciences and helped Wisconsin become a leading graduate program in the social sciences and economics. At the same time, along with John R. Commons and other Wisconsin faculty he became active in the Progressive movement. He served for a number of years as an adviser to Governor Robert M. La Follette and worked to promote the passage of Progressive legislation. Indeed, it is his involvement with Progressivism that links Ely with George H. Mead as a Progressive critic of Veblen.

After Ely's retirement in 1924, he went to Northwestern University, where he headed a research institute that specialized in the study of land economics and public utilities. In Evanston he met William Jaffe, who held an academic post in the Department of Economics, and his wife, Grace. Although William Jaffe (1898–1980) was to make his reputation as a scholar specializing in the study of the life and work of Leon Walras, he had a lengthy intellectual flirtation with the work of Veblen. According to his biographer and the executor of his literary

estate, Donald Walker, "Veblen's work interested him because of its
socialistic implications which had taught him to distrust economic theory."[47] Jaffe not only read Veblen's published work but attended one of
his courses at the New School of Social Research. While studying at
the University of Paris in the early 1920s, he became concerned because most French economists had never heard of Veblen, so he selected a dissertation topic that dealt with Veblen's social and economic
thought. In 1924 he published the dissertation and was gratified to
receive a letter of congratulation regarding it from Veblen himself.[48]

Grace Mary Spurway (b. 1897) was an Englishwoman who met and
married William Jaffe in France. While he wrote his dissertation on
Veblen, she wrote a dissertation on the labor movement in Paris during
the French Revolution. After her husband joined the economics faculty at Northwestern, Richard Ely invited her to become his chief research assistant. When Ely was a young professor at Johns Hopkins he
had written what became a very popular textbook entitled *Outlines of
Economics*, which was first published in 1893. From time to time Ely
would publish new editions of it. One of the tasks assigned to Grace
Jaffe was to edit another edition of the text. However, he also asked
that she "write a brief, historical account of Thorstein Veblen."[49] This
is her view of what followed:

> I accepted with alacrity, and foresaw little or no difficulty, since I was quite
> familiar with Bill Jaffe's thesis on the controversial American economist. I
> reread Veblen with some care, and found that his strange language no
> longer presented me with any difficulty. In order to get a picture of the man
> himself, I corresponded with one of his sisters, who wrote to me in terms of
> fulsome praise of her distinguished brother. I finished my account of Thor-
> stein Veblen's economic theories and handed it in to Dr. Ely. . . . It was then
> that I discovered that Ely hated Veblen from the bottom of his heart. True,
> I had noticed when, some years previously, I had asked Ely what he thought
> about Veblen, the old man had turned his back on me and pronounced his
> verdict: "Woman trouble."
>
> The story of Veblen's marital and extra-marital adventures is too well
> known to need recounting here. In this day and age, they seem quite insipid.
> The real reason for Dr. Ely's opinion of Veblen had, I think, little or nothing
> to do with sex. He saw Veblen as a serious rival and, a victorious one at that,
> in the field of economics.[50]

It is important to note that, however disgruntled Ely may have been
with Jaffe's essay on Veblen, he intended to use it in "The Story of
Economics in the United States." The unpublished manuscript in the
Ely collection clearly indicates this; indeed, in the preface Ely himself
acknowledged

the constant help that I have had for the past two years from my associate Dr. Grace M. Jaffe. There is no part of the book which has not received the benefits of her knowledge and her illuminating insight. The chapter on Veblen which I believe is a valuable contribution to the history of American economic thought is entirely and wholly her work, apart, of course, from suggestions that I have made from time to time, and it appears over her own name.[51]

In view of the fact that Veblen had been William Jaffe's dissertation topic some years earlier, it is very likely that Jaffe influenced his wife's interpretation of Veblen. It is difficult to know to what extent Ely's views on Veblen were incorporated into the manuscript, but as Ely indicated above, he clearly felt he played a role in its development.[52] Therefore, the contributions of the Jaffes and Ely, whatever they may have been, will be treated as one and referred to as the "Jaffe-Ely" authorship. While Grace Jaffe was undoubtedly the main author and should be so credited, the input of both her husband and Richard Ely cannot be ignored.

William Jaffe's doctoral dissertation[53] is essentially congruent with the Jaffe-Ely interpretation. However, there is little about his analysis of Veblen that is original, unique, or critical. With two exceptions, the study is little more than a descriptive-narrative presentation of Veblen's ideas to Frenchmen who know nothing of them. The one major criticism Jaffe made of Veblen is that he put forward no constructive proposals for changing the American economic system.

In *The Engineers and the Price System*, Veblen had argued that production should be in the hands of technicians, and that a soviet of technicians should replace the existing soviet of finance. However, Jaffe claimed that Veblen did not tell how the technicians should be chosen, to whom they should be responsible, or how they should be financed. He also thought Veblen exaggerated the teleological and animistic traits of neoclassicism, an opinion shared by his wife and Ely. Nevertheless, much of Jaffe's analysis is so commonplace that today similar presentations can be found in undergraduate textbooks on the history of economic thought. In short, while his dissertation on Veblen advanced ideas that undoubtedly influenced his wife, and through her, Ely, it is so nonjudgmental as to be compatible with all but the most arbitrary interpretations of the corpus of Veblen's writings.

The Social Philosophy of Ely and Veblen

In contrast to the radical Veblen, Ely can best be described as a conservative, genteel reformer, who wanted to leave private property largely undisturbed and have reform guided by the "better" classes. This was evident in his preference for incremental, amelioristic efforts to change capitalism and slightly modify property rights, as compared with Veblen's demand for the abolition of absentee ownership. Ely's definition of "vested interest" as "economic interests which are legally recognized to be such that they cannot be impaired by public action, directly or indirectly, without indemnification"[54] must be contrasted with Veblen's definition of "vested interest" as "a marketable right to get something for nothing."[55] Indeed, in "The Story of Economics in the United States," Jaffe and Ely, after alluding to Veblen's definition, commented that "latterly among democratic thinkers a tendency has shown itself not so much to fight the vested rights as to extend vested rights and thereby a stake in social stability to the lower middle class and skilled workers."[56] Clearly it was not Veblen's "industrial republic" that they anticipated but the broadening of "vested interests" to include other social strata. However, Ely's increasing conservatism with age did not turn him against the New Deal when it came, since on the whole he supported it.[57] His conservative bent did, however, make him strongly apologetic at times about corporate enterprise.[58]

Ely was able to accommodate himself to changing circumstances and personalities in ways that were beyond Veblen's powers of adaptation. For example, Nicholas Murray Butler, president of Columbia University, was instrumental in having Ely named Honorary Associate in Economics at Columbia, and Ely bestowed upon Butler accolades such as "the man I am proud to call chief."[59] This was the same Nicholas Murray Butler who was notorious in certain academic circles for hounding dissenters and interfering with academic freedom and the man who instigated the vilification of Veblen for writing *The Higher Learning in America.*[60]

Ely's brand of reform economics was heavily laced with Protestant Social Gospel Christianity. He was critical of laissez-faire economics because he felt it was not compatible with the Golden Rule, which formed the ethical core of Christianity. Indeed, while he was at Johns Hopkins, Ely even led student devotional meetings for the Young Men's Christian Association (YMCA).[61] In view of his caustic comments regarding the YMCA and his negative view of religion, it is hard to imagine Veblen presiding over such prayer sessions. While Veblen watched with interest the Bolshevik Revolution and its aftermath and satirized the frenetic reaction to it, Ely, in 1919, wrote that the menace to a league of free nations was no longer autocracy, but bolshevism, which was a more serious menace than the czars and kaisers were in the last century. He then commented, "In our work in this state we have three watch words, namely, patriotic, sanely progressive and anti-bolshevik."[62]

During this same period, Ely, attempting to secure funds for the support of his Institute of Economic Research, found it necessary to appeal to the prejudices of potential donors. Indeed, his dependence on the donations of men of wealth appears to have shaped his responses to social issues. In reply to a letter from George Roberts, assistant to the president of the National City Bank of New York, he wrote:

> If the bankers of the country could only know how serious the threat of Bolshevism is and could also realize two things, namely that landed property is always first attacked, and that furthermore the rights of private property in land cannot be seriously diminished without bringing ruin to the credit of the country, I believe, I would have no difficulty in securing the funds that I want.[63]

The difference between Ely and Veblen was also evident in their views on the toleration of dissent by domestic radicals during the First World War. While Veblen was defending the right of the I.W.W. to oppose the war, Ely was a militant supporter of the Wisconsin Loyalty Legion and took its pledge to protect the soldiers from attack by enemies at home, identify and punish traitors, hold slackers up to public contempt, and teach and practice a broad, vigorous American patriotism.[64]

In summation of the different ideological positions of Veblen and Ely, it is evident that Veblen's radicalism and Ely's moderate reformism provide considerable contrast. It is important to note, however, that Jaffe and Ely, while predictable in their analysis of Veblen within their own ideological predilections, occasionally stray from their parameters. It is in these brief detours that they often exhibit the doctrinal ambiguity of American liberalism in the 1930s.

Veblen as a Social Scientist

The authors dealt briefly with the question of whether Veblen was a success as an economic scientist, or whether his work was essentially propagandistic in nature. As they put it, "Are we, then, forced to conclude that Thorstein Veblen was a sort of modern Savonarola, posing as a scientist?"[65] Their answer to this question was a qualified yes, but they made this judgment in part by rejecting Veblen's own tongue-in-cheek professions of value neutrality and scientific objectivity. In their words, "Veblen, judged by his own scientific standards, was very far . . . from being a scientist or from looking upon human activities with the same kind of detachment displayed by the natural scientist."[66] The authors believed he was filled with animosity toward American businessmen, but they were uncertain why, owing to "his habit of expressing his indignation only through the medium of thinly veiled satire [which] made it very hard to say with any measure of certainty what led him to take just the attitude he did."[67] With good reason, Jaffe and Ely remained skeptical about Veblen's disclaimers of evaluating economic institutions from the ethical or utilitarian point of view. They were unconvinced that his intent was to examine the "economic life process" with complete detachment and dubious of his claim that his view of science "knows nothing of policy or utility, of better or worse."[68]

The authors believed Veblen's caricature of conventional economic theory was taken too seriously by younger institutionalists. To paraphrase them, for a time it seemed as though the strong reaction against this type of economic theory might hamper the progress of economic science in the United States, but fortunately this was no longer true. Now only a few ideologues of the institutional school still failed to perceive the scientific and practical value of neoclassical economics. At the same time, however, the evolutionary approach to economics was capable of standing on its own merits.

The authors believed Veblen refrained from open denunciation and took refuge instead in satire. They contended that Veblen would be a more "scientific" economist if he had expressed his denunciations with the clarity of a John Ruskin, on the one hand, while creating a "heroically theoretical" system with the logical prowess of a John Bates Clark, on the other hand. In short, Veblen's empirically valid insights and value-laden doctrines were so interwoven as to seriously compromise the scientific integrity of his work.

Jaffe and Ely also included comment on Veblen's use of anthropological data and literature in *The Theory of the Leisure Class*, which indicated their belief that the book belongs in the category of prescientific anthropology. They broke prescientific literature into two main types. One is the type associated with John Locke and Jean-Jacques Rousseau, both of whom accepted the idea of a remote golden age, when peaceful, propertyless savages inhibited the earth. The other is that of Thomas Hobbes, who described the life of primitive man as "nasty, brutish, and short." The authors believe Veblen subscribed to the view of Locke and Rousseau rather than to that of Hobbes:[69]

He saw a primitive culture

virtually without weapons, whose gods are mothers and whose religious observances are a ritual of fecundity. He infers from the available evidence that the early neolithic culture of Northern Europe had a prevailingly peaceful complexion. He sees the members of primitive communities cooperating to the common gain and to no one's detriment, since there is substantially no individual or private gain to be sought.[70]

In Jaffe's and Ely's eyes, Veblen painted an idyllic picture of the early neolithic culture of northern Europe. Although they did not claim to be anthropologists, they regarded his anthropology as little more than conjectural prehistory based upon a dislike of modern, pecuniary civilization. Veblen may have been right that if primitive men had not been peaceful, cooperative, and endowed with the instinct of workmanship and parental bent, economic evolution could not have come about. However, the authors pointed to the evidence for a much less pleasant hypothesis regarding economic evolution, that of group selection through warfare. On balance they seemed to think that this view has more to recommend it than Veblen's.[71]

Veblen as Critic of Classical and Neoclassical Economics

Veblen is often regarded as an acute and original critic of classical and neoclassical economics, although some scholars believe he was unfair to such luminaries of the economics profession as John Bates Clark, Irving Fisher, and Alfred Marshall. His work in this area has received so much attention from Veblen scholars that it would be difficult to say anything new regarding his critique of mainline economics. However, most of these commentaries were published after Jaffe's and Ely's collaborative effort in the early 1930s; thus the authors' critique of Veblen is of significance to historians of economic thought interested in primacy and originality of interpretation.[72]

The authors claimed, like many other economists near the center of the political spectrum, that Veblen was more effective as a critic of the received economic doctrines than as a constructive theorist. Nevertheless, they believed Veblen forced "most of his younger contemporaries and co-workers to look with newly-opened eyes upon their preconceptions and assumptions."[73] But Jaffe and Ely believed Veblen and his followers went too far in their attacks on conventional economics "in claiming that all the systematic theory of the older type was obsolescent" (ibid.). The institutionalists of the 1930s had little respect for the concept of idle curiosity and were apt to regard the elaboration of theories as one of Veblen's idiosyncratic specialties. Thus it was apparent that Veblen had little in common with those institutionalists who were atheoretical.

The authors believed that Veblen's identification of "taxonomy" with "natural-theology," which was accepted uncritically by some of his followers, temporarily retarded the progress of scientific economics in the United States. As they put it: "His claim that *all* the modern sciences are evolutionary is manifestly absurd. His prejudice against 'taxonomy' probably arose, as already suggested, from a desire to free economic theory from Natural-Theology" (ibid.). However, according to Jaffe and Ely, only a few ideologues were still among the blind who failed to perceive the value of the "taxonomy" to which even Veblen paid a passing tribute while appropriating its method of procedure, which he regarded as obsolescent (ibid.)! In fact, in the opinion of the authors, Veblen's "taxonomic" theories, as presented in *The Theory of Business Enterprise*, are "among his most valuable contributions to economic thought" (ibid.).

Is this statement to be interpreted as a barbed comment on the inconsistency of Veblen's own description of the neoclassicists as mere "taxonomists"? Or is it, instead, to be viewed as a serious commentary on the nature of Veblen's own "constructive" theory? The authors have left the reader uncertain of their intent at this point in the manuscript. Later, however, they explained what Veblen meant by a "taxonomy."[74] "Taxonomy," as Veblen defines it, contains two separate and distinct elements, which he thinks neoclassicists mistakenly confuse with one another. These elements are that (1) logically consistent propositions are based upon certain postulates, and (2) the "normal" or desirable relations of things is the actual state of affairs (ibid.). The authors believed that the two are analytically different from each other in the work of many neoclassicists and that Veblen exaggerated their tendency to confuse the two.

Jaffe and Ely then turned to Veblen's criticism of the theory of marginal utility, in which he claimed that it fails to explain economic change since it is essentially a "static" theory (ibid.). The authors believed Veblen identified the theory of marginal utility with hedonistic psychology in much the same way as he identified "taxonomy" with the old "natural-theology" habit of mind. The neoclassicists believed, according to Veblen, that man always seeks to attain satisfaction with as little trouble as possible (ibid.). In point of fact, man is too optimistic, for he always thinks he is going to derive more satisfaction from his efforts than he actually does. There is always an unanticipated surplus of "disutility" rather than of "utility." Thus the authors shared Veblen's belief that the theory of marginal utility can offer no explanation of the fact that men have worked hard for thousands of years and have produced the whole series of inventions that led to the industrial revolution (ibid.). In pointing out its limitations and in rejecting its hedonistic psychology, Veblen thus rendered a real service to economic theory.

What of Veblen's other contention that marginal utility analysis is based upon a faulty conception of human nature? Veblen's rejection of the old "hedonistic" psychology was accepted as justifiable by the authors. But they pointed out that, as Herbert Davenport has shown, marginal utility analysis can be divested of its "hedonistic" garb. Admitting that most of our actions are habitual rather than rational or "hedonistic," the fact remains that goods are purchased or otherwise acquired on the basis of imputed desirability. As for Davenport, he believed that "there is no one single essential doctrine in the system that might not, without substantial impairment or change of economic bearing, be stripped of its psychological or ethical implications."[75] But even if the marginal utility analysis is separated from its "hedonistic" psychology, Veblen's contention that the theory is of a static nature and would not explain economic evolution, seemed undeniable to the authors.

How, asked Jaffe and Ely, can the existing social and economic order be explained without knowing how it came into existence (ibid.)? The importance of studying changing economic and social institutions cannot be denied, for economic phenomena can be explained only through the evolutionary and institutional approach advocated by both Veblen and the German Historical School. The authors believed that Veblen's critical-genetic approach to economics stands on its own merits. But they cautioned institutionalists against ignoring the value of the older type of economic theory that takes a cross-section view of the economic order as it exists at a given time and analyzes that order as a "going concern." Much can be learned from the classical economists and from their intellectual descendants, the marginal utility theorists, through this type of analysis.

Jaffe and Ely scolded Veblen because they believed no serious contemporary economist believed in any kind of "natural law" that is "felt to exercise some sort of coercive surveillance over the sequence of events."[76] They contended that since this feature of economic theory, which Veblen attacked with much force and satire, had passed out of existence, the evolutionary economist must rationalize his position in other ways. Nevertheless, the authors believed that Veblen was justified in claiming that mid-nineteenth-century classical theory was based on "an uncritical conviction that there is a meliorative trend in the course of events, apart from the conscious ends of the individual members of the community" (ibid.). However, they remained skeptical of Veblen's view that such opinions are still held by conventional economists.

Veblen and the German Historical School

Both Veblen and Ely were influenced by the economists of the German Historical School; the former as a result of reading and translating their works, the latter by having studied with Karl Knies, one of its leading figures, when he took his doctorate at Heidelberg. The influence of the Germans was evident in their dissatisfaction with both the sterility of English neoclassical economics and the laissez-faire dogmatism of the American economics profession. However, Veblen was more radical in his criticisms of conventional economics than Ely and less supportive of the German contribution.[77] Veblen admitted that the Germans had abandoned the older type of theory, but he claimed that they failed to substitute new theories for the older doctrines, contenting themselves, instead, with mere historical and statistical investigations. On the one hand, Jaffe and Ely believed that Veblen accused the Germans of not offering a theory at all. On the other hand they claimed that the goal of the German Historical School was very similar to his own in that both were trying to turn economics into an evolutionary science. The authors noted that while Veblen criticized the German Historical School for being atheoretical, he leaned rather heavily on the theories of Karl Knies in relation to credit.[78] Since Veblen referred to Knies's *Geld und Credit* in his footnotes, they presumed that his criticism was not directed against the work of Knies, who in their view was the outstanding representative of the German Historical School, but against the other members of it.[79]

To the view of economic theory introduced by the German Historical School, Jaffe and Ely thought Veblen added the Marxian idea of the inevitable decay of capitalistic enterprise and the no less inevitable growth of socialism. However, the main difference between Veblen and the German Historical School, besides Veblen's penchant for socialism, resided in their attitudes toward economic theory. While some of the Germans, Gustav Schmoller, for example, stressed investigation rather than the formulation of theories, Jaffe and Ely believed that Veblen avoided the atheoretical bias of Schmoller through his willingness to generalize from empirical data. On the whole, however, Jaffe could see little difference between the German Historical School and the contemporary American institutionalists.[80]

Veblen, Marx, and the Future of Capitalism

Jaffe and Ely believed that Veblen's "taxonomic" theory of business enterprise was far removed from the concept of "natural harmonies," which was an important feature of American economics from the time of Henry C. Carey to the time of J. B. Clark. On the contrary, Veblen offered economists a "dismal science," for he had no panacea to relieve human suffering. While the economics of Karl Marx is similar in many respects to that of Veblen, these two writers differ rather widely in one respect. Marx believed that if only the rule of the proletariat were inaugurated, a reign of peace and joy would begin, but Veblen took no such optimistic view. On the other hand, while he rejected the utopian element in the Marxian philosophy, Veblen thought that some form of socialism must be the outcome of the development of technology and that it would be coupled with the growth of the modern, matter-of-fact attitude of mind. Jaffe and Ely then quoted Veblen to this effect: "Among those classes whose everyday life schools them to do their habitual serious thinking in terms of material cause and effect, the preconceptions of ownership are apparently becoming obsolescent through disuse and through supersession by other methods of apprehending things."[81] The authors believed this was an intriguing but unproven hypothesis. In any case, the decisive difference between Veblen and Marx lay in their respective attitudes toward socialism. For while Marx regarded socialism as the ultimate goal of civilization, Veblen saw socialism as but one phase in the economic evolution of society. Jaffe and Ely believed, however, that Veblen's concept of economic evolution was teleological, for he looked upon socialism as the immediate, though not ultimate, telos of economic evolution. The classical economists like Ricardo, for example, assumed that the existing order will endure more or less forever, whereas Veblen assumed that "the natural decay of business enterprise" was only a question of time.[82] Those who read his *The Theory of Business Enterprise* in 1904, without tasting the proverbial grain of salt, must have felt that a collapse of the capitalistic system was imminent.

Veblen, J. B. Clark, and Industrial Organization

Since Veblen never wrote a systematic treatise on industrial organization, his views on the subject remain ambiguous even for Veblen scholars. However, according to Jaffe and Ely, he developed a theory that stressed the "disharmonies" of a competitive system with the same meticulous care that the neoclassicist J. B. Clark elaborated his theory of economic "harmonies." The main differences between Clark and Veblen lay in their respective premises rather than in their method of procedure. To illustrate, Clark started with the premise that free competition, if enforced, will produce beneficial results. Veblen, on the other hand, started with the premise that some form of monopoly is the only way out of a chronic depression that he sees as a result of modern business enterprise operating under a competitive regime. Ely and Jaffe believed that some form of monopoly thus seemed to Veblen both inevitable and economically desirable.[83] However, the authors believed it inappropriate to say that Veblen's theory is right and Clark's is wrong, for both interpreted facts in the light of certain underlying postulates.[84] One of Clark's postulates is that free competition and private enterprise are essential to all modern, progressive societies. Veblen's main postulate, on the other hand, is that free competition and private enterprise, although well adapted to the handicraft era, are incompatible with the modern machine era.

Jaffe and Ely believed that Clark identified free competition with the normal or desirable condition of affairs, while also making a state of perfect competition his logical starting point. Thus Veblen was partly justified in his attack on Clark for confusing these two elements, for the latter had indeed confused them. However, to paraphrase the authors, such an identification was not essential to systematic economic theory. It was quite possible to work out a theoretical system of distribution under conditions of perfect competition without believing that, in actual fact, free competition was necessarily "normal" or "desirable." Similarly, it was possible to work out a theoretical system of distribution under monopolistic or socialistic conditions without concluding that either of these regimes would necessarily ensure the greatest good of the greatest number.[85] The authors believed that Veblen's view that a state of business depression was normal under a regime of free competition seemed inconsistent with his idea that the businessman tended to absorb a larger and larger portion of the national income. There was, however, no contradiction. For Veblen claimed that while in brisk times most of the gain in material wealth accrues to the larger businessmen, he also thought that in times of depression most of his gain is simply transferred to those businessmen "who come out of the subsequent liquidation on the credit side."[86]

Veblen's familiarity with Ely's work and his own attitude toward it were expressed in *The Theory of Business Enterprise* in which Veblen discussed the varying degrees of monopoly in the railroad industry and the practice of "charging what the traffic will bear."[87] Veblen concluded that "it is very doubtful if there are any successful business ventures within the range of modern industries from which the monopoly element is wholly absent."[88] In a footnote, Veblen then commented,

> The economic principle of "charging what the traffic will bear" is discussed with great care and elaboration by R. T. Ely, *Monopolies and Trusts. . . .* Monopoly is here used in that looser sense which it has colloquially, not in the strict sense of an exclusive control of the supply, as employed, e.g., by Mr. Ely in the volume cited above. This usage is the more excusable since Mr. Ely finds that a "monopoly" in the strict sense of the definition practically does not occur in fact.[89]

Later Veblen was to return to the subject of industrial organization in his anticipation of the theory of monopolistic or imperfect competition, but the authors did not deal with this aspect of his work in "The Story of Economics in the United States.[90]

Conclusion

In view of Veblen's notoriety, it is surprising how few systematic, scholarly treatments of his economics by economists actually existed in 1932. However, there were two critical evaluations of Veblen's attacks on conventional economics that antedated the unpublished Jaffe-Ely chapter.[91] In addition, there were a few prior efforts to treat him as a social philosopher and theorist.[92] Nevertheless, had the chapter on Veblen been published when it was completed in 1932, it would have been a significant contribution to American economic thought, and not simply because Ely was an eminent economist. Nowadays, the salient points the authors made are commonplace, but that should not detract from their achievement when viewed in the context of existing Veblen scholarship sixty years ago.

While impressed with certain of Veblen's claims, the authors believed that his obsession with the morbid aspects of business enterprise blinded him to the wholesome side of it. They suggested that while Veblen was a master of locating traces of teleology in others, he nevertheless fell prey to it himself. Veblen's attacks on orthodox economics were regarded by them and by many American economists as too extreme. An opinion commonly voiced by others and shared by the authors was that Veblen should have improved upon orthodox economics instead of calling for its abandonment. Critics besides Jaffe and Ely also assessed Veblen's contribution to the methodology of economics and charged him with making disguised value judgments while at the same time claiming scientific objectivity.[93] While there was no doubting Veblen's brilliance as an original thinker, his critique of orthodox method in economics was the subject of debate, much of it negative.

The Jaffe-Ely interpretation of Veblen and the Institutional school provided an interesting commentary on the state of Veblen scholarship in the 1930s as well as on the ideological predilections of American economists.[94] The doctrinal ambiguity of American liberalism in the 1930s manifested itself in their analysis of Veblen, for just prior to the start of the New Deal they wrote, "The idea of public utility regulation and of social control of those monopolies is in close harmony with Veblen's theory of business enterprise."[95] Here they claim Veblen as an advocate of incremental reformism, an interpretation at odds with the rest of their analysis, but one in keeping with much subsequent liberal scholarship on Veblen and the New Deal. One virtue of their treatment of him is that typically they recognized the nonliberal tenets of his thought, but at this point their occasional insensitivity toward his radicalism misled them into portraying him as an advocate of public regulation and, perhaps, antitrust policy. Unfortunately, there is little in

Veblen that indicates he believed the positive state could reform capitalism piecemeal, nor much reason to anticipate all of the policies of Franklin D. Roosevelt in his writings; with inadequate justification Ely and Jaffe were on the edge of interpreting him as the doctrinal source of what was soon to become the New Deal.[96]

During the depression, several economists urged realization of the degree to which Veblen's work paralleled that of John Maynard Keynes.[97] Most of the time Jaffe and Ely did this, however, without sharing the characteristic liberal illusion that Veblen had a common doctrinal orientation with other liberals and belonged politically and ideologically to their camp.[98] The authors were well aware of their own ideological differences with Veblen. For example, in replying to Jaffe's letter of 3 November 1931, Ely wrote, "So far as I can gather, your thinking in regard to Veblen corresponds to mine. I also think we should bring in the factor that he was consciously trying to undermine our economic civilization by indirection. We can strongly bring out the fact."[99] It is clear, then, that Jaffe and Ely understood, without endorsing, Veblen's belief that neoclassical economics was irretrievably wrong-headed, neoclassical economists were apologists for the vested interests, and the price system they defended was "imbecile."[100]

EPILOGUE

Although Veblen is often treated by historians as a "progressive" intellectual he was significantly more radical during the Progressive era than most of the other thinkers who are often lumped in with him to form an unleavened mass, such as Oliver Wendell Holmes, James Harvey Robinson, John Dewey, and Charles A. Beard. However, Mead and Ely shared much of the same political and ideological ground during the Progressive era with other Progressives, although Ely became increasingly conservative with age. Nevertheless, as Progressive intellectuals, they defended most of the Wilsonian New Freedom domestic reforms and enthusiastically supported American entry into the war. On the other hand, it is difficult to tell precisely what Veblen thought about Wilsonian Progressivism or U.S. entry into the Great War, since he was not very judgmental in his writings about either.

As far as generic domestic reform is concerned, however, enough is known as regards Veblen's analysis of capitalism and the structure of his values to warrant asserting that he envisioned more radical changes in the system of property relations and more thoroughgoing displacement of the market mechanism and price system than either Mead or Ely. It is also evident that he did not anticipate reforms necessarily occurring under the auspices of the capitalist state, while the other two men simply took this for granted.

Veblen perceived patriotism in a negative light as a form of false consciousness that increased the manipulability of the common man in the hands of the vested interests who were promoting war. But Mead and Ely, on the contrary, mostly saw the positive aspects of patriotism because they viewed it as an other-regarding bonding agent essential to the well-being, if not the survival, of the American community. In the case of Ely, even the persecution of dissenters from the war effort was justified on the grounds that dissent impeded successful prosecution of the war by spreading disaffection in the underlying population. Veblen, whatever he thought about the Allied war aims, strongly defended the rights of dissenters, and even became an activist in their cause. Veblen looked with more sympathy on the Bolshevik Revolution than either Mead or Ely. Consequently, he was much more critical of the postwar settlement than either man because of its conservative nature, which he believed aimed at preserving vested interests and checking the spread of radicalism.

Veblen was a colleague of Mead's at Chicago for a dozen years or so, a student of Ely's at Johns Hopkins for one semester, and an occasional correspondent with him thereafter. He did not appear to have been particularly interested in the thought of either man, yet their ideas did not escape his attention altogether. However, both were very interested in his work and, perhaps, recognized his as a seminal mind of the first order, although in Ely's case his attitude toward Veblen was soured by personal jealousy. But, what ultimately separated Mead and Ely from Veblen was the latter's social and political radicalism and his estrangement from American life and culture.

Chapter Six

LIBERAL CRITICS: THE INSTITUTIONALISTS

ALTHOUGH Veblen was the single most influential figure in the development of institutional economics, other institutional economists in the earlier part of this century did not hesitate to criticize both his theoretical position and his occasional policy prescriptions. Paul Homan, John Commons, Wesley Mitchell, and John Maurice Clark are all examples of holistic, heterodox, or institutional economists who, although influenced by Veblen, nevertheless, developed a coherent critique of him detailed enough to be worth analyzing. All were politically more conservative than the radical Veblen and thought of themselves as liberals or Progressives. All, at the time they wrote on Veblen, advocated a more extensive social control of industry, more effective countercyclical macroeconomic policy, and more equitable distribution of income, and additional social welfare services.

The common thread that runs through their interpretations of Veblen is that his analyses and his policy prescriptions are too radical in that they lack political realism; too drastic in assuming a basic dichotomy between business and industry; and too extreme in demanding change in the existing price system and market mechanism. Perhaps, also, although they were less explicit about this, they feared the social dislocations that might result from an attack on absentee ownership. Instead of a collectivistic, egalitarian economy, the institutionalists preferred a system of government controls that would offset the coercive power of business and thus make the price system work with less waste and without depressions. This, of course, was New Deal liberalism and it legitimized a mixed economy that preserved private property within the matrix of welfare and regulatory state capitalism.

Homan, Commons, Mitchell, and Clark were all aware of the fact that Veblen's ideological predilections placed him among the ranks of those who were principled opponents of major aspects of capitalism. Indeed, what primarily distinguished Veblen from the Marxists was the fact that the intellectual antecedents who provided the major organizing principles in his thought were Charles Darwin and American visionary socialists like Edward Bellamy, rather than Marx and Hegel. Much of Veblen's writing suggests that he had more in common with other radicals than with reform liberals.

This is not to claim, however, that Veblen's institutionalist critics may simply be lumped together into a amorphous mass without identifiable political or theoretical differences. It is to suggest, however, that they occupied ideological turf a little to the left of center as proponents of reform capitalism. It was from this angle that they viewed the radical implications of his social theory with jaundiced eyes.

WESLEY C. MITCHELL

It would be misleading to suggest that Wesley Mitchell (1874–1948) engaged in a long and intense ideological confrontation with Thorstein Veblen. On the contrary, much of his writing on Veblen was of a laudatory nature and there can be no doubt of his admiration and respect for him. As a former student and long-time friend, Mitchell had an intimate knowledge of the man and his ideas.[1]

Lucy Sprague Mitchell remembered her husband's "great admiration for Veblen's brilliance, imagination, artistry and erudition [which] dated from the time he studied under Veblen at the University of Chicago."[2] Yet she also pointed out that while Mitchell believed that in comparison with other economists at Chicago, Veblen was a "giant," Veblen "got nothing more certain than the classical economist by his dazzling performance with another set of premises."[3] Joseph Schumpeter's analysis paralleled Mrs. Mitchell's when he observed that "before long he [Mitchell] also took Veblen's measure and if for the rest of his life he continued to emphasize the difference between making goods and making money he soon tired of the glitter of the more dubious Veblenite gems."[4]

A number of Veblen's surviving letters to Mitchell are revealing of their personal and professional relationship. For example, in 1909, Veblen who was at Stanford, wrote to Mitchell in Berkeley to inform him that he was unable to come visit with him the following Monday. Earlier he had sent Mitchell a draft of "Christian Morals and the Competitive System" and he now commented that "I have some notion of sending the Christian paper to the *Journal of Ethics*, for a chance. So the ms. should be returned to me some day soon. And if it should not tax you unduly I would be very glad of an expression of opinion as to the propriety or expediency of so doing and as to whether it is fit to print anyway."[5] A little later Veblen wrote again to Mitchell to tell him he was coming for a visit with him and that he hoped to "get all the latest on economic theory."[6]

On 6 September 1908, Veblen wrote to Mitchell, who was apparently interested in moving from the University of California to Chicago, that he had corresponded with J. Laurence Laughlin, chairman of the Department of Economics and told him that "for all I know you are all right as a teacher; that you are fond of Berkeley; and that you have assurances of a substantial advance in pay when you return to work."[7] Veblen's concern for his former student was often reciprocated. For example, in 1924 Mitchell wrote to Leon Ardzrooni in terms that were revealing regarding Mitchell's financial relationship with Veblen, his health, and current research interests.

> Once more I am writing to you about the Veblen Fund. You may have heard that Veblen became very tired of teaching last year and is at present taking a sabbatical. He is eager to go to England for two years in order to study British imperialism. To do so he needs a subvention. A Mr. Kaplan, about whom I know nothing, has promised to contribute $1,000 per annum toward such a trip. I can maintain my annual contribution of $500. Do you feel disposed toward joining in this scheme? Veblen has come back from a summer at his island, followed by a long session with the dentist in St. Paul, looking and seemingly feeling rather well. I have persuaded him to present a paper at the forthcoming session of the American Economic Association in Chicago on "The Prospects of Economic Theory in the Calculable Future." All his thoughts seem to be centering nowadays around the problems which he feels he can study to advantage only in England. For his happiness as well as for the benefit of the world, I think we should help him to get there if we can.[8]

Mitchell and Leon Ardzrooni were both former students and long-time friends of Veblen who aided him in various ways after he was forced to leave Chicago. Their relationship with him was sustained not only by their interest in his ideas but by some personal bond that has never been adequately explained. Clearly, they and Herbert J. Davenport were the best friends he had outside his immediate family.

Political Activism and Veblenian Satire

Mitchell was a political activist who was often involved in civic affairs and professional organizations that aimed at social amelioration. Perhaps this was what led him to critically comment that "Mr. Veblen has an eerie detachment from current political issues that is as disconcerting to most readers as Mr. [Walter] Lippmann's immersion in them is comfortably natural."[9] Although Mitchell admired Veblen's aloofness and objectivity in scholarly matters, he did not favor his lack of involvement in the active promotion of political reform. Mitchell found Veblen's satire amusing and enlightening, and his satirical abilities left a lasting impression:

Such phrases as "conspicuous waste" the great phrase of that particular book have become almost a part of language. The book was read by the intelligent public at large quite as much as by the economic fraternity. Indeed, a good many economists were inclined to take it as primarily a brilliant satire upon prevailing habit and not necessarily a serious contribution to an understanding of the modern phenomena of consumption. Veblen took it in the latter fashion. He was a born tease and greatly enjoyed the uneasy feeling which his discussion of our current habits of thought produced in many of his readers.[10]

Mitchell found wisdom in Veblen's critique of neoclassical economics and much art in his writing style, but he was unwilling to accept Veblen's teachings at face value. As he put it, "Veblen took a whimsical pleasure in making orthodox economics appear in the light of his workaday world as airy rationalizings, spun from conceptions that live below the threshold of consciousness and that wither in the light of common day."[11] Mitchell thus remained skeptical of Veblen's more extreme claims regarding neoclassical economics as well as his more doctrinaire assertions about American capitalism. Cautious empiricist that he was, Mitchell naturally concluded that not all the evidence was in. Consequently, Mitchell thought that the more dogmatic claims of both Veblen and the neoclassicists were not adequately substantiated. That he was never able to overcome his skepticism regarding Veblen's parody is evident in his comments that "there is much of the satirist in him; but it is satire of an unfamiliar and a disconcerting kind. Professedly, he seeks merely to describe and to explain our cultural traits in plain terms. But he likes to put his explanations in a form that will make the commonplaces of our daily lives startling and ridiculous to us. It is this histrionic foible which gives his writing its peculiar flavour.[12] Mitchell thus emphasized Veblen's ability to interpret human behavior in ways that dramatize emancipation from the conventional wisdom. But he remained dubious regarding his ability to empirically substantiate many of his hypotheses.

Methodological Strictures

However, it was not Veblen's satire that Mitchell ultimately found unsatisfying. It was Veblen's critique of the methodology of conventional economics and the methods he used or failed to use in his own work. In lectures at Columbia University in the mid-1930s, Mitchell commented on Veblen's approach to the study of economics, stating,

Veblen himself at times makes casual implicit use of orthodox economic theory. For instance, if you look carefully at the brilliant chapter of his on the theory of modern prosperity in which he is discussing business cycles, you will find him explaining how a rise of prices at the beginning of a period of prosperity spreads from its source to other lines of industry, spreads from prices of commodities to the price of labor, the price of loans, and so on. And in that discussion he is taking for granted that you the reader as well as he the writer understand the theory of prices as it is expounded in our ordinary text-books, for the view that he gives of the process of this spread of rise in prices is a view which can be reinterpreted if you like in ordinary terms of supply and demand theory.[13]

These comments are significant because they indicate that the iconoclast Veblen was, nevertheless, capable of using the analytic and conceptual apparatus of neoclassical economics in a manner acceptable to an eminent economist much closer to the neoclassical mainstream. Mitchell here portrayed Veblen, not as an inveterate enemy of conventional economics, but as an occasional practitioner of orthodoxy, which, of course, blended well with Mitchell's own reformist liberal bent. Mitchell was aware that Veblen was no archetype New Dealer, but he was not above using Veblen to satisfy the needs of his own political and ideological agenda. Indeed, he went even further in his efforts to show that Veblenian economics are useful to reform liberals of his own doctrinal ilk. He commented that

[if Veblen] feels comparatively slight sympathy for this effort to throw away the whole body of economics on the basis of reasoning and to resort merely to observation and then to induction from observation, it is not so much because he thinks their methods as such were wrong as it is because he thinks they have applied their methods in an unsatisfactory way, particularly because they were led astray by a very artificial conception of human nature.[14]

As for Veblen's own work in economics, Mitchell made related criticisms that, interestingly, find Veblen guilty of the same sins for which he criticized the classical and neoclassical economists:

It must also be said that Veblen's general method of work is closely akin to that of the classical economists in the sense that he reasons things out on the basis of his own suppositions and his general knowledge of the world and makes very little effort to check his conclusions by direct observation or by a more elaborate procedure of mass observation which statistics makes possible.[15]

Mitchell believed Veblen fell into the same errors as the neoclassicists he criticized in that he generalized on the basis of insufficient evidence. As Mitchell put it:

Or take again Veblen's proposition that Socialism does not spread far beyond the circle of machine tenders, that its scope is substantially the scope of the classes who are disciplined in the machine process. Now that is a proposition that presumably was suggested to his mind by observations of the Socialist movement in different parts of the world, though of course it did not seem to fit very well with American conditions because though we have a highly developed machine process, we did not have a highly developed Socialistic movement. It is a proposition that Veblen makes no formal effort to prove beyond citing certain of the German evidence that is compatible with his notion. He was, in laying down rules of this sort, proceeding very much in the fashion in which the classical economists and their successors had proceeded.[16]

Mitchell failed to acknowledge that Veblen believed that industrial workers were subject to countervailing social forces that placed them in a cultural environment characterized by crosscutting cleavages. Specifically, they were torn between the pressures exerted by the machine process that pushed them toward socialism loosely defined and the massive system of invidious distinctions and status emulation that he described in *The Theory of the Leisure Class*. If the machine process triumphed in shaping their habits of mind, then what lay ahead was the industrial republic, but if status emulation carried the day, then the proletariat would submit to chauvinism and predatory exploit. Veblen was uncertain of the course of events that was to come.

Mitchell admired Veblen's massive learning and his creation of what, perhaps, constitutes a new theoretical system. But Veblen was not really an economist of his own persuasion, although his work contained fruitful suggestions and insights for further research, some of which Mitchell carried out on his own.[17] Thus he questioned Veblen's method of reasoning and verifying more than his institutional analysis.

The Veblen Dichotomy

The Veblen dichotomy between business and industry, that is, between making money and making socially useful goods, had a lasting impact on Mitchell, who used it in his own work. He well recognized that goods made and purchased for emulatory reasons might command a high price but be of little real value to the buyer. Large profits might result, but little serviceability be provided. Mitchell illustrated the significance but also the weakness of the Veblen dichotomy by analyzing his use of it in attacking the advertising industry.

So too, he points out that advertising has become a branch of business which requires the use of a very large amount of capital, which employs the efforts of tens of thousands of men, and he asks of what use is advertising to satisfaction, to what human wants does that contribute. . . . Veblen in his indictment does not pay perhaps sufficient attention to the defense of advertising which is sometimes advanced seriously on economic grounds that while it is not itself a means of satisfying wants it does after all contribute to an expansion of the market for certain types of goods and therefore makes it possible to produce them on a large scale and so to organize production at lower cost.[18]

As the last sentence in the quotation indicates, Mitchell found more virtue in basic capitalist practices, in this case advertising, than did Veblen. The Veblen dichotomy is correct in pointing to the fact that advertising is wasteful and misleading, yet Mitchell concluded that he had exaggerated. Veblen's ideas must be deradicalized in order both to achieve maximum heuristic value and serve as the basis for policy prescription by liberal reformists such as Mitchell.

Charges of "technocratic elitism" emanated from many of Veblen's liberal critics and Mitchell was no exception. He did not stress this alleged facet of Veblen's work as much as some other liberal writers, yet he believed the industrial economy was interpreted by Veblen in such a manner as to highlight the role of the engineers and technicians. Worse yet, he believed Veblen would place these occupational groups in control of the economy if he had the power. As Mitchell put it:

The high priests of this aspect of economic life are our engineers; they are the people who know how to make things. And from Veblen's point of view if our economic life were really organized for the purpose of satisfying our wants, it would seem to be the sensible thing to turn the direction of our labor and our capital over to these experts, the men who are both best trained and best fitted to organize industrial processes, to make proper choice of materials on technical grounds, to understand the designing of machine processes, the men who are great experts in making goods.[19]

Like scholars of all ideological persuasions, Mitchell found much in Veblen's use of the term *instinct* that is objectionable. He pointed to both the inconsistency and ambiguity of Veblen's usage, but in the final analysis conceded his explanation of human behavior was not fatally flawed by his use of a vocabulary in transition.

There is one point however, at which we may fairly ask Mr. Veblen to modify his language. . . . Veblen seems mistaken in saying that instincts (in his usage) are "hereditary traits." . . . As parts of the original nature of man, instincts are inherited; but instincts "as they take effect in the give and take of cultural growth" have important acquired elements in addition to the elements which are inherited. Perhaps Mr. Veblen's explanatory clause, the instincts are inherited "as spiritual traits *emerging from* a certain concurrence of physiological unit characters" is a sufficient defense against this criticism.[20]

Strictly speaking, objections to Veblen's use of *instinct* are not of necessity rooted in a particular ideological framework of the left, right, or center. Scholars from all parts of the political spectrum criticized his incorporation of it into his social theory and explanation of human behavior. However, environmental determinists who take the side of nurture in the nature versus nurture controversy are more likely to come from the left side of the doctrinal continuum than the right. Thus it is not surprising to see liberals and radicals focus more on this deficiency in Veblen than conservatives.

Veblen's analysis combined a penetrating critique of liberal market societies with an enticing vision of human potentialities. Mitchell recognized this without sharing the mainstream liberal contention that the communal bias of his theory would germinate the seeds of an authoritarian destruction of individual freedom. Of course, Mitchell's view differed from radical criticisms that emphasize Veblen's retention of so much liberal individualism in his theorizing that he cannot generate the revolutionary doctrine or locate the social forces needed to implement the industrial republic he advocated. But that is a problem to be taken up later in connection with radicalism and Veblen's attitudes toward the working class and mass political action. In any case, a systematic treatment of the relationship between theory and action lay outside the parameters of Wesley C. Mitchell's reform liberalism.[21] In the latter's view, Veblen provided an inventory of useful analytical and conceptual tools combined with a outsider's detachment from conventional bias. But, in the final analysis, his theories lacked an adequate empirical basis that limited their usefulness in the making of public policy.[22]

Conclusion

At times Mitchell made criticisms of Veblen that reveal important components of the ideological structure of his own liberalism. Indeed, Mitchell's commentaries on Veblen reveal as much about his own social and economic doctrine as they do about Veblen's. The following summation of Mitchell's methodological approach by A. B. Wolfe is particularly revealing in this regard:

Men in the mass, at any given time and in any given culture-complex, be-
have in certain standardized ways, according to uniform but not simple patterns; these patterns undergo an evolutionary drift which can be roughly
measured by the statistical device of time series and which with adequate
empirical analysis is amenable to some degree of rational control and direction.[23]

Those familiar with Veblen's work will immediately recognize the difference between his broad-gauged theorizing and Mitchell's sometimes narrow-gauged empiricism. Yet Veblen's influence was intermittently present in his work. Paul Homan has written that "his
dissent from orthodox economics is not original. It is taken from Veblen. . . . The cathartic effect of Veblen's early influence cleared his
system of tradition and left him with a hearty appetite and sound
powers of absorption for innovating and progressive thinking in the
social sciences."[24]

There were at least three parts of Veblen's thinking that were of
great importance for Mitchell. First, he adopted Veblen's perspective of
the evolving, organic nature of society. He thus emphasized the complexity of economic phenomena and was highly critical of simple theories. Second, Mitchell believed that theories that assume that consumer tastes or preferences are given are deficient because they fail to
scrutinize either the origins of the wants or the effects of their satisfaction. Finally, Mitchell held that Veblen's distinction between business
and industry, between the pecuniary and technological phases of the
economy, was a valid one although, unlike Veblen, he never contemplated a radical displacement of the price system.

Given the parameters of Mitchell's liberalism, his personal gentility
and civility, and his long-time friendship with Veblen, it was predictable that Mitchell's analysis would not be caustic or direct. However, he
was less certain than Veblen about what constituted the generic ends
of life and, consequently, he was less judgmental regarding the quality
of consumer tastes and preferences and expenditure of leisure time
and waste. Although he valued Veblen's own pursuit of idle curiosity,
he nevertheless believed that much of his theorizing was speculative
rather than empirical. Indeed, aspects of Mitchell's life work may be
interpreted as efforts to empirically test Veblen-generated hypotheses.

It is clear that in the 1930s, when Mitchell did the bulk of his writing
about Veblen, that he was essentially a liberal reformist. Both his connection with New Deal planning and work relief agencies and the doctrinal bent of his work indicate he never seriously contemplated radical
changes in the price system, market mechanism, or structure of prop-

erty relations. In fact, Mitchell was much closer to the institutionalist mainstream than Veblen himself, even though the latter was the intellectual founder of the movement.

PAUL HOMAN: EARLY ANALYST OF VEBLEN

The American economist Paul T. Homan (1893–1969) was once a student of Herbert Davenport, who, in turn, had been a student and long-time friend of Veblen. Homan was a professor at Cornell when he did the bulk of his work on Veblen, including a lengthy analysis published two years before the latter died in 1929, but he continued to write about Veblen and the literature on him until 1953.[25] His work on Veblen is important, for not only was he a liberal critic of Veblenian economics, but he was also a competent student of Veblen's influence on institutional economics and a discerning commentator on the development of institutionalism.[26]

Homan, while very critical of Veblenian economics, was even more ideologically antagonistic toward Veblen's conservative critics, such as Richard Teggart. Indeed, he described the latter's study of Veblen as "entirely unsympathetic," complained also that it contained "unkind misrepresentation," and concluded that it exhibited a "conscientious refusal to find merit in Veblen's work."[27] Those comments by Homan are of interest because they reveal the difference between the principled opposition of conservatives like Teggart, who see no merit in Veblen, and the less dogmatic reaction of liberals who admire his work, although ultimately disagreeing with the fundamental thrust of his attack on capitalism and neoclassical economics.

Veblen's Methodology and Veblen on Methodology

Homan's commentary on methodological aspects of Veblen's work is the most penetrating aspect of his confrontation with him. Homan believed, however, that Veblen's methodological strictures were more important for their freshness of approach than for substance. Indeed, his methodological critique must be separated from his own methods of inquiry. As he put it,

> Any careful estimate of his work demands that a sharp distinction be made between the approach which he devised and the questions he has raised on the one hand, and the methods he has used and the conclusions he has

reached on the other hand. The obvious criticism, of the sort that have been recounted, refer primarily to the latter aspects of his work. He is there stimulating and enlightening, but also, one would say, often far-fetched and prejudiced, and at time merely absurd.[28]

Specifically, Veblen's own methodological sins included making

abstractions of most of man's mental traits and of many of his institutional arrangements. He has given attention only to such phenomena as could be crowded into two rigid categories, constructed to include, respectively, such phenomena as promote and such as hinder the adequate provision of the material means of life to the group. And with equal readiness in the art of classification, he has divided the eternity of past time into four quite arbitrary eras, on the basis of certain putative relationships between the technological and pecuniary aspects of the prevailing culture. Veblen, in short, is somewhat the master of the use of the "taxonomy" which in others he so sarcastically criticizes.[29]

Homan believed that Veblen's attack on the received body of economic doctrine was occasionally exaggerated and did not deal with many issues and problems.[30] Nevertheless, his methodological critique of classical and neoclassical economics has considerable force and its corrosive effects were immense. His assault on the method of deductive logic undermined the faith of economists in its scientific validity. Homan summarized Veblen's case against the methodological bias of conventional economics by commenting that

he has attacked the concept of normality as a metaphysical hold-over, scientifically untenable. He has riddled the hedonistic implications of economic theory and demonstrated the insufficiency of a normalized competitive institutional situation as a postulate of theory. He has denied the coincidence of acquisition and production; developed a capital concept in which capital is merely capitalized earning-capacity but little related to industrial plant; and riddled the connection between utility and consumption.[31]

Unfortunately, Veblen's desire to discredit the methods and doctrines of orthodox economic theory led him to "an exaggerated insistence upon the evolutionary viewpoint."[32] Homan suggested, however, that those economists like Veblen who possess "an evolutionary bias, who have been so scornful of the 'preconditions' of earlier economists, are themselves faced with the necessity of adopting positions the actual correctness of which is quite as incapable of proof."[33] This comment is evidence that Homan had difficulty conceptualizing economics as a discipline much different than it was, or an industrial economy organized in another way than the American or British in the mid-1920s. Yet, on the whole, he approved of the New Deal when it came. In any case, the Soviet planning experience and industrialization drive were just beginning, so he had no other working models to compare with what he took to be the Veblenian scheme.

Veblen's methodological strictures were faulted on still another count, namely that in formulating them he fell into "obvious grossness and absurdity that fostered a smug conservatism upon the part of his intended victims. Out of this controversy has sprung much sterile discussion of what constitutes scientific method in economics."[34] The clear implication of Homan's claims is that if Veblen made more measured and balanced criticisms, his influence would have been deeper and more enduring. Judging by the subsequent development of mainline economics, however, it is at least as likely that he would have been ignored. Homan was insensitive to the fact that Veblen aroused both Irving Fisher and Frank Knight sufficiently from their dogmatic slumbers that the former tried to rebut Veblen directly and the latter sniped at him intermittently for the rest of his life. Nevertheless, Homan raises some important questions regarding the proper role of the dissenter in the economics profession that are not easy to answer, for neither Fisher or Knight incorporate Veblenian theory into their formal theoretical work.

Most commonly, critics charge Veblen with both defining and conceptualizing economics in too broad a fashion. Indeed, a typical criticism is that Veblenian economics is so broad that it is sociological in nature. Interestingly, Homan made just the opposite criticism.

> Having, however, insisted upon the idea of the life-process, he is faced with a certain methodological difficulty. This lies in the necessity of separating from the life-process certain portions which can be specifically labeled "economic," and which can be studied in isolation. . . . Veblen accomplishes this feat of prestidigitation heroically and a little cavalierly by defining economic as having to do with provision of the material means of life for the group, and by tacitly assuming that the rest of the life-process can be shelved while the human traits and institutions bearing upon this problem are separately examined.[35]

If there is any American economist who stressed the interaction of economic and noneconomic institutions, it was surely Thorstein Veblen. Homan's claims in this regard cannot be authenticated through textual exegesis of his writing.

Much of Veblen's critique of classical and neoclassical economics stressed their pre-Darwinian nature and suggest an evolutionary eco-

nomics as an alternative to them. But Homan believed that "in introducing the evolutionary approach, Veblen claimed too much for it" (p.
258). Homan reasoned that it is not true that the "scientific social studies must proceed by a method analogous to that of biology" (p. 258). It
is questionable that "the life of society is comparable to that of a biological organism" (p. 258). Homan also complained that "the mere device
of adapting the evolutionary approach . . . cast doubt upon the 'static'
and 'dynamic' analysis of orthodox economic theory" (p. 258). It is easy
to understand why Homan believes Veblen's evolutionary approach is
incompatible with static equilibrium analysis, but why would this also
preclude dynamic analysis? The evolutionary approach stressed
change over time and, although the pace of change may be glacial,
Homan did not explain why dynamic and evolutionary analysis are incompatible—indeed, he did not even attempt to do so.

However, what distressed Homan the most is not simply the nature
of Veblen's value judgments, but his efforts to conceal them behind a
supposedly scientific, that is, ethically neutral facade. Perhaps Veblen's attitudes would have been less objectionable to Homan if he were
more candid regarding his value commitments. The latter summarized
his strictures on Veblen's role as an economic scientist by stating that

> it is obvious that Veblen cannot be rated very high as a scientist. His task is
> carried out with none of the cold objectivity which, in his own view, distin-
> guishes the scientific spirit. With consummate skill in selecting and coloring
> his facts, he has succeeded in building up his central antithesis between
> business and industry, between obstructive and invidious acquisition on the
> one hand and humanly useful production on the other. With his tongue in
> his cheek and under cover of a sophistical scientific pose he has accom-
> plished a covert ethical damnation of the dominant modern economic insti-
> tutions. (P. 261)

However, it is difficult to avoid the conclusion that what Homan objected to were not simply Veblen's subterfuges but his moral and political values. Perhaps this was the essential meaning of his claim that
Veblen was too clever a polemicist to be rated high as an economic
scientist. Often critics denigrate the "scientific" quality of Veblen's
work when what they really object to is his satirization of their consumption patterns and the social institutions they hold dear.

Social Value and the Generic Ends of Life

Veblen's rejection of the neoclassical view of value as subjective preference was based on his claim that the human life process has certain
generic ends. But Homan complained that Veblen believed

that the greater material gain is preferable to the lesser, with its corollary that the most desirable form of economic organization is that which will maximize material output. In short, he knows no canon of welfare except maximum output of material goods, certainly a very narrow interpretation of the "generically human" ends of life. (P. 260)

Veblen did lay great stress on maximum output of goods and services. But they are to be produced and used for noninvidious, that is, nonemulatory purposes, which Homan failed to mention at this point in the text. Also, much of Veblen's work described and analyzed the generic ends of life that take the form of idle curiosity, altruism, and workmanlike proficiency. However, Homan also complained that Veblen "refuses to discuss the justice of distribution" (p. 249) as if he systematically avoided this topic. This reaction to Veblen's attack on leisure-class waste and frivolity was tempered, however, by his comment that

nevertheless, the force of his caustic satire is forever turned against those contaminating institutions and habits of thought which hinder the working out of the generically human ends of life. These ends, which, if not "good," are at least advantageous to group-survival, are, it should be noted, always expressed in terms of technological proficiency, of bulk of output in weight and tale. (P. 249)

It is important to note that even when Homan did focus on Veblen's "generically human ends of life," he emphasized that they were advantageous primarily for purposes of group survival. He ignored Veblen's view that these values not only have group-survival value, they have intrinsic value for individuals and communities that aim at fullness of life. Indeed, Veblen may have believed that he had located transcultural ethical imperatives and social processes.

Although at every opportunity Veblen made scientific pretensions that are unconvincing, his satire and criticism are nevertheless valuable. In Homan's words:

Adroitly and wittily, he exposes to view the deficiencies of the law, the imbecility of our thinking, the futility of our habits of consumption, and the amazing ineptitude of our economic institutions. Overly maintaining the pose of following out an objective analysis of the process of cumulative institutional change, unrelated to any norms of ethical validity, he is in reality telling the world exactly what Veblen thinks of it. (Pp. 154–255)

In Homan's eyes, Veblen's value-neutral posturing gives way at times to transparent revelations of his own aesthetic, moral, and political values.

Social Control

Homan was just as skeptical about Veblen's attitudes toward the social control of the economy as he was toward his view of the generic ends of life. He wrote:

> And his scheme for attaining welfare is as debatable as his idea of the content of welfare. With no more concrete suggestion than a vague plan for the supervision of the economic system by a hierarchy of technical experts, he merely succeeds in evading the problem of economic guidance and the problems of value and distribution, which lie within the sweep of the price-system. He thinks the "mutual defeat" inherent in the present economic order should be escaped in the interest of material welfare and of race survival. But no intelligible theory of social ends, no adequate account of social forces, and no tenable scheme of social control are anywhere advanced.[36]

It is likely, however, that the only "tenable scheme of social control" of which liberal critics such as Homan would have approved are those like the New Deal that came on the heels of his analysis of Veblen. Apparently Veblen is faulted for failing to anticipate and outline the welfare and regulatory mechanisms of the American New Deal and post–New Deal periods. Or, at the very least, he is charged with failure to forecast and articulate the social control mechanisms that are now characteristic of other Western political economies.

Conclusion

That Homan's critical view of Veblenian economics was no flash in the pan, but rather the considered reflections of a mature scholar is evident in a review Homan wrote of David Riesman's study of Veblen in the mid-1950s. Nearly thirty years after his major study of Veblen, he still saw the same deficiencies in the Veblenian system and agreed with the liberal Riesman's attack on them:

> As to the substantive elements in Veblen's work, Professor Riesman outlines the basic ideology and examines in turn the argument of each of the principal works. His critical method is to check Veblen's categories and conclusions against the present contemporary scene. The effect is to make a considerable shambles of the Veblenian structure of thought—as science, as relevant social criticism, as prophetic progress and as social engineering. The critical commentary is most efficiently done with respect to the more broadly sociological aspects of Veblen's thought.[37]

Homan believed that in the past, American intellectuals and economists read Veblen as an important part of their development; but this meant learning to separate the wheat from the chaff in his work. Again Homan concurred with Riesman's judgments that

> his social criticism was highly topical and contemporary. His psychological and anthropological categories are obsolete. The course of industrial civilization did not develop according to the "evolutionary" pattern which, from his turn-of-the-century viewpoint, he prognosticated. His dramatically posed antitheses of interest and outlook no longer provide the terms in which radical reformers face up to the conventions and prescriptions of the social order.[38]

Homan believed that even though Veblen remains an interesting and important figure in American intellectual history, his influence is primarily as "a satirist, much impressed with the comic or futile aspects of human life."[39] Although he was a brilliant phrasemaker and wordmonger, the scientific character of his analysis was sacrificed to the demands of his "striking, even flamboyant, diction" and he defended "weak positions" by "blandly adapting a position of the shadiest scientific authenticity."[40] In the final analysis, Homan viewed Veblen as an important social critic and philosopher who nevertheless failed as a "scientific" economist. Was this evidence of the way scientism had infected Homan's own brand of liberalism, or did it simply reveal his dislike of Veblen's value-neutral posturing? Perhaps, it was both, with scientism providing the undergirding for Homan's rejection of Veblen's methodological and epistemological deviousness.[41]

JOHN R. COMMONS

John R. Commons (1862–1945) and Veblen were clearly the two leading institutional economists in the United States in the first third of the twentieth century. In several respects, Commons' penetrating critique of the radical Veblen revealed the characteristics of the ideological structure of American liberalism in the interwar period. It is interesting to note, however, that while Commons wrote extensively about Veblen's work, Veblen paid little attention to Commons. Indeed, while they played leading roles in the theoretical development of heterodox economics, they apparently never corresponded, although they may have encountered one another at conferences.[42] However, Commons was in reading contact with Veblen before *The Theory of the Leisure Class* was published in 1899; and Commons's last book, *The Economics of Collective Action*, published posthumously in 1950, contains a reference to Veblen.[43] Veblen's ideas, then, were, at least, of intermittent interest to Commons over a period of fifty years.

The differences between Veblen's radical brand of institutionalism and Commons's more conservative institutionalism are significant.[44] To illustrate, while Veblen focused on emulatory consumption and institutional rigidities, Commons emphasized individual volition and collective choice; whereas Veblen stressed waste and exploitation, Commons anticipated social amelioration and the institutionalization of reasonable value. Veblen engaged primarily in broad-gauged theorizing, while Commons, himself a theorist of considerable stature, was also given to empirical investigation. Commons feared the loss of freedom and efficiency that might result from radical changes in the existing order, but, apparently, Veblen did not share his fears. Commons looked upon the state as an instrument for the incremental reform of society, but Veblen believed the pre–New Deal state to be a tool of the vested interests. Commons viewed trade unions as fundamental agencies for improving the lot of working people, but Veblen thought the craft unions in the AFL were part of the vested interests. With these contrasts in mind, then, Commons's critique of Veblen can profitably be viewed as a characteristic ideological expression of liberal reformist attitudes toward an authentic American radicalism.

But juxtaposing Commons's liberalism with Veblen's radicalism is not a fully satisfactory way of making an assessment of his critique of the latter's theoretical system. For Commons's "instrumental presentism" aimed at using the history of economic thought, including Veblen's contribution to it, to build a new theoretical system that would shed light on present economic processes and issues.[45] It would thus be an error to assume that Commons's exegetical approach to Veblen aimed at understanding him on his own terms or even on the terms on which other economists understood him. Indeed, Veblen's doctrines were of interest to Commons because the latter was a highly eclectic thinker who borrowed ideas from others primarily on the basis of their utility for concept formation and theory construction. It is to an analysis of the method he used to accomplish this and the role that his liberalism played in this process that we now turn.

Intangible Property

What was the idea of "intangible property" as Veblen developed it, aside from its function as a device for getting "something for nothing?" Commons put it this way:

> This historical explanation of Veblen's cynical antithesis of business and industry is in the failure to trace out the evolution of business customs under the decisions of courts, as he has traced the technological customs. Such an

investigation reveals the evolution of his "intangible property" which has consisted in making the distinction, not allowed by Veblen, between good-will and privilege, goodwill being the reasonable exercise of the power to withhold, and privilege being the unreasonable exercise of that power. . . . It is just because this fact of evolution in the decisions of courts is not observed by Veblen that he does not arrive at a concept of reasonable value.[46]

Commons stressed the fact that two diverse theories of modern intangible property have been developed since 1890. The first is the exploitation theory of Veblen; the other is the reasonable value theory of the courts. It was the latter that Commons endorsed, which is not surprising since radical exploitation theories do not fit within the doctrinal parameters of liberalism. This is not to suggest, however, that liberalism lacks a theory of exploitation. Rather, its exploitation theory is different from Veblen's in that it focuses on the exercise of monopoly power, the efforts of legislatures to curb monopoly through regulation and antitrust and of the courts to adjudicate it through the doctrine of reasonable value. To illustrate, Commons agreed with Veblen's interpretation of the creation of the United States Steel Corporation, which was brought about by the purchase of the Carnegie Steel interests in a financial deal underwritten by the House of Morgan.

> This difference of 225 million dollars could not be ascribed, on the traditional theory of economics, as the value of the corporeal property. Nor was it incorporeal property since it was not a debt owed to Carnegie. The only other name that could be given to it was "intangible property" the name given by the financial magnates themselves. Veblen rightly interpreted this intangible property as merely exploitation or "hold-up" value, because it arose solely from the need of all competitors to remove Carnegie from the price-cutting competition which it was known he would initiate.[47]

But unlike Veblen, Commons did not think such transactions are characteristic of business deals; in fact, he believed they are uncommon. Consequently, generalizations made on the basis of them distort reality by exaggerating their prevalence. Furthermore, these transactions were increasingly coming under the control of new working rules developed by the courts through the concept of intangible property.

> Thorstein Veblen, to his great credit, was introducing the same idea of intangible property into economics during the period following 1900, and it was mainly on this ground that he became known as an "institutional" economist. But the difference was that Veblen obtained his case material from the testimony of financial magnates before the United States Industrial Commission of 1900, so that his notion of intangible property ended in the Marx-

ian extortion and exploitation. But my sources were my participation in collective action, in drafting bills, and my necessary study, during these participations, of the decisions of the Supreme Court covering the period; so that my notion of intangible property ends in the common-law notion of reasonable value.[48]

Commons believed that Veblen made a valuable contribution to economics with his notions of intangibility, but he, nevertheless, contrasted his own heuristic methods, information sources, and policy prescriptions with Veblen's; which provides evidence of Commons's doctrinal affinities with the main drift of ideological liberalism. In any case, Commons saw progress in its melioristic form in the newly emerging public policy, while Veblen merely observed change.

Another key point at which Commons differed with Veblen was over the role that intangible property plays in the modern political economy. He agreed, however, with Veblen's definition of intangible property. As he put it:

> Veblen could move from the metaphysics of entities, with foreordained goals, to the Darwinian idea of a process, only by changing from the Marxian and orthodox concept of corporeal property to the new and indeed post-Marxian concept of intangible property. The latter is a process itself of buying, selling, borrowing, lending, and augmenting the pecuniary value of property rights; while corporeal property has, in itself, no power of buying or selling, and its augmentation is only the increase of use-values by the labor process of working and invention.[49]

Commons also wrote that

> Veblen, when he changes from entities to processes, must change from corporeal property which contains no pecuniary process by buying and selling, to intangible property which is none other than the pecuniary process itself. Correspondingly, when he changes from Marx's social labor-power he must substitute an orderly process of the creation of material wealth, uncontrollable by the pecuniary process. This we name the expected orderly repetition of Managerial Transactions. Veblen named it the Instinct of Workmanship.[50]

Commons further explained the historical development and contemporary significance of intangible property:

> It was not until the new idea of "intangible property" arose out of the customs and actual terminology of business magnates in the last quarter of the Nineteenth Century that it was possible for Veblen and the Supreme Court to make the new distinctions which clearly separate from each other not only

the ownership of materials and the ownership of debts, but also the owner-ship of expected opportunities to make a profit by withholding supply until the price is persuasively or coercively agreed upon. This ownership of ex-pected opportunities is "intangible" property.[51]

Veblen's concept of intangible property was thus based on the pre-sent value of the future bargaining power of capitalists. He had en-larged the definition of both *property* and *capital* from that of corporeal property to that of expected earning capacity.[52] Commons complained, however, that Veblen had not investigated the decisions of the Su-preme Court. The Court gradually came to rest its decisions on this same new phenomenon of intangible property, not on Veblen's theory of exploitation, but on its own "historic concept of reasonable value."[53]

The Dichotomy between Business and Industry

Commons's admiration for aspects of Veblen's work is evident in his writings on him.[54] Nevertheless, Commons did not accept Veblen's main thesis regarding capitalism, at least in the radical form he articu-lated it. This thesis, of course, focused on the ceremonial-technological dichotomy in which, as Commons put it, "a complete line of business or pecuniary employments has been separated off from industrial or mechanical employments."[55] The capitalist thus "makes his gains, not by workmanship which is serviceable to the community, but by busi-ness which is not serviceable."[56] Commons complained, however, that Veblen's analysis ended "in a cynical dualism of materials and owner-ship."[57] This reasoning was also found in his analysis of trade unions.

> Veblen opposed trade unions just as he opposed combinations of capital. Each was collective restraint of trade. Each is a pecuniary instinct, and each is the intangible property of bargaining power. The difference between capi-talists and workmen is not that the former have the pecuniary instinct and the latter do not, but that the power to withhold, vouchsafed by the laws and customs of property, is perhaps greater in capitalistic organizations than it is in labor organizations. . . .there is no good reason for separating them into two entities, the idealized instinct of workmanship and the bedeviled in-stinct of acquisition.[58]

Commons failed to acknowledge the complexity of Veblen's views on organized labor. The latter was strongly critical of the craft unions in the American Federation of Labor, which he regarded as part of the vested interests. Yet he clearly admired the Industrial Workers of the World for their radical egalitarianism and militant opposition to capital-ism.[59] In Veblen's eyes, it was the "bedeviled instinct of acquisition," which was embedded in the craft unions and the "idealized instinct of workmanship," which characterized the Wobblies. But in Commons's view, Veblen was guilty of lumping all unions together as business unions marching under the banner of the pecuniary vested interests.

Exploitation versus Reasonable Value

Commons well recognized the radical nature of Veblen's analysis of the concept of intangible property. He wrote:

> We can thus see the highly different conclusions reached by Veblen and the Supreme Court upon the newly arrived concept of intangible property which each of them was investigating at the same time after its recognition by the court, in the year 1890. The Veblen conclusion reaches a theory of exploitation, the Court reaches a theory of reasonable value. Veblen reaches it suddenly in a book; the court reaches it experimentally by investigation.[60]

Commons was correct in stressing that Veblen did not arrive at the theory of reasonable value as defined by the courts. The reason was that he was unwilling to accept court definitions of reasonable value as such, since he used values that were still largely external to the judicial process. These included proficiency of workmanship, scientific curiosity, and altruism, and they were not adequately encapsulated in public policy by what he perceived as a big-business-oriented court system. Indeed, it is well to remember Veblen's sardonic view of law itself considered as both an intellectual discipline and cultural artifact.

> The name of science is after all a word to conjure with. So much so that the name and the mannerisms, at least, if nothing more of science, have invaded all fields of learning and have even overrun territory that belongs to the enemy. So there are "sciences" of theology, law and medicine . . . and there are such things as Christian Science, and "scientific" astrology, palmistry and the like.[61]

In the ceremonial-technological dichotomy that was derived from Veblen's original distinction between business and industrial pursuits, can the study and practice of law be classified as ceremonial or instrumental? Veblen appeared to have differed from Commons in stressing the ceremonial aspects of law and lawyering while the latter apparently believed that the study of law, the legal profession, and the federal courts were becoming steadily more instrumental in their orientation and social function. The critic may object, however, that it makes little sense to ask whether the law is ceremonial or instrumental. Rather, the question might be posed in another way by asking whether the

processes of lawmaking, both legislative and judicial, utilize ceremonial or instrumental criteria? Commons clearly felt that the common
law, in particular, based on the concept of reasonableness, was instrumental. The weaknesses of the judicial system were lack of investiga-
tive ability and the effect of the "habitual assumptions of judges,"
which might be out of date. Commons dealt less sympathetically with
legislative decision making, although even there, he did not present
the process as totally ceremonial. Thus, on balance, Veblen was more
inclined than Commons to stress the ceremonial rather than the instrumental criteria used in the processes of lawmaking both legislative
and judicial.

Value and Purpose in Economics

Commons believed that Veblen rejected the role of human purpose or
aim in economics as unscientific. As he put it, "Veblen strongly contended that a science of economics, like other sciences, does not properly permit the introduction of purpose."[62] It is likely that Commons
took Veblen's tongue-in-cheek statements regarding his own value
neutrality too seriously, although it is difficult to ascertain what Veblen
actually thought about the role of value judgments in economics. Veblen was skilled in detecting even the minutest trace of teleology in the
work of other economists. Yet he often teased his readers with value
judgments of his own while disclaiming any ideological bias or commitment. Unfortunately, Commons failed to make a distinction between what Veblen taunts other economists for, namely their failure to
achieve value-neutrality and, despite Veblen's disclaimers, the powerful and compelling role that value plays in his own work.

The role of purpose is central in Commons's work for he believed
economic evolution is, in fact, driven by what he calls "artificial selection." This is why Commons believed that economics is inherently a
volitional science, that is, a study of how human volition produces effects, not an "evolutionary science" in the manner that Veblen outlined. In short, Commons criticized his faulty conception of social science, which is not to assert that Veblen actually overlooked the role of
purpose in institutional evolution, but only that Commons perceived
him to have done so. Commons always emphasized that purpose drives
the process of institutional evolution and hence is a characteristic of
actual institutional arrangements, while for Veblen much of social evolution is due to sheer, blind drift. On occasion, Veblen did analyze action within a given institutional framework in terms of the given purposes of decision makers. But he did not want to portray institutional

evolution as a matter of deliberative or purposive actions to alter institutions. His explanations, instead, ran in terms of habituation to changed material circumstances, but to Commons his "behaviorism" was unsatisfactory. Of course, Commons tended to the opposite extreme, putting much emphasis on deliberative processes of change.

Power and Control

Commons viewed American capitalism as a particular kind of power system, and in one sense his perspective converges with Veblen's. He asked, how it is that the rights of ownership have an earning capacity and a value apart from the value given to commodities by the technological aspects of production? Commons suggested that Veblen's answer to this question was that corporate enterprise has the power to withhold goods from producers and consumers. While the growth of the industrial economy increases the supply of goods and services, ownership withholds the supply. Corporate enterprise can stop the machines from running and its exercise of this power compels its constituency to abide by the owners' terms.[63] Or as Commons also put it, it is assumed that the owner has the right "to command the behavior of those whom he admits on his premises."[64] However, Commons believed ways exist to modify the system of power relations even though these are not Veblen's:

> There is not in Veblen, an analysis of bargaining transactions as they have, for example, been developed in Anglo-American decisions of the common law, the law arising from the customs of the people. Managerial and rationing transactions, based, as they are, on the legally Superior and Inferior, lead to a social philosophy of dictatorship and its social psychology of Command and Obedience. But bargaining transactions, based on the concepts of willing buyers and sellers, and therefore on an ideal of persuasion versus coercion between those who are deemed to be equal before the law, lead to a social philosophy of freedom of the will in non-discriminatory choice of opportunities, in fair competition and in reasonable bargaining power under the protection of due process of law.[65]

It was evident, then, that Commons believed that authoritarian power structures might be ameliorated with the development of what he called "bargaining transactions," by which he meant processes such as collective bargaining. Veblen, however, did not usually focus on ameliorating existing institutions through incremental change. Rather he looked to fundamental transformations in power and property relations, which was often camouflaged by his pessimistic portrayal of the futility of a human existence encapsulated by imbecile institutions.

The Distinction between Time as Interval and Time as Flow

Commons believed that Veblen did not adequately distinguish between time as interval and time as flow. As he put it:

> The terms of a selling-buying transaction are agreed upon at a point of time, when the minds meet and titles are transferred; but, if an *interval* of time is agreed upon between negotiations and the future performance or payment, then Lapse of Time is of the essence of the case. An increment of profit or loss occurs, and each increment is a *flow* of time. Hence an *interval* of time is not of the essence of profit. But if the product is bought *now* and sold 30 days from now, the interval of time is of the essence of interest. The interval appears, indeed, both as risk and as waiting, and each has an effect on present valuation. But Veblen eliminates the waiting and attends only to the risking.[66]

In the history of classical and neoclassical economics, three different arguments have been used to explain and to justify the receipt of income from property. The first, and perhaps oldest, was the idea of abstinence; the second was the notion of risk; and the last the view of time as waiting. It was this last one that Commons believed Veblen failed to grasp. As he put it:

> He thereby made Time an essential fact of economics. But . . . he could not see the difference between *change* and *waiting*—which is the difference between a moving point of time in the ever-present, when change occurs, and an interval between a present point and a future point of time, when waiting occurs. The first may be named a flow, the second a lapse of time. The two go together, but it was Veblen's failure to recognize the distinction that permitted him to eliminate the incorporeal expected beneficial transactions.[67]

Indeed, Commons believed it was Veblen's inability to distinguish between change and waiting that doomed him to grasp the risk but not the waiting argument. Commons thus claimed that

> his "intangible property" does, indeed, look to future earning capacity, and it is properly named intangible, but that earning capacity is solely an expected *repetition* of business transactions along a risky *flow* of time, not an expected *postponement* of income during a *lapse* of time. His meaning of the term "lapse," which he uses, is really the meaning of "flow." This, we have seen, is exactly the difference between intangible and incorporeal property. Incorporeal property is waiting until a debt is paid; intangible property is the expectation that profits will be obtained from future transactions.[68]

It is evident at this point that Commons had conceptual axes to grind that brought him closer to convergence with neoclassical theory and showed him to be a much less virulent critic of conventional economics than Veblen.

Technical Elitism

Like many liberal critics of Veblen, Commons believed that his theory led ultimately in the direction of technical elitism. Interestingly, it was in this context that he related Veblen's instinct of workmanship to Frederick Taylor's notions regarding scientific management:

> Taylor's idea of scientific management was solely the engineer's idea of measurement applied to labor as it had been applied to machinery. The manager determined by his superior position just how much and how the laborer should produce. Veblen in 1914 revolted against this idea and built up the contradictory idea of the idealized workman, whether manual, scientific, or managerial, carrying forward the traditions of good workmanship. For these reasons Veblen became the intellectual founder of all the modern schemes which would place the engineer, instead of the capitalist, at the head of the social process.[69]

Veblen was perennially on the lookout for a revolutionary social change agent. Early in his career he thought it might be the blue-collar workers or the Bellamyite Nationalist organizations. Later, according to Commons, he decided it was the engineer and technician. Ultimately pessimism and futility regarding the likelihood of large-scale structural change became apparent in Veblen's work. However, Commons was too confident in his claim that after Veblen lost faith in the conventional radical agents of social change, he seized on the only remaining group potentially capable of overturning the existing order, namely the engineers and the technicians. Commons believed that the technical elite had always been present in embryonic form as a harbinger, if not determinant, of progressive social change in Veblen's analysis. It was only when Veblen abandoned his faith in other social forces that the embryo developed into a conviction that the technical elite should (and could) assert their control over the economy. This would be done by disallowing absentee ownership and expelling management from control over the corporate structure and organizing the work process with the support of the labor force and the underlying population. In short, Veblen's rejection of capitalist property and power relations was rooted in a disbelief in the equity and efficiency of the existing system and, more importantly,led him to search for social change agents that could drastically alter it. In Commons's view, *The Engineers and the Price System* only brought to fruition tendencies already present in Veblen's early work.

It is difficult to justify Commons's emphasis on *The Engineers and the Price System* as the most authentic expression of Veblen's long-term projection of the course of social evolution and industrial relationships. Michael Starr was closer to the truth regarding Veblen's intent when he described it as a "clever expository device" intended not as a serious proposal for economic reconstruction but as an indictment of the waste caused by absentee ownership, predatory management, and business unionism.[70] Often, Veblen's satirical intent has not received its just due because of the ideological ax-grinding of his critics and interpreters who sought to discredit his work in order to achieve their own political objectives. Although Commons was not among this group, he apparently believed that Veblen undermined a more pragmatic politics and more realistic ideals by focusing on the technical elite instead of adjusting his sights on realizable goals.

Critics often cite *The Theory of Business Enterprise* (1904) in an attempt to show that Veblen's stress on the emancipatory impact of the machine process is linked to his other call for an industrial system operated by engineers and technicians who have most thoroughly assimilated technological values. They also cite portions of *Absentee Ownership* (1923), Veblen's last book, in an effort to demonstrate that Veblen did not abandon his focus on the liberating role of the engineers and technicians after the publication of *The Engineers and the Price System* (1921).[71] It seems, however, that the overall thrust of *Absentee Ownership* is largely an expression of Veblen's despair over his failure to locate social forces that promote radical change. The technical elite play an insignificant role in it because Veblen had returned once more to an indictment of absentee ownership and the cultural and ideological superstructure that support it.

Veblen scholars often wish Veblen had not written *The Engineers and the Price System*. Although it began as a series of articles published in *The Dial*, a politico-literary journal read by liberal intellectuals who were not economists, and was then published in book form, it cannot be ignored or explained away. So Commons was correct in insisting that the reality of its publication be faced and that it be related to the rest of Veblen's work. But this can be done most accurately by viewing it as an expository device expressing satirical intent, not as a serious plan for economic reconstruction. But given his tongue-in-cheek style of presentation and convoluted rhetoric, who can be sure of Veblen's intent?

Conclusion

Commons's discussion of Veblen's ideas occurred in the context of Commons's development of his own theory of reasonable value. He clearly used Veblen to highlight his belief that economic analysis must incorporate a more sophisticated understanding of property. Hence the critique of Veblen's interpretation of intangible property, which Commons alleged did not incorporate an understanding of the true role of working rules. This also led to Veblen's failure to understand the role of law and the final authoritative agency in determining its content, the Supreme Court. Commons criticized Veblen's failure to grasp the significance of scarcity to property and argued that his inability to understand the nature of bargaining transactions was due to his preoccupation with "real" phenomena. This was reflected in Commons's assessment of Veblen's theory as a "physical theory" that neglected the inescapable second aspect of all transactions in a system where there is ownership and in his critique of Veblen's inadequate incorporation of time into property concepts. The critic should also note how Commons lumped Veblen's theory with other "physical theories" that Commons obviously considered inadequate to the understanding of a money economy. According to Malcolm Rutherford, Commons believed

> institutions evolve under pressure from the requirement of workability. Workability involves a degree of efficiency and a distribution of benefits and burdens that allows the system to survive, but inefficiencies and injustices may remain. Workability is an entirely pragmatic requirement; there must be a set of rights and rules, some authority for enforcing rights, and some degrees of adherence to common customs or norms. Commons was quite aware of the role of power struggle, sometimes leading to war and revolution, in institutional history, but social order, for Commons, required both a balance of opposing interest groups and the existence of a system of common belief.[72]

What was most important to Commons was ensuring that the power of one individual or collective was not used to control the behavior of others in an unreasonable fashion. In practice, that could be done only be creating new forms of collective action and working rules designed to equalize power, provide representation of interests, and emancipate those presently operating under coercion, duress, or unfair competition. Veblen showed little direct interest in such matters, perhaps because he had little faith in incremental reform and, in any case, viewed the kind of trade unions Commons was most familiar with as a vested interest in their own right.

From Commons's perspective, Veblen failed to provide a satisfactory analysis of the decision-making process, of why and how it is that groups adopt some practices and abandon others, and of how new social morals are formed and become embedded in particular legal and political forms. Commons believed that high ideals were often the enemy of the realizable good, and he voiced his opposition to utopians who based their reconstructive efforts upon rational, abstract principles. As he put it:

> They turn, according to character and circumstance, perhaps into able supporters of the most conservative reactionary capitalism; or perhaps into despondent pessimists holding that "nothing can be done;" or perhaps into a deistic or materialistic faith that an over-ruling Providence, or the great inherent forces of natural law, can be trusted to work out these reforms . . . to which they have formerly devoted their lives.[73]

Although none of these categories are adequate portrayals of Veblen's state of mind, it is likely that he fell into the utopian category in Commons's analysis. This characteristic posture toward radical critiques of American capitalism is deeply rooted in the doctrinal structure of liberalism, in that small-scale, incremental change is viewed as the only feasible method of improvement. But Veblen's view was that drastic reorganization of the economic system was required, and his prescriptions to fulfill this end have a strongly radical flavor. Commons thought that more realistic objectives could be achieved by regulating the sphere of collective action of bargaining groups, such as the trade union and the business corporation, and at the same time expanding the economic powers of the state and federal legislatures. Commons spent his life promoting and drafting legislation on unemployment and accident insurance, and on minimum wage and public utility regulation. He studied changes in the laws brought about by judicial decisions, and constructed economic theories to harmonize with these decisions from the standpoint of their relevance to a capitalism that was evolving from individualistic competition to collective organization and bargaining.

The main thrust of Commons's institutionalism was thus different from Veblen's. It was more optimistic, in part, because it stressed adaptation by choice, for Commons emphasized volition and will-in-action as a prime mover in social relations, while Veblen focused more on drift and institutional rigidities. In Commons's social theory, behavior was purposive and manifested a large concern with future results. Perhaps he remained more faithful than Veblen to the American belief that human intelligence, if properly directed, could ameliorate the important issues of social life. For Commons, theory had to serve as a call to action, while for the withdrawn, at times detached, Veblen, it was enough at least in the short run to understand the situation.[74] Commons held that institutions can be made suitable to the present and future, whereas Veblen's theory of cultural lag stresses the continuous maladjustment of institutions in past, present, and future.[75]

This treatment of Commons as a critic of Veblen makes the claim that his critique is, in certain respects, an ideological expression of reform liberalism, albeit a very sophisticated one. Commons utilized both the analytic apparatus of a self-devised conservative institutionalism and the assumptions of legal realism to expose weaknesses in the Veblenian system. Yet much of what he expressed represented efforts not merely to understand the evolving American economic and legal system, but to reach an accommodation with it, an accommodation he articulated by endorsing the reforms of the New Deal era.[76]

Commons's criticisms of Veblen may seem esoteric because they were clothed in the jargon of law and economics as well as in his own idiosyncratic conceptualizations and hair-splitting distinctions; yet, at bottom, his criticisms were political and moral, a point that has often evaded his interpreters. Court decrees regarding "reasonable value" were portrayed as representing strong progress toward ultimate "social equity," high wages paid to skilled craftsmen because they are unionized and can engage in collective bargaining were viewed by Commons as socially just. Returns to capital were sometimes legitimized by arguments that could easily have originated in the minds of Irving Fisher or Frank Knight.

However, Commons's most important deficiency as a critic of Veblen was his failure to come to grips with the latter's most important contribution to microeconomics, namely his theory of status emulation, with the massive waste and invidious social distinction this signifies. Indeed, if Commons had any serious objections to neoclassical assumptions regarding consumer sovereignty, he kept them well-concealed in his critique of Veblen. Apparently, this was because he did not believe that the American economy seriously misallocated resources by producing commodities largely for purposes of status enhancement.[77] Related to this, of course, was Commons's dismissal of the important Veblenian distinction between making money and making socially useful goods as "cynical." Given Commons's broader perspective, this cannot be interpreted as a moral, political, and perhaps even aesthetic endorsement of whatever is, is right. More likely, it is merely the fatalistic resignation of an elderly man who believed he had more important differences with Veblen to explain in the process of constructing a new theory of institutional economics.

John Maurice Clark

At Carleton College, Veblen was once the student of John Bates Clark (1847–1938), who became an eminent American neoclassical economist. Veblen was highly critical of the doctrinal structure of Clark's neoclassicism, but Clark never responded in print to his attacks.[78] While Veblen attacked Clark's work, he, nevertheless, spoke highly of Clark the person. Clark was proud of having had Veblen as one of his students and after Veblen achieved notoriety with the publication of *The Theory of the Leisure Class*, he noted with satisfaction that Veblen had fulfilled his potential.

It was John Maurice Clark (1884–1963), J. B. Clark's son, who was both influenced by and critical of Veblen.[79] Indeed, it was in his occasional references to Veblen, rather than in his father's work, that the Clark family's ideological confrontation with Veblen occurred. Nevertheless, Clark's work resembled Veblen's in that as a social economist he suggested that value itself is social in nature and that the part takes its price from the value of the whole rather than the whole getting its price from the utility of the marginal part. Such organic social valuations, made independent of institutions of competitive exchange, were most basic in Clark's analysis of the economy and gave him common ground with Veblen, although he stopped short of the radical economic and social collectivism that the latter favored. Addison Hickman summarized the evolution of Clark's attitudes toward the social control of industry and economic stabilization during the period that he did most of his work on Veblen:

> Clark's early conviction that much of this stabilization, especially regularization of employment, could be accomplished by actions of industry never completely disappeared. Beginning in 1926, however, his emphasis shifted firmly toward what the larger society, through government, could also do. His preferences were always for mild rather than drastic measures; for indirect instead of direct controls; and for action that would complement rather than supersede or negate the efforts of the private sector. Yet, he was advocating by the early 1930's policies clearly in anticipation of Keynes, and in subsequent years he apparently grew increasingly comfortable with the macroeconomic policy.[80]

Hickman's description of Clark's political and economic philosophy indicated that he was once a classical liberal who had moved toward collectivism by the time he wrote on Veblen. Indeed, by the 1930s, his early preference for economic individualism had given way to acceptance of many of the New Deal reforms.

Clark's Methodological Strictures

Veblen's own methodology as well as his critique of the methodology of neoclassical economics was subjected to critical scrutiny by many of the liberal scholars who examined his work. Clark was no exception and he was of the opinion that "even though Veblen neglects scientific procedure in proving his detailed conclusions, he is still a great apostle of scientific method."[81] Specifically, Clark claimed that

> [Veblen's] contribution is in a conception of the problem, the range of data to be envisaged and the kinds of results to be looked for. Perhaps these are the most important things, and the tactics of weighing data may be governed by the character of the data that are sought and the nature of the questions asked about them. Possibly it needed someone of Veblen's temperament to teach the more conventionally-minded what economic dynamics really includes, and how it is likely to alter not merely static doctrines, but static definitions, conceptions and classifications; and to try out sample theories of evolutionary economics. It certainly needed someone of his iconoclastic humor to challenge the complacencies of nineteenth-century liberalism. His work of orientation has fulfilled itself in the studies and work of other men more adapted to plodding induction and detailed verification.[82]

The ideological structure of Clark's own thought was evident in his insistence that such broad-gauged theories as Veblen's be submitted to the tests of induction and verification. Interestingly, Clark wrote that Veblen did not understand that

> an observed sequence of events is not identical with a relation of cause and effect and that historical observation is too limited to prove relations of cause and effect with scientific completeness. Hence Veblen's own conclusions as to cause and effect are based fundamentally on judgment or insight, rather than on scientific demonstration. . . . And if he is to be criticized it is for not noting that . . . failure is inherent in any attempt to discover relations of cause and effect in an historical sequence only, or for implying that the relations of cause and effect which are suggested by such study are the only ones worthy of scientific attention.[83]

Indeed, Clark suggested that Veblen's ultimate contribution to methodology is found not in his own work, but incorporated in that of his student Wesley C. Mitchell. He wrote: "Here we have a type of inquiry such as Veblen's doctrines suggest, carried out with a thoroughness of induction and a full presentation of data such as Veblen never attempted. The result is sufficiently realistic to afford a more practicable basis for policies of control than had yet been achieved."[84] Of course,

Veblen did little of the kind of research in which Wesley Mitchell so ably engaged. Worse yet, he lacked an unambiguous approach to the problem of objectivity in the social sciences. As Clark put it:

> Veblen's analysis, then, is not the completely objective tracing of impersonal sequences of cause and effect which his essays on method call for; but is—as anything human must probably be—a matter of selected aspects. One of the unanswered puzzles about this intriguing thinker, at least to those who did not know him intimately, is his own attitude toward this subjective element entering into his avowedly objective treatment.[85]

Once again, the question arises as to what Veblen's attitudes were toward the role of values in social science inquiry. How seriously is his eschewal of value judgments to be taken? Judging by his use of his own values to make judgments about other values and institutions, not too seriously. Indeed, his efforts to persuade his readers that his position was value-neutral and thus "objective" often were either comic relief or satirical efforts at diverting attention from his own utilization of a particular set of values to flail his ideological opponents.

Interestingly, the broader problem of valuation was also evident in Clark's penetrating comment that

> when one understands the conflict between Veblen and Neo-Classicism sufficiently to see that Veblen's dogmas of waste and the Neo-Classical dogmas of serviceability both contemplate very similar ranges of ultimate facts, and differ chiefly in what they choose to call "normal"—when one has carried his appreciation thus far, he would be foolish to ignore either range of facts or to refuse to admit both types of things as the results of natural laws in the economic world.[86]

The ambiguous nature of Clark's liberalism was evident in his perception of the "reality" of "Veblen's dogmas of waste and the Neo-Classical dogmas of serviceability." He failed to express a preference for either view and indicated to his reader that since both sets of facts were relevant, there are no grounds upon which to demonstrate the superiority of one over the other. At times, it is apparent in Clark's appraisal of Veblen that the doctrine of subjective preference that badly infected neoclassical economics had also produced intermittent moral agnosticism in him. Thus he could not formulate a preference either for Veblen's attacks on "waste" or neoclassical defenses of it. The moral paralysis that other institutionalists avoided thus marred Clark's critique of Veblen, at this point, indicating that he was less of a dissenter than these heterodox economists.

On the other hand, Clark was critical of the hedonistic postulates of neoclassical economics, but not as critical as Veblen. Once again, the ambiguity of his position was perhaps a reflection of the value conflicts and value inconsistency of liberal doctrine in the 1920s and 1930s. He wrote that

> The marginal utility theory of value is based on hedonistic psychology and falls to the ground with it, while the marginal productivity theory of distribution is a tautology. This last is a debatable point but is not debated. It would be much nearer the truth to claim that the marginal theory of price is a tautology: it certainly becomes one when it tries to rid itself of every taint of hedonism, like some ascetic striving to free his spirit from the bonds of the body. (P. 243)

In his methodological critique of Veblen, Clark also made the intriguing comment that what "impels Veblen to discover unity underlying differences is his genetic method of study" (p. 247). To illustrate, Veblen's critical genetic method permits him to see the continuity and underlying "unity" of the organization of Viking piracy as an early example of a "trust" or contemporary monopoly and also the unity between "our class standards of consumption and those of a warlike and predatory aristocracy" (p. 247). The similarities that exist between predatory and invidious behavior from one generation to the next were thus tied together by Veblen but, as Clark noted, at the risk of overgeneralization.

The Business-Industry Dichotomy

The value inconsistency of Clark's liberalism is also evident in his equivocal attitude toward Veblen's condemnation of the parasitical function of the business community. Clark wrote that

> this inverse normalizing method of Veblen's enables him to characterize parasitic gains as the essential nature of the institution of Business, while any successful pursuit of workmanlike efficiency which may persist does so in spite of the essential nature of the institution, not because of it. Most readers will enjoy his implication without afterthought: the more analytical will appreciate the adroitness with which he reverses and uses the weapon on his adversaries, normalization (which he has himself characterized as not fully scientific) and they may be moved to speculate whether one use is not quite as legitimate as the other. (P. 244)

Clark also believed that Veblen often failed to make any "finer distinctions than the orthodox economics" (p. 247). For example, his definition of *sabotage*, which included all "withholding of efficiency" and consequently became a blanket term that encompassed "strikes, limitation of output by labor or employer, adulteration and protective tariffs" (p. 247). In Clark's view, this indiscriminate approach ignored important distinctions that deserve consideration and there was little reason to prefer it to the neoclassical approach.

If the norm of business is parasitism, then any real service that is "rendered is rendered incidentally"[87] rather than because of the intrinsic nature of business enterprise. Orthodox economists take just the opposite tack and regard parasitism not as a norm but as an "incidental perversion of the true spirit of the institution."[88] But, in contrasting Veblen with orthodox economists, Clark argued, in terms that revealed his own ambiguity, that

> they are not so much contradicting each other as selecting different things to talk about. Veblen is talking about the nature of the pursuit of profits; and the beneficial effects of competition, where competition works beneficially, are an incidental and very partial check (and possibly a temporary one) on the natural tactics of the pursuit of gain. Orthodox economics is talking about the nature of competition (or rather of an "ideal" form of competition) as a check on human selfishness in the pursuit of profits and to them any failures of competition to produce its full effects appears as incidental disturbances. In a general way most economists admit the same general mass of facts, but pick out different ones as the central axioms of their systematic economic theorizing.[89]

As a reform liberal, Clark favored "scientific" extension of social control of industry. Indeed, he believed that in certain respects this was also the perspective of Veblen, although "of course it need not imitate wholly his bias as to the disserviceability of private business."[90] Clearly, Veblen's analysis was too radical, for, in Clark's view, there was little justification for large-scale changes in the existing price system, market mechanism, or system of property relations.

The organic view Veblen held of the industrial economy emphasized the interrelatedness of all economic activities, and the collective legacy of technology as social in nature. Naturally, he concluded that parasitical class control and use of the means of production, exchange and distribution were unwarranted. As Clark put it:

> It means that everyone is dependent upon everyone else in many ways which the market can never trace and measure, and that one's apparently independent contribution is really a joint product, with society as a partner in production. Thus the system of distribution under free exchange does not represent either the contributions of the parties, the ultimate results of what

they do or their equitable claims. This doctrine does not aim to abolish individual rights, but it discredits the competitive arbitrament of them, and leaves an indefinite scope of policies of a mutualist color.[91]

At this point, Clark's comments exhibited the ideological bias of liberals, for he did not complain of Veblen's radicalism, which was his characteristic stance toward him. Instead, he attempted to deradicalize him by placing an amelioristic gloss on his writing that made it difficult to distinguish him from other modern liberals.

Veblen's attacks on the "waste and futility" of capitalism were, in Clark's eyes, inadequate because Veblen had a

certain reluctance to search for alternative systems which might remove these wastes, thus leaving the conservative in considerable doubt whether they are wastes at all, in the practical sense of being avoidable. And when Veblen does face the question of alternatives he takes the position that an automatic regeneration is possible by negative means, through abolishing existing "vested interests" in "absentee ownership."[92]

At this point, Clark preferred the conservative analysis to Veblen's, because as he put it, "Both ignore some things which require analysis, though in this respect Veblen's position is the more at fault, for the orthodox position means something in terms of present behavior and the present requirements of industrial efficiency, while it is hard to tell whether Veblen's does or not."[93] Again, the ambiguity of Clark's own liberalism manifested itself in the uncertainty that characterized his reading of Veblen. Some of this uncertainty was, no doubt, a natural reaction to the circumlocution of Veblen's style. The rest, however, appears to be evidence of the value inconsistency and value conflicts of liberal ideology and represented vacillating efforts on Clark's part to realize his own doctrinal and political agenda. The parameters of this agenda rest on the uncertain assumption that there are no viable alternatives to private ownership and control of the means of production and use of the existing market mechanism and price system.

The Price System, Market Mechanism, and Allocation of Resources

Many liberal critics, and Clark was no exception, expressed grave reservations regarding Veblen's attitudes toward the price system. Some of their misgivings were based on his views in *The Engineers and the Price System*, that *bête noire* of the Veblenian corpus. Others stem from conclusions implicit in the general logic of the dichotomy between business and industry. Clark's own position, however, was that of uncertainty: "There is nothing in Veblen's inquiry into socialism to indicate that he would dispense with the price system. On the other hand, the reviewer is not aware of any positive indications that he would use a price system, or, if so, with what modifications."[94] On other occasions, however, Clark did imply that Veblen intended to displace the price system. For example, he commented in his review of *Absentee Ownership* that "Veblen does not explain . . . how the technician can measure net income—the excess of product over cost in purely technical terms, as he calmly assumes."[95] Clark also claimed that Veblen believed

> that an economic organization of society is possible in terms of technical facts and values alone, without any substitute (or any formal substitute) for the scheme of prices whereby the incommensurable human values are graded and precedence determined among them. His only recognition of this need is to put some economists (of the institutional school) on the council of his proposed soviet of technicians.[96]

Clark now exhibited one of the characteristic traits of the liberal ideologue in that he misrepresented Veblen's critique of the price system by claiming that he advocated its complete displacement, which, of course, he portrayed as irrational. In short, Clark took Veblen's "proposals" in *The Engineers and the Price System* too seriously, indeed, more seriously than Veblen ever took them, judging from his tongue-in-cheek articulation of them. Indeed, Clark's parting comments represented a sophisticated form of red-baiting, itself a sport at which a particular kind of liberal has long been adept: "For any intellectual sins he may have committed it would be adequate and appropriate punishment to live under a soviet system, to probe its characteristic wares and futilities as only he could probe them, and to be forcibly silenced by the new spokemen of edification."[97] This last sentence, written in 1924, sentenced Veblen to life under the Soviet system replete with oppression as a punishment befitting as intellectual suspected of sympathy with the early Bolshevik regime and bold enough to author *The Engineers and the Price System*.

Conclusion

Clark believed that Veblen exaggerated the power that capital has over the economy, as well as the benefits that it extracts at the expense of labor. He put it this way:

> Capital and labor are both dependent on the "state of the arts," but the observed facts do not indicate that capital alone "corners" the results of current

progress, still less the "wisdom of ancients" as Veblen has suggested. Capital absorbs part of the effects, but labor absorbs still more, and this is definitely borne out by the figures before us.[98]

Some of the difference in ideological perspective between Veblen and Clark may be attributed to Clark's view that Veblen dealt in half-truths, particularly when he wrote about capitalism. He complained that

> While Veblen admits a modicum of serviceability under private enterprise, he does not seriously undertake to explain how this provision of the essentially parasitic nature of business enterprise comes about. He does not focus attention on the nature of the checks on selfish exploitation, embodied in customs, morals, rights of property and person with the negative and positive duties they involve, and in that complex, self-contradictory but very real institution of economic competition.[99]

Clark believed that Veblen's "instinct of workmanship," while perhaps a misnomer, was an important concept. As he put it:

> Even the courts [are] under the powerful influence of the judicial form of that "instinct of workmanship" which a reader of Professor Veblen's very valuable book tempts one to define as a "bent toward mistaking the means for the end" . . . for this perversion of Veblen's terms I hope to be forgiven, on the ground that it is no worse than those perversions of the instinct itself which form so large a part of his book, and which he shows to be inherent in the nature of the instinct.[100]

Clark also suggested that Veblen overlooked the deficiencies of the instinct of workmanship in fixating on its positive qualities. In fact, he argued that workmanship carried to extremes is wasteful as measured by price because workers driven by a desire for perfection would invest too much time and take too many pains; in short, work would become an end in itself instead of simply a means.[101] At this point, however, Clark, while pointing to the microeconomic limitations of the instinct of workmanship had also, perhaps unwittingly, articulated the dubious moral stance of neoclassicism toward craftsmanship.

Like most of Veblen's liberal critics Clark believed that there are no equitable or efficient alternatives to capitalism and that, in any case, Veblen did not give adequate attention to the positive aspects of the system. In this sense, Veblen was not a constructive critic. As Clark put it:

> Was Veblen "constructive?" Not in the sense of constructing a "system" of defined levels of equilibrium or other definitive results. . . . Not in the sense of making his work an outgrowth of previous orthodoxy; that was not to be expected. Not in the sense of furnishing his followers a complete substitute

for that orthodoxy in the form of propositions with which to solve all problems. . . . He was not constructive in the sense of explaining the socially constructive forces in the world of private business. . . . And not in the sense of proving to what quantitative degree business is governed by the principles he assumes—that test is only beginning to be applied to any of our doctrines.[102]

Yet the ambiguity of Clark's liberalism also surfaced, for he found value in Veblen's iconoclasm when he wrote that "if an independent explanation of important and neglected ranges of economic facts be constructive, Veblen meets the test in generous measure."[103] However, in rebuttal of Clark's broader critique, Veblen could not unfairly claim that Clark's own descriptive analysis of the American economy contained much that is merely rationalization for the status quo. He was ready to do patchwork here and there on its design and performance, but its essential equity and efficiency were largely taken for granted after the reforms of the New Deal era. Indeed, Clark was more concerned to defend the existing institutions and policies of the New Deal and post–New Deal periods against conservatives than to answer the criticisms of radicals like Veblen. This, of course, is a characteristic of an American liberalism that rarely takes indigenous radicalism seriously, since its concern is with the obstructionism of the political Right.

THE INSTITUTIONAL ECONOMISTS AND VEBLEN

The vein of radicalism that runs through Veblen's work struck a discordant tone in the ear of his conservative critics but was less of an irritant to the institutionalists. In his debate with Fisher, Veblen claimed that the latter's work lacked the "breath of life" and it is this charge that he now faces from otherwise sympathetic evolutionary economists who question the "realism" both of his analysis and his policy prescriptions. Also, the tone of moral superiority that sometimes emanates from Veblen irritates the institutionalist critic, particularly when it exceeds the conventional boundaries of social satire.

In view of the many criticisms leveled at him by the institutional economists Mitchell, Homan, Commons, and Clark, why is Veblen generally conceded to be the father of institutional economics? Even assuming that all were influenced positively by him in various ways, what is the common thread, that is, the doctrinal and theoretical bond that lends coherence to this school of thought? The answer seems to be that institutionalism itself is an amalgam of different theoretical sources and tendencies. Even more important is the fact that political and doctrinal divisions have long existed in the movement, even if they have gone unnoticed or been submerged. This is not to suggest that institutionalism has been latently polarized into ideological camps; it is to state, however, that Commons and Veblen, for example, held widely divergent views. It was largely the need for institutionalists to present a united front against political conservatives and neoclassical economists that prevented them from adequately recognizing their own diversity and squarely facing its political and ideological implications. The criticisms of Veblen by institutionalists themselves provide powerful and compelling evidence of the fact that he held significantly more radical views than most other evolutionary economists of the time.

Chapter Seven

LIBERAL CRITICS: THE NEOINSTITUTIONALISTS

MOST "neoinstitutionalists," meaning those institutional economists who did the bulk of their writing after World War II, were not very critical of Veblen's work. Instead, they were more concerned to defend him from critics and more interested in explicating his theories than engaging in doctrinal confrontation with him. What distinguishes neoinstitutionalists Clarence Ayres (1891–1972) and Allan Gruchy (1906–1990) long-time professors of economics at Texas and Maryland, respectively, from other neoinstitutionalists is that they were significantly critical of Veblenian theory and doctrine.[1] Ayres and Gruchy, particularly the latter, found spongy, incomplete, or erroneous claims in the corpus Vebleniana and, at times, probed them tellingly. Indeed, Gruchy's work on Veblen is among the most penetrating commentaries ever written. Ayres, himself, rarely wrote systematically on Veblen, but he spent a lifetime reflecting on his ideas. On occasion, when not consumed with the application of his synthesis of Deweyan and Veblenian social value theory to institutional analysis, he made insightful comments on Veblen's doctrines. It is to Gruchy's and Ayres's criticisms of Veblen that we now turn. But it should be remembered that both were greatly influenced by him and regarded his as a seminal mind.

GRUCHY'S METHODOLOGICAL CRITICISMS

Like many of Veblen's critics, Gruchy found him inconsistent in his methodological prescriptions, particularly in his failure to take his own advice. Veblen seemed to advocate an inductive approach to economic studies, yet as Gruchy put it:

> Veblen left it to others to do the painstaking work of marshalling the facts and fitting them into intricate patterns of price behavior. Had he possessed a greater capacity for the statistical handling of economic data, Veblen could have done much to provide a firm inductive foundation for many of his broad generalizations. But he makes no use of the devices of statistical analysis, nor does he seem to have been interested in grappling with the kinds of problems that are subject to statistical measure.[2]

Like other critics, mostly liberal or conservative, Gruchy thought Veblen concentrated too exclusively on the more complex levels of abstraction in economic analysis.[3] Gruchy's methodological strictures thus stressed Veblen's lack of interest in statistical analysis and his failure to investigate the more mundane aspects of economic behavior, two deficiencies that are closely related to each other.

The Engineers and the Price System

Although Gruchy took Veblen's "proposals" in *The Engineers and the Price System* too seriously, he made some astute comments regarding the problems that might arise were the scheme to be implemented. The first question he asked concerning its equity and efficiency was "what is the possibility that Veblen's regime of workmanship will be a democratic form of economic organization?" (p. 129).

Like other critics of *The Engineers and the Price System*, Gruchy was wary of what may be its totalitarian implications. The self-appointed or self-selected soviet of technicians would govern with the support of the industrial rank and file. Yet Gruchy believed that Veblen had ultimately failed to come to grips with the problems of democratic accountability (p. 129). He put it this way:

> Veblen has little to say about the preservation of democratic values and procedures in the disposal of the community's scarce resources. It is plain, however, that the discipline of the new industrial technology has no special power to cause men to function in a democratic manner, or to make them see democratic goals with a special mental clarity. The machine can improve neither the human reason nor the democratic leaning of those whom come in contact with the new technology. The achievement of a democratically functioning economic society is more a psychological than a technological problem. (P. 130)

Many of Veblen's critics attacked *The Engineers and the Price System*, but few focused so penetratingly on its weaknesses, although Gruchy assigned it a centrality of importance out of proportion to its actual role in the corpus of Veblen's writings. In any case, he stressed Veblen's failure to come to grips with the impact of politics on economic activity, for the latter left his readers with the impression that the democratic economy of the future, if implemented, would not have to resolve political issues. With reason, Gruchy thus charged him with not inquiring deeply enough into the political basis of his new industrial order (p. 103).

Another aspect of *The Engineers and the Price System* that Gruchy found wanting was Veblen's failure to adequately explain how income would be distributed in his new industrial republic. He believed that Veblen thought that

> the only really functional claimants to the net surplus product of industry are the technicians and the workers; and, in the socialistic economy of the future that he envisions, the surplus product of industry would be distributed between these two groups. Veblen, however, does not make any detailed inquiry into how socialistic economy would remunerate only those who contribute to the national income of real goods or economic values. All that he has to say on this important question is that there should be "an equitable distribution of the consumable output" among the workers and the engineers. (P. 115)

Gruchy pointed to a lacunae not only in Veblen's proposal of 1921 for reconstructing the economy but to his larger failure to specifically address the problem of income distribution in industrial society. Veblen's sympathy for abolition of absentee ownership and his egalitarian values suggested that he favored more equality than presently exists, but he offered no explicit formulas, standards, or criteria by which to guide the redistribution of income. However, he did suggest an approach that is essentially Darwinian, that is, evolutionary in nature. But Gruchy demanded more specificity from a Veblenian perspective that is not adequately oriented toward policy prescription.

Veblen's Social Psychology

The deficiencies of Veblen's social psychological analysis are objects of considerable interest to Gruchy. Part of his critique focused on Veblen's view of the social psychology of Karl Marx. As Gruchy put it:

> In criticizing Marx's rationalistic psychology Veblen overlooks the extent to which Marx went in working out a social psychology. He makes little reference to the relations between Marx's economic interpretation of history and his theory of human behavior. Veblen ignores the whole discussion by Marx of the social or environmental influences that shape human behavior. While it is true that Marx makes much of human reason and little of human instinct, it is hardly justifiable to confine him to the simple rationalistic psychology accepted by the classical English economists. In this connection Veblen's criticism appears to be more sweeping than correct. (P. 78)

However, Gruchy's primary focus is not on Veblen's critique of Marx; rather he criticized the inadequacy of Veblen's psychological theory. Gruchy lay great stress on the fact that "Veblen seems to have limited his psychological analysis to the progress in psychology that had been achieved by 1914" (p. 127). This was the year Veblen published *The Instinct of Workmanship*, and, according to Gruchy, the idea of instinct was still dominant in his psychological theory, which was unfortunate because "the concept of instinct remains vague and unmanageable, the recent practice of social psychologists has been to pass hurriedly over the instinctive basis of human behavior, and to turn to psychological data which are more amenable to scientific handling" (p. 128).

Critics have often attacked Veblen's use of the term *instinct* as the basis of his psychological theory. Although he moved some distance away from his most naive use of it in *The Theory of the Leisure Class*, he never completely abandoned it. However, perhaps under the influence of his Chicago colleagues John Dewey, George H. Mead, and Jacques Loeb, he did modify his use of the concept of instinct. In this regard, Gruchy's criticisms of Veblen's use of psychology for purposes of economic analysis were focused and penetrating.

> If Veblen had devoted more of his time and energy to analyzing his concept of economic status and the economic attitudes which are associated with class behavior, he would have been spared much of the criticism that has been levelled at "instinct psychology." But Veblen makes no painstaking effort to locate economic attitudes, to determine their order of development, or to measure their respective significance for the explanation of human conduct. (P. 28)

Without explicitly invoking the cultural lag theory that Veblen used to belabor his opponents, Gruchy claimed that

> since these cultural situations can be handled more objectively than the human instincts, the interests of modern social psychologists center in them rather than in the instincts. Although Veblen had a grasp of many of the elements of the new integrative psychology, he was unable to divest himself of his deep interest in the role of instinct. . . . Veblen did not find it easy to keep up with the trends in the development of sociopsychological analysis after 1914. As a consequence much of the psychological emphasis underlying his evolutionary economics is both inadequate and outmoded. (Pp. 128–29)

It might be added that part of the reason for this was Veblen's tendency in later years to write on nonpsychological aspects of economics. Also, a larger part of his writing after 1914 tended to be of a polemical or propagandistic nature in which the subtleties of recent psychological theory would have been submerged anyway.

Conclusion

Gruchy commented that while Veblen's writings "do not lack unity, unity is never displayed within the limits of one treatise" (p. 126). Unlike the first volume of Marx's *Capital*, or Smith's *The Wealth of Nations*, Veblen's socioeconomic theories cannot be adequately understood by reading *The Theory of the Leisure Class*. One important reason for this is that

> Veblen, Commons, Mitchell, and their followers have not matched their specialized research work with similar endeavors in the fields of classroom instruction and popular education. They have made few attempts to invade the fields of elementary instruction where they would have to compete with the writers of orthodox economics textbooks. Had they done otherwise, these heterodox economists would have felt the need to move from the realm of specialized research to that of general or synthetical analysis. (P. 613)

Gruchy focused on the lost pedagogical opportunities that to this day impede understanding of the Veblenian creed and neo-Institutionalist doctrine. Most efforts in recent years to present evolutionary economics in textbook form have not been conspicuously successful and in the years 1891 to 1963, there were few efforts at all. Veblen thus failed to write at a level that was intelligible to the common man and never presented the bulk of his ideas in a single treatise, which, in Gruchy's view, explained the limited scope of his influence.

Gruchy's other criticisms of Veblen, include the claim made in several contexts that "Veblen was not himself especially interested in problems of economic policy" (p. 124). His skepticism and utopianism were in turn, no doubt, a source of his sardonic attacks on the virtues of the middle class of his time, which may also explain his failure to aid the middle-class reform movements that existed between 1890 and 1925. Basically, he remained detached from those economic and political struggles, the understanding of which was, nevertheless, one of his major intellectual achievements. In this vein, Gruchy also commented that "as in so many other instances, Veblen has introduced an important problem, but he has failed to examine it with any degree of thoroughness. When it comes to concrete suggestions for collective action, Veblen has nothing or, at the most, little to say" (p. 115). Gruchy believed that Veblen remained largely aloof from political involvement and social militancy both because of personal temperament and because he did not think the time ripe for change. Normally Veblen did not involve himself in partisan political movements, but functioned as a social change agent through both scholarly and polemical writing.

CLARENCE AYRES

Clarence Ayres's critique of Veblen, like Gruchy's, was an abbreviated one because he was more interested in using Veblenian doctrine as a component in the development of his own neoinstitutional economics than he was in criticizing Veblen. Indeed, he rarely wrote systematically about Veblen, since he focused on selective aspects of his work that possessed heuristic value or potential for theory construction. Rather than use Veblen as the focal point of a scholarly monograph, he preferred to use Veblen's ideas in eclectic fashion so long as they were congruent with Deweyan instrumentalism. One of the few instances when he wrote in detail about central Veblenian concepts was in his essay to commemorate Veblen's one-hundredth birthday. His main criticism was that Veblen had misunderstood and misused the term *instinct*. As he put it,

> It is now quite conclusively established that no such complex behavior patterns are in any literal sense "inborn." We now know that such patterns are wholly cultural. Hence the problem of their origin is indissociable from the problem of the origins of culture. We know also that Veblen was wrong in supposing . . . that workmanship prevailed from the beginning, so to speak, and that sportsmanship, or ceremonialism, developed only when a supposedly idyllic "savage" state was supplanted by "barbarism." Archeological evidence is conclusive that ceremonial burial, for example, goes as far back as any human remains.[4]

In *The Theory of Business Enterprise*, Veblen argued that interaction with the machine process fostered a matter-of-fact state of mind in the industrial worker that stripped him of respect for convention, authority, status, property rights, and perhaps religion. But as Ayres put it, "Throughout Veblen's work there runs an implication that the common man is somewhat less addicted to ceremonial behavior than his masters, dynastic and capitalistic—an implication which contemporary social scientists would judge to be contrary to fact."[5] Ayres's political liberalism was thus linked with his conviction that the minds of American industrial workers are just as encrusted with ceremonialism as other social strata. Perhaps, for this reason, he had less confidence in the social change potential of the working class than did social critics to his left.

Ayres's correspondence with John Dewey indicated his skepticism toward other of the more dubious Veblenite gems. In Ayres's view, one problematic claim was the Veblenian assertion of the transference of habits of thought from one realm to another. In 1928 Ayres wrote to Dewey:

> Isn't the Veblenian notion another incarnation of the transfer of training? I wonder if a matter-of-fact habit of thought is really transferred from one set of activities to another. . . . An acquaintance of mine here is a really fine automobile mechanic. . . . He thinks nothing of regrinding cylinders to micrometric degrees of nicety. And he has another local distinction: he is a highly prized and much sought "water witch." That is, he has great powers of locating underground water—the site for a well—by the willow twig method of incantation. No transfer there. It does seem to be that the transfer of authority or prestige is much easier than an actual transfer of technical habits.[6]

Ayres's own corrective to Veblen's claims in *The Theory of Business Enterprise* was thus to assert that it was easier to transfer ceremonial ideas rooted in authority and prestige than to transplant technological habits of mind.

In another context, Ayres developed still further his critique of Veblen's social psychology based on the cultural incidence of the machine process:

> The machine is by its essential nature matter-of-fact; and consequently, Veblen argued, habituation to the use, operation, and maintenance of machines is bound to develop matter-of-factness that will extend to every aspect of human experience. He thought of this process as reaching its highest intensity in the experience of factory hands. In this he was misled, in part, perhaps, by the narrowness of his focus of the whole technological process upon the machine, and also in part by his personal sympathy for wage earners. It is very doubtful if factory hands are the most matter-of-fact members of the community. The cultural incidence of "the machine" is very much more subtle and pervasive than that.[7]

Whether or not the social psychological theory advanced by Veblen in *The Theory of Business Enterprise* was intended by him to be definitive or merely suggestive is unclear. But Ayres did not believe that the transference effects of working around machines were as enduring or as qualitatively distinct as he claimed.

More evidence of Ayres's ideological bent is found in his treatment of Veblen's claims regarding "industrial sabotage":

> We should first of all recall Thorstein Veblen's dictum that the gains of business enterprises are proportional, not to the magnitude of their creative achievements, but "to the magnitude of the disturbances they are able to

create." Applied to all business activities, this is of course a prodigious over-statement.[8]

To Ayres, Veblen's indictment of capitalism and the unearned gains of capitalists provided by disruption of the industrial apparatus was another example of where one keen insight was massively exaggerated to highlight the shortcomings of the entire system. Ayres looked with jaundiced eye on an analysis that called for a radical alteration of the price system, market mechanism, and system of property relations to reduce the amount of capitalistic sabotage.

He also wrote much like other conventional liberal critics regarding Veblen's use of the data and literature of anthropology. As he put it,

> Indeed Veblen's (conjectural) derivation of status from the "war-like" and "predatory" bent of "the barbarian culture" suggest that he did not conceive it to have been a feature of the earlier and "peaceful" society of "the savage level of culture" and so did not regard it as universal. In this he was misled in part by mid-nineteenth-century anthropology (in which Rousseau's "noble savage" was still kept alive).[9]

Ayres, as a liberal critic of Veblen, found it necessary to evoke the "primitivist" image of a Veblen beset with visions of an idyllic, halcyon state of human innocence. But unlike more extreme critics, he did not suggest that Veblen wished literally to restore the "golden age" in an industrial setting.

Ayres believed correctly that there were similarities between Veblen's and John Hobson's views on underconsumption. But Veblen's failure to devise a strategy for ameliorating the problem of underconsumption through income redistribution gave Ayres an opportunity to make a broader criticism regarding his inability to move from theory to policy prescription.

> The "underconsumption fallacy" has never in the past appeared to flow directly from any systematic analysis of the industrial economy of which it was the inescapable conclusion—from any way of thinking of which income redistribution was the characteristic expression. . . . Even Veblen, whose thinking more than that of any other economist did afford a systematic theoretical foundation for such a strategy, failed to carry through at all from analysis to policy. It was his chief failure, and one that has not yet been rectified.[10]

Ayres's own policy solution was logically in keeping with his liberal amelioristic outlook, in that he advocated a moderate leveling out of the income stream of the community, not a radical change in the system of property relations. Consequently, Ayres endorsed what later came be known as the "negative income tax," not the abolition of large-scale absentee ownership as proposed by Veblen.

Finally, Ayres seems, at least in 1952, to have believed that there were racist tendencies in Veblen. In his scattered criticisms of Veblen he concluded that "worst of all, perhaps, was his tentative addiction to racism. He was somehow persuaded that 'the dolicho-blond race' was possessed of certain peculiar propensities which shaped its culture— an idea which present-day anthropologists most decisively reject."[11] Allegations of "racism" in contemporary usage indicate personal animosity toward representatives of other racial groups. There is no evidence of this in Veblen's work. Ayres should have used the term *racialism* to denote the biogenetic determinism that is most conspicuous in *The Theory of the Leisure Class*. The cultural and intellectual milieu of later nineteenth and early twentieth century Western society was greatly influenced by racialist arguments and theories whose roots were often traceable to pseudo-Darwinism. What Ayres was really suggesting was that Veblen came to intellectual maturity in this environment and only gradually worked his way out of it.

Conclusion

In summation of Ayres's brief against Veblen, it can be concluded that the potency of transference effects induced in the psyche by the machine process was exaggerated; his use of the concept of instinct was vague and misleading, and he failed to adequately link economic analysis with policy prescription. Veblen mistakenly thought in terms of "unilinear evolution" and imputed to the "savage stage" of human existence much of the rudimentary communism of Rousseau's "noble savage."[12] Finally, it was Ayres's opinion that a theory of value was never adequately developed by Veblen, so that it was imperative to move beyond his discussion of pecuniary and economic values by introducing Dewey's concept of value.[13]

Ayres's last extant letter to John Dewey, written in 1949, contains interesting commentary contrasting Veblen's pessimism in old age with Dewey's optimism. Dewey had just turned ninety when Ayres wrote to thank him for having sent a reprint of "Has Philosophy a Future?"

As I read "Has Philosophy a Future?" I couldn't help thinking of Veblen's paper on the future of economics, one of the last he did, though he had several years more (six, I think). How different yours is. I'm sure you won't think I am likely to underestimate Veblen's contribution if I say that in the end he seemed to give way to cynicism. Certainly there is nothing but cyni-

cism in that paper; whereas yours looks to the future as eagerly and hope-
fully as though you were twenty instead of ninety.[14]

Ayres was referring to Veblen's "Economics in the Calculable Future"
published in the *American Economic Review* in 1925, in which the
latter argued that economists would continue to be apologists for the
price system with all that implies in the Veblen lexicon of satire. However, Ayres failed to mention the fact that Veblen's last years were
largely spent in modest material circumstances and scholarly neglect,
while Dewey lived comfortably and enjoyed every honor that could be
bestowed on America's greatest living philosopher.

Chapter Eight

LIBERAL CRITICS:

HARVARD AND COLUMBIA STYLE

TALCOTT PARSONS, David Riesman, Daniel Bell, Pitirim Sorokin, Robert Merton, and Louis Schneider, six eminent Harvard- or Columbia-trained or -affiliated sociologists, all assessed Thorstein Veblen's contributions to social theory at some point in their careers. Parsons mostly wrote about him in the 1930s and 1940s; Riesman analyzed his life and thought in the 1950s as did Merton; Schneider wrote about him throughout his career; Bell focused on him briefly in the early 1960s; and Sorokin casually alludes to his work on many occasions. All except the conservative Sorokin were political liberals at the time they wrote and, ultimately, all except Merton and Schneider reacted negatively to his work. However, there are sufficient differences in both their approaches and their evaluations of him to warrant treating their critiques separately. Bell's and Riesman's attitudes toward Veblen appear to be ambivalent, although more negative than positive; Parsons's and Sorokin's views are almost wholly negative; while Merton and Schneider represent special cases. Each was an important theorist in his own right, thus giving their attacks on Veblen a significance they would not otherwise have. Parsons and Sorokin were on the Harvard faculty when they wrote on Veblen; Riesman was at Chicago; while Bell, Merton, and Schneider were at Columbia. Nevertheless, all six of these critics were sociologists and spent a substantial part of their academic careers either in Cambridge, Massachusetts, or Morningside Heights in New York City. For these reasons they are referred to as Veblen's "Harvard and Columbia Critics."

Assessing Veblen's treatment by these social scientists is important for several reasons. First, the sociologists considered are influential and have helped define the parameters and agenda of American sociology. Second, it is evident that mainline sociology under the influence of its dominant figures has often abandoned social criticism in favor of approaches that study existing structures, and in the process, justify them by showing that various institutional configurations perform necessary functions in some natural sense. Third, the field of sociology is briefly surveyed and conclusions reached respecting Veblen's position among mainline sociologists. The dominant mode of post–World War II sociology was such that the ideas of radical critics—Veblenian,

Marxist, Millsian, or otherwise—were ignored, rejected, or trivialized in order to justify more orthodox analyses of social structures. This critique provides an opportunity to show why this was so, for the conventional treatment of Veblen is indicative of the bias of mainline paradigms and theorists.

Before analyzing the work on Veblen by these prominent American liberal sociologists it is essential to explain why so many other sociologists simply ignore Veblen altogether. There are several reasons for this. First, it is not clear to many that Veblen was a sociologist as well as an economist, for he is commonly regarded as the latter. Second, since Veblen is widely known as a social critic and satirist whose work was heavily laden with value judgments, he is thought to have little to say to "empirical" social scientists. Third, in the post–World War II era, research grants have been primarily available to those doing empirical work who were able to convince grant-givers that their work was value-free, that is to say "scientific." Veblen, in spite of tongue-in-cheek posturing as an "objective" social scientist, provided little aid or comfort to those engaged in "value-free" or "scientific" approaches to the study of society.[1] Fourth, Veblen's iconoclasm was professionally unacceptable to many purveyors of the conventional wisdom who were looking to more orthodox analyses of existing social institutions. Iconoclasm is not "enlightening" when it threatens the basic social fabric and values that liberals hold dear.

Although interest in Veblen's work has varied from one period to another, his name is clearly not a household word among sociologists. Nevertheless, Veblen's contributions to sociology have not gone unnoticed in certain quarters. Specialists in social deviancy and criminology, social theory, political sociology, social psychology, industrial sociology, social stratification, social anthropology, and the sociology of knowledge have all paid heed to his work, if only to mention it in passing. However, there is a strong tendency for many scholars to simply mention Veblen and one or two of his ideas without systematically incorporating the ideas into their analysis. Does this reflect a selective and politically judgmental reaction of American sociologists who find Veblen too radical to take seriously? Or does the answer lie elsewhere? An analyses of the work of six leading American sociologists on Veblen may provide answers to these questions.

DAVID RIESMAN AND THE
REDUCTIONIST INTERPRETATION OF VEBLEN

David Riesman (b. 1909) treated Veblen as an eccentric outsider, which is ironic in view of Riesman's own inability to gain acceptance

within the inner sanctum of the sociology profession. He is all the more
relevant here because he has published more about Veblen than other
sociologists. Riesman's well-known psychoanalytic study, *Thorstein
Veblen: A Critical Interpretation*, was accomplished, as the saying
goes, "without benefit of couch." His disclaimers to the contrary, Riesman did not heed his own words when he wrote:

> I do not feel that Veblen's intellectual achievement can be reduced to the
> tangle of motives that produced it. (And I must remind the reader that I can
> only surmise what these motives were; to be surer of my ground I would
> need to know much more than I do about Veblen, his parents, his many
> siblings, his whole development.) In what follows, therefore, I shall proceed
> without further speculation as to Veblen's personality. . . . There will be no
> absence of ambiguities, but they will be those of Veblen's published thought,
> not the ambivalences of his inner life.[2]

Unfortunately, much of Riesman's work on Veblen is rife with a reductionism that psychologizes or sociologizes the latter's ideas. Used
in this context, *reductionism* means a refusal to deal with the substantive content of a theory, explaining it rather in terms of its author's
family background, occupational environment, and ethnic and religious affiliations. Riesman investigated Veblen's relationship with his
two wives; his role as a professional economist; and his interaction
with other faculty, students, and administrators. Much of Riesman's
speculation is intriguing, but by his own admission it is based on
scanty evidence that he often uses as a way of avoiding serious analysis
of the independent merit of Veblen's ideas. Indeed, what Riesman unwittingly demonstrates is his liberal political bias and his ambivalence
toward his own values.

At the beginning of his study of Veblen, Riesman justified what he
was about to do. He wrote:

> We are led to look to the idiosyncratic elements in him for what they will tell
> us about his ideas. Of course, it does not help determine the truth of a doc-
> trine to penetrate into its personal and psychological sources in its origina-
> tor. . . . However, such analysis can sometimes help us trace connections in
> a man's thought that might otherwise escape us.[3]

In the first of many examples that could be given, Riesman argued that
the influences on Veblen's thinking were conditioned by the fact that

> Veblen, having early handed in his resignation to life and being in many
> ways a very dependent person, seems to have felt that the "struggling ambi-
> tious human spirit" could neither found a scientific system nor change the
> world, even though, as in many fatalistic schemes, this discovery heartened

him to espouse, with a very personal style, the claims of impersonality and, with a very unexpedient life, the mandates of expedient adaptation and determinism.[4]

This allowed Riesman to avoid direct confrontation with Veblen's tongue-in-cheek allegations that he was engaged in "scientific," that is, value-free analysis of the work of other scholars and the existing social order. Veblen's posturing in this respect is certainly open to question, but what is gained by explaining away his position with reference to his personality traits?

Veblen's study of *Imperial Germany and the Industrial Revolution* has been widely praised by scholars in several disciplines, both for its explanatory power and its prophetic qualities. It has also been criticized by German historians. But, instead of dealing with Veblen's substantive arguments Riesman argued that "Veblen's ill-disguised and quasi-racial dislike of the Germans may have less intellectual roots than here suggested: it may go back to hostility between German and Norwegian Lutheran groups in Minnesota and Wisconsin."[5] In this book Veblen made major contributions to development theory by advancing his theory of cultural lag, pointing to the advantages of industrial backwardness and the "penalty of taking the lead," and prophesying the resurgence of right-wing authoritarianism. Instead of dealing squarely with the main elements of Veblen's analysis, Riesman again engaged in reductionism—this time we were told that what "really explains" Veblen's work is the ethnic conflict that existed in the community where he was reared!

Veblen's egalitarian sympathies are evident in his attacks on the vested interests who function at the expense of the common man. Riesman refused to articulate his own position on the issue of equality in contemporary America and then "explained" Veblen's egalitarianism by asserting that "Veblen was so frightened of one human being taking precedence over another that at times he seemed willing to repress all equally."[6] Veblen's alleged psychological traits were now substituted for serious analysis of the exploitative mechanism upon which he claimed capitalism rested.

Resorting to Veblen's relationship with his parents in yet another example of his psychoanalytic treatment, Riesman wrote:

> The mother was a softer person, whimsical and imaginative; she enjoyed folktales and the Bible. . . . Much of Veblen's work may be read as an internalized colloquy between his parents; between one who calls for a hard, matter-of-fact, "Darwinian," appraisal of all phenomena and one who espouses the womanly qualities of peaceableness, uncompetitiveness, regard for the weak. I am inclined to think that Veblen is at his best when he takes the side of the one who is maternal, and is destructive when he tries to be

"hard." Like many bright boys, he seems to have been impressed by the male who had the power and authority in his home to give commands, while at the same time developing unexpressed resentments against power and command of any sort. When, late in life, he saw in the hard-boiled, mechanically-adept engineers an elite who would take over the country and run it as a no-nonsense industrial republic, one may sense the return of his father in a Technocrat's uniform.[7]

Riesman accounted for Veblen's alleged technocratic elitism by pointing to his father, who was a "hard" man. He also explained Veblen's "destructive" (read "radical") polemics in the same manner. If only Veblen had been more influenced by his "soft" (read "liberal") mother!

Much of Riesman's analysis of Veblen revealed more about academic liberalism in the 1950s than it did about Veblen. Indeed, politically it is an ideological form in which a facade of objectivity and detachment is employed that avoids any substantive criticism of the American social system and political economy. Riesman, however, perceptively acknowledged that "it is a measure of Veblen's strength as a social critic that no rounded judgment of his work can be made that is not also a judgment of American society, now as well as then."[8] Why, then, did Riesman not integrate this idea more effectively into his study of Veblen? The gist of his disagreement with Veblen can be summarized by saying that Riesman approved of American institutions and deemed them fundamentally sound and wholesome, although slightly in need of repair, while Veblen, in contrast, thought these same institutions in his own day to be "imbecile." There is much ambiguity and ambivalence in Riesman's own social thought, much more, in fact, than in Veblen. Indeed, it is Riesman's vacillation that vitiates his critique of Veblen and precludes any structural criticisms of American society. Is Riesman the 1950s prototype of the social scientist that C. Wright Mills criticized for engaging in the institutionalization of equivocation?

Riesman explained some of Veblen's more vitriolic attacks on the rich by his jealousy of their success, ambition, and social station. That is to say, Veblen's satirical treatment of the leisure class was made to appear to be the result of his first-generation "Norskie" Midwestern-farmer background. But how would Riesman have explained the psychological roots of other Veblenian concepts such as the "penalty for taking the lead?" Here he saw no need to "equalize" owing to a fear of failure of lack of "commitment." Also, could not Veblen's indictment and analysis of the university have been shared by a professor who was tenured, published, well-paid, and highly regarded by students, colleagues, and administrators? Perhaps Veblen was not alone in his feelings toward the "higher learning?"

Like Daniel Bell and other postwar critics of Veblen, Riesman was eager to label much of Veblen's work "utopian." He felt, for example, that Veblen's works on economic planning had "something about them anticipatory of Brave New World."[9] Also, "Veblen could have lived . . . in a brave new world where all consumption would be guided by Consumer's Research, all production by Technocrats, and living itself by a kind of Fordism, a code of simple and invariant rigor."[10] Riesman also commented:

> For in spite of his disclaimers and in spite of his skepticism, Veblen does ally himself . . . with the progress-minded thinking of the 19th century rationalist. He envisages a society cleansed by the machine and its presumptive accompanying case of thought of all ritual, reliquary, and rite. The problem of how such a society, if conceivable at all, would hold together never seems to bother him.[11]

Curiously, Riesman cast himself in the role of defender of the status quo, including institutional religion, absentee ownership, and status emulation.

The implication of psychobiographies such as Riesman's are all to obvious and even dangerous; if and when a dissident voice is heard, a respected and responsible member of the profession will come forth to draw connections between the dissident's ideas and his or her personality. The "analysis" might not only result in a diminution of the dissident's reputation, but might also render their ideas impotent, crushed by the sheer weight of conventional thought. Better, perhaps, that in some hypothetical context, books, articles, programs, and suggestions be unsigned, so that all forebear the temptation to discredit through reductionism, and instead, be forced to meet the arguments therein on their own merits. Riesman's study of Veblen failed to advance the cause of the sociology of knowledge and simultaneously performed a disservice by portraying Veblen as a hopeless eccentric. In this skirmish, the dissident's attack was beaten back by subtle yet emotional appeals to conventionality and respectability. Not surprisingly, the dominant political ideology was once again confirmed as legitimate and sensible.

TALCOTT PARSONS'S CRITIQUE OF VEBLEN AND INSTITUTIONAL ECONOMICS

Talcott Parsons (1902–1979) was introduced to Thorstein Veblen's writings and doctrines by Clarence Ayres and Walton Hamilton, two eminent institutional economists, while an undergraduate at Amherst.[12] Although Parsons's writings on Veblen are not extensive, it is evident that Parsons was familiar with Veblen's work and with some of the subsequent literature in American economics produced by the institutionalist movement.[13]

Several penetrating studies of the ideological structure and political aims of Parsonian sociology now exist. Two of these studies explicate the latent and manifest ideological functions of Parsons's work and are revealing in the sense that his analysis of Veblen can now be seen as a logical outgrowth of his systematic social theory.[14] Indeed, given the parameters of Parsons's theory of social action and the constraints imposed by his political objectives, the basic outline of his attack on Veblen could have been anticipated before it was written.

What were the imperatives imposed by his theoretical structures and political aims? As William Buxton pointed out, Parsons had a particular view of the mission of the intellectual in advanced capitalist countries, for the role of the intellectuals was an active one and "by contributing to the cultural matrix, they could help ensure the regulation of action, the continuation of the social system, and the generation of overall stability."[15] Buxton also argued that Parsons "was not only acutely aware of the problems of social control faced by capitalist nation-states, but regarded the professionalized social sciences as important contributors to the process of 'rationalization.'"[16] The ideological nature of Parsons' political and social commentary thus cannot be disaggregated from his more abstract and formalized theoretical endeavors. Even more important, however, Parsons's use and abuse of the history of social thought, including Veblen, to achieve his own political and social goals cannot be overlooked.

The only significant usage of Veblen's ideas that can be found in Parsons's work—and the ideas were not acknowledged—was in an article he wrote in 1945 as a contribution to the Report of the Conference on Germany after the War. A group of psychiatrists, anthropologists, and sociologists, which included Parsons, met in New York City in the late spring of 1944, and he used this opportunity to speculate on the state of Germany after the war and the nature of any reconstruction program likely to be successful. Without citing or even mentioning Veblen, Parsons employed his analysis in *Imperial Germany and the Industrial Revolution* (1915).[17] Finding Veblen's definition of a "vested interest" useful, he modified it slightly and, like Veblen thirty years before, he called for the dispossession of particular vested interests, such as the Junker class, and the confiscation of their estates. This display of social radicalism, unusual for Parsons, clearly had its roots in Veblen's analysis and prescription of methods for eradication of Prussian militarism after the Great War. It is important to recognize, however, that Parsons did not acknowledge Veblen's influence and did not use any of his ideas this directly again. Clearly, Veblen had little lasting impact on him of a positive nature, although much of Parsons's theoretical and professional orientation was shaped by the debate between the institutionalists, such as Veblen, and the neoclassical economists.[18] In any case, the atmosphere at Harvard during much of Parsons's long tenure was not particularly conducive to heterodox social science, although figures there such as John Kenneth Galbraith and Arthur Davis took more than a passing interest in Veblen's life and work.

An eminent sociologist with a negative view of Veblen's achievements who was a Harvard contemporary of Parsons was the conservative P. A. Sorokin (1889–1968). In the mid-1930s Professor Underhill Moore of Yale University attempted to raise money for a portrait of Veblen and asked Sorokin for a contribution. Sorokin wrote in response to Moore, "I am sorry not to be able to contribute to the portrait of Thorstein Veblen. There are so many claims on me here that I cannot go far afield in making gifts; and, candidly, I do not think of Thorstein Veblen as a great scholar. I trust you will pardon my frankness."[19] Sorokin's opposition to Veblen was based on his own rejection of monocausal and dichotomic theories. As a result, it was not simply Veblen whose monocausal and dichotomous theorizing he attacked, but other social scientists such as Marx who used similar approaches.[20] However, Sorokin wrote little regarding Veblen and does not appear to have been particularly interested in his work.

Parsons's Attack on Veblen

One explanation for the neglect by Americans of native "founders" of social science like Veblen has been the profound influence of European social science. Parsons's claim that Max Weber said everything Veblen said, and said it better, is symptomatic of that influence.[21] His preference for European social theory is also evident in his attacks on other influential American theorists.

Parsons attempted to undermine radical critiques of the American national power structure by labeling the normative aspects of them as "utopian." This was evident in his analysis of both C. Wright Mills and Veblen, whom he lumped together as having basically similar but fallacious views of the existing power structure.[22] Unfortunately, Parsons confused two theories that are substantially different by failing to distinguish Mills's power elite theory from Veblen's ruling class hypothesis. More important, however, he charged the two men with having unrealistic views of possible alternatives to the existing system of power, and further, with a highly selective treatment of the whole complex power problem.

Both were alleged to be guilty of exaggerating the importance of power by holding that it was only power that "really" determines what happens in a society. Parsons also maintained that Mills and Veblen were inclined to think of power as "presumptively illegitimate; if people exercise considerable power, it must be because they have somehow usurped it where they had no right and they intended to use it to the detriment of others."[23] Summarizing the case against Mills and Veblen, Parsons wrote,

> This is a philosophical and ethical background which is common both to utopian liberalism and socialism in our society and to a good deal of "capital-ist" ideology. They have in common an underlying "individualism" of a cer-tain type. . . . Both individual and collective rights are alleged to be promoted only by minimizing the positive organization of social groups. Social organi-zation as such is presumptively bad because, on a limited, short-run basis, it always and necessarily limits the freedom of the individual to do exactly what he may happen to want. The question of the deeper and longer-run dependence of the goals and capacities of individuals themselves on social organization is simply shoved into the background. From this point of view, both power in the individual enterprise and power in the largest society are presumptively evil in themselves, because they represent the primary visible focus of the capacity of somebody to see to it that somebody else acts or does not act in certain ways, whether at the moment he wants to or not.[24]

Parsons thus claimed that Mills and Veblen so distrust social organiza-tion of any sort that they can be lumped together with most of the other extremist critics, right and left, who want to minimize social organiza-tion so that individualism can flourish.

According to the Parsonian interpretation of the radical critique, all existing social restraints vanish in the "utopia" so that anarchy pre-vails. Parsons espoused an antiradical political viewpoint, and refused in his own work to allow any serious normative consideration to forms of social organization that differed significantly from those already ex-isting in the United States. The social property and egalitarian power system that Veblen and Mills saw as alternatives to the dominant form of corporate ownership and control could, therefore, be labeled "uto-pian" by Parsons.

Parsons saw little of value in any of Veblen's major contributions to modern social theory. For example, he disagreed with the emphasis Veblen allegedly placed on the role of technology in bringing about social change. As he put it,

> Some schools of thought, as of Veblen and Ogburn, give the former (technol-ogy) unquestioned primacy. This is at least open to serious question since it is only in relatively highly developed stages of the patterning of functionally

specialized roles that the most favorable situation for the functioning of scientific investigation and technological application is attained.[25]

Parsons suggested, rather, that the mobility of resources made possible
through property and market relations, and the institutions of personal
freedom all greatly facilitate the influence of technology. In Parsons's
principled pluralist explanation of social change, greater emphasis
was placed on the role and value of the institutions of early capitalism
and Veblen was faulted for exaggerating the role of science and technology.[26]

Parsons was also highly critical of institutional economics, and, implicitly, Veblen, for repudiating the conceptual apparatus of orthodox
economic theory without recognizing the possibilities of using its analytic tools even in a different economic system.[27] The denial of the legitimacy of analytical abstraction in economics was a serious error according to Parsons. And in a broader sense, the institutional movement
was abortive and spread disillusionment because it "undoubtedly exaggerated the distance between the two disciplines. The combination (to
us) of not very good sociology and a negative attitude toward economic
and almost any other theory made this movement a poor entering
wedge for exploring interdisciplinary relations on a theoretical level."[28]

Parsons found Veblen's distinction between business and industrial
pursuits, what is today known as the "ceremonial-technological dichotomy," to be greatly exaggerated and destructive of the positive role of
the business community.[29]

> Symptoms of disturbance appeared, e.g., the "technological" view of the de-
> structive consequences of business . . . machinations as interfering with "ef-
> ficiency," utopian exaggerations of the results to be obtained from abandon-
> ing "business" altogether and becoming purely "technological."[30]

Parsons argued that Veblen's application of the ceremonial aspect of
the dichotomy to consumer behavior seriously distorted the significance of that behavior. He charged Veblen with believing that consumption under capitalism serves primarily a status function, and, is,
therefore, a form of status emulation. Parsons wrote that

> the very ready tendency to derogate such symbolism often takes the form
> immortalized by Veblen in the phrase "conspicuous consumption," with the
> allegation that people lived in comfortable and tasteful houses, or wore at-
> tractive clothes, in order, for instrumental motives, to enhance their pres-
> tige. This was then held to be a dishonorable motive with no "intrinsic" con-
> nection with the "real" functions of the unit.[31]

Parsons continued to the effect that "the aspect of the problem which needs to be noted here is that it arises wherever generalized media of interchange are involved in human action."[32] Parsons held that status emulation would occur wherever there is economic inequality and where money is used as a medium of exchange.[33] Parsons failed to note that status emulation is more intense in some societies than in others, and that advanced capitalism is more effective, in part owing to mass advertising, than other kinds of societies in inducing such behavior. He thus assumed that status emulation on a massive scale is an inevitable feature of all industrial societies, about which little can be done.

Parsons believed that Veblen, in *The Theory of the Leisure Class*:

> called attention to some of the relevant features of the role of women but did not relate it in this way to the functional equilibrium of the social structure. Moreover, what Veblen means by "conspicuous consumption" is only one aspect of the feminine role and one which is associated more with certain elements of malintegration than with the basic structure itself.[34]

Women's ostentatious display of goods, through which their men obtain vicarious status gratification, is not interpreted by Parsons as it was portrayed by Veblen, as "normal" behavior on the part of the leisure class and those who would emulate it. Instead, it is seen as evidence of "malintegration" with the basic social structure. Presumably, when women are more adequately integrated into the social structure, such behavior will significantly diminish in intensity. Other than mere assertion, Parsons provided no evidence that this has occurred since Veblen's day, nor was there recognition in his analysis of the waste and predation such behavior signifies. Parsons also wrote that

> high progressive taxation, both of incomes and of estates, and changes in the structure of the economy have "lopped off" the previous top stratum, where the symbols of conspicuous consumption were, in an earlier generation most lavishly displayed. A notable symbol of this is the recent fate of the Long Island estate of the J. P. Morgan family, which had to be sold at auction in default of payment of taxes. One wonders what Veblen would say were he writing today instead of at the height of the "gilded age."[35]

In keeping with the postwar tenor of American liberalism, Parsons argued that progressive taxation had significantly reduced conspicuous consumption by limiting the financial resources available for ostentatious display. Apparently, he believed this made Veblen's theory of status emulation obsolete.

Parsons indiscriminately lumped together different forms of emulatory behavior, thereby making them appear to be "normal" and generalized features of all societies. He did not adequately consider the waste and deprivation created by some forms of status emulation. Indeed, his systemic explanation of its functioning came perilously close to a justi-fication or defense of it, although its most objectionable features were probably viewed by Parsons as having been modified by the tax welfare and regulatory system created by the New Deal.

Parsons would, no doubt, have replied that there exists no scientific or agreed-upon standard that would allow social scientists to condemn those practices Veblen described. The upshot of all this is that sociol-ogy of the Parsonian variety can brook no criticism of social action; what is, and what happens, exist and occur in some natural sense. Criticizing conspicuous consumption is as scientifically pointless as denouncing shifts of rock strata or the movements of planets.

Parsons was highly critical of Veblen's theory of instincts and habits. Yet nowhere did he attempt to go beyond the mere expression of these terms to draw out any further significance they might have. Veblen had cautioned against possible misinterpretation of his use of *instinct* and *habit*, and several observers since have pointed out that these terms are best understood in some other sense than the terms imply. Janice Harris, for example, claimed that "Veblen's position on 'in-stincts' and 'habits' comes far closer to what Erich Fromm calls 'nor-mative humanism' postulating a plausible relationship between basic drives and cultural determination, than to the tenets of biologistic de-terminism."[36] The best that Parsons could do was to label Veblen's sys-tem as quite "simple." Considered in the light of Parsons's own com-plex social theory, that may be true, but, nonetheless, to Veblen's credit.

Interestingly, Parsons recommended a fusion of aspects of neoclas-sical economics with the social theories of several of his favorite Euro-pean thinkers.

> The older institutionalism has been essentially positivistic empiricism, un-fortunate in its rejection of the solid achievements of the older economic theory and at best very one-sided in the factors put in its place. There is a great opportunity for a "new institutionalism" based on an enlightened and mutually respectful cooperation between the best and methodologically most sophisticated, of the orthodox economic theory, and the newer socio-logical theory of such men as Pareto, Durkheim, and Max Weber and their successors. In the understanding of concrete economic activities neither can get on without the other.[37]

Parsons simply dismissed Veblen and American institutionalism as ir-relevant to the development of a new and more adequate Institutional Economics. Few traces of Veblen were to permanently color his think-ing and no residues of institutional economics were visibly embedded in his social theory.

ROBERT MERTON'S ATYPICAL ANALYSIS OF VEBLEN

A sociologically utilitarian employment of Veblen was that of Robert Merton (b. 1910). Trained at Harvard by Talcott Parsons, he became a leading proponent of structural-functional theory, and served for many years as chairman of the Department of Sociology at Columbia. Merton was also an advocate of "presentism," a view in which social-scientific writings of the past are seen in terms of contemporary sociological pre-occupations and concerns. The development of social-scientific ideas was thus thought to proceed incrementally, with the current state of knowledge representing the culmination of this process.[38] According to Merton, the "systematics" of sociology, in the form of the empirically validated residues of earlier theories, ought to be distinguished from the "history" of the field, as embodied in "the false starts, the now archaic doctrines, and both the fruitless and fruitful errors of the past."[39] As William Buxton put it:

> Merton views the history of sociology from the standpoint of the current state of knowledge, with the thoughts and ideas of the past validated against the standards of the present. Merton selectively reads the history of sociology in terms of those theoretical notions that have empirical relevance to contemporary sociological concerns.[40]

Indeed, it is in this context that Merton's attitude toward Veblen and his use of his ideas must be understood, for it was through this particular employment of him that he stripped Veblen's theory of status emulation of part of its political and moral significance. It was in his separation of structure from function that he, perhaps unwittingly, became one of Veblen's critics.

Talcott Parsons deplored the unfortunate fact "that at present few economists and sociologists have even a modicum of interest or competence in each other's subject matter."[41] On the same page, reference is made to the "great synthetic minds" of such luminaries as Alfred Marshall and Vilfredo Pareto, but no mention is made of Karl Marx and Thorstein Veblen.[42] It is evident that while Parsons neglected, or paid only peripheral attention to, seminal thinkers such as Simmel, Mannheim, Marx, and Veblen, his contemporary and former student Robert Merton took a greater array of ideas from a broader variety of sources. Merton's skillful and judicious use of Veblenian concepts vividly demonstrates Veblen's potential for incorporation into a continually evolving and eclectic (in the nonpejorative sense) social theory.

Merton's use of Veblen is most evident in regard to the distinction between manifest and latent functions that Merton popularized in American sociology. Indeed, Merton argued that the Veblenian analysis has entered "so fully into popular thought, that these latent functions are now widely recognized." Merton's analysis in this respect bears further elaboration, for it led to perhaps the most astute employment of Veblenian concepts in the literature of mainline American sociology.

It is often remarked that "necessity is the mother of invention," but Merton approved of Veblen's inversion of this idea and its role in both manifest and latent conceptualizations of function. He wrote that "It is more often the case, as Veblen has remarked, that invention is the mother of necessity. The ulterior consequences of the more important mechanical inventions have been neither foreseen nor intended, though they have commonly demanded a whole series of institutional and technical adjustments."[43] Merton also suggested, in another context, that scientific data may have had only a latent function in ordinary, everyday activity, but a manifest function when part of scientific discourse. He credited Veblen with this insight: "Thorstein Veblen has put this with typical cogency: 'All this may seem like taking pains about trivialities. But the data with which any scientific inquiry has to do are trivialities in some other bearing than that one in which they are of account.'"[44] However, Merton's most important use of Veblenian ideas resided in his skillful explanation of status emulation from a functionalist perspective. In Merton's words:

> However, says Veblen in effect, as sociologists we must go on to consider the latent functions of acquisition, accumulation and consumption, and these latent functions are remote indeed from its naive meaning (i.e., manifest function) that the consumption of goods can be said to afford the incentive from which accumulation invariably proceeds. And among these latent functions, which help explain the persistence and the social location of the pattern of conspicuous consumption, is its symbolization of "pecuniary strength and so of gaining or retaining a good name." The exercise of "punctilious discrimination" in the excellence of "food, drink, shelter, service, ornaments, appeal, amusements" results not merely in direct gratifications derived from the consumption of "superior" to "inferior" articles, but also, and Veblen argues, more importantly, it results in a *heightening or reaffirmation of social status*.
>
> The Veblenian paradox is that people buy expensive goods not so much because they are superior but because they are expensive. For it is the latent equation ("costliness – mark of higher social status") which he singles out in his functional analysis, rather than the manifest equation ("costliness –excellence of the goods").[45]

Bearing in mind Parsons's rejection of Veblen's theory of conspicuous consumption, the startling difference between Parsons's treatment of Veblen and Merton's handling of him is apparent. Even if, for the sake of argument, one were to agree with Parsons that Veblen's works were shot through with utopianism, could he not have taken a concept such as conspicuous consumption, and found in it heuristic value or theoretical illumination? Parsons had dismissed Veblen too quickly, and that amounted to a loss for sociology.

Notice, on the other hand, Merton's careful analysis of Veblen's famous concept. Rather than reject it out of hand, Merton removed it from its "utopian" environment and put it to work. He refined the notion, gave it greater precision, and applied it to a number of situations—with the felicitous outcome that social theory has been enriched.[46]

However, by treating Veblen as a functionalist, Merton allowed himself to ignore the political significance of his work. Thus Veblen's radical critique of capitalism was simply absorbed into mainline sociology. Merton's emphasis on function rather than structure became a device for stripping Veblen of radical import and ultimately rendering his work conservative. While a sympathetic interpreter of Veblen such as Merton may praise his originality and utilize his insights, Merton nonetheless deradicalized Veblen's most important ideas and, perhaps inadvertently, became his critic.[47]

Louis Schneider and the Freudianization of Veblen

One of the most significant comparisons of Veblen's thought with that of a European contemporary was *The Freudian Psychology and Veblen's Social Theory*, published in 1948 by the American sociologist Louis Schneider (1915–1979). Schneider, who had been a student of Merton at Columbia, was then an assistant professor at Colgate and was later to spend many years at Purdue, Illinois and the University of Texas, Austin.[48] Schneider found in Veblen's work much of value that he put to use in his own theorizing. To illustrate, he was impressed with Veblen's theory of cultural lag as it applied to Imperial Germany, particularly the advantages of selective technological borrowing minus institutional encumbrances.[49] He also praised Veblen's employment of irony, paradox, satire, and contradiction. In Schneider's view, Veblen's ideas about conspicuous consumption had more than a mere intellectual impact on his readers, for there was evidence that it pricked the conscience of status emulators and, perhaps, affected their behavior as consumers. Nevertheless, there was much in Veblen that Schneider could not accept. Indeed, Schneider commented with regard to *The Theory of the Leisure Class* that it

> is not characterized by much respect for evidence. Its anthropology is casual and somewhat vague and often gives the impression of being a homemade product designed to support Veblen's special crotchets. There is a bit of foolishness about "dolicho blonds." Veblen is not always very neat conceptually. The term "institutions" is herewith in this review set down in quotation marks for the second time, to stress Veblen's rather loose way with it. Really careful delineation of stratification schemes instead of Veblen's "poetic" approach to them would have been helpful.[50]

In keeping with the main focus of this book which is the history and analysis of the confrontation between Veblen and his critics, attention is now directed at the negative aspects of Schneider's appraisal of Veblen's social theory.

The Problem of Social Order

A fundamental line of criticism voiced by Schneider against Veblen focused on the problem of social order and the creation and maintenance of structures of organization. Schneider repeatedly claimed that there is a powerful strain of romantic and utopian anarchism in Veblen preventing him from adequately considering the need for organizing processes and stabilizing institutions that channel and direct behavior. In fact, Schneider focused on the ambiguity of Veblen's whole attitude toward institutions.

> It remains very unclear just how a society could exist without institutions and it is likewise unclear whether any institutional apparatus at all would be found in the savage state or whether a re-building in strict, exclusive accord with the instinct of workmanship would produce any recognizable institutional apparatus.[51]

Schneider believed that, except for biological evidence that Veblen failed to specify, there is little basis for believing in his first evolutionary stage of primitive savagery, which was characterized by an anarchic and egalitarian culture. Yet it is from this stage of social development that Veblen drew his conclusions regarding the disutility of authority structures and organizing principles. As Schneider put it in contrasting Veblen with Freud, "Veblen's anarchism is less final, in that the dissolution of institutions would make a more livable life, although, of course, such an outcome is purely fantastic."[52] Thus Veblen was repeatedly charged with ignoring the entire problem of social order, including the role of authority and structure both in industry and society at large. Schneider commented that

> the problem of organization in industry is left entirely to take care of it-
> self. . . . The instinct of workmanship and the parental bent, with the coop-
> erative disposition that the latter involves, could presumably organize the
> work of industrial research. . . . There is no reason to think industrious and
> cooperative workmen would be produced by the resiliency of ancient in-
> stincts if merely the "dead hand" of absentee ownership were removed. . . .
> Given his anarchism, Veblen could not plainly see the necessity of norms of
> some kind to hold any society together.[53]

Schneider stressed Veblen's opposition to all authority and structure
because as a liberal he could not foresee any alternative to existing
institutional patterns that did not involve large disparities of power and
status. In the process, he largely ignored the ceremonial-technological
dichotomy used by Veblen that evaluates the role of authority on the
basis of functional imperatives rather than ascriptive status. In Veblen's Darwinian view, inequalities of power are justifiable only if they
promote the instrumental adaptation of the community to the changing environment.

The Nature of Human Nature

The reader will recall that Veblen postulated the existence of two type-
forms, the peaceful and the predatory. The instincts of workmanship,
parenthood, and idle curiosity were dominant in the peaceful type
while the sporting and pecuniary instincts were characteristic of the
predatory type. It was Schneider's view, however, that in the Veblenian
scheme the peaceful traits were more primary and fundamental than
the predatory traits. As he put it:

> Insofar as Veblen argues for the higher biological authenticity of the first set
> of instincts—which may therefore be called the primary instincts—he intro-
> duces a romantic, "optimistic" strain into his theory. Instincts that are more
> deeply ingrained, of greater antiquity, more "indefeasible," should "in the
> long run" triumph over other instincts.[54]

Schneider thus believed that Veblen put too much into man's "original"
or "archaic" nature, which became the source of the anarchism that is
often observed in Veblen's writings. An anarchist society is, of course,
possible only if it can be shown that mankind is capable of internalizing
adequate norms that make external coercion unnecessary. Such
norms must therefore be an intrinsic part of the human psyche, which
is essentially what Schneider charged Veblen with teaching. Ultimately, he concluded that

it is a very common device for a critic of society to implement his criticism by describing human nature in such a way as to make it appear to give support to the ideals he holds. Then society can be made over to conform to the human nature posited, and the particular ideals will be realized. An element of this sort is undoubtedly present in Veblen's social theory, although it does not stand by itself. If the critic insists, as Veblen did, that a "scientific" description of human nature be *forced* to give support to his ideals, there is always a good chance that the view he gives of human nature will be subject to severe strictures.[55]

Schneider thus suggested that Veblen's view of human nature is a form of ideological ax grinding constructed so as to achieve in theoretical form his political and moral goals. However, the same charge may be leveled at Schneider, for the latter's criticisms of Veblen may also reflect his own political aspirations for American society. It is, no doubt, true that Veblen's "human nature" would make good raw material for either an anarchist society or an industrial republic. Yet since he accented the plasticity and malleability of human nature, the contamination of the peaceful instincts by the predatory instincts is also a distinct historical possibility. How else could his prediction of the rise of right-wing authoritarianism before the advent of Hitler and Tojo be explained? Schneider had conveniently chosen not to make a point of this, for it would have obviously weaken his argument by showing that there is *no* fundamental instinctual-normative layer in the human psyche that is more primary than any other in Veblen's analysis. The characteristic liberal ideological ploy that Schneider used was to make it appear as if all radical schemes for social reconstruction are based on unrealistic views of human nature rooted in some as yet untapped repository of altruistic virtue.

The Problem of Rationality in Veblen

Schneider interpreted Veblen as believing that men have "rationality" in the functional but not the substantive sense. By this he apparently meant that they are endowed with a sense of means-ends congruence, but not with ability to make calculated choices between alternative ends. The consequence of this, according to Schneider, is that Veblen, having deprived men of their substantial rationality, was driven "in the direction of his own brand of romantic optimism."[56] As Schneider put it:

> If a humanly "favorable" outcome is insisted upon in a theory, and the faculty of human reasoning and calculation cannot be relied on to produce such an outcome, and if, moreover, structural irrationalities or their equivalents

are postulated, there is little recourse except to a presumption that something in the "nature of man" constrains to the favorable outcome. Had Veblen been a perfectly consistent "Darwinian," and at times he almost was, he could have left out the romantic element in his thought, and society would have appeared as a utterly aimless, goalless process *a priori* as likely to have one upshot as another.[57]

Schneider, like many of Veblen's liberal critics, was eager to display his own "realism" and "antiutopianism," in short, his "pragmatism" while denying the existence of these traits in radicals. This "toughminded" intellectual posturing was a common trait of liberals in the late 1940s and 1950s because they were under pressure either externally imposed or internally generated to mark off their own ideological turf from radicals, including both Stalinists and democratic socialists. To illustrate the point, there is massive textual evidence in Veblen that what could lie ahead for mankind is not a resurgence of egalitarianism in a cooperative commonwealth, but a revision to rightist authoritarianism—what may loosely be labeled "fascism"—a predatory, dynastic state capable of using science and technology to achieve its own inhuman ends. Schneider downplayed the counterutopian aspects of Veblen's thought because, like several of Veblen's other liberal critics, he had his own political agenda to pursue and related ideological axes to grind, in which there was little room for interpretive balance.

Veblen's liberal and conservative critics, including Schneider, persistently sought a biological metaphysics, an embedded instinctual norm, and an underlying teleological premise that holds the Veblenian key to the riddle of social evolution. They found a normative substratum located in the psyche of Veblenian humans that they used to indict his alleged faith in the primitive goodness of early man and his Rousseauian optimism regarding the revival of the Golden Age. Underlying all Veblen's discussion of tropisms and instincts must be an undeclared conviction that "real" human nature is good and will ultimately reveal itself in an ungraded commonwealth of masterless men. More important, however, than the question of whether textual exegesis of his writings will support such claims is the political and ideological function of this interpretation.

The Problem of Rationality

Veblen advanced the claim in 1904 in *The Theory of Business Enterprise* that the machine process had a new and unique impact on the industrial work force. As Schneider put it:

The workman in contact with the forces given by the machine industry is trained to think in "matter-of-fact" terms, in "cause and effect" terms, and there is a carry-over of "matter-of-fact" thinking from its origins in the machine discipline to other types of activities. This is rather definitely a psychological view of the effects of the machine process on the workman, and the outcome of the process is a rational, "scientific" workman. Veblen even presumes "transfer of training." It is hardly necessary to argue that there is little evidence for Veblen's view, taken at face value. (P. 121)

Schneider then added that "obviously the distinction of substantial rationality and functional rationalization" originally made by Karl Mannheim would weaken Veblen's argument considerably (p. 122). Veblen's liberal critic also believed that "'Matter-of-fact' has reference to a normative scheme that, Veblen considered, somehow took its rise in the machine discipline. The workman's rationality is not only sheer reasoning power, but reasoning power definitely oriented toward anti-leisure class and anti-business norms" (p. 122). Schneider thus focused on both the ambiguity and the inadequacy of Veblen's claims about the impact of technology on human rationality. Mannheim's distinction between functional and substantial rationality did bring into question Veblen's argument since it focused on the issue of whether any "transfer effect" occurs and, if so, in what ways. Was Veblen asserting that industrial workers develop understanding of means—ends congruence (functional rationality), or was he claiming a greater ability to understand complex sets of alternative ends (substantial rationality), or both? Schneider believed that he made both claims, but that there is little empirical evidence to show that the machine process produces such transfer effects in the human psyche. Contrary to Veblen, Schneider thought that the impact of technology is confined to the industrial setting and that the only rationality it inculcates in the labor force is narrowly functional, if that (p. 122). *The Theory of Business Enterprise* certainly lent itself to the view that the machine process induces both functional and substantive rationality, but Veblen's liberal critics dissent from this claim.

Value as Technological Efficiency

In a criticism of Veblen and Clarence Ayres, Schneider commented that

technological efficiency is a very limited goal, one, moreover, that cannot even answer the question of *what* specifically shall be produced. Yet Veblen never gave this serious consideration, and a position substantially similar to his is also taken by a contemporary Veblenian. Clarence E. Ayres, after an eloquent criticism of price theory, comes out on the question of value precisely where Veblen did: productivity is somehow good in its own right. Ayres . . . distinguishes technology from ceremony and status, and definitely holds that what is not technological must impede technology. Technology is the "locus of value." Even if it is granted that "price" is merely "price" and a very dubious measure of "value," a norm of productivity is obviously still only one, requiring supplementation by, and integration with, others, if a community and a functioning economic system are to exist. (Pp. 128–29)

Schneider failed to recognize that when Ayres (and Veblen) suggested that technology is the "locus of value," they were not simply referring to the physical capacity of machines to produce, as though this by itself is the full measure of value. Rather they were including continuity of life, creation of noninvidious community, flourishing of scientific curiosity, growth of other-regardingness, and excellence of craftsmanship as both cause and consequence of efficient utilization of technology. In their view neither machine efficiency nor price were adequate measures of value.

Schneider criticized Veblen for attempting to settle aesthetic and moral issues from a purely "economic" point of view. He charged Veblen with ignoring the functional role of religion, for example, by focusing on its waste of resources through unwarranted consumption of goods and labor, thus causing a lowering of the physical well-being of the community.[58] Schneider could not accept Veblen's radical indictment of institutional religion on account of its waste, yet that was only part of his assault on it. Clearly, Veblen also believed that the doctrinal claims of the Church were false and the Church itself a source of superstition that bred a kind of false consciousness in the community.

However, Schneider was also critical of Veblen's claims about waste in other contexts than religion. He believed that Veblen offered no adequate explanation of his claim that in the modern industrial economy "the margin of admissible waste probably always exceeds 50 percent of the output of goods."[59] Admittedly, Veblen was extravagant in his claims about the amount of economic waste, but, in a broader sense, he defined waste as the result of both unused industrial capacity and emulatory consumption. Schneider complained, however, that "to argue that what is waste" in the economic respect "is not necessarily" waste "in other respects does not clarify the general concept of waste."[60] He summed up Veblen's prejudices, including his hatred of waste, in this manner:

Veblen "didn't like," so to put it, business enterprise, the price system, ceremonialization of status, status itself, luxuries, the national establishment, or religion; he "liked" very little besides technology or technological efficiency;

most of the rest was likely to be of the nature of "waste." As Freud never adequately explained the cohesion or existence of any society, so Veblen failed to explain how a society could maintain itself or continue to exist on the basis of a mere avoidance of "waste."[61]

Because Schneider failed to understand Veblen's approach to value, he could not accurately link his values with the problems of waste and waste avoidance. Clearly, economic activities of an invidious nature were, in Veblen's eyes, wasteful. More significant, however, was Veblen's view of waste as detracting from the achievement of the generic ends of life, impersonally considered. According to Veblen, these ends were idle curiosity, other-regardingness and competency of workmanship. Waste, then, is behavior that unnecessarily impedes or constrains the development of these traits. Schneider saw only the negative or waste-avoidance aspect of Veblen's analysis because he never understood the positive aims that the latter thought the community should pursue with its economic resources.

Schneider's purpose in examining Veblen was to show how a kind of theorizing shared by Veblen and Freud was grounded in a preference for a society free of all social restraints, that is, devoid of socialization and social structure, in particular.[62] Thus, Veblen's views on the "repression" of a modern industrial society, like Freud's, contrasted as they were in both instances with the presumed "healthier" kind of person that might be produced in a "nonrepressive" order, were found wanting because, in effect, this sort of "health" is impossible. Once again, a liberal critic had tried Veblen for being a utopian visionary and found him guilty.[63]

BELL'S ATTACK ON VEBLEN AND RADICAL UTOPIANISM

The most contemporary of Harvard's Veblen critics is Daniel Bell (b. 1919).[64] In order to understand the nature of Bell's attack on Veblen, it is necessary to recognize Bell's own drift away from radicalism toward neoconservatism and his critique of "totalizing" ideologies and large-scale programs for social and economic reconstruction.

Bell came to political awareness during the depression and joined the Young People's Socialist League in 1932, at the precocious age of thirteen. In the late 1930s, while a student at C.C.N.Y., he thought of himself and was perceived by others as a democratic socialist, not a Trotskyite or Stalinist. But ultimately it is neither the "radical" period before Bell wrote on Veblen or the period after he wrote on him that is of concern. Rather, it is the immediate aftermath of the publication of

The End of Ideology (1961), and the ensuing years of the Kennedy administration that provide the intellectual milieu and political backdrop for Bell's critique of Veblen. Indeed, his analysis is an ideological barometer of related ideas and events that transpired in the era of the New Frontier and is best understood in that context. By way of explanation of Bell's attitudes, he once wrote:

> During its crusading Bolshevik phase, Marxism became a total ideology, as I used the term: "a total ideology is an all-inclusive system of comprehensive reality, it is a set of beliefs, infused with passion, and seeks to transform the whole of a way of life." This commitment to ideology—the yearning for a "cause" or the satisfaction of deep moral feelings—is not necessarily the reflection of interests in the shape of ideas. Ideology . . . in the sense used here is a secular religion.[65]

Bell never charged Veblen with subscribing to a total ideology. Nevertheless, it is the more exuberant ideological and programmatic aspects of Veblen toward which he is antagonistic. For he objects to any intellectual perspective that utilizes a totalizing critique of society that calls for large-scale reorganization of the social structure and political economy. In *The End of Ideology* Bell wrote that

> Few serious minds believe any longer that one can set down "blueprints" and through "social engineering" bring about a new utopia of social harmony. . . . In the Western world, therefore, there is today a rough consensus among intellectuals on political issues: the acceptance of a welfare state; the desirability of decentralized power; a system of mixed economy and of political pluralism. In that sense, too, the ideological age has ended.[66]

However, Bell shrewdly qualified this statement by arguing that

> The end of ideology is not—should not be—the end of utopia as well. If any, one can begin anew the discussion of utopia only by being aware of the trap of ideology. The point is that ideologists are "terrible simplifiers." Ideology makes it unnecessary for people to confront individual issues on their individual merits. There is now, more than ever, some need for utopia, in the sense that men need—some vision of their potential, some manner of fusing passion with intelligence. Yet the ladder to the City of Heaven can no longer be a "faith ladder," but an empirical one: a utopia has to specify *where* one wants to go, *how* to get there, the costs of the enterprise, and some realization of and justification for the determination of *who* is to pay.[67]

These observations were intended as an indictment of both political extremists and particular kind or radical utopianizing. Bell himself had ceased to engage in utopianizing or advocacy of large-scale structural change of any kind. Indeed, while his ideological odyssey from the left to the center of the political spectrum was occurring, he engaged in free-lance journalism, editing for *Fortune Magazine*, and professoring in sociology at Columbia where he resided at the time he wrote on Veblen. It is also interesting to note that his colleague there was C. Wright Mills and that Bell's reaction to Mills's work converged markedly with his treatment of Veblen. This was predictable given the ideological similarities between the two and the degree of doctrinal consistency that characterized Bell's own work.

Although not as negative in his judgments of Veblen as either Riesman or Parsons, in the final analysis, Bell found it necessary to emphasize the essentially "utopian" nature of much of Veblen's thought. However, to obtain a balanced view of Bell's interpretation, it is necessary to mention briefly aspects of Veblen's work he praised or incorporated into his analysis of Western societies. Bell recognized the partial validity of Veblen's assertions about status emulation and its impact on consumption patterns, employed Veblen's ideas regarding the "penalty of taking the lead" as this pertains to the disadvantage of early industrialization, and acknowledged the value of Veblen's famous distinction between business and industrial processes. He also praised Veblen's arguments that what ultimately provides direction for the economy is not the price system, but the value system of the culture in which the economy is embedded.[68]

Of more interest, however, are Bell's efforts to pin the label of utopian on Veblen for his alleged lack of realism and Bell's further claim that the utopia Veblen espoused was a dangerous one, if taken seriously. In Bell's words:

> Central to all this—to return to our earlier theme of the new class—is the elitist image, which was given its most mechanical shape in the doctrines of technocracy. Most of Veblen's admirers have sought to discredit similarities, but the resemblance is clear, and while Veblen's doctrines cannot be held accountable for the later phase of technocracy—which flared again briefly in 1940 as a quasi-fascist movement, replete with gray uniforms and monad symbol—the "elective affinity" between Veblenianism and technocracy is evident not only in the formal content of the ideas but in the temperamental derivatives: the qualities of inhuman scientism and formal rationalism, which in the end become an attack upon culture itself.[69]

Veblen is thus accused of indulging himself in the "technocratic dream," for in Bell's eyes, he is clearly another technocratic elitist in the tradition of Henri Saint-Simon, Augustin Cournot, and Frederick Taylor. Furthermore, his reiterated emphasis on technology also reveals the one-sidedness, or inadequacy, of the Veblenian system. He was indifferent to the social relations within the factory—both the elements that created bureaucracy and those that, as in the case of the engineers, made for insistence on professional status as one means of overcoming the impersonality that the rationalization of work imposes on modern life.[70]

Yet Bell managed, unlike Talcott Parsons, to find positive elements in Veblen's system. While Bell paid little heed to the egalitarian aspects of Veblen's thought, he did not ignore the contributions made by Veblen to social theory. Ultimately, however, Bell's critique of Veblen has the effect of disarming Veblen's attack on capitalism by making the assault appear utopian. Of course, this is a standard device frequently employed by those close to the political center, whether liberal or conservative, for discrediting radicalism. It takes three forms. The first is to claim that the radical's criticism of capitalism are exaggerated or unwarranted. The second is to assert the alternative ways of organizing the social system and political economy endorsed by the radical are "unrealistic." And the third is to misconstrue the actual nature of the radical proposal for social reorganization. Bell managed to do all three. His analysis is unconvincing both because it distorts Veblen's proposal for economic reconstruction and because it treats him as a hopelessly utopian theorist.

Bell's portrayal of Veblen as a "technocratic elitist" was logically connected with his ideological stance toward Veblen's egalitarianism, for, in his eyes, Veblen has none of the flattening or leveling tendencies attributed to him by other writers. Bell paid little heed to Veblen's sympathy for the abolition of absentee ownership through a constitutional amendment. Also, the powerful egalitarian strain in his anthropology, as expressed in his admiration for primitive men in the stage of "savagery," made no impression on Bell; nor did Veblen's preference for an "ungraded commonwealth of masterless men."

Veblen believed that neoclassicists confused or conflated the fulcrum with the lever in analyzing the price system, which only served to mystify its actual role. But Bell, like other liberals, has little tolerance for fundamental criticisms of the price system, which is perhaps why he does not think that Veblen or institutionalists understand its essential nature. However, Veblen's real objection was not to price data but to the neoclassical view that price is an objective measure of value, which is itself a matter of subjective preference. Veblen believed, to the contrary, that there were generic ends of existence best served by continuity of life and the recreation of noninvidious community. He disagreed with the moral agnosticism of neoclassicism because to him value was not a privatized phenomena of a purely subjective sort; rather, its nature was impersonal and its impersonality made it subject to external standards of comparison, empirical scrutiny, and public observation. Bell misunderstood Veblen's fundamental criticism of the price system, which aims not at the disregard of price data but at the confusion of price itself with real value—value that serves the generic ends of life impersonally considered.

Veblen did not always cite sources or adequately acknowledge the contribution of earlier thinkers on the formation of his own thought. Nevertheless, it is inaccurate to claim as Bell did that he never cited sources or footnote references. To the contrary, *The Theory of Business Enterprise*, *The Instinct of Workmanship*, and *Absentee Ownership*, all have scholarly appendages. Many of Veblen's published articles also are replete with citations, although some were not written for scholarly journals and consequently lack the accoutrements Bell considers essential. Of his books, *The Theory of the Leisure Class* is perhaps the most conspicuous example of an American classic that largely lacks a scholarly apparatus; perhaps it is this work upon which Bell based his generalizations.

However, even more important than Bell's factual errors and lapses of scholarly judgment are his claims regarding Veblen's intellectual pedigree, for which he offers little supporting evidence. He believes that the main sources of Veblen's ideas as expressed in *The Theory of the Leisure Class* are Rousseau, St. Simon, Fourier, and Adam Smith. Certainly Veblen had read the major works of Rousseau and Smith. Perhaps he also possessed a passing familiarity with Fourier and St. Simon, but few Veblen scholars would claim the kind and the degree of influence over Veblen that Bell attributed to the latter two. Bell's ideological ax grinding is again apparent because in order for Veblen to be convincingly portrayed as a technocrat, technocracy must be located in his doctrinal background and few better examples can be found in the nineteenth century than the two Frenchmen. Bell's attribution of influences on Veblen are often greatly exaggerated or simply wrong, for Bell ignores the influence of Edward Bellamy, the I.W.W., and the evolutionary biology of Charles Darwin in favor of French sources that reinforce his technocratic elitist interpretation of Veblen.[71]

Examination of Bell's professional career and his published work leads to the conclusion that he has a particular political, occupational and ideological agenda to fulfill.[72] Bell's agenda aims at discrediting radical intellectuals by attacking their theoretical work and their political and social criticism. Closely related to this are his efforts to undermine all ideological systems that endorse large-scale social reconstruction or political transformation. One rhetorical device by which to accomplish this is to claim that in Weber's words, only an "ethic of responsibility" can serve as the basis of a defensible politics since an "ethics of conscience" leads to absolutist political philosophies and to political extremism. This intellectual and political strategy thus delegitimizes all parties, movements, and ideologies that are either very far left or right. This leaves intact only a politics that hovers around the center, which, of course, is ideologically fulfilling for Bell. Like the other liberal Harvard and Columbia sociologists, Riesman, Parsons, Merton, and Schneider, he stakes out his turf slightly left of the political center, which in turn flavors his efforts to repel all theoretical and doctrinal alternatives. Bell's writing on both Veblen and C. Wright Mills offers valuable documentary evidence on how the liberal mind reacted to an authentic American radicalism in the postwar period.

Chapter Nine

RADICAL CRITICS: THE FRANKFURT SCHOOL

MOST OF THE scholars attached to the Frankfurt Institute for Social Research found it necessary to leave Germany after the Nazi Revolution. Three of the most important of them emigrated to the United States and, subsequently, evinced some interest in Thorstein Veblen and institutional economics. They were Herbert Marcuse (1898–1979), Max Horkheimer (1895–1973), and, most important in terms of understanding Veblen scholarship, Theodor Adorno (1903–1969).

In recent years, the critical theory of the Frankfurt School has attracted wide notice in scholarly journals in the Anglo-Saxon world. In the 1960s, one member of the school, Herbert Marcuse, received much attention in the popular news media as one of the intellectual leaders of the New Left. It is thus surprising how little attention has been paid to the Frankfurt School's 1941 analysis of Thorstein Veblen.[1] Even though Veblen was perhaps America's leading radical thinker, and the proponents of critical theory in the Frankfurt School were among Europe's most prominent theorists, their analysis of his work has been largely ignored. In view of the importance of both critical theory and institutional economics in the United States, it would be useful to examine the treatment given by the Frankfurt School to Veblen's work.

Veblen's Darwinism versus Critical Theory's Dialectics

The Frankfurt School is generally of the opinion that Veblen's philosophical roots lie in American pragmatism. The major weaknesses of pragmatism, according to the Frankfurt School, are its heavy reliance upon natural science as a model for philosophical analysis and its rejection of Marxian dialectics in favor of Darwinian evolutionism or some other form of empiricism.[2] Hence, in his critique of Veblen's social theory, Adorno tended to treat Veblen as a pragmatist whose work suffered from many of the same deficiencies found in John Dewey, William James, and C. S. Peirce.

The pragmatist, in Adorno's view, is too often the captive of mere facts. In his refusal to employ dialectics as a tool of social analysis, the pragmatist ignores the possibility of understanding as potential for positive social change. To Adorno, pragmatism's "scientism" precludes uncovering the hidden or partially manifest patterns of human behavior that dialectics might illuminate. Moreover, pragmatism is always "conscious of the perennial limits put upon men's attempts to go beyond the existent limits set to both thought and action."[3] The methodological conservatism of pragmatism is further evidenced in the fact that it hypothesizes the present "situation as an eternal one."[4] Adorno attempted to drive this point home by suggesting a contradiction in the Veblenian concept of adaptation:

> The concept of adaptation is the *deux ex machina* through which Veblen tried to bridge the gap between what is and what ought to be. But adaptation implies the rule of the ever equal. If dialectics, on its side, were to understand the next step as adaptation, it would be surrendering its very case, the idea of potentiality. But what can the next step be if it is not to be abstract and arbitrary, if it is not to be the brand of those Utopias which the initiators of dialectical philosophy have rejected? Conversely, how can the next step obtain its direction and its aim without one's knowing more than merely what is pregiven?[5]

In other words, Veblen's adamant commitment to Darwinian empiricism did not provide a sufficient concept of praxis, for he failed to demonstrate the relationship between man as a conscious being and the demands for thought that social change requires.[6] Adorno took the position that, for Veblen, all social change is the result of mere animal-like adaptation, devoid of conscious decision making concerning means and ends. Hence, any talk of an abstract ideal, as a normative social goal, is impossible. The Darwinian scheme of evolution suggests only blind, cumulative causation, not that optimistic future promised by the Marxian reconstruction of Hegelian dialectics.

Veblen's view was that selective adaptation can never keep pace with the constantly changing social situation; hence "each successive situation of the community in its turn tends to obsolescence as soon as it has been established. When a step in the development has been taken, this step itself constitutes a change of situation which requires a new adaptation; it becomes the point of departure for a new step in the adjustment, and so on interminably."[7] Veblen's theory of selective adaptation, according to Adorno, failed to provide a sound basis for his normative principles; indeed, Veblen's Darwinism appears to contradict his avowed normative framework.

To highlight the difference between Veblen and Adorno, consideration should be given to the reasons behind Veblen's rejection of dialectics and Adorno's attempts to refute what he saw as positivism in the methodology of the social sciences. Veblen found Marxian dialectics to be romantic, unjustifiably optimistic, and unscientific. He could see no historical support for the class struggle doctrine, which was "essentially an intellectual sequence and . . . therefore of a teleological character."[8] Similarly, the Marxian doctrine of progressive proletarian misery also had to be rejected. From a Darwinian point of view, it was impossible to determine whether the proletariat would establish socialism or once again "sink their feet in the broad sands of patriotism."[9] Adorno, in contrast, was firmly committed to the position that social theory must be critical and dialectical in nature. It became clear that, in Adorno's opinion, Veblen's use of Darwinian evolutionary theory did not accord to man what is due him in the process of conscious historical change. Adorno thus viewed Veblen's theory of adaptation and obsolescence as unduly pessimistic and latently conservative. Unfortunately, Adorno had mistaken Veblenian institutionalism for the incremental ameliorism of more politically conservative types of pragmatism. Veblen's sharp polemical attacks on absentee ownership, organized religion, the price system, the state, and patriotism made it evident that he was no advocate of mere adaptationism.[10] Instead, it would be nearer the truth to interpret Veblen's work as principled opposition to capitalism as well as supportive of large-scale structural change.

Implicit in the Frankfurt School's critique of Veblen is the idea that his social theory suffered from philosophical poverty,[11] an allegation evident in Adorno's disapproval of Veblen's rejection of Hegelian dialectics in favor of Darwinian science. One might mistakenly infer from this that Veblen was somehow too conservative for Adorno's taste. However, at times Adorno appeared to be less critical of capitalism than was Veblen. The latter was at his most vitriolic in his attack upon capitalist culture, while Adorno explained dialectically and sometimes rationalized those aspects Veblen dislikes. Perhaps this curious twist can be explained by Adorno's faith in the dialectical process of social evolution: Whatever exists does so for a reason and can be illuminated through the power of dialectics.

Conspicuous Consumption and Status Emulation

Veblen, with his penchant for efficiency and dislike of waste, was unable to understand, in Adorno's view, the reasons or motives behind conspicuous consumption or superfluous show. For Veblen, the "false castle is nothing but a reversion."[12] For Adorno, "conspicuous consumption is actually a realm of artificial imagery . . . created by a desperate compulsion to escape from the abstract sameness of things by a kind of self-made and futile *promesse de bonheur.*"[13] The idea of "show," as understood by Adorno, was not simply a "false statement of labor"; it was, rather, an attempt to "summon into reality the idea of that which cannot be exchanged."[14] Thus did Adorno endeavor to demonstrate a weakness in Veblen's argument. That which cannot be justified by criteria of efficiency can be understood as an attempt to negate the social and cultural by-products of industrial uniformity.

Adorno noted that Veblen disliked conspicuous consumption because it aimed not at the satisfaction of true wants, but at social prestige or status. Adorno certainly recognized that conspicuous consumption exists, but his analysis differs radically from Veblen's. While Veblen sees conspicuous consumption as "mere ostentation" (Adorno's words), Adorno sees a need to transcend the drudgery of industrial life.[15]

Veblen's attack on status emulation and conspicuous consumption aroused the antipathy of Adorno. The latter not only offered an alternative explanation of these phenomena, but also was sympathetic toward them, at least in his 1941 analysis, if not later. Adorno asserted that Veblen did not grasp the manner in which the individual's needs are satisfied through emulatory consumption patterns. Adorno also believed that Veblen's use of the ceremonial-technological dichotomy is inadequate and that his technological criteria of value are unsatisfactory. Related to this is Adorno's lack of enthusiasm for mass culture. He believed that it is sordid, tawdry, and vulgar and the result of manipulation by vested interests. Thus, it is not surprising that he sympathized with attempts to "transcend" social station even if these attempts take the form of status emulation and conspicuous consumption. However, critical theory's position itself seems ambiguous if not contradictory. As Langdon Winner wrote:

> With each new invention or innovation it becomes possible to awaken and satisfy an appetite latent in human constitution. What if all the wrong needs are awakened? Marxists grapple with this dilemma in their analyses of "false consciousness" and "commodity fetishism" trying to explain how the proletariat should have taken such a serious interest in the debased consumer goods and status symbols of bourgeois society. Much of the neo-Marxian criticism of the Frankfurt School . . . focuses on the corruption of Marx's vision of human fulfillment in technological societies.[16]

Curiously, some of the Frankfurt Marxists, especially Adorno, defended or rationalized the patterns of behavior that Veblen stigmatized. Also, it is ironic that in later years critical theory's analysis of consumption patterns in advanced capitalism should more closely parallel Veblen's view, rejected earlier. In particular, Marcuse's position in

One Dimensional Man converged with Veblen's interpretation in *The Theory of the Leisure Class* in its recognition of the artificiality and manipulated nature of consumer tastes and their links with the national system of status and power.

Anti-Intellectualism and Social Intermediaries

While claiming to recognize the historical importance of Veblen's sociology, Adorno maintained that attention must be given to the "objective motives underlying his thinking."[17] Indeed, much of Adorno's criticism of Veblen centered around the latter's personality and intellectual experiences. For example, he claimed to detect a great deal of spleen in Veblen's work. Moreover, "melancholy lurks behind" Veblen's critique of society, along with an attitude of "disillusionment" and "debunking." Adorno continued:

> The splenetic attitude clings obstinately to the alienated world of things and makes the malicious object responsible for evil. The debunker follows through. He is the "man with the knack," who does not allow himself to be cheated by the malicious objects but tears the ideological cover from them in order to manipulate them more easily. He curses the damned swindle. It is not accidental that the debunker's hatred is always directed against intermediary functions. The swindle and the middle-man belong together. So, however, do mediation and thinking.[18]

Adorno qualified this by saying that "Veblen's consciousness was quite free from this hatred. To be sure, anti-intellectualism was objectively implied in his struggle against intermediary functions as well as in his denunciation of 'higher learning.'"[19] Adorno attempted to explain the "narrowness" of Veblen's thinking in this regard by reference to the "zealotry of Scandinavian Protestantism which does not tolerate any intermediary between God and inwardness and trains itself to serve the purpose of a society which liquidates the intermediary functions between the omnipotent production and the forced consumer."[20] Adorno also noted that Veblen in *Absentee Ownership*, compared the functions of the clergyman with those of the salesman. However, Adorno exaggerated the degree to which Scandinavian Protestantism repudiated the social intermediary function of the clergy. He should have recognized that in certain of the Lutheran traditions the post-Reformation ministry has possessed a diminished, but not insignificant, role in administering the sacraments, instructing the laity, and counseling the disturbed. Adorno's efforts to attribute Veblen's "anti-intellectual tendencies" to his Lutheran background showed an incapacity to distinguish between the radical forms of Protestantism that abolished the social intermediary functions of the ministry and the more conservative traditions, such as the Anglican and Lutheran, which did not. It is but a modest exaggeration to suggest that, to Adorno, all Protestants look alike. Adorno's efforts to attribute Veblen's views to his Lutheran background reveal an interesting contrast between the perceived parochialism of the American-born Norwegian farm boy and the undeniably elitist proclivities of the cosmopolitan Adorno.

Indeed, the possibility, perhaps the likelihood, of class bias is evident in Adorno's family background, his circle of friends, his life-style, and his failure to experience capitalist aesthetics from the position of working-class consumers. What Adorno did to Veblen can be done to Adorno by linking his social theory with his personality and background.[21] While it is true that Veblen preferred efficiency, thrift, and a flattened society devoid of status distinctions, is it not also the case that Adorno, wellborn and well-bred, urbane, an aesthetic intellectual, would be more disposed to prefer those things Veblen found objectionable? In the last analysis, the differences between the two were the differences between two cultures and traditions. One was urban, Jewish, and intellectual; the other rural, Protestant, and egalitarian. These two men represented the difference between the Europe of the late 1920s and early 1930s, which gave birth to critical theory, and the America of the late nineteenth century, which spawned Veblen. One was largely the intellectual by-product of the culturally scintillating Weimar Republic. The other was a "son of the middle border," whose immigrant family wrested a living from the soil with their own hands, and whose intellectual outlook was shaped by the struggle between the corporate interests and the farm-labor community that culminated in the Populist revolt.

Adorno's Critique of Veblen's Aesthetics

Adorno attributed to Veblen a rather one-sided analysis of culture. Veblen's "misanthropy," his "obsession" with explaining culture in terms of display of booty, power, and appropriated surplus value, precluded a fuller understanding of those cultural phenomena "which go beyond this display."[22] In short, Veblen "explains culture through the trash, not vice versa."[23] Nor did Veblen pay attention to those cultural objectives that Adorno felt are different from today's commodity culture. In a penetrating way Adorno was able to show the extremism of Veblen's assault on culture; Veblen's dislike of waste seemingly led him to condemn all leisure class cultural and aesthetic values and objects. Veblen's parsimonious aesthetic (when pushed to its logical extreme) would indict as mere manifestations of ceremonialism the paintings of Rembrandt and Hals, the poetry of Shelley, and the sculpture of Rodin, as well as his own example of the medieval Gothic cathedral. Or would it? Veblen never clarified his theory of aesthetics, and it is difficult to tell how far he would have pushed his technological criteria of value, or how he could have applied it without destroying aesthetic values altogether.

It may be that Adorno was not objecting to Veblen's technological criteria of value as such, but to his indiscriminate efforts to use it where inapplicable. It is difficult to disagree with Veblen's indictment of women's clothing and fashion when these obviously interfere with workmanlike efficiency or personal comfort. In Veblen's day, such encumbrances as whalebone corsets and beaver hats were detrimental to the industrial efficiency that Veblen viewed as intrinsic to the life process of mankind.

Perhaps Adorno was suggesting that the Veblenian technological criterion of value is an important standard by which to measure economic and engineering processes, but is inappropriate for evaluation in the aesthetic realm. While it is evident at this point that Adorno was less critical of capitalistic cultural processes and values than was Veblen, Adorno made some telling points in his critique of Veblen's functionalist aesthetic and pointed to the weakest part of the American's cultural critique of capitalism. Adorno saw waste and tawdry vulgarity as closely tied to capitalism and, to him, Veblen's position resembled more that of the puritanical capitalist than of the aesthetic socialist. Yet, Veblen's functionalist aesthetic linked wasteful consumption to unproductive employment in a way that illuminated the dynamics of capitalism more effectively than did Adorno. The latter's critique of Veblen's aesthetics was penetrating as aesthetic criticism, but it was not so successful in linking aesthetics with structural aspects of the political economy.

Veblen—a Primitivist?

John Diggins has argued that Adorno depicted Veblen as "searching for mythic norm that is more basic than immediate reality; he wants to establish the validity of an ideal on the basis of its antiquity."[24] Actually, what Veblen wanted to establish were certain norms whose value arose from their ability to enhance the life process of mankind and were not simply a function of their age. Adorno mentioned Veblen's faith in the norm found in the primitive history of mankind, for "Veblen the technocrat, longs for the restoration of the most ancient."[25] Assuming Veblen's debt to Rousseau's "ideal of the primitive," Adorno contended that Veblen's introduction of the instinct of workmanship was merely incidental "in order to bring paradise and the industrial age to their common anthropological denominator."[26]

In summary, the accusation made against Veblen by Adorno was that he was a primitivist who wanted to revert to a golden age a la Rousseau's noble savage. This is a mistaken view. Veblen attempted to show how the institutional matrix of a particular society would bring forth the traits of either the peaceful or the predatory type. If it is the former that emerges, the instinct of workmanship, the parental bent, and the pursuit of idle curiosity would become manifest; egalitarian and pacifist traits would dominate. If it is the latter, the traits that would come forth are the pecuniary and sporting instincts, with their militaristic, exploitative, and superstitious results. Veblen preferred the peaceful type but even though he thought that type dominated in primitive times, this should not be interpreted as a preference for the restoration of some idyllic, primitive state of existence. Instead, he endorsed a resurgence of the traits of the peaceful type within the framework of a modern industrial society. Adorno's charge of primitivism against Veblen thus seems incongruous with his claim that Veblen was a technocrat. Veblen wanted to restore the pristine virtues of ancient communal society, but not in the Luddite sense. He can, however, be faulted for not making the normative aspect of his theory more explicit.

Adorno believed that the images of barbarism that Veblen uncovered in the cultural display of the nineteenth century contradicted Veblen's "optimistic belief in progress," that his last writings do an injustice to culture owing to his "fascination of the impending doom" of Western society. This pessimism of Veblen's stems, presumably, from the melancholy underlying his thinking. Although there is a strain of pessimism evident in Veblen's later writings, it is difficult to tell whether he is predicting stagnation and inertia as the future course of capitalist development in America, or the collapse of civilization, as Adorno has suggested.[27]

Exploitation, Waste, or Both?

Adorno argued that "what Veblen dislikes about capitalism is its waste rather than its exploitation."[28] It is more accurate to assert that Veblen disliked capitalism *both* because it is exploitative and wasteful and because, in his view, waste and exploitation are causally related. Veblen's attacks on the Marxian labor theory of value should not be permitted to hide his fundamental egalitarianism and his belief that private property is the source of exploited labor. His attack on absentee ownership

was based on the conviction that it both causes waste of industrial resources *and* leads to exploitation. Despite his contempt for institutional
religion, his view paralleled both the American Protestant emphasis on
avoidance of waste and the general Christian strictures against
sweated labor. As an early theorist of oligopoly and price administration, before these terms were popularized by economists, Veblen realized that laborers received less than they were worth and consumers
were overcharged. Veblen did give more emphasis to waste than to
exploitation, but this was not because he dismissed the inherent ex-
ploitativeness of capitalism. In its way, Veblen's criterion of value was
as critical of exploitation as is the Marxian labor theory of value, but
for different reasons. Adorno did not fully grasp the meanings of waste
and the roles that it plays in the Veblenian system. Waste is not just the
superfluities consumed by the leisure class or the excesses resulting from status emulation on the part of the underlying population, as
important as these are. Waste also reflects the inability of capitalist
economies to run industrial plants at capacity and the tendency of the
system to squander increasing amounts of economic resources on advertising and salesmanship. As Veblen made clear, the institutional
processes and forms that make waste inevitable are linked with the
exploitative mechanisms that are rooted in absentee ownership. Waste
and exploitation are an integral part of a system that is structured to
produce both on a grand scale. Adorno's contention that Veblen was
more concerned with waste than with exploitation must be understood
in light of Adorno's more fundamental but mistaken complaint that
Veblen was a "technocrat" and "adaptationist" and not a dialectical
thinker.

Sport

The few critics and contemporary sociologists of sport who are familiar
with Veblen's work perceive him as a radical critic of sports, both competitive and noncompetitive. For him, sport was merely another unjus-
tifiable form of competitive ranking of human beings based on invidious distinctions that are wasteful of time and economic resources; in
short, it is a realm of human endeavor rooted in force and fraud. As he
put it:

> Sports—hunting, angling, athletic games, and the like—afford an exercise
> for dexterity and for the emulative ferocity and astuteness characteristic of
> predatory life. So long as the individual is but slightly gifted with reflection
> or with a sense of the ulterior trend of actions—so long as his life is substan-
> tially a life of naive impulse action—so long as the immediate and unre-

flected purposefulness of sports, in the way of an expression of dominance, will measurably satisfy his instinct of workmanship. This is especially true if his dominant impulses are the unreflecting emulative propensities of the predaceous temperament."[29]

There is little evidence in Veblen's work, however, that he was opposed to physical culture as such, but this claim needs qualification. Indeed, one of his most penetrating comments was that "football bears much the same relationship to physical culture that bullfighting bears to agri-culture."[30] Implicit in this remark is his view that football was so invid-iously organized, ostentatiously displayed, and brutally conducted that it defeated the very ends of physical culture for which it was ostensibly created. But Adorno's deep revulsion for sport was rooted in his inabil-ity to see it as anything other than a manic syndrome of pathological attitudes and instincts. Indeed, Adorno's only complaint about Veb-len's portrayal of sport as a savage and even vicious primitivism was that it failed to grasp sport's sadistic and masochistic elements. Ath-letes enjoy having pain inflicted on them by others, particularly in a fascist state! To quote Adorno in more detail:

> According to Veblen, the passion for sports is of a retrogressive nature: "The ground of an addiction to sports is an archaic spiritual constitution." But nothing is more modern than this archaism; athletic events were the models of totalitarian mass rallies. As tolerated excesses, they combine cruelty and aggression with an authoritarian moment, the disciplined observance of the rules—legality, as in the pogroms of Nazi Germany and the people's repub-lics. Veblen's analysis, of course, should be expanded. For sport includes not merely the drive to do violence to others but also the wish to be attacked oneself and suffer. Only Veblen's rationalist psychology prevents him from seeing the masochistic moments in sports. It is this which makes sports not so much a relic of a previous form of society as perhaps an initial adjustment to its menacing new form.[31]

Adorno could only interpret sports in any form as leading to a cult of the body, and as fulfilling a masochistic desire to inflict suffering on one-self, or a sadistic impulse to inflict it on others. Adorno also wrote in his essay on Veblen that "Modern sports, one will perhaps say, seek to restore to the body some of the functions of which the machine has deprived it. But they do so only in order to train men only the more inexorably to serve the machine. Hence, sports belongs to the realm of unfreedom, no matter where they are organized."[32]

The irony of the title of Adorno's critique of Veblen, which includes the phrase "attack on culture," should now be evident. This phrase is surely more befitting Adorno's own attitudes toward culture, particularly sport, than much of what Veblen wrote as a critic of culture. It is another example of the way that the Frankfurt School's obsession with fascism, however justifiable at the time, led to its one-sided critique of Veblen.

THE PROBLEM OF RATIONALITY

Herbert Marcuse's analysis of Veblen was based primarily on the latter's survey of the impact of technology on human rationality. In his article, "Some Social Implications of Modern Technology," Marcuse quoted approvingly from Veblen, noting that he was "among the first to derive the new matter-of-factness from the machine process, from which it spread over the whole of society."[33] Veblen realized clearly the social consequences of this new mode: The modern workman had become an attendant to the machine process; his work merely supplements it; and, in stronger terms, the machine utilizes the workman. The new attitude, according to Marcuse, results in a "highly rational compliance" on the part of those living under the new technology. "The facts directing man's thought and action are not those of nature, which must be accepted in order to be mastered, or those of society, which must be changed because they no longer correspond to human needs and potentialities. Rather are they those of the machine process which itself appears as the embodiment of rationality and expedience."[34] Marcuse's own idea of technological entrapment, and what Veblen called the "cultural incidence of the machine process," were used by Marcuse to suggest a convergence of viewpoint as to the effects of modern technology on human rationality. However, divergence is also apparent in Marcuse's view of the industrial process as having a debasing and enslaving effect, whereas, in Veblen's early work the effects are interpreted as emancipatory and as possibly leading to the development of socialist consciousness.[35]

Specifically, Veblen's thesis is that workers interacting with the machine process under the conditions of modern industry develop the capacity to think in terms of regularity of sequence, precise measurement, and impersonal cause-and-effect relationships. In short, they become secular in orientation, matter-of-fact, irreligious, unmoral, and less given to patriotic ideals. Egalitarian beliefs become more prevalent, as does skepticism toward existing property rights, social status, and power. Militaristic, bellicose, and coercive values diminish in influence among workers as they take on the attributes of Veblen's "peaceful type."[36]

Marcuse conceded that in certain ways Veblen correctly explained the impact of the machine process on the industrial labor force. He fundamentally disagreed, however, with the moral and political ramifications of Veblen's analysis. In this respect he concurred with Adorno's statement:

> Mitchell sums up Veblen's psychology of the industrial worker as follows: "They (the masses of factory hands) tend to become skeptical, matter-of-fact, materialistic, unmoral, unpatriotic, undevout, blind to the metaphysical niceties of natural right." One could not give a more adequate description of the cynical frame of mind of very large sections of the population in present day Germany. It ought to be noted in particular that even the term patriotism has fallen into disfavor with the National Socialist regime.[37]

Given the world situation in 1941 and the desperate circumstances of European Jewry, it is not surprising that Marcuse should have focused on the role of technology in the Nazi system and the weakness of Veblen's theory in this respect. Marcuse wrote:

> Technology . . . is a mode of organizing and perpetuating (or changing) social relationships, a manifestation of prevalent thought and behavior patterns, an instrument for control and domination. Technics by itself can promote authoritarianism as well as liberty, scarcity as well as abundance, the extension as well as the abolition of toil. National socialism is a striking example of the ways in which a highly rationalized and mechanized economy with the utmost efficiency in production can operate in the interest of totalitarian oppression and continued scarcity.[38]

Veblen was misguided in his uncritical faith in the emancipatory potential of the machine process; in Marcuse's view, modern technology is as likely to enslave and oppress as it is to liberate. In Veblen's defense, however, it should be noted that he predicted a resurgence of authoritarianism in Germany and Japan long before it occurred because he doubted that institutions and values of feudal origin could successfully adjust to the logic of the machine process. Indeed, Veblen anticipated the fusion of archaic social institutions with modern science and technology in a chilling forecast of what was to come. His point was that when ruling classes or elites use their power to misuse technology, it is because their own minds have not yet adjusted to the logic of the machine process. In short, they have not yet fully assimilated technological criteria of value. However, Veblen assumed the truth of what Marcuse challenged when he made a distinction between "technological" and "critical" rationality. Marcuse wrote that the idea of compliant efficiency perfectly illustrates the structure of techno-logical rationality. Rationality is being transformed from a critical force into one of adjustment and compliance. Autonomy of reason loses its meaning in the same measure as the thought, feelings and actions of men are shaped by the technical requirements of the apparatus which they have themselves created. Reason has found its resting place in the system of standardized control, production and consumption. There it reigns through the laws and mechanism which insure the efficiency, expediency and coherence of this system. . . . Rationality here calls for unconditional compliance and conse-quently, the truth values related to this rationality imply the subordination of thought to pregiven external standards. We may call this set of truth values the technological truth, technological in the twofold sense that it is an in-strument of expedience rather than an end in itself, and that it follows the pattern of technological behavior. (Pp. 422–23)

In contrast, critical rationality does not subordinate thought to pre-given external standards or machine efficiency. It implies the use of reason to criticize the established order and its dominant set of ideas (pp. 422–23). Critical rationality also suggests an ability to understand complex sets of social relationships and empathize with humanistic values. Implicit in Marcuse's analysis is the view that Veblen failed to distinguish between technological and critical rationality. He did not adequately differentiate between an ability to understand means-ends congruence and master technical skills, on the one hand, and the ca-pacity to engage in acts of critical rationality, on the other hand. It was characteristic of Veblen to confuse the two different kinds of rationality in his analysis of the mentality of industrial workers. The critical ra-tionality essential to the development of a socialist ethic proved too weak in the psyche of the Western proletariat to achieve a mass social-ist consciousness, a fact that Veblen admitted in his later writing.

Although Marcuse did not specifically criticize Veblen in his "Some Social Implications of Modern Technology," it was his conviction that Veblen did not adequately come to grips with the role technology played. Rather than it having an emancipating or liberating role, tech-nology was "a mode of organizing and perpetuating (or changing) so-cial relationships, a manifestation of prevalent thought and behavior patterns, an instrument for control and domination. Technics by itself can promote authoritarianism as well as liberty, scarcity as well as abundance, the extension as well as the abolition of toil" (p. 414).

Veblen was conceded by Marcuse to have been one of the first to understand that a new matter-of-factness was derived from the ma-chine process that spread throughout society. But, again, Marcuse suggested that Veblen's analysis was inadequate because this process thus "dissolves all actions into a sequence of semispontaneous reactions to perceived mechanical norms. . . . Individualistic rationality has developed into efficient compliance with the pregiven continuum of means and ends" (p. 419).

Yet, at this point, Marcuse was not so much a critic of Veblen as he was a user of Veblen's ideas, in part, to show their own contemporary inadequacy, for as he put it, "technological rationality . . . is being transformed from a critical force into one of adjustment and compliance" (p. 422). Marcuse concluded that encapsulated within modern industrial culture were

> two different sets of truth values and two different patterns of behavior: the one assimilated to the apparatus, the other antagonistic to it; the one making up the prevailing technological rationality and governing the behavior required by it, the other pertaining to a critical rationality whose value can be fulfilled only if it has itself shaped all personal and social relationships. (P. 423)

To Marcuse these two sets of truth values were neither wholly contradictory nor complimentary to each other. He revealingly commented, and pointed to a weakness in Veblen's analysis, that because the distinction between the two sets was not rigid "the content of each set changes in the social process so that what were once critical truth values become technological values" (p. 423). In Veblen, of course, there was often no real point of division between technological and critical truth values, because he compressed the two together so closely that no real qualitative distinctions were possible. Technological rationality signifying mean-ends congruence was thus fused with substantive rationality, that is, for example, the ability to manipulate and adjust bodily motions to machine technology was linked with the development of skepticism toward conventional property rights and religious belief.

HORKHEIMER ON VEBLEN

Max Horkheimer's often vague and sometimes convoluted piece "The End of Reason" was unambiguous on only one topic—fascism. His contempt for it was penetrating, powerful, and absolute. Unfortunately, the article did not mention Veblen by name and it is necessary to read between the lines to relate Horkheimer's central themes to him. However, in the preface to the third 1941 issue of *Studies in Philosophy and Social Science*, Horkheimer wrote that the article on Reason and the one on Veblen represent the fruit of a joint effort of their authors. It became clear to us that thorough study and earnest analysis of Veblen, America's great sociological critic of culture, would help us better to understand the catastrophic change in human nature, outlines of which the article on Reason attempts to sketch.[39]

Thus, there can be little doubt that Horkheimer, Adorno, and Marcuse intended to analyze Veblen's work, however obliquely, in this issue of their theoretical journal.

Essentially, Horkheimer treated Veblen as a pragmatist who stressed the adaptationist power of the species as expressed instrumentally through its survival. The species may have to strip itself of all worthwhile qualities in order to survive—gallantry, nobility of character, aesthetic and moral sensitivities—yet, in Veblen's view, survive it must! This crudely Darwinian portrayal of Veblen's evolutionary social theory saw him as advocating, indeed, exhalting in survival at any cost. Horkheimer indicted life in industrial society and, perhaps, Veblen's "sanction" of it when he wrote: "Previously, men were appendages to the machines, today they are appendages as such. Reflective thought and theory lose their meaning in the struggle for self-preservation."[40] Horkheimer argued that the prevailing means of production, economic planning, and stress on efficiency led to a form of intellectual enervation in which thought had been removed from philosophy by reducing "the latter to the technique of organizing, by reproduction and abridgement, the matters of fact given in the world of sense. In positivism reason sustains itself through self-liquidation."[41]

Was this simply an indictment of the corporate state as it developed under fascism? Did Horkheimer intend that the indictment be expanded to include reform capitalism, as in the New Deal? Or was it an attack on Veblen's claims that the machine process has a emancipatory impact on industrial workers? Probably, it was intended to be all three, since in the Frankfurt view they are all more or less expressive of the same underlying techno-bureaucratic forces.[42]

Veblen believed that the machine process fostered both functional and substantive rationality in the labor force. Although he did not use the term *functional* or *substantial* in connection with "rationality," it is evident in *The Theory of Business Enterprise* that industrial workers have induced in them by machine technology both the ability to understand means-ends congruence (functional rationality) and compare alternative sets of ends (substantial rationality). However, it is clear that the Frankfurt School believed that only functional rationality is present in the labor force, because "reason" (substantial rationality) has been liquidated. The growth of bureaucracy, totalitarian propaganda, and subservience to the machine and the machine's masters, be they monopoly capitalists or the state under the control of the Party, are the reasons why.

Given the desperate situation created by the fascist advance in Europe in 1941, the Frankfurt School's denial of the emancipating impact of machine technology was understandable and their obsession with defeating nazism laudable. However, the consequence of this fixation was to ignore or at least downplay the accuracy and relevance of Veblen's analysis in those systems not under fascist dominance. But it appeared that the School believed that his claims were no longer valid, if they had ever been, under conditions of monopoly capitalism whether fascist or not. Reason had thus been usurped or liquidated by the institutional imperatives of advanced industrial society and Franklin Roosevelt's America and Winston Churchill's Britain were no exception to the rule.

Horkheimer, like Adorno and Marcuse, succumbed to the temptation, not to directly link Veblen with fascism, but to suggest that his uncritical attitudes toward technics and technology reflected a blind spot in his sociology of culture. This blind spot made it unlikely that he would understand how technology could be used by antidemocratic, reactionary, and oppressive forces. This was a strange comment for critical theory to make in view of Veblen's prediction that unless Imperial Germany and Japan were subjected to structural renovation after the War, they would revert to right-wing authoritarianism. His writings on the Hohenzollern and Meiji dynasties with their stress on the unstable and dangerous fusion of modern science and technology with obsolete social institutions went largely unnoticed.

Chapter Ten

RADICAL CRITICS: *THE MONTHLY REVIEW*

Paul Sweezy

S INCE ITS founding by Paul Sweezy and Leo Huberman in
1949, the *Monthly Review* has been a politically independent
organ of the extreme left in the United States. Started to both
combat the Cold War and promote socialist doctrine, the journal had
an explicitly Marxist orientation. It differed in several ways from the
other two left-leaning journals whose audience also consisted mostly of
radical and left-liberal intellectuals.

It was distinguishable from the other Marxist journal, *Science and
Society*, in that it was a monthly rather than a quarterly, and its format
and substantive content were more polemical than scholarly. However, many of the same individuals wrote for both journals, so there
were few doctrinal differences between them, since Marxism was
clearly the focus of both. Indeed, it was evident that a main reason why
the journals occasionally featured material on Veblen was on account
of the perceived convergence between his thought and that of Karl
Marx.

The third left-wing journal, *Dissent*, was founded by a group of
mostly Jewish, New York intellectuals and led by the literary critic
Irving Howe. It was much more eclectic than either *Monthly Review* or
Science and Society and covered a broader spectrum of political opinion
and cultural interests. Its main appeal was to the anti-Stalinist left and
many who wrote for it belonged to what remained of the Norman Thomas Socialist party.

Monthly Review was for many years the most influential Marxist
periodical in the United States and described itself as an "independent
socialist magazine." Although Paul Sweezy and his journal took
strong, often revolutionary ideological and political stands on issues of
the day, they had no formal affiliation with any political party or movement. In this sense only could Sweezy and his journal be said to be
"nonpartisan." Sweezy is well-known in the Marxist intellectual community, both as a political journalist, scholar, and theoretician.[1] Indeed, his and Paul Baran's *Monopoly Capital* (1966) is perhaps the
most influential book ever written by American Marxists. Attention
here, however, is focused on his and Baran's writings on Veblen, which
are treated separately.

In the summer of 1957, Sweezy's journal *Monthly Review* devoted a double special issue to an evaluation of the life, work, and contemporary relevance of Thorstein Veblen.[2] Various radicals, including Arthur Davis, were invited to contribute on the centennial of Veblen's birth, and their essays are of considerable value in understanding the ideological underpinnings of American Marxism in the mid-twentieth century. It is important to notice, however, that no institutional economists were asked to contribute. This was explained by co-editor Leo Huberman and Sweezy in their introduction: "Those who call themselves Veblenites or who have made a special study of his work are for the most part not, in our judgment and for reasons which we hope will become clearer to the reader as he proceeds, the ones best qualified to make the kind of reappraisal we think needed."[3]

Almost simultaneously, Douglas Dowd edited a centennial volume on Veblen with sixteen different contributors, only one of whom was an avowed Marxist at the time, and that was Sweezy himself. The unwillingness of institutional and other heterodox economists, most of whom were political liberals, to interact even on a scholarly basis with Marxists and the equally rigid attitude of Marxists toward liberals was indicative of the fragmentation of the American left during the early years of the Cold War. In any case, Sweezy's analysis of Veblen revealed the degree of his alienation from "liberal reformist economics" which is what he and Paul Baran believed institutional economics had become. Probably, also, it is a commentary on the extent to which both men believed the institutionalists had become assimilated into the Keynesian mainstream and Cold War politics. It is important to remember that the Association for Evolutionary Economics and its publication, the *Journal of Economic Issues*, evolved some years later; and to Sweezy and Baran most institutional economists were indistinguishable from other economists of liberal persuasion who were both converts to Keynesianism and combatants in the international confrontation with the Soviet Union and its allies. In the same vein, although Sweezy did not agree with the common Marxist view of Veblen as a petit bourgeois reformer, he and Huberman explained how other critics could plausibly reach this conclusion:

> There is no doubt that by appropriately picking and choosing quotations from Veblen's extensive literary output, one can build up a plausible case for this view. Strong elements of racism and technocracy, a specially fervent hostility to finance capital—these and other characteristic petty [sic] bourgeois ideas and attitudes can certainly be found in Veblen, and a skillful critic can weave them together to form an all-too familiar picture.[4]

In explaining Sweezy's interpretation of Veblen, it is important to recognize both the stress Sweezy placed on his personal alienation and the role played by his followers who were institutional economists. He wrote that

> in addition to being a stranger Veblen was a rebel, and American society, for all its protestations to the contrary, has no use for rebels. The plain fact, which it requires a sociologist not to see, is that Veblen's isolation was imposed upon him because of his ideas, and not that his ideas arose out of his isolation. Nor is it any answer to point out that from a fairly early date he was usually surrounded by a clique of admirers. Offering him adulation rather than understanding or stimulation, these cliques served rather to intensify his isolation; and as the individuals grew older and escaped one by one into respectability they were careful to take with them only such elements and aspects of "Veblenism" as would be thoroughly safe and sound in a rapidly developing monopoly capitalist society.[5]

Veblen's followers were thus portrayed as careerists and opportunists who lacked the courage of his convictions and used the residues of his thinking only after his ideas were, first, denatured and, secondly, deradicalized. However, those familiar with the career and thought of such "Veblenians" as Clarence Ayres, Walton Hamilton, and John Kenneth Galbraith may find it difficult to accept this view of their moral and professional character. Although, Huberman and Sweezy named no particular individuals, it is evident that they have in mind such heterodox economists; having excluded them from participation in the centennial issue, it was also apparently necessary to collectively denigrate them.

The Theoretical Unity of Veblen's System?

Only the undiscerning could fail to recognize Sweezy's belief that most of what is valuable in Veblen is so because of its convergence with Marx. Marx remained his standard to measure theoreticians against and Veblen was valuable primarily because he supplemented, reinforced and occasionally updated Marx's insights. Sweezy commented on the positive side that

> No one understood so clearly the growth of monopolistic (or, if you prefer, oligopolistic) big business with its ramifications and implications in such fields as advertising, distribution, and popular culture. No one grasped so thoroughly the unity of economics and politics. Above all, Veblen was and remains unique in the way he assigns a decisive role in the development of capitalism to the reciprocating interaction of business principles and national politics. Others have described the economic impact of war, the psychological effects of militarism, the cultural incidences of nationalism; and none can deny that these forces have become increasingly important, if not

actually dominant, in the world of today. Yet only Veblen has built these elements into a reasoned and coherent theory.[6]

Yet at another point in his writing on Veblen, Sweezy commented on "his unsystematic and often highly frustrating way of theorizing."[7] On balance, perhaps what he meant is that, while there is more coherence in Veblen than in most of his contemporaries, the standard rendered by Marx is beyond his grasp.

The Distinction between Pecuniary and Industrial Pursuits

A characteristic Marxist evaluation of Veblen's famous dichotomy between business and industry is expressed in the following words:

> Genius is not enough in the social sciences unless it is armed with a system, as Veblen was. Indeed, he suffered from having too rigid rather than too amorphous a system: thus the excessive sharpness of his distinction between the pecuniary and industrial elements in business enterprise goes a long way towards explaining the worst mistakes he made on the American economy and on imperialism.[8]

Marxists are sometimes impressed with the Veblenian distinction between industrial and pecuniary pursuits, but nevertheless find it both overdrawn and misleading. Sweezy apparently believed that the distinction is an exaggerated one and, worse yet, that it leads to the conclusion that what is wrong with capitalism is its waste not its exploitation. Instead of focusing on the extraction of unpaid labor time from one class by another, Veblen mistakenly stressed the role of pecuniary pursuits that elicit the production and consumption of goods and services that do not enhance the generic ends of life impersonally considered.[9] Implicit in Veblen's analysis, however, is his conviction that those who engage in pecuniary pursuits are exploiting the underlying population. References sprinkled throughout his writing to the "kept classes," who are bent on "getting something for nothing" by living off absentee ownership of stock or "charging all the traffic will bear," make inescapable the conclusion that American capitalism is both wasteful and exploitative. This was Veblen's way of avoiding the metaphysics of the labor theory of value without having to abandon exploitation as a class phenomenon rooted in capitalist property relations.

The Business Cycle

Although they are appreciative of Veblen's attack on neoclassical economic theory, his Marxist interpreters find Veblen's ideas concerning the business cycle to be, while at times perceptive and innovative, ultimately deficient. Arthur Davis, for example, wrote that "in some respects, Veblen was a pioneer in the field of business cycle theory. Aside from Schumpeter, Keynes, and the Marxian, no other major economist so clearly grasped the inherently changing and crisis-generating nature of capitalism."[10] And Sweezy told us, "his overall vision and detailed insights were unsurpassed since Marx—no American economist will even stand comparison."[11]

Despite rating Veblen highly as a thinker, Sweezy was of the opinion that in certain respects his economic analysis was "weak and misleading" and that his views regarding the nature of capitalism were one-sided, because Veblen saw only the negative aspects of capitalism and failed to supply a thorough historical treatment of the institution.[12] He faulted Veblen for restricting capitalist activities to finance and "sabotage" and for postulating the industrial engineer as the only progressive element in the new order. According to Sweezy, this theory paid insufficient attention to the fact that capitalist accumulation "can take place only through the steady expansion of means and employment of more labor" and that the capitalist is in a dominant position with respect to the industrial engineer.[13]

The major weakness in Veblen's economic theory, however, lay in his failure to analyze fully the process of capital accumulation.[14] This failure, according to Sweezy, prevented Veblen from "developing an adequate theory of employment and business fluctuations in general,"[15] not to mention its adverse effect on his theory of imperialism. Sweezy suggested that

> the root of the trouble was that Veblen, like must of his contemporaries, never gave any serious thought to working out a usable income-expenditure theory. He habitually and naively assumed the operation of Say's Law in the extreme form in which total income is automatically spent and remains constant over time. And he equally habitually wrote about phenomena—depression, inflation, deflation, and the like—which could not possibly happen if the assumption were valid.[16]

Sweezy is also dissatisfied with Veblen's theory of chronic depression, which figured so prominently in *The Theory of Business Enterprise*. For Veblen, the force behind depression is progressive lowering of costs, which undermines capital values through technological advances. Sweezy commented that while Veblen did not detail the process, this presents no serious difficulty for his theory because "declining prices, bankruptcies, and the like, can exercise a dampening effect on new investment; and a low level of investment can, in turn, keep income and employment at depression levels."[17] Veblen's explanation of why the system does not collapse is that consumption expands, especially unproductive public consumption, and monopoly takes the places of competition.[18]

It is at this point that Sweezy expressed surprise that Veblen turned his attention to the growth of monopoly and dropped the problem of chronic depressions, which he felt "would disappear along with free competition."[19] Sweezy suggested that this problem could have been avoided had Veblen "thought in terms of the determinants of consumption and income and investments (hence of total income and demand)."[20] Continuing in this vein, Sweezy wrote:

> There is one crucial problem left over from *The Theory of Business Enterprise*, however, which Veblen fails to come to grips with, let alone solve, in *Absentee Ownership. This is the relation between the monopolization process and the tendency to chronic depression.* Veblen's answer to the problem . . . would have been that the economic dispensation brings with it fairly stable *business* prosperity on the one hand and a persistent and grinding form of *industrial* depression on the other. It seems clear that he expected neither the upswing of output and employment which characterized the later twenties nor the collapse of 1929–1933. In this view, the absentee owners were perfectly satisfied with the status quo, and there was little that the underlying population could do about its condition except revolt.[21]

Veblen was wrong about these developments, said Sweezy, because his overall theory of monopoly was faulty. Nonetheless, it was in his discussion of the emerging economic patterns at the turn of the century that "Veblen made some of his most brilliant and original contributions to economic theory."[22] He treated concepts such as monopolistic or imperfect competition before other economists. Veblen is likewise to be credited with envisaging the tremendous growth of salesmanship in American life and tracing its roots to a decaying competitive system.[23] And "no one," Sweezy asserted, "grasped so thoroughly the unity of economics and politics."[24] While others have written on the impact of war on economics, militarism, and nationalism, "only Veblen has built all these elements into a reasoned and coherent theory."[25]

On the whole, Marxists seem more impressed with Veblen's ability to link internal economic dynamics with state intervention, the fostering of nationalism, and the outbreak of war than with his explanation of other causal factors relating to the business cycle. Generally, they view his overcapitalization theory of business cycles as insightful but incomplete and thus inadequate to support the burden he placed on it.

Veblen's Theory of the State and Nationalism

Veblen theorized about the capitalist state during a period when it could reasonably be argued that the Western republics had a ruling class that consisted primarily of large-property holders. According to Sweezy, "Veblen regarded practically all government economic policies as absurd and harmful."[26] "His views on the economic functions and policies of the state were necessarily one-sided and frequently have a strong air of unreality about them."[27] These policies, in Veblen's eyes, aided only the capitalist ruling class, which, nevertheless, could count on the support of the common man. But what would happen if the underlying population, stimulated by its material interests and disciplined by the machine process, should stop wanting business leadership and refuse it support? Sweezy commented that

> Veblen, however, made no direct attempt to answer this question—though of course any complete theory of the state would have to do so—but instead concentrated on what the vested interests could do to prevent matters from reaching this pass. And it is here that his theory of "national integrity" (one of a number of expressions used to convey the same idea) enters into the picture.[28]

Sweezy suggested that Veblen underestimated the importance of both war and imperialism as methods of dealing with surplus capital, while at the same time he overemphasized the role played by nationalistic sentiments.[29] He noticed Veblen's tendency to present a one-sided analysis of those institutions and practices which he then condemned. For example, in the case of nationalism, Sweezy remarked that Veblen could see only its negative aspects—predation, chauvinism, and duplicity. But Sweezy failed to recognize that Veblen's focus was on the reactionary nature of nationalism as it is manifest in developed societies, not on its role in the underdeveloped world. Veblen's sin, if any, was one of omission not commission. But in his "unhistorical" treatment of the subject, Veblen overlooked the crucial fact that nationalism can also serve as a vehicle for liberation from oppressive forces, and Sweezy used modern Chinese nationalism to illustrate his point.[30]

Veblen and the Engineers

All Veblen scholars must ultimately come to terms with his book *The Engineers and the Price System* and with his stress on the social conflict between engineers and technicians on the one hand and capitalists and corporate executives on the other. Sweezy's manner of accomplishing this was to ignore Veblen's satire and take literally what he claimed was Veblen's belief in the potential revolutionary class consciousness of engineers and technicians. Sweezy believed that Veblen came to view "the industrial engineer as the truly progressive factor in the modern economy and to postulate the existence of a basic conflict between the capitalist and the engineer."[31] Sweezy complained of four basic weaknesses in this theory, commenting that:

(1) it ignores, or at best slurs over, the capitalist's fundamental urge to add to his wealth as distinct from consuming it; (2) it entirely fails to see that accumulation by the capitalist can only take place through the steady expansion of the means of production and employment of more labor; (3) consequently it fails to see that the capitalist in effect calls into existence the industrial engineer, pays him and gives direction to his work; and, finally, (4) it inverts the relationship of engineer to capitalist, which is in reality one of dependence of the former on the latter, and makes it appear as a relation of conflict.[32]

Sweezy thus assumed in characteristic Marxist fashion that ownership and control of the means of production are synonymous, and that engineers and technicians are structurally dependent on the will of the capitalists and their agents. The managerial revolution thesis, present only in embryo form in Veblen's *Absentee Ownership*, asserted the divorce of ownership from control in the corporate structure. The thesis was then developed into its mature form in the early work of Gardiner Means and Adolph Berle. But Sweezy believed that the severance of ownership from management, even if this has actually occurred, will do little to alter corporate behavior.

Conclusion

Sweezy claimed to find little or no trace in Veblen of the theory of surplus value.[33] He was correct in that Veblen was critical of the labor theory of value because it originated in eighteenth-century versions of natural law and was thus tainted with residues of the natural law tradition. It should be noted, however, that Veblen articulated an equivalent that he labeled the "economic surplus," which was above and beyond what the community needed for its functional and biological sustenance. This surplus was appropriated by the leisure class and its satellites for their own invidious uses. Briefly, Sweezy's inventory of Veblen's other weaknesses include using outdated anthropological information and projecting prehistory into the present,[34] using a repetitive style that as often defeated as achieved its purpose,[35] and failing to adequately understand "that war is now completely dependent on science, and science increasingly takes both its problems and its material support from the military."[36] Sweezy also complained that Veblen "only partly realized that cultural lags are reservoirs of strength as well as of weakness to dominant economic groups, to whose end they can be adapted or bent."[37] In Sweezy's discussion of Veblen's theory of imperialism he commented that "his most serious failing is his systematic underestimation of the economic basis of imperialism which leads him badly astray in his discussion of the German search for markets and colonies. His work dates here more than anywhere else."[38]

Sweezy's writings on Veblen are thus an important radical documentary of mid-twentieth-century American Marxist attitudes toward him. Unfortunately, despite his inconsistent criticisms of Veblen for insufficient systematization, Sweezy's writings on Veblen are not systematic or detailed enough to fully reveal the nature of his opposition to him. Nevertheless, despite his fundamental criticisms of him, he was more influenced by Veblen's theoretical work than any other Marxist intellectual in the post-World War II era except Baran. But it should not be forgotten that Sweezy viewed Veblen as a valuable thinker primarily because he updated, expanded and complemented the work of Karl Marx. Like many Marxists, he believed that Veblen lived in Marx's shadow and assumed importance primarily when he contributed to the Marxian legacy.[39]

Paul Baran

The doctrinal components of Paul Baran's thought are Marxist and his interpretation of Veblen is thoroughly structured and stylized by this.[40] Although Baran's critique of Veblen represented a more rigid and doctrinaire Marxist perspective than the analysis of Sweezy, the two men shared a similar theoretical perspective that was cogently expressed in their co-authored *Monopoly Capital* (1966). However, despite their convergence, they treated different facets of Veblen in *Monthly Review* in 1957, which provides a rationale for treating their criticisms of Veblen separately.

Baran believed Veblen greatly overstressed the uniformity of class exploitation throughout the ages. He thus failed to distinguish the different forms exploitation takes and the varying consequences this has for diverse social orders. As Baran put it:

> Thus having observed correctly that since time immemorial an upper class has been in a position to appropriate a more or less sizable share of the social product, Veblen never tires of stressing that the existence of the class has been always based on exploitation, that its rich endowment with leisure and worldly goods has been always secured by fleecing the underlying population. In his morbid engrossment in this sameness of iniquity he never attempts, however, to distinguish clearly between different upper classes that at different times appropriate, on the basis of different social relations, different shares of different social outputs produced in different stages of the development of productive resources.[41]

Unfortunately, Baran's intriguing comments were not followed by any systematic effort to explain his criticism of Veblen, although he conceded that there are worse consequences of exploitative systems than exploitation itself. Presumably, what he had in mind in this regard was the arbitrary misuse of power, or economic stagnation, or cultural deprivation. Baran indicated that even though Veblen could not grasp the totality of the social order he detested, "he saw the existing misery without fully realizing at the same time that it is this very misery that carries in itself the objective chance of its abolition" (pp. 90–91). Perhaps it was Veblen's pessimistic belief in the persistence of atavistic continuities, that is, his radical conservativism that Baran here opposed. Indeed, it is evident throughout his essay that a key weakness in Veblen's thought, in Baran's eyes, was his resort to "bourgeois" ideological devices instead of a transcendence to dialectics and materialism:

> Veblen's wisdoms of last resort are always of a biological or psychological nature, have always something to do with "basic" racial characteristics of men or with the no less "fundamental" structure of their motivations. Leaning heavily on the psychology of William James, he conjures up a number of "instincts" conveniently tailored to suit his particular requirements, and treats them as permanent characteristics of the human race. (Pp. 85–86)

That Baran did not agree with the main thrust of Veblen's analysis is evident from still other accusations he made (pp. 88–89). For example, he thought that Veblen believed that "all forms of resource utilization that draw on the economic surplus or that lead to smaller output are necessarily irrational or wasteful" (p. 90). The inescapable consequences were an attack on culture, which Baran denounced in tones reminiscent of the Frankfurt School's critique of Veblen in 1941:

> Holding that would mean nothing less than viewing all of human culture as an involved and protracted process of waste and profligacy, nothing less than considering all the paintings, music, literature, architecture created in the course of millennia by the genius of mankind to be but a series of violations of the principle of productivity and frugality. Once more, what is decisive is not that an activity is supported out of economic surplus, that an activity detracts from the process of production, or even that an activity is rewarded in what might be considered an excessive way. What is decisive is the content of that activity, the nature of the performance to which it leads, the impact that its results have on the unfolding and enrichment of human potentialities. (P. 90)

Like Theodor Adorno, Baran failed to grasp Veblen's apparent view that not all cultural and aesthetic activity leads to waste and futility, only that which is invidious. Cultural and aesthetic values and processes that are noninvidiously meaningful, that is, not expressive of emulatory strain toward power and status are logically congruent with the Veblenian doctrinal system.

Baran's fundamental misunderstanding of Veblen's theory of status emulation makes much of his sermonizing on it seem unnecessary or irrelevant. However, Baran's misrepresentations of it are instructive:

> There is no more justification for considering all conspicuous consumption and luxury to be the inventions of the devil. For in the first place all consumption is, and always was, not merely (and not even primarily) private business but a social act. Being always in society, with society, and of society, consumption has always been conspicuous, that is, shown to many, observed by many, shared by many, deriving indeed a vast share of its pleasurability from being an aspect of the individual's social existence. What matters, in other words, is not the conspicuousness of consumption but its concrete contents, not that it takes place in society but the kind of society in which it takes place. . . . There surely would be nothing to deplore if people were habitually endeavoring to excel their neighbors in reason, knowledge, appreciation of arts and sciences, devotion to the commonweal, and solidarity in collective efforts! (P. 89)

At this point it is difficult to take Baran's criticisms of Veblen seriously because he had no real disagreement with him. He had mistakenly concluded that Veblen opposed all emulatory behavior regardless of its origins or consequence when, in fact, all he opposed was such behavior when it had invidious intent or result. "Invidious" means status-enhancing and, or course, in the Veblenian analysis this is determined primarily by price—the higher the price of the commodity, the more the status bequeathed to its purchaser. Thus not all imitative behavior is regarded by Veblen as invidious, as Baran mistakenly believed, only that which aimed at status enhancement by virtue of the display of ability to pay.

Baran's failure to adequately grasp Veblen's fundamental values is also evident in his accusatory rhetoric regarding the value of frugality and productivity.

> Since the question is always and inexorably: productivity for whom? frugality for what?—the call for productivity and frugality in socialist societies has a radically different meaning and plays an altogether different role than in the advanced capitalist countries where the development of productive resources has progressed so far that meaningful leisure could be substituted for a good part of currently enforced toil and that plenty could take the place of artificially maintained want. (P. 89)

Baran believed that Veblen saw frugality and productivity as ends in themselves rather than as the means to a better life based on cultural and aesthetic awareness and self-realization. It had not occurred to Baran that Veblen had ends in mind other than constant husbanding of resources and intensification of already frenetic work patterns. Baran believed Veblen did not understand the ideological role that the values of frugality and productivity have played, both in the primitive stages of capital accumulation and later in the development of capitalism. If he had understood it, Veblen might have seen that

> this glorification of both frugality and productivity constituted an ideology making a virtue of a necessity, a means of asserting the preponderance of a social class whose rise to affluence and power was inseparably bound up with austerity and hard work—at first of itself and its hired help, before too long of the hired help alone. (P. 87)

Perhaps unintentionally, then, Veblen's ideological function was that of maintaining cultural hegemony and upper-class domination. Baran seemed to have lost sight of Veblen's attack on absentee ownership, but like Adorno he believed that Veblen's objections to it were based on its wastefulness, not its exploitative character. Such is the doctrinal stock-in-trade of Marxists who see evidences of puritanism everywhere in American culture. Even Veblen, but particularly Veblen, is not exempt from such criticism.

Conclusion

While many Marxists conceded that Veblen was a keen student of emulatory processes, Baran believed that Veblen thought emulatory behavior was rooted in human nature. He complained that "he does not see that it has very little to do with biotic and psychic 'instincts' and with the 'basic' nature of man. It is clearly a product of an economic and social order which is rent by the irreconcilable conflict between accumulation of capital and its very apposite: consumption of goods and services" (p. 88).

Baran argued that Veblen was guilty of employing a faulty biological-psychological theory of instincts. Moreover, Veblen's theory of "institutions," in Baran's eyes, became a "slippery psychological notion" of "habit of thought," no more profound than Weber's "attitude of rationality and calculations" or Sombart's "spirit of capitalism." Baran alleged that Veblen relied too heavily on James's psychology in developing his theory of instincts, which he then treated as "permanent characteristics of the human race" (p. 86). Baran would have Veblen abandon his "psychological" theory in favor of a thoroughgoing historical and dialectical approach. Indeed, for all Veblen's talk of evolution, he was nonetheless "a stranger to the historical method, never truly committed to placing a thorough morphology of the historical process at the center of his analytical efforts" (p. 84). If, Baran suggested, Veblen had actually utilized a dialectical-historical mechanism, he might have illuminated the "far-reaching changes and transformations that set apart century from century" (p. 87). Had Veblen gone further "he would have transcended himself and taken the decisive step to materialism and dialectic" (p. 91).

Although Veblen's stages of history might have been ambiguous as well as conceptually inadequate, Baran told us little about them except that they were not Marxist. When his words are decoded he had simply stated that only Marxism provided adequate analysis of the transition from one historical epoch to another. Implicit in Baran's critique was the charge that if Veblen had utilized a dialectical approach to conspicuous consumption, he might have understood that the phenomenon was not entirely wasteful or the mere manifestation of useless display (p. 91). In brief, Veblen's method prevented him from grasping the dialectical processes at work that allowed a fuller understanding of the behavior he ridiculed.

Baran's strictures were rooted in his belief that Veblen did not subscribe to a rigorous or consistent materialist perspective. For other Marxists, and certainly for Baran, this implied that Veblen was guilty of eroding the ties between the mode and the means of production on the one hand and the ideological superstructure on the other hand. In Baran's eyes, the instincts of workmanship, idle curiosity, and parental bent were mere epiphenomena and Veblen's focus on them detracted from a more realistic appraisal of their origins and effects. He endowed his own system of value with absolute validity because he had not adequately examined the historical circumstances that gave rise to it. Had he done this, Baran believed that

> he could also have established that the pomp and circumstance of the feudal courts, the castles, fortifications, monuments, and palaces of worship erected at the behest of worldly and ecclesiastic potentates, far from constituting an expression of a mysteriously evolving "habit of thought," reflected the hard, stubborn demands of the economic and social systems rooted in slavery and serfdom. (P. 87)

Baran thus felt that Veblen's attacks on excess consumption and luxury were misdirected because

> what squandering, waste, and snobbery call for is not a proscription of consumption or a condemnation of luxury but an effort to ascertain and to estab-

lish conditions in which abundance will supersede both want and waste, in which on the basis of greatly transformed needs poverty will become a fossil of the past, and a measure of luxury will become attainable to all. (Pp. 90–91)

Baran thus charged that Veblen subscribed to the gospel of efficiency by endorsing an economy of constant economic quantities. This also carried over into his view of the role of government. Baran complained that

Veblen resembles an embittered shopkeeper irate about his burden of taxation and therefore decrying violently each and every kind of government spending. Yet there is good government spending and bad, there are outlays on hospitals and roads, and TVAs as well as expenditures on armaments, on imperialist intrigues, on the support of foreign and domestic parasites. Ranting against both types of government activity is tantamount to criticizing neither, just as attacking as waste all forms of consumption except the knife-and-fork variety destroys all possibility of exposing effectively the prevailing system of irrational and destructive employment of human and material resources.[42]

The irony of this statement is striking because in making it Baran sounded like the New Deal liberals he consistently attacked. Paradoxically, Veblen more closely resembled a doctrinaire Marxist defending the ruling-class theory of the state than the newly emergent "pluralist" Baran.[43] The latter ignored the fact that Veblen died in 1929 and had no opportunity to observe the changes in public sector expenditures that occurred during the 1930s. Veblen was thus faulted for not understanding the social impact of shifts in the quantity and composition of government spending that characterized the New Deal even though he was not alive to witness it.

ARTHUR DAVIS

Although Arthur Davis (b. 1916) was not a prominent American sociologist, his extensive writings on Veblen are of considerable interest and value. For there are important political similarities between his early interpretation of Veblen and that of Talcott Parsons in that both shared liberal ideological predilections that negatively influenced their view of our central figure.[44] Davis is also significant in this study because he is the only scholar whose views underwent a pronounced ideological shift from liberalism to radicalism while he was writing on Veblen.[45] Indeed, his last writings on Veblen were laudatory, although couched in cautious language on account of the authoritative nature of the entry he wrote for the *International Encyclopedia of the Social Sciences*.

It is interesting to note that when he largely abandoned liberalism and liberal attitudes toward Veblen, Davis's attitudes toward Marx and the Marxian tradition were simultaneously changing. More important, he was now to "acknowledge Veblen as a notable and original contributor to the Marxian tradition" whose work had a "Marxian character and source."[46] It is significant that Davis found little of theoretical importance in the American radical tradition and had to, instead, fasten the Marxian label, however loosely, on Veblen in order to reassure himself that the latter was doctrinally sound.[47] Indeed, Davis would have been more impressed by Veblen were the latter's work not flawed by American ideological contaminants such as populism and utopian socialism of the Bellamyite variety.

The transition in Davis's thought, however, involved more than rejecting the static frame of reference at the time characteristic of conventional academic sociological theory. There also was a strong shift in the ideological structure of his thought—a transition to a doctrinal position on the left hastened by the influence of Marxists such as Paul Sweezy and journals like *Monthly Review*.[48] By 1957, issues involving imperialism, capitalism, war, peace, and racism were approached from the perspective of a militant socialist rather than viewed from the armchair of the conventional academic liberal theoretician. Nevertheless, in spite of his newfound admiration for Veblen, Davis complained of "Veblen's lack of systematic economic analysis, his underestimation of the role of the state, his backhanded terminology, and the obscurantist influence of anarchism and populism upon his thought."[49] Apparently, Davis's Parsons-inspired early criticism of Veblen had eroded and its place was taken by radical critique. By the mid-1950s, Davis found himself able to write that

> in the works of Thorstein Veblen are many of the best etchings of the American social landscape that we possess. . . . With the passing of time he looms ever larger as one of the handful of really great minds of the modern world. He is surely the most original and prophetic figure in American academic circles: history may yet judge that he is the greatest social thinker this country has so far produced.[50]

These words are reminiscent of C. Wright Mills, who also believed that Veblen was the best critic of the United States that it has so far produced, and they indicate a fundamental change in Davis's attitudes toward Veblen.

Order and Authority

However, Davis's early criticisms of Veblen were rooted in a Parsonian model of the social order, with emphasis on an action theory of human behavior. The bias of this doctrinal stance was particularly evident in Davis's criticisms of Veblen for his failure to articulate an adequate theory of social order. Davis expressed this criticism in several ways: "Existing institutions appeared to Veblen as obstacles to Utopia. . . . A society without institutions such as Veblen sometimes leans toward, is a contradiction in terms. . . . Social life without organized institutions is tacitly assumed to be not only possible but ideal.[51] These criticisms of Veblen's attitude toward the problem of social order closely parallel Talcott Parsons's critique of both Veblen and C. Wright Mills which is not surprising since Davis wrote his doctoral dissertation under Parsons and shared most of his theoretical and ideological biases at this point in his career. Indeed, Davis succinctly summarized his and Parsons's case against Veblen when he commented that "Veblen theory is highly consistent, but its main failing is the lack of an adequate concept of institutions. His explicit scheme leaves unsolved the problem of order."[52] Davis consistently found what he thought was a "latent strain of naive philosophical anarchism in Veblen's thought"[53] that was rooted in his belief that contemporary technology and science are incompatible with all existing institutions. He put it this way:

> The three benevolent Veblenian instincts which would emerge as the decisive elements in action after the demise of current predatory institutions are wholly inadequate as substitute institutional structures despite their implicit normative content. The problem of order in Veblen's future machine age therefore becomes exceedingly acute. On the institutionalization or integration of value patterns depends the very possibility of social order, organization, and stability. A society without institutions is inconceivable.[54]

Davis thus claimed that idle curiosity, proficiency of workmanship, and the parental bent, Veblen's three "instincts," "cannot begin to solve the inevitable and omnipresent problems of authority, property patterns, distributive standards, and punishment—reward patterns."[55] Yet Davis failed to explain how any viable social order could exist for long without those value traits so esteemed by Veblen.

He complained that Veblen did not understand the need for or the methods by which fundamental social and cultural values were inculcated in the underlying population by basic socialization processes. Because he was so committed to the "generic ends of life," which emphasize "peaceful solidarity" and "maximum production," he could only view contemporary institutions as causing wasteful and predatory behavior. Apparently, at this point in his career, Davis believed that respect for authority, subservience to the existing social order, and an uncritical loyalty to the status quo must take priority over Veblen's normative goals. Davis was correct that Veblen failed to solve the problem of social order, but then its conventional resolution was of no particular concern to him.[56]

However, understanding the legitimization of social order and institutionalization of authority was a focus of Parsonian structural-functionalism as well as of Veblenian institutionalism. Even in Davis's later radical writings on Veblen, there was a focus on both processes. To illustrate, he wrote that

> workmanship may produce goods; and the parental bent, good will. But how are goods to be distributed? How are new members of society to be trained? How are rights and duties to be formulated and enforced? How adjust to change? To rule-breakers? How are leaders to be chosen and trained? It is not that Veblen merely neglected to answer such questions: the point is that his theoretical system leaves no place for them at all.[57]

Davis believed that Veblen's views were ultimately rooted in his account of cultural evolution, starting with a primitive stage of savagery that he would have liked to restore.[58] Unfortunately, this caused him to give no heed

> to such problems as allocation, the criteria of distribution, the organization of power. In short, his projected state of technological abundance had no provision for such indispensable institutions as property and authority. They are phenomena of culture lag, which would not exist in a society governed by the sense of workmanship.[59]

Davis also criticized Veblen's failure to deal with the problem of social order and morality. As he put it:

> So broad a concept as the parental bent could never be an instinct. Its unadulterated altruism in part expresses Veblen's personal rejection of the highly competitive and self-interested values of contemporary society. Its formlessness springs from Veblen's lack of an adequate concept of a social system. Solidarity in the real world is not uniformly omnipresent but channelized in specific relationships—in patterns of moral obligation (rights and duties) which vary in content and extent in time and place.[60]

Veblen was thus criticized for his lack of specificity, which overlooks the fact that, in a generic evolutionary schema of the kind he constructed, specificity is not essential; indeed, it may even thwart a better understanding of the development of more adequate ideal-types, or "type forms" as Veblen called them.

Status Emulation and Emulatory Consumption

Davis was critical of the best-known of Veblen's theoretical contributions, namely, his theory of status emulation. Interestingly, he believed that "in emphasizing competitive emulation, Veblen was universalizing a characteristic of modern American society by reading it back into antiquity. To the sociologist, history is a number of different social systems, more or less or not at all interrelated, depending on the particular case."[61] Veblen's history and his prehistory was thus infected with his view of the contemporary United States. He saw the past through lens encrusted with the American present and, as a consequence, this past was permeated with emulatory consumption and invidious distinctions.

Another related weakness Davis found was Veblen's "exclusive concern with the invidious effect of contemporary life [which] entirely overlooks the cohesive function of consumption habits in expressing the basic values of the group."[62] But the "cohesive function of consumption habits in expressing the basic values of the group" may be just as destructive of the generic ends of life as those coercively imposed from the top down. Davis's comments were of little value in helping determine whether the basic values of the group are authentically expressed or simply represent manipulated consensus.

It is also the case that the moral agnosticism characteristic of Davis's early liberal work on Veblen provided no standards by which to measure the proper development of the social order. Even in his later writings, Davis complained that "Veblen is one-sided about consumption motives. His streak of Tolstoyan austerity probably reflects his populist idealization of the countryman. But a neatly cropped lawn, for instance, is not necessarily wasteful; it can express a positive value as well as an invidious one."[63] However, Veblen carefully qualified his attack on emulatory consumption by pointing to *both* the emulatory and the functional, that is, utilitarian role of most commodities.

Davis gave a different stress to status emulation than most Veblen scholars who emphasize conspicuous consumption because, instead, he stressed conspicuous waste and conspicuous exemption from useful labor. As he put it:

> Leisure activities tended to divert time and resources from production, hence they ran counter to Veblen's idea of social welfare. He cited many examples: sports, war, religion, the study of Latin, gambling, idle wives,

servants, government, anything above a fairly austere level of living. Such phenomena he presented as archaic survivals of earlier predatory traits.[64]

Perhaps Davis gave stress to this aspect of Veblen's thought because he rightly saw that it is as important to system maintenance as the more socially visible kinds of emulatory consumption, particularly in more traditional societies that have not yet reached the stage of mass production and consumption. In his early writing on Veblen, Davis also stressed the cultural lag aspect of Veblen's theory, which he believed weakened it. This was particularly true of *The Theory of the Leisure Class*:

> His analysis is vitiated by the fact [that] he saw only the invidious aspect of the conspicuous consumption pattern and not its positive side. It is further weakened by his view that this pattern is an archaic survival, a culture-lag phenomenon long since obsolete from the standpoint of the sense of workmanship and technological efficiency.[65]

Davis again failed to note Veblen's view that many goods and services serve both an invidious and noninvidious role, that is, have both a functional or utilitarian significance as well as an emulatory one. Davis then went to considerable lengths to find merit in emulatory behavior.

> But his definition of conspicuous activity as waste is highly arbitrary. All activity that did not contribute directly to the production of material goods, all expenditure incurred on invidious grounds—Veblen styled wasteful. The test is whether the expenditure contributes to the "generically human ends of life." Exactly what these ends are Veblen nowhere specifies. . . . The unmistakable drift of his writings suggests that he considered all consumption notably above the level of subsistence as wasteful—a notion which scarcely comports with his ideal of technological abundance. Even his critical view of conspicuous display as a mere invidious competition for esteem may be questioned; surely the esteem of one's fellows is a "generically human end of life."[66]

Davis was still in his "liberal" stage when he wrote these lines in 1944, as the last sentence in the quotation makes abundantly clear. Nevertheless, he raised important questions about which values are most generically human and why this is so. Mostly, Veblen assumed that the prime values of life are critical intelligence, proficiency of workmanship, and altruism. But Davis was insistent on knowing why these ends of life are more important, for example, than the desire for esteem, even if it is achieved through invidious competition and conspicuous display. The issue may admit to no easy resolution, but in

Veblen's view humanity must be seen as something other than atom-ized globules of desire, each trying to maximize their own utility.

Interestingly, Davis also criticized Veblen's theory of status emula-tion in an attempt to discredit Veblen's satire on women's dress

> This "wasteful" aspect is most clearly shown in women's dress, according to Veblen. The skirt and the high heel sharply underline the nonproductive role of women, whose chief function is to symbolize the pecuniary status of their husbands. Here again Veblen gives a one-sided picture of women's roles in our society. Differentiations in dress are primarily reflections of the segregation of sex roles in our society. Likewise, the rapid change in women's fashions is due more to the institutionalized definition of women's roles than to the seesaw struggle between the sense of workmanship and the norm of conspicuous waste which Veblen collaborates.[67]

Once again the theoretical influence of Parsonian structural-function-alism was evident in Davis's belief that even women's dress is system-sustaining; all social processes have a purpose or they would not ex-ist. Apparently, it does not matter if emulatory behavior and invidious distinction adversely affect the well-being of the community.

Cultural Lag and Economic Self-Interest

In his last writings on Veblen, Davis commented that "Veblen made less of vested interest and more of culture lag in explaining contempo-rary institutions."[68] Davis believed this was unfortunate in that Veblen mistook economic self-interest in the form of exploitative and preda-tory behavior for archaic survivals. Davis believed that

> Veblen clearly perceives the discrepancy between yesterday's theory and today's practice. But he one-sidedly attributes it to "culture lag." This throws the emphasis on inertia, ignorance and habit, at the cost of underestimating conscious exploitation of society by Big Business. Veblen isn't wrong, of course—only incomplete. His stress on culture lag neatly supplements the overemphasis common among Marxists on conscious exploitation.[69]

The theoretical consequence of Veblen's position was that "the con-cept of culture lag may give undue weight to factors of ignorance and drift, at the expense of vested interest rationality."[70] Davis be-lieved Veblen was so preoccupied with cultural lag that he failed to de-velop an adequate conception of the imperialist state.[71] He did not sufficiently recognize that social customs "survive not only because of inertia and culture lag but also because certain groups profit from their survival."[72] It is interesting to note that in his later writings on Veblen,

Davis criticized Veblen's use of the cultural lag concept for its evasion of the realities of class interest and class conflict. Yet in his early Parsonian period, he attacked it for not leading Veblen to the truths of structural-functionalism! He commented that:

> sociology considers a social phenomena not as survivals but as elements having definite functions, manifest or latent, in a social system. Survival as used by Veblen implies cultural lag—a conception which hinders more than it helps, because it obviates further analysis. The current sociological significance of social phenomena cannot often be explained by the study of their origins. Veblen's "genetic" method offers neither an adequate functional analysis nor a proof of causality. Indeed, it prevented him from seeing a social system as a functioning whole.[73]

The societal apologetics of Parsonian structural-functionalism are nowhere more evident than in Davis's insistence that "survivals" be accepted because they perform latent or manifest functions. The moral agnosticism of liberalism is also apparent in Davis's vacillation and, at times, refusal to judge whether the functions are positive or negative and can be contrasted with Veblen's emphasis on whether or not the generic ends of the community are being served. To Veblen, "survivals" were ceremonial in nature when they are destructive of the life process impersonally considered. To the Parsonian Davis, who lacked criteria by which to evaluate institutional growth and development, survivals, whether their functions be manifest or latent, were seen as equilibrating processes in the social system, and that ends the inquiry. Davis's interest in further investigation of the processes is, of course, a later story and is connected with his political radicalization.

In certain respects, Veblen's cultural lag concept was utilized more intensively in his study *Imperial Germany and the Industrial Revolution* than elsewhere in his work. But this was not what attracted Davis's attention in his early writing on Veblen. Instead, once again showing the influence of Parsonian structural-functionalism, he stressed the role of value consensus and shared attitudes among commoners as the bulwark of support for the Hohenzollern regime; and it was this aspect of Veblen's analysis of Imperial Germany that impressed him. Davis wrote that "he took pains to emphasize the underlying meanings which the humans attached to their authoritarian behavior. He demonstrated the impossibility of making pure coercion as the essential cohesive factor in German social organization."[74] But if coercion was not important in coagulating the social and political fabric of the German community, what was its effective bonding agent? Davis answered that

Veblen argued that coercion is not the mainspring of the Dynastic State, as an American observer might assume. Instead, its intense patriotism is part of a common value pattern furnishing positive cohesion to the German state. Such coercion as exists is a symptom thereof rather than the essence. Unlike many political scientists of his day, Veblen looked beneath the external forms of government structures.[75]

Davis's early writings on Veblen thus manifested the influence of Parsonian structural-functionalism to such an extent that Veblen drew praise from Davis primarily when his analysis converged with it. However, Davis never quite laid his own ideological cards on the table. He came tantalizingly close to articulating the Parsonian theory as his frame of reference without explicitly endorsing it.[76] For example, he commented on "the lack of recognition of the absence in Veblen of a comprehensive conception of a functioning social system. The last is the basic weakness, shared by many institutionalists."[77] To this complaint against the institutionalists Davis added that

> the last-mentioned type of category, having social referents, permitted further analysis. An adequate theory of change in social science must be stated primarily in terms of analytical social elements. Where, as in Veblen's case, the use of nonsocial and particularly normative elements have implicitly crept into such concepts as instinct and habit.[78]

On several occasions, Davis argued that Veblen's "evolutionary view of history, with its corollary of culture lag and his vein of Utopian anarchism . . . prevented any consideration of a social system as a functioning whole."[79] But what is meant by the claim that Veblen was not able to explain the social system as a functioning whole? First, Davis meant that the fulfillment of Veblen's radical political vision could not be achieved within the framework of the existing social order. He claimed that Veblen believed that

> contemporary institutions were not competent media for conveying socialist attitudes. Actually, both the vagueness of the socialists and Veblen's own indefiniteness are due mainly to the negative character of their own sociological orientations. No specific institutional substitutes were offered because neither Veblen nor the socialists realized the necessity for such a program. In brief, they had only an incomplete idea of a functioning social system and its component elements.[80]

In short, Veblen's political hopes for the system were incompatible with a scientific (read Parsonian) understanding of it. Also, Davis believed his radical empiricism and his Darwinian bias made it impossible to develop his insights on a theoretical level.[81] Veblen's empiricism "accounts for the baffling vagueness" in his work[82] and the Darwinian elements sow confusion and inconsistency.

Related to these problems was Veblen's critical-genetic method, which Davis claimed could not adequately explain causation.

> Temporal sequence established nothing about causality. Veblen's genetic method can produce only a descriptive history of socio-economic developments. Indeed, by focusing on an indiscriminate succession of concrete events, and by tending to overemphasize the causal role of one or a few elements, geneticism hinders the analytical consideration of a social system as a functioning whole.[83]

Of course, the opposite deficiency is often found in Parsonian theory where pluralistic conceptions of causation make causal factors and processes so diffuse and scattered that the main agents of social change cannot be identified.

Yet structural-functional models, since they focus on social stasis or equilibrium as a "normal" state of affairs, see an adaptive or integrative role for every social structure and process. The "objective" social scientist can make no statement of moral or evaluative preferences between them. For this reason Davis also found Veblen's attitudes toward religion to be inadequate. He wrote that

> Veblen implied that scientific knowledge, through the occupational discipline of industry, is increasingly becoming man's sole orientation to his situation—nonscientific sources of orientation such as religion being the result of ignorance or error. This untenable view is to some extent characteristic of evolutionary and positivistic social thought.[84]

The clear implication of Davis's own position is that it is "unscientific" to make judgments regarding the validity of religious beliefs, thus providing evidence once more of the epistemological underpinning of his brand of liberalism.

Science, Ethics, and Objectivity

Like many liberals, Davis, in his early work on Veblen, claimed that "criticism of his scientific work should not obscure the value of his ethical insight."[85] But when his work on Veblen prior to 1957 is probed to find the nature of these ethical insights, they evaporate and what takes their place is a barrage of criticism. In the main Davis found Veblen guilty of confusing social science and social ethics. As he put it, "Veblen was justified in feeling that science and ethics should draw closer together. His mode of relating them was wrong, for he mixed the two categories indiscriminately."[86] And yet, Davis admired Veblen's work on Imperial Germany despite the latter's misconceptions regarding objectivity in the social studies. Davis commented that

> his best work, such as that on Germany and the stabilizing of peace, represents a preliminary attempt at co-operation between social science and policy. The answer to his shortcomings is not the relapse of science into academic isolation and esoteric specialization. Scientific objectivity, specialized analytical development, knowledge for its own sake—these are still as indispensable as ever. Yet they must make their contribution to the necessary ethical awakening, to social reorganization, and to the universal view.[87]

These are interesting comments for a liberal social scientist to make in the 1940s and 1950s because they do not indicate an epistemological commitment to the value neutrality then in vogue, but rather a social activist conception of praxis. This may be the intellectual bridge that led to fundamental shifts in Davis's attitude toward Veblen and to Davis's radicalization by the mid-1950s.

Whatever the case, Davis perceptively wrote that "no discussion of his thought can avoid the problem of the relationship between social science and social ethics, for his ideas are a blend of those two categories."[88] The important role of the normative element was thus becoming more fully recognized in part because of Veblen's focus on it.[89] The attitude of Davis toward other facets of Veblen's values was more characteristically liberal, however, for he objected to the use of technological criteria to measure social welfare. He wrote,

> Contrary to his belief, maximizing social welfare, which meant for him the highest possible output of physical goods, is not solely or even largely a technological problem. . . . His emphasis on technological abundance as the criterion of welfare ignores elements crucially important to every functioning social system.[90]

Unfortunately, however, these comments were not accompanied by development of a more detailed critique of Veblen's alleged technological theory of value or of alternatives to it. Veblen's theory of value is only technological at one level of analysis, and that is where instrumental rationality or means-ends congruence dominates. Veblen had other more substantive values that lay beyond mere instrumental rationality, including idle curiosity, proficiency of workmanship, and altruism. Unfortunately, many Veblen scholars, including so important a sociologist as Karl Mannheim, did not adequately recognize this and accused Veblen of confusing substantive and instrumental rationality.[91] Some of this was Veblen's fault, because his criticisms of capitalism implied that no criteria except avoidance of waste matters. But it was the American business community that proclaimed its own efficiency, and Veblen was simply showing that it did not adequately fulfill this cherished American value.

Davis was sensitive to Veblen's endorsement of idle curiosity and recognized that it was expressive of a large element in Veblen's own moral perspective that valued learning and science.[92] Davis critically commented, however, that in spite of Veblen's praise of objectivity in science "his own practice, in his study of the leisure class, was so one-sided that it became almost an exposé, though not without significant scientific contributions."[93] This comment, written early in Davis's career, betrayed the influence of scientism on liberal sociologists, causing them to exaggerate the degree to which the social sciences require value-neutrality. Or, put another way, Davis did not adequately appreciate the manner in which social inquiry is inescapably value-laden.

Imperialism

As Davis turned left politically in the 1950s, he began to see more validity in Marxist and Marxist-Leninist ideas regarding capitalism, imperialism, and military conflict. He began to use these ideas as measuring rods in his evaluation of Veblen's work on the same topics and, not surprisingly, Veblen was found wanting. Now, however, instead of attacking Veblen from the perspective of structural-functionalism, he adopted a dialectical perspective.

> Little or nothing does Veblen say about the actual struggles of various groups for greater social and economic security, or about the concrete impact of science, urbanization, and industrialization upon religion and the family and particular occupations. This is perhaps the greatest flaw in his work, and the most important difference between Veblen and the Marxians. The latter make it their central concern to show specifically how actual interests and pressures inherently impel certain elements of capitalist societies to range themselves increasingly against capitalism. Veblen's failure to come up with anything better than "contagious magic" as an explanation of the decline of capitalism seems primarily due to his overemphasis on culture lag, and to the utopian vein in his thinking which allowed him to oversimplify his social analysis.[94]

Once again, Veblen was perceived as a cultural lag theorist by a radical critic who believed that he was not able to adequately link superstructural phenomena with the economic foundation because of his failure to understand and use dialectics. This was apparently what Davis meant when he approvingly quoted Paul Sweezy to the effect that "Veblen consistently underestimates the importance of war and imperialism in providing outlets for surplus capital."[95]

Praxis

In his liberal stage, Davis paid little heed to Veblen's detachment and aloofness from overt political activism. As he turned further to the left, he became more interested in Veblen's lack of involvement in political affairs. Indeed, in his last writing on him, he commented that

> Veblen took no direct part in any social movement. Although basically criti-
> cal of modern capitalist institutions and culture, he claimed to be a detached
> observer, above the battle. His ironic wit did not spare his friends; if he did
> not chastise them as much as he did his foes, he did so enough to support
> plausibly his claim to objectivity.[96]

But worse than Veblen's own personal noninvolvement was his elitist view of how change was to occur.

> Revolutionary change is to come about more or less by fiat from above as a
> result of educational enlightenment, sparked by elements of the upper
> class—the professions. True, the educational appeal is to be directed at the
> underlying population instead of to the ruling class, as was the case with
> most of the earlier utopians. But for active revolutionary leadership Veblen
> looks to a lesser segment of the privileged elite.[97]

Once Davis was radicalized, he also criticized Veblen for failing to accurately locate agents of revolutionary social change. Apparently, Davis accepted Marxist premises regarding the political potential of the working class, or at least was convinced that broad-scale progressive social forces could be harnessed to overturn the existing social order. For these reasons he commented negatively on Veblen's thesis in *The Engineers and the Price System*:

> Our chief criticism of this scheme is its utopian character. Ruling classes
> rarely step down on request. Nor are engineers as a group very revolutionary.
> In a capitalist economy, they are subject to the decisions of capitalists on all
> matters of basic economic policy. And being rewarded socially and economi-
> cally, considerably above the average occupational group, they are in general
> to be ranked with the privileged elite. Veblen's "soviet of technicians" must
> be classified as a modern version of utopian socialism, to be enacted from
> above by fiat, and relying for its acceptance on its appeal to reason. His kin-
> ship here is not with Marx, but with pre-Marxian socialism.[98]

Davis overlooked the fact that Veblen suggested, perhaps satirically, that a massive strike might be necessary to change the system. This hardly constitutes a polite request to the ruling class to step down.

In his earlier writing, Davis found Veblen's detachment from political activism to be a normal mode of behavior for academics not worthy
of more than casual mention. In his later radical phase, it became a

source of indictment, for Davis claimed that, unfortunately, Veblen (1) limited his political action to his writings and lectures instead of engaging in overt political action; (2) held elitist rather than egalitarian views of the likely sources of radical social change. He inaccurately identified engineers and technicians as possessing radical political potential, thus ignoring the revolutionary mission of the working class as a progressive social force.

Conclusion

It is doctrinally significant that social scientists select one of Veblen's books as better, or more important than the others. To illustrate this point, in his dissertation, Davis nominated *Imperial Germany and the Industrial Revolution* and *The Nature of Peace* as Veblen's best, meaning most lastingly insightful. Later he concluded that this judgment was wrong and named *Absentee Ownership* and *Essays in Our Changing Order* as more important because they were "pregnant with insights into the terminal disease of the United States of America. The name of the disease? Dementia Praecox."[99] This mental state is definable as "precocious insanity" and Davis is here making reference to the mind-set that Veblen suggested had taken hold of the underlying population at the end of the Great War. But why the shift in judgment on Davis's part? Perhaps it was due to the less inflammatory nature of the studies of Germany and international politics and the more polemical and radical tone of *Absentee Ownership*—a tone more in keeping with Davis's own increasingly strident denunciation of American capitalism by the 1950s. *Imperial Germany* and *The Nature of Peace* have a detachment about them that is somewhat more congruent with a liberal view of the world, but *Absentee Ownership* is more in accord with a structural critique of corporate America. It is not surprising that as Davis moved further to the left politically, he would find more of value in the latter than in the former.

In his radical phase, Davis believed that Veblen, while basically close to the Marxian tradition, was infected with "bourgeois pessimism—which had been manifest in Western literature for many decades."[100] This was also apparent in his careerist ambitions and the ideological mind-set this characteristically induces in American academic liberals. As Davis put it:

> Scepticism also represents Veblen's bourgeois aspirations, his keen interest in an academic career. American professors are ordinarily expected to be committed to capitalism, but occasionally one may get by with a sceptical lack of commitment to *any* order, since this doesn't directly challenge the

powers that be. Scepticism therefore tends to become, among liberals, as rigorous a dogma as any capitalist or socialist commitments by other factions. Hence Veblen duly criticized both capitalism and socialism.[101]

Davis failed to point out, however, that Veblen was far more critical of capitalism in both theory and practice than he was of socialism. Most of Veblen's social theory, as well as his social criticism, had a doctrinal structure and political thrust that cannot be explained away by professional opportunism or careerist expediency. In certain respects, Veblen's ability to raise important questions in the right way and his partial successes as a prophet and seer greatly impressed Davis. But even this praise was qualified by him in his liberal phase, as in his comments that "in his posing of challenging issues lies most of his claim to greatness, for his answers to those problems were often untenable."[102] Yet, in his radical phase, Davis was so impressed by Veblen that in 1957 he wrote that "Among modern academic Western economists, only Keynes rated comparison with Veblen. In technical analysis, Keynes, a many-sided genius in his own right, is incomparably the greater. But in general insights concerning broad *social* realities, Veblen's superiority is beyond doubt."[103]

In characteristic liberal fashion, Davis was unable, at first, to concede the validity of Veblen's insights regarding broad social realities. Indeed, it was only when he turned left politically that the Veblenian system offered analytic and conceptual insights that converged with his newfound Marxism à la *Monthly Review*. Davis's work on Veblen can only be properly understood when the change in his own philosophy is taken into consideration.[104]

Chapter Eleven

RADICAL CRITICS: MARXISM,
TROTSKYISM, AND SOCIAL DEMOCRACY

B Y THE mid-1950s, there were only three principal clusters of independent left intellectuals remaining in the United States. One was an amorphous group headed by Bernhard Stern, who wrote for *Science and Society*. Another were the already-mentioned Marxists who wrote for *Monthly Review*, while a third were the anti-Stalinist democratic socialists gathered around the New York-based journal *Dissent*, which was started in 1954. The latter included such figures as Irving Howe, Lewis Coser, and a professor of sociology at the New School for Social Research, Bernard Rosenberg. In addition to these three clusters of radical intellectuals, there were remnants of Trotskyism, which once had as its theoretical organ *The New International*. For a time this journal carried the writings of John Wright, who proved to be an intransigent critic of Veblen.

Founded in 1936, *Science and Society* was a scholarly journal of Marxist orientation without partisan political affiliation or party attachment. Edited during much of its existence by Bernhard Stern, it occasionally featured analyses of Veblen and institutional economics by radical social scientists. The two most important of these critiques appeared in 1938 and 1957, and the authors were Addison T. Cutler of Fisk University in Nashville, Tennessee, and Randolph H. Landsman of New York City, respectively.[1] Both authors used Marx as a yardstick by which to evaluate Veblen and institutional economics. It is also interesting to note that although the two pieces were written almost twenty years apart, Landsman was significantly more doctrinaire than his predecessor Cutler in his use of Marxism.

Addison Cutler was a student of Clarence Ayres at Amherst in the early 1920s. Although he was further to the left politically than Ayres, his radicalism in the late 1930s reflected the intellectual training he received at Amherst from Ayres and Walton H. Hamilton, the other institutional economist who taught there. After reading Cutler's article on institutional economics in *Science and Society*, Ayres wrote to his former student. He did not agree with what Cutler had written on Veblen and institutionalism, but felt they were within "hailing distance" of each other anyway. Some of their differences had to do with Veblen's

treatment of the received economic doctrines. Cutler believed that
Veblen's attack on classical and neoclassical economics was indiscriminate. As he put it,

> He lumped the classical writers with the neo-classical, assailed them both
> for unreal assumptions and their "animistic" bent, and in so doing failed to
> recognize the progressive features of the classicists. The significance of the
> fact that Adam Smith and David Ricardo had directed their theories toward
> the unleashing of the productive forces of their time, thus representing the
> progressive tendencies of capitalism on the upgrade was lost to Veblen. Far
> from considering neo-classicism a regression, Veblen appeared to consider it
> a slight, but unsatisfactory, advance as compared with classical political
> economy.[2]

However, in his letter to Cutler, Ayres attempted to rebut this interpretation of Veblen by arguing that

> while it is true that Adam Smith and David Ricardo were not such dogma-
> tists as Mill, Jevons, or Marshall but were engaged in active vigorous revolt,
> it may still be true that the ideology employed by them in that revolt—how-
> ever effective it may have been as a literature of revolt—was nevertheless
> metaphysical and teleological; and in that case the predicament of later
> economists is that of men who went on spreading war propaganda after the
> war was over. As I understand it, Veblen is not disparaging [the classicists]
> but he is pointing out that the system of ideas elaborated by those men for
> those purposes contains a lot of hum-bug, and that the same hum-bug has
> been in circulation ever since.[3]

Ultimately, however, what separated the two men was not their disagreement over Veblen's competence as a critic of the received economic doctrines. Rather, it was over Marx and Marxism, both as to its
efficacy as socioeconomic theory and its political significance. The positive and important idea that Ayres believed defined the institutionalist
perspective was

> Veblen's principles of analysis of the present economic order and the whole
> process of its development in terms of technology and institutions. Of
> course, this represents a pretty fundamental difference with an adherent of
> Marxian mythology of the class struggle. But both positions are equidistant
> from capitalism and both sets of principles represent an attempt to deal with
> the same problem: that is, how can the present economic order and its devel-
> opment be considered when capitalism and classical economic theory are
> wholly dispensed with. To my mind the real tragedy of institutionalism is the
> little that has been done to realize the prodigious possibilities inherent in its
> basic idea.[4]

However, Cutler could not accept Ayres's denigration of the class basis of Marxian analysis. On 6 January 1939, he responded to his former professor's letter, commenting sardonically, "Your passing reference to the 'Marxian mythology of the class struggle' seems to me a bit of *Petitio Principis*. . . . Anyway I think the class struggle is a lot more than mythology."[5]

The most significant of Cutler's other comments was that Veblen's "interest in finding likenesses between different historical cultures led to a reading back of capitalist contradictions into precapitalist forms."[6] Although Cutler believed this a weakness in the Veblen analysis, it is arguable, instead, that it provides a useful analytical tool for the evaluation of economic development in economic systems in earlier stages of growth. Leonard Dente, in particular, showed the value of the Veblenian dichotomy in identifying waste and predation in the developing countries, while Ayres used Veblen's theory of cultural lag in explaining why technological potential is or is not exploitable in various cultural and institutional settings.[7]

Class Structure, Consciousness, and Conflict

While occasionally applauding Veblen's class analysis, Marxists nevertheless found serious deficiencies in his work on class structure, conflict, and consciousness. As Cutler put it, "Veblen's theory foundered because of faulty class analysis."[8] Marxists also charged Veblen with misunderstanding the composition of classes in America. They believed that he sloughed off serious class cleavages by lumping together classes with opposed economic interests, was vague when contrasting the "vested interests" with the "common man," and naive in making unwarranted assumptions of an existing harmony of class interests. Although less extreme, these accusations were not very different from the Marxist indictment of liberalism. They were, in fact, indicative of the tendency of Marxist commentators to portray Veblen as an exponent of advanced bourgeois liberal ideology.

While sometimes appreciative of his theoretical efforts to link false consciousness with status emulation, Marxists were also generally critical of Veblen's explanation of class consciousness, especially his failure to identify those classes most likely to foster opposition to upperclass domination. This was directly related to the Marxist tendency to fault Veblen for his pessimism in failing to recognize the political possibilities of a working-class breakthrough to socialism. They believed that he devoted most of his attention to superstructural aspects of society and failed consistently to analyze the underlying dynamic forces of social development. His critics conceded that Veblen's concept of "vested interests" has some value for superstructural analysis, but . . . he does not adequately distinguish between major and minor interests and their relative importance, nor does he recognize the concept's limitations in terms of the more general and decisive class interests and class struggle.[9]

Cutler believed Veblen reached the point of considering how the forces of production would break down restrictive property relations. But, here again, Veblen's theory foundered because of faulty class analysis. In the transition to socialism, he envisioned the engineers in the vanguard. Supporting the engineers would be the skilled workers, for Veblen ignored the unskilled workers. In fact, Cutler claimed that in *The Theory of Business Enterprise*, Veblen aligned the unskilled workers and the farmers on the side of bankers and business promoters. This allegation distorted Veblen's analysis, for what he argued was that the machine process made radicals out of workers; the kind of occupational skill, if any, mattered little. However, in Cutler's eyes such a coalition at best was a confusion of the temporary ideological backwardness of workers and farmers with their basic class interests. At worst it was unacknowledged support of fascism.[10]

According to radical V. J. McGill, who also wrote for *Science and Society*, Veblen could envisage the economy under the control of engineers, but he found pecuniary traits too deeply embedded in the mass psyche to permit any such outcome in the near future. In short, because Veblen "underestimated" the power of trade unions and other forces opposed to corporate control, he concluded that business domination would compel conformity in the underlying population even though per capita income was declining.[11] Radicals like McGill and Cutler paid little heed to Veblen's claim that unions, especially craft unions, had been co-opted by business into the national power system and were themselves a vested interest.

RANDOLPH LANDSMAN AS CRITIC

Also typical of the critical Marxist approach to Veblen's methodology was that of Randolph Landsman. Landsman focused on Veblen's "psychology," which "stands out as the bulwark of current philosophical attacks on Marxian socialism."[12] The coupling of Darwinian biology with behaviorism might be expected of a machine-age instrumentalist. Veblen's method was thus faulted, as it ignored "the psychology inherent in the materialism of Marx, the relation between class and habit, between class and thinking, between class and memory, all on the materialist basis."[13] Further, Veblen's psychology lacked viable historical roots,[14] for his own purview was the "age of the machine, the age of business and industry under capitalism."[15] Landsman charged that Veblen "never introduces the historical fact of the rise of capitalism out of feudalism, nor the kind of thinking appearing, historically, in this social continuum."[16]

Of course, Landsman assumed that Marx provided the only valid way to describe the transition from feudalism to capitalism; he also failed to recognize the possibility that capitalism incorporates more of the traits of the feudal order than Marx imagined it did. Indeed, the existence of such atavistic continuities between feudal and capitalist epochs was a main theme in Veblen's economic history.

Put simply, Veblen, as perceived by Landsman, was a behaviorist and pragmatist who did not envisage the possibility of new modes of thought, such as would develop in different historical epochs. Veblen belonged essentially to the nineteenth century and had arrived at an arrested stage of development. His method was neither feudal nor socialist; it, concluded Landsman, stood for liberalism and a modified capitalism, a conclusion that recalls the words of Trotskyite John G. Wright, written twenty-five years earlier. However, in view of Veblen's desire to abolish absentee ownership, his polemical attacks on the nature of the capitalist state, and his criticisms of incremental reform, it would be difficult to substantiate the claims of Wright's and Landsman's commentary.

Veblen did not think the ideological unification of the proletariat was historically inevitable or, later in his career, even likely. Instead, he strongly emphasized the importance of prestige and status influences that divided classes and weakened their ability to engage in anticapitalist politics. Thus Veblen concluded that the working class is exploited, but is still not revolutionary or radical because it is manipulated and propagandized by the ruling class and is unable to escape the false consciousness of bourgeois culture. However, his Marxist critics claimed that this position failed to identify serious oppositional efforts and tendencies within the working class. Hoodwinked, brainwashed, and bribed the proletariat may be, but parts of it still manifest a socialist consciousness that enable it to engage in anticapitalist actions.

Landsman believed that Veblen and his contemporary John Dewey are transition figures who function ideologically and politically "in behalf of a liberal or liberalist philosophy, most suitable to a 'modified capitalism.'"[17]

> Veblen thus represents a transition figure in philosophy, economics, psychology and education. As a thinker he belongs to the period between the decline of capitalism and the rise of socialism. He saw, indeed, many phases

of the corrosion of capitalism, but still clung to the hope of two "instincts" of man: workmanship and idle curiosity. His recourse to Darwinism was to the narrowly biological; his recourse to psychology was to the behavioristic. In either case, he failed to move forward and beyond both his biology and his psychology. . . . And in education, he could see, most clearly, the menace of business control, but never moved beyond that to realize that a new social order was demanded, so that we might move to a new education beyond pragmatism. Minus a theory of the state, a theory of history, Veblen was obliged to remain immured within the present: he had no clear-cut view of the future, of the very future he most desired for humanity.[18]

Landsman, in the final analysis, thus viewed Veblen as a "museum piece" seized upon by "nostalgic socialists" who lacked the courage and conviction to move forward on the basis of Marxism.[19] His critique of Veblen was much like that of Trotskyite John Wright which follows, although it was couched in less caustic language.

John G. Wright: A Trotskyite View of Veblen

Perhaps the most ideologically antagonistic Marxist portrayal of Veblen, one that exceeded Baran and Landsman in its polemical, confrontationist tones, was published in 1936 by John G. Wright in the *The New International*, the organ of Leon Trotsky's Fourth International.[20] His critique is of considerable value because, while brief, it is systematic and consistent in its treatment of Veblen's ideas. Wright portrayed Veblen as a sometimes effective liberal opponent of the prevailing conservatism in vogue in American culture and the academic social sciences in his lifetime. Otherwise, however, he saw no real virtue in Veblen's thought. He believed that Veblen, instead of listening to Marx, was influenced by revisionists such as Edward Bernstein and by classical liberals such as Herbert Spencer. Like Baran, only more vehemently, he charged Veblen with "idealism." As Wright put it:

> To Veblen the primary motive force is the human mind. "Social evolution is a process of selective adaptation of temperament and habits of thought under the stress of the circumstances of associated life." When Veblen says that the development of societies is the development of institutions he implies that the development of institutions is the development of human motives. He does not at all imply what Marx maintained—that the development of the institutions and therefore of society is governed by laws not only independent of human will, consciousness and intelligence, but rather, on the contrary determining that will, consciousness and intelligence. Veblen accepts no such law.[21]

Wright's allegations of idealism against Veblen were developed in such a manner as to reveal the reductionist nature of his own Marxism. Indeed, he commented that

> one may easily read into Veblen, an outright idealist, a standpoint—i.e., Marxism—altogether alien to him. Thus, when Veblen asserts that "the cornerstone of the modern industrial system is the institution of private property," he does not at all subscribe to the Marxian standpoint. To him the substance of this cornerstone is psychological. It is made of mind-stuff because all institutions, including private property are in substance only habits of thought.[22]

Wright continued his assault:

> Veblen recognized only cumulative and correlative changes in nature, and in human nature. But his attempt to explain the causes that underlie the variation of human nature is as age worn as the mummies of the Pharaohs. Far from being scientific, it boils down to the animistic formula of explaining a phenomenon in terms of the spirit. Human nature varies because it is its nature to vary; or, more exactly, the amiability of human nature is due to the stability of human nature. In Veblen's own words, "this variation of human nature . . . is a process of selection between several relatively stable and persistent ethnic types or ethnic elements."[23]

It was important to proponents of a codified dialectical materialism, such as Wright, to make certain that ideological opponents, such as Veblen, were discredited according to canonical procedures and methods. One of their stock-in-trade devices was to label the political enemy "idealist." This demonstrated that a thinker such as Veblen believed that ideas are biologically rooted in human instincts or else plucked out of the spiritual atmosphere to be used in an improvisatory, opportunistic fashion. Wright did not really come to grips with Veblen's theoretical system on the basis of its own premises and consequently judged it entirely by the positivist, reductionist Marxism that was his only point of reference.

Wright also found Veblen guilty of sexism and in a heavy-handed attempt at satire commented:

> From this original invidious distinction between the occupations of men and women—whose occupations coincide with the difference between the sexes—there sprang up those institutions which tended to repress variant A in favor of variant B. For obviously, under the regime of exploitation, emulation and competition, the individual fared better in proportion as he had less of the gifts of human nature A. In his appraisal of women, Veblen agreed not only with the poets but with the patriarchs, among them Spencer who held

that "the slave class in a primitive society consists of women." Worst yet, women are directly responsible for the institution of private property: "the earliest form of ownership is the ownership of women by the able bodied men of the community." Destructive, damnable, deceitful woman![24]

To his growing list of Veblen's sins, Wright thus added charges of sexism, despite the fact that Veblen was an early advocate of female emancipation and women's rights whose biases ran counter to invidious distinctions of any kind.[25]

Wright apparently found little of value in Veblen's theory of status emulation. Once more, Veblen was the focus of his derisive comments, which were aimed at the core of his social theory.

With the dawn of modern enterprise social evolution enters a stage unknown to natural evolution, or anyone else save Veblen. He shares with no one the honor of formulating this discovery: "Under modern conditions, the struggle for existence has in very appreciable degree been transformed into a struggle to keep up appearances." As a consequence, the evolution of economic life "takes such a turn that the interests of the community no longer coincide with the emulative interests of the individual." To millions in the world today who are being forced to keep up the appearances of being alive while unemployed this might sound like satire, but no satire was intended. The formulation is a logical one, the logic pertaining to what Kant called psychologic logic.[26]

The main thrust of Wright's satire appears to be that it is immoral for Veblen to focus on status emulation when the main problem for the masses is keeping alive. His views may have been logical but they lacked realism at the level of physical existence and continuity of life. It had not occurred to Wright that, in Veblen's analysis, the waste caused by emulatory behavior was causally related to economic deprivation.

Wright continued his polemic, but now shifted to the eternal problems and issues of war and peace:

Veblen agreed not only with Spencer but with the revisionists that under the modern regime "life is generally occupied in peaceful intercourse with fellow citizens." Peaceful intercourse and the struggle for existence are mutually incompatible. And this is how peace came to man. Originally type B had to specialize in both force and fraud, mostly force. With the passage of time, and the gradual improvement of industrial efficiency, predation turned more and more in the direction of fraud. From being ferocious, the barbarian by natural selection tended to become a specialist in perfidy. Thus the era of rapine passed into the quasi-peaceable stages, until finally the modern peaceful epoch of fraud was attained. So peaceful that wars had become

implausible. Spencer, too, was sure that "the vast increase of manufactu-
ring and commercial activity must lead to a long peace." All this is pure
psychology.[27]

Again, Wright's analysis may have been pleasing to the satirist, but
it misrepresented Veblen's thinking on the modern era with regard to
war and peace. He failed to recognize the Veblenian assumption of the
contamination of the values of the peaceful type by the exploitative and
sporting proclivities of the predatory type. Furthermore, Veblen assumed the possibility of the persistence of atavistic continuities if not
a resurgence of barbarism itself. Wright's implicit claim that Veblen
believed war was a relic of the past is impossible to sustain through
exegesis of his texts, especially *The Nature of Peace*. His propagandistic aspirations overrode Wright's scholarly judgment but in ways that
were ideologically revealing.

Like many Marxists or Marxist-Leninists in the 1930s, Wright appeared to believe that social behavior can be explained by already existing scientific laws or lawlike generalizations found in germ form in
Marxism. Given these assumptions, Veblen's theoretical work could
only appear to Wright to be a form of political opportunism and bourgeois mystification. Wright commented that

> Veblen unquestionably accepted his own approach as scientific. It is equally
> incontestable that he attempted to analyze economic life as a process. His
> attempts, however, did not pass beyond criticism. He thought himself that
> his own generalizations were in part novel—and in so far as American
> thought of his day was concerned this is correct. For this reason he is re-
> puted by many to be a modern iconoclast. By imputation Veblen's views have
> been interpreted as an attack upon existing institutions. However, while
> there is much in Veblen that runs counter to convention, essentially his
> work can serve only as a basis for liberalism because his theoretic approach
> is founded on pre-conceptions and not laws.[28]

Wright's view here that Veblen's "work can serve only as a basis for
liberalism because his theoretic approach is founded on pre-concep-
tions and not laws" reveals the ideological gap that existed on the left
in the interwar period between revolutionary Marxists such as Wright
and radicals like Veblen. The latter never claimed that his theories de-
served the status of scientific laws and he satirized the work of those
who made such claims for Marx.[29] However, it was inconceivable to
Wright that Veblen's ideas could have the potency attributed to them
by his disciples. For they could not systematically strip away the ideological veil that masks capitalist property and power relations. Nor
could the Veblenian analysis be used to reconstruct the existing social

order and political economy. Thus in the final analysis, Wright believed Veblen and Veblenism provide no basis for structural change. Indeed, given the ideological structure of his own thought he could only regard Veblen as an advocate of the status quo.

> It may be argued that Veblen was no supporter of the existing system since he forecasted that the social engineers would build an industrial structure "on a system different from either status or contract." One may just as well argue that neither was Spencer, since he also forecasted that the future type of society would be a type differing as much from the industrial as this does from the militant.[30]

Once more, it is difficult to square what Wright said about Veblen's political perspective with what Veblen stated in his own writings. To illustrate, Veblen suggested the undesirability of absentee ownership, the displacement of management in the major corporations, and viewed with sympathy the revolution in Russia and the disallowance of American property holdings overseas. His attitudes toward institutional religion and emulatory consumption are so well-known as not to need reiteration here. What, then, is the basis of Wright's claim that he was a proponent of the established order?

This is not merely a rhetorical question, for it is a serious error to assume that textual exegesis of Veblen's works would demonstrate to Wright that he was in error. The reason is that his writing on Veblen was an ideological device aimed at undermining non-Marxist-Leninist political alternatives; it was not a serious scholarly effort to come to grips with Veblen's ideas and their role in American political life. Wright believed that ideas are weapons, and that, since only revolutionary socialism promised to overturn the existing social order, any kind of ideological compromise with this order was a betrayal of the working class. Veblen's ideas regarding frugality and productivity reeked of bourgeois ideological hegemony to Wright and his stress on the evils of emulatory consumption was an exclusionary elitist rhetoric aimed, wittingly or not, at depriving the proletariat of a decent standard of living.

Conclusion

Wright complained that Veblen's work could only function as a basis for liberalism because his theoretical position was founded on preconceptions, not laws. Of course, the view that Marxism, or for that matter any other theoretical system, provides "scientific" laws of human behavior may strike the reader as a doctrinaire, if not naive, claim. Nevertheless, Wright further argued that to the extent that Veblen's method was based on Spencer rather than on Marx, it failed to go beyond mere assertion. While Veblen may have differed from Spencer factually, the two are methodologically akin in their attempts to apply Darwinian concepts to the study of society.[31] Wright also pointed out that Veblen had rejected Marx's dialectical method as unscientific and chose, instead, to speak favorably of the revisionist attempts to update Marx. Wright considered this a serious error and added that "there is no foundation for the opinion that Veblen was guilty of attributing social change to 'habits of thought,' human nature, dispositions, and motives."[32] This alleged "idealist" position Wright invidiously compared to the Marxian conception of societal development governed by laws independent of "human will, consciousness and intelligence."[33] Moreover, Veblen's postulates of polar types of human nature and wants were unsupported by scientific evidence. His famous laws, such as conspicuous waste, were to Wright mere "embroideries upon conventional economics."[34] In sum, Veblen's critique of society and its institutions was unsound. This fact, coupled with Veblen's dissatisfaction with Marxian dialectics revealed, for Wright at least, a conservative streak in his thought that ultimately made Veblen a proponent of the status quo.[35]

BERNARD ROSENBERG AND *DISSENT*

Peter Clecak, a penetrating contemporary critic of the American left, accurately described the orientation of the *Dissent* group when he wrote that "for these critics liberal democratic norms became the overriding criteria of political action and historical evaluation."[36] It is from this anti-Stalinist left perspective that Bernard Rosenberg (b. 1923) and his interpretation of Veblen must be understood, for there was more stress in Rosenberg on polity, culture, and bureaucracy than on socialism as an economic phenomenon. The same can be said for most of the other writers for *Dissent*, which is not to question the sincerity of their motives or the authenticity of their aims. It is to suggest, however, that unlike some other socialist groups at the time, socialization of the means of production was not an overriding objective of the *Dissent* group.

Over a fifteen-year period from 1948 to 1963, Rosenberg made an important contribution to Veblen scholarship.[37] Indeed, he was among the first to systematically compare the social theories of Marx and Weber with Veblen.[38] Although critical of certain aspects of Veblen's work, he also found value in it. On the whole, he believed that there is "some seriously faulty thinking, some second hand ideas that are worn out altogether, and a quantity of vagueness and haziness," but when his theory is compared with contemporary social science it "stands up remarkably well."[39] Rosenberg's mixed reaction to Veblen's ideas were summarized in his comment that "there is an astonishing predictive value in Veblenism that the new social scientist would scarcely expect from the flimsiness of its empiricism."[40] Rosenberg also expressed his appreciation for the inimitable Veblenian prose "since Veblen was a powerful writer and an extraordinary satirist, he deserves our attention on purely aesthetic grounds."[41] However, it will soon become evident that Rosenberg, who was further to the left in the political spectrum than conventional liberals, nevertheless, largely shared their view of Veblen.

Methodological Considerations and Considerations of Method

Unlike several Veblen critics who are economists, Rosenberg was not critical of Veblen's writings on methodology. Instead, he focused on deficiencies in Veblen's own methods and found that Veblen was guilty of both hypostatization and stereotyping, two closely related methodological errors. Rosenberg felt these tendencies were most evident in his dichotomous formulations of an anachronistic ruling class and the common man, and of business and industry. They were also found in the pecuniary and sporting instincts, as contrasted with the instincts of idle curiosity and workmanship. Rosenberg believed Veblen gave a life and an independent existence to these processes and traits that grossly exaggerated their actual divergence from each other.[42] He also commented that

> in marking off prehistorical and historical epochs, Veblen veers dangerously close to Comtianism for he does not always see the mixture of metaphysical, rational, and positive components that make up scientific method. Deduction is no longer to be disposed of in the cavalier manner of Auguste Comte; by de-emphasizing it, Veblen approaches an untenable empiricism. As Kaufmann has pointed out so well, science combines synthetic judgments and analytic judgments.[43]

Since Rosenberg believed Veblen's method was suspect because it produced exaggerated dichotomies, it is not surprising that he would focus on the business-industry dualism also.

> Here are the familiar antinomies. Modern civilization is comprised materially of the machine process, which is good, and investment for a profit, which is bad. The norms are implicit but unquestionable. That these two forces are exclusive of each other is as unambiguously stated in *The Theory*

of Business Enterprise as in any of Veblen's books. This assumption is at least arguable and probably invalid, for businessmen contribute something to production even if they do not want it to be entirely unimpeded.[44]

Veblen's dichotomy between business and industry may have been an exaggerated one but Rosenberg did not adequately explain why. Businessmen may contribute to production but he did not indicate even generically the nature of their contribution. Interestingly, Rosenberg also failed to distinguish between the different roles businessmen play depending on the type and size of their firm. The characteristic demand for specificity is thus conspicuous by its absence from his own analysis.

Bureaucracy versus the Classless Society

Perhaps the most original contribution Rosenberg made to Veblen scholarship lay in his perception of the relationship between Veblen's and Weber's ideas regarding bureaucracy. No other writer stressed Veblen's work on bureaucracy to the degree Rosenberg did. He treated Veblen as both a theorist and a prophet of a bureaucratized society; not surprisingly, his own views on bureaucracy coincided with what he said were Veblen's views on the subject. In addition he linked Veblen's views on bureaucracy with what he asserted was his belief in the unlikelihood and undesirability of a classless society. It is thus difficult to avoid the conclusion that Rosenberg was reading his own values and prophecies back into Veblen when he wrote that

> bureaucratism is the main datum with which Veblen works, when he notes its presence in American universities, when he refers to trained incapacity as a trait of business administrators, and when he foresees cultural configurations to come. The bureaucratization of society was a side issue to Marx; it is a central decisive one to Weber and Veblen. . . . Even conservatives believe that what lies before the world is a choice between Marxist socialism and free enterprise capitalism. Veblen is the first important social scientist to deny this choice and to detect the emergence of a new class whose dominance is de facto already and may soon become de jure as well. . . . the societal form now universalizing itself is neither socialism nor capitalism but bureaucratic collectivism.[45]

As noted, Rosenberg compared Veblen and Weber favorably with Marx in that the former recognized the likelihood of a permanently stratified society structured along functional-bureaucratic lines, while the latter did not. As Rosenberg put it:

How best to stratify a society for scientific purposes remains, of course, an open question. But that society is objectively stratified into classes and will be restratified on a new basis in the future now goes without saying. We must credit Veblen with realizing that the next step would not be Marx's classless society, but still another class society, with its bureaucrats on top as the new men of power.[46]

Rosenberg relied heavily on *The Engineers and the Price System* and *The Higher Learning in America* to make the case that Veblen was both a theorist and a prophet of bureaucracy. This led him to conclude that "Veblen was the first major sociologist to detect an emergent class whose dominance is now de facto and could become de jure as well."[47] Rosenberg stressed the bureaucratization of higher education, in particular, commenting that the bureaucrat is institutionalized in the American university and endorsing Veblen's alleged belief that "as for bureaucratized institutions of learning, they will not be freed—they will be further bureaucratized."[48] In higher education and in the rest of industrial society, Veblen predicted the triumph of the organization man, the managerial revolution, the white-collar employee, and bureaucratic collectivism. At this point Rosenberg appeared to have mistaken Veblen for C. Wright Mills, an easy error to make given the similarities between the two;[49] for the thesis he advanced regarding Veblen more accurately depicted the theses of *White Collar* and *The Power Elite*. Apparently, Rosenberg mistook the effects of the division of labor that Veblen stresses for an endorsement, or at least an acceptance, of the inevitability of the bureaucratic form of organization.[50] Veblen was not convinced that hierarchy, power disparities, and inequalities of income were either necessary or inevitable accompaniments of large-scale industrial organization. Of course, this contradicted Rosenberg's claim that Veblen believed that bureaucratization would continue its remorseless growth and result in a permanently stratified social order. As he put it:

Like Weber, he neither especially wants nor in any sense predicts a classless society—and his negative vision is being borne out all over the world. Society has not ceased to be stratified (least of all where lip-service is paid to Marxism); it is merely stratified in a new way. This is an age that calls for the specialist, the expert, the technician, the engineer. It can literally be said that bureaucratism and not egalitarianism is inevitable . . . it is certain that the bureaucrat will rule us. . . . In Veblen's work he is the main character. The industrial specialist and his scientific compeers are a real General Staff in an economic army that cannot do without them.[51]

Rosenberg believed that Veblen was not an egalitarian, for he repeatedly made the point that Veblen did not endorse or anticipate the coming of a classless society. Like Daniel Bell, he made little effort to relate such claims to Veblen's support for abolition of absentee ownership, his stress on the wasteful life-style of the upper classes, or his consistent praise of the egalitarianism of primitive societies. Perhaps he failed to come to terms with Veblen's egalitarianism because equality is incompatible with Rosenberg's own pessimistic vision of the inevitability of a permanently stratified bureaucratic society.

Rosenberg was aware of interpretations of Veblen that stressed his primitivism and his anarchism, but he did not recognize the extent to which these traits were connected with his egalitarianism and were the outgrowths of a mind that sanctioned no invidious distinctions among men. But functional distinctions based on the division of labor were, in Rosenberg's eyes, the basis of Veblen's theory of stratification and inequalities of power, status, and income were their inevitable accompaniments. Although he believed that the technocracy of the 1930s was a distortion of Veblen's plan, the latter was no equalitarian with his eye on the creation of a classless society.

Religion and Functionalism

Rosenberg portrayed Veblen as a philosophe descended from the enlightenment with all the antireligious bias that usually connotes. It is, of course, true that Veblen included the Church when he spoke of "imbecile institutions." As Rosenberg put it:

> It will be remembered that ritualists of every variety are berated by Veblen and that he regards religion itself as impermanent and on the wane. In this role he is preeminently the Rationalist. Veblen always seems to be saying: unreason is rampant and it must be extirpated. The same cry resounds through so much late nineteenth century thought, notably as it comes down to us in psychopathological theory by way of Freud. Veblenism does not differ appreciably on this heap from Freudianism: for either the religious "illusion" should certainly be doomed with science making more and more headway.[52]

Rosenberg believed that Veblen, like Marx, was unable to adequately explain why and how religion has such a pervasive hold on the human mind. He attributed to him a belief that religion is a form of superstition resulting from the deceit and dupery of priests, a view that is incapable of explaining the continuing religiosity of the underlying population. Indeed, Rosenberg commented that "Veblen's functionalism has a number of blind spots of which religion is the most serious. It is affiliated scientifically with the early anthropology and philosophically with the Enlightment."[53] The sociologist in Rosenberg criticized Veblen for failing to recognize "that from the very beginning society and religion were practically identical, or more correctly, that one was an expression of the other."[54] Rosenberg then showed his own hand, although admitting this to be a debatable point, when he commented that "religious organizations—like family structure—is *sui generis*, a completely neutral phenomenon."[55] This passage is reductionist in the sense that it portrays religious belief and practice in the same way that it does family structure. It is as though both were equally "natural" phenomena and permanently rooted in the human psyche and the social order. Rosenberg's own cultural relativism appears to be in conflict with his acceptance of the family and the church as permanent and integral parts of society.

Patriotism, War, and Peace

Rosenberg also evaluated Veblen's views on international politics and found them to be more realistic and subtle than those of Marx and his followers. He cryptically commented that "no devotee of Marx could, to begin with, have categorized patriotism as a part of the substructure, which is really what Veblen did."[56] But he then argued that

> Veblen was afflicted with ambivalence, and even in this book reverted occasionally to the other phase of his temperament. It is impossible to believe with any logical consistency that this was simply foisted upon the people by businessmen who profit from it and, at the same time, that it was as the result of patriotism which cannot be exercised from the psyche. Yet Veblen alternately defended both points of view, and his gloom seems justifiable to use, irrespective of how soundly he has analyzed the total pattern.[57]

A different reading of Veblen based on a synthesis of his later writings would stress the latent convergence of the corporate profit motive with the patriotic sentiments of the underlying population. But Rosenberg argued in another context that Veblen could not make up his mind whether war was a cultural phenomenon or whether it was due to inherent impulses.[58] Consequently, Rosenberg believed Veblen was caught between believing that

> On the one hand, patriotic devotion is falling into disuse, is little more than an archaic affection; on the other hand, it is a permanent and indissoluble part of human nature. To be sure, the first view appears more often and is stated more forcefully than the second. But together they reveal profound ambiguity in his thinking.[59]

When he treated Veblen's explanation of patriotism, war, and peace and the linkages between them, Rosenberg lay great stress on the ambivalence, indeed, inconsistency in his view of human nature. As regards the nature versus nurture controversy Veblen, alas, could not make up his mind.

> As usual he is hard put to it to explain the persistence of such an untoward habit as patriotism. He does so in *The Nature of Peace*, by dismissing it as an instinct. This is the line of least resistance for Veblen at all times, the tautology that affords salvation. That it does violence to technological determinism is obvious. For clearly, some causal agent takes primacy over the state of the industrial arts. A quality of human nature exists, we learn—ubiquitous, intimate, and ineradicable—prior to technology. This view however, erroneous it may be, contradicts Veblen's customary hypothesis.[60]

Of course, if patriotism has indestructible roots in the human psyche, there is little hope for permanent peace and Veblen's pessimism is fully justified. On the other hand, if generic man is sufficiently plastic and malleable, then perpetual peace is at least conceivable. Rosenberg thus believed there is no clear or consistent portrayal of human nature in *The Nature of Peace*.

Instinct Theory and Human Nature

Rosenberg's interpretation of Veblen's view of human nature was inconsistent. At times he presented Veblen's views as instinctivist, but, contradictorily, he also represented them as stressing human plasticity and malleability.[61] Ultimately, however, despite his inconsistency (and Veblen's) he came down on the side of nurture in interpreting Veblen's ideological position in the nature versus nurture controversy.

> Instinct theory has bedeviled us for too long and Veblen may be numbered among those who have added to rather than detracted from the general confusion. Ordinarily instincts connote rigidity or inflexibility or the irreducible psychological and physiological elements in human behavior. This is the case with instinctivists like MacDougall; it is no longer the case with Veblen for whom human nature approaches something close to infinite malleability.[62]

Rosenberg believed that other liberal critics of Veblen, such as Talcott Parsons, attempted to discredit his work by focusing on his theory of instincts and, worse, by misrepresenting it. He put it this way:
Veblen knew that instinct theory was in disrepute, that

"it is a concept of too lax and shifty a definition to meet the demands of exact biological science." So he debiologizes, and sociologizes it. Where the biologists and the individual psychologists had ignored culture he plays it up; where they had slighted "habit" he gives it centrality; where their conception of man were inflexible his is plastic. From this it should be evident that the glib dismissal of Veblen as a theorist who subscribed to instinct psychology is altogether unfair.[63]

In spite of this defense of Veblen, Rosenberg did not find his instinct theory to be an adequate one for he argued that "four basic 'instincts' inhere in Veblen's schemata: the parental bent, the predatory bent, the bent of workmanship, and idle curiosity. There is vastly more to man than any composition of these instincts, and the first, third, and fourth are not as unqualifiedly beneficial as Veblen believes."[64] At this point the classical liberal residues in Rosenberg's thought manifested themselves as he questioned the value and consequences of altruism, proficiency of craftsmanship, and critical intelligence. By implication, does this also mean that the predatory bent, in the form of the sporting and pecuniary instincts, are more beneficial than Veblen supposed? Such an interpretation is consistent with Rosenberg's analysis.

Altruism and the Family

Rosenberg did not agree with Veblen's views concerning the family and the altruistic moral and behavioral traits that he alleged it supports. Veblen wrongly found nothing but virtue and sustenance in the family and viewed it as a nearly universal source of positive traits and other regardingness that congealed in the "parental bent."

> It is supposed that some such polarity does exist, that collective satisfaction can only proceed from personal dissatisfaction, and that society should be served over the individual—conceding all these unverifiable assumptions, it is still not possible to support Veblen. The family as a social institution is neither the unmitigated evil that Marxists make it out to be nor the unmitigated good that it becomes in Veblenian psychology.[65]

Rosenberg believed that whether or not the family plays a positive role in society will vary greatly from one culture to another.

> A modicum of evidence about prehistorical times is enough to puncture the Noble Savage and reduce him to a kind of brutishness unfathomable to the Romantic mind. Infanticide is known to prevail in many primitive cultures— which does not argue very strongly for an innately beneficent parental bent. . . . If it is unrealistic to rhapsodize about primitive altruism in the

family, then consider Western Culture with its oedipal affections? Relativistic norms govern the family structure in its irregular fluctuations from one gestalt to another; as comparative anthropology amply demonstrates, it may be constructive or destructive.[66]

Rosenberg appeared to believe that there are some universal purposes and values that families should serve, but he was vague about what these might be. Consequently, it is difficult to tell what standards he used to measure the performance of the family and Veblen's attitudes toward it. Nevertheless, he criticized Veblen for uncritically sanctioning the family structure by assuming that it is the fountainhead from which altruism flows. Indeed, Rosenberg claimed that

> the dedicatory spirit of parents for their children is culturally conditioned to a greater extent that Veblen imagined. He romanticizes primitive life, as we shall see from his anthropological precepts, and so it seems to him that preliterate peoples were selfless and devoted where civilized man with his narrow familism feels comparatively few parental obligations.[67]

Rosenberg failed to indicate to the reader what binding traits and values the family should protect and nurture. The extreme value-relativism *cum* moral agnosticism of modern secular liberalism had so infected his thinking that he was unwilling to articulate the very values he charged the family with betraying in certain cultures. On the one hand, he criticized Veblen's endorsement of the family because it does not foster certain values that Rosenberg prized. But, on the other hand, he was unwilling to adequately state these values. Is this additional evidence of the tendency of postwar liberals to obfuscate when analyzing and prioritizing values? If so, what does this moral posturing indicate about the structure of their own ethical values?

Rosenberg also criticized Veblen for his one-sided treatment of the family, which "obscures the reciprocity of a child-parent relationship."

> He would scorn the mother who neglected her son, but the one who cares for his mother is abetting conservatism and stagnation. Gerontocracies obstruct any innovation which would jeopardize their social supremacy. Veblen implies that reverence for elders is the cause of seniority, authenticity, tutelary oversight, class tabus, autocracy, chieftainship and aristocratic government; that this contention is specious can be shown by the ease with which other equally plausible causes could be summoned to explain the same effects.[68]

Unfortunately, Rosenberg did not tell what these other "equally plausible" causes might be. He also exaggerated the causal relations that Veblen thought existed between reverence for elders and various undesirable social traits and processes.

Veblen's Attack on Culture: Role of Aesthetics and Athletics

Many writers of various ideological persuasions agreed with Rosenberg's criticisms of Veblen's narrow focus, which allegedly utilized rigid criteria of waste-avoidance to measure the role of aesthetics. It was *The Theory of the Leisure Class* that caught their eye, for it was in that work that Veblen most fully developed his functional aesthetic.

> Veblen gives himself away by referring to economic beauty which he inferentially equates with beauty itself; while chuckling over the aphorism that "cheap clothes make a cheap man" he practically says that cheap clothes make a fine man. The one is as manifestly wrongheaded an aesthetic as the other. If longer lasting goods made with a machine are scorned in favor of fragile handwrought goods, this indeed is laughable. But handwrought goods are not "intrinsically ugly" and that they are so marked by Veblen immeasurably weakens his excellent case against conventional taste.[69]

Rosenberg also found it objectionable that Veblen wanted to completely rationalize all other social processes. He complained that

> Veblen defines conspicuous leisure as the *non-productive* consumption of time—i.e., as conspicuous waste. His excoriation of almost everything not purely economic blights the book. For there are areas which cannot sensibly be classified as wasteful or as economic; yet in *The Leisure Class* and elsewhere Veblen tends to ignore them.[70]

Veblen's attitude toward competitive sports and athletics was, of course, to focus on their waste and predation. His best-known comment in this regard from *The Theory of the Leisure Class* was that "the relation of football to physical culture is much the same as that of the bull-fight to agriculture."[71] Rosenberg complained that Veblen did not understand that sports and athletics provide physically wholesome escapes from boredom. However, he admitted that

> Veblen would probably reply that this was all well and good for the boys with their surplus energy, but quite unbecoming for an adult who should work not to better his own physique but to perfect the body social. Veblen can see no critical difference between primary and secondary conflict; he does not speculate about a moral or an amoral equivalent of war? It is enough the exhibitions of prowess are irrational. Ergo, they may be written off as undesirable. The issue of athletics gives us a clue to *The Leisure Class* which, from this angle, could be viewed as a brief in favor of total rationalization.[72]

Rosenberg's criticism was that Veblen favored "total rationalization" of society and this meant total elimination of all economic waste regardless of sources or consequences. But what if Veblen believed that only

aesthetic and athletic endeavors which aimed at invidious comparisons be eliminated and that those activities that are noninvidiously
meaningful to the common man be retained? Unfortunately, Rosenberg overlooked the latter possibility in his eagerness to convict Veblen
of wanting complete rationalization of all social processes and institutions. For some forms of physical culture and aesthetic endeavor may
be noninvidiously meaningful to the underlying population and can be
spared in a drive toward total rationalization of social life. Unfortunately, Veblen did not advance beyond the functional aesthetics of his
first book in which his theory of aesthetics is not fully developed. Indeed, he rarely turned his attention to aesthetics again, leaving the
casual reader with the impression held by Rosenberg that waste avoidance and satire were the sum total of his contribution.

Borrowing and Imperial Germany

Rosenberg was intrigued by Veblen's work on Imperial Germany in
which he focused on the rapid industrial growth of Germany, which
was facilitated by the borrowing of technology and techniques from
more advanced economies such as Great Britain. As Rosenberg put it:

> Veblen argues that Germany became industrially more efficient than her
> predecessors, England, France, Holland, and Belgium, just because she
> came after and borrowed from them. England paid "the penalty of taking the
> lead" while Germany and Japan profited from "the merits of borrowing."
> Belated entrance into the so-called concert of industrial nations imposes
> something of a handicap, but it also provides an extraordinary advantage.
> Germany could and did take over a ready-made technology. There was no
> obsolete equipment, no large capital investment in tools the continuance of
> which could only retard economic expansion, no conventional restrictions to
> hamper enterprise.[73]

There was nothing unusual in Rosenberg's interpretation of Veblen's;
at this point it differed in no essential way from other conventional
portrayals. However, Rosenberg also wrote that "there were values
Veblen held to be higher than economic efficiency and productivity.
And these values—above all, freedom, the exercise of idle curiosity,
elbow room, self-fulfillment in creative activity—are in his judgment
directly jeopardized by too rapid a rate of industrialization."[74]
    To this list, Rosenberg should have added the "parental bent," that
is, other-regardingness or altruism. However, a more serious problem
of interpretation lay in his explanation of the causal factors that thwart
fulfillment of the values Veblen cherished. It was not as Rosenberg
suggested—that the machine process and technology caused this—in

Veblen's view, it was the institutions of capitalism fused with the dynastic authoritarian traits of Imperial Germany that were responsible. Rosenberg, mistakenly focused on the autonomy and impact of industrial technology while Veblen, who was often charged with "technological determinism," emphasized, instead, the institutional framework that channels and directs the techno-economic development of society. Rosenberg failed to see that the evils of rapid industrialism were traceable to institutions, not technology, in Veblen's analysis.

Rosenberg was also critical of Veblen's analysis of Imperial Germany because of his exaggerated dichotomy between business and industry. As he put it:

> Veblen finds himself overanxious to account for German industrial supremacy in terms of his preconceived division between malign pecuniary interests and benign industrial interests. He must deny that the Kaiser Reich permits conspicuous waste because the price system is an essential accompaniment of *late* capitalism. This is why he closed his eyes to the waste that must have been obvious to any other detached observer of Imperial Germany. Veblen's own analysis indicates that tardy industrialism, because it is too precipitate, will lead to military appropriations which are more completely wasteful than any other form of expenditure.[75]

A more accurate reading of *Imperial Germany and the Industrial Revolution* would acknowledge that Veblen saw waste in both systems, but excluding the costs of militarism he saw more in England than Germany. He was not unaware of the costs of the German monarchy and aristocracy, the extravagances of the Church, or the dissipation of resources in emulatory consumption, but he felt that the British expenditures on the like exceeded them by a significant margin.

Conclusion

Rosenberg's own doctrinal stance was particularly evident in his use of Veblen's analysis of class to show the futility of trying to promote militant, class-based political socialism. His perception of the potency of status emulation was thus evident in his claims that

> regardless of whether polo should be played or should be banned, it is factually accurate to say that the leisure class plays this game and that the underlying population would like to play it. Veblen could save the Marxist organizer from exercising his larynx in a futile attempt to convince the worker who only wants to emulate his superiors that really he ought to revolt. Refusal to recognize one's "objective" class is tantamount to destroying its social reality, at least on the level of revolutionary political action.[76]

At times, however, Rosenberg was ready to engage in anticapitalist rhetoric, or at least to endorse Veblen's radical assault on aspects of the capitalist system.

> In retrospect one can legitimately accuse him of naiveté. For he knew that the establishment of a league or of federation in itself would mean nothing unless certain features of capitalism disappeared. It seemed to him, as he doffed his rose colored glasses to don dark ones, that the common man was not much worse off in an imperial state than here in America. Our nominally representative government operates with a view to the advantage of one class. The business man, for whom Veblen is always seeking a new and more scurrilous appellation, is finally called the gentleman gone to seed.[77]

Rosenberg carefully observed that most of the population was subject to business influence and manipulation that greatly reduced the likelihood of radical change; to this he added the Veblenian view that radical political action was further undermined to the extent that emulatory consumption engulfed the underlying population.

Rosenberg claimed to see much of contemporary value in Veblen's writings in his last comments on him in the early 1960s. Yet he also stated that "his several errors of fact, the occasional contradictions, his theoretical limitations, all required criticism."[78] These criticisms probably reflected Rosenberg's conviction, shared by many American sociologists, that, while Veblen was an important social scientist, he never achieved the stature of Marx or Weber.

Rosenberg's stress on Veblen's role as a theorist and prophet of bureaucracy exaggerated Veblen's interest in it. Indeed, it revealed more about the ideological structure of postwar American sociology than it did about the author of *The Theory of the Leisure Class*. However, Rosenberg used Veblen as a seer and analyst of bureaucracy not simply because bureaucracy was a popular topic among sociologists under Weber's influence, but because he now perceived bureaucracy as a major obstacle to genuine socialization of the means of production. While Rosenberg regarded himself as a democratic socialist, he believed that the realization of an egalitarian society was likely to founder on the shoals of inevitable bureaucratization. His ultimate portrayal of Veblen was that of a thinker whose focus on the division of labor and the hierarchy of skills and power assumed the permanent forestalling of an egalitarian society. The description of Veblen as a prophet and theorist of bureaucracy reinforced Rosenberg's own doubts regarding the feasibility of socialism, doubts ultimately expressed in his caricature of Veblen as a theorist of bureaucracy who believed that the arrival of the bureaucrat in industrial society was a harbinger of the indefinite postponement of the classless society.

LEWIS COREY AND JOHN HOBSON

An additional militant Marxist critic of Veblen was Lewis Corey (Fraina) who, in certain respects, was a representative radical interpreter of him. Writing in the short-lived *Marxist Quarterly* in 1937, Corey found much of value in Veblen in those theoretical realms where he converged with Marxism. As Corey put it, "all that is vital in Thorstein Veblen may fulfill itself in Marxism and Socialism."[79]

However, he also found much with which to reproach Veblen. First, there were elements in Veblen's work that made it susceptible to vulgarization; thus the technocrats in the 1930s misinterpreted his theory of social change by giving it an elitist twist that neglected Veblen's emphasis on the fact that technicians as leaders of a social revolution needed the support of the labor force. Nevertheless, Corey argued that "Veblen did speculate, wrongly, on the technicians being a peculiarly revolutionary force" (p. 163). He was thus guilty of overemphasizing "the technological factor and of not analyzing precisely the class-economic elements of social change" (p. 184). Corey believed Veblen had severely undermined the assumptions of conventional economic theory, but had not really developed a theory of his own. Worse yet, "his analysis of institutional changes and mutations lends itself to the belief that one may tinker with institutions pragmatically, for there is no theory to guide action" (p. 164). The consequence of this, of course, was that the New Dealers could claim that Veblen was an important source of doctrinal inspiration for them (p. 164).

Corey was very critical of Veblen's interpretation of Marx and argued that "unlike Marx, Veblen neglected the factors of consciousness and purposive struggle in human history, despite his emphasis on the psychological approach to the study of culture" (p. 165). Veblen's "mechanical materialism" robbed the working class of its ability to overturn the existing order for, while the concept of vested interests is valuable, "Veblen does not recognize its limitations in terms of the more decisive class interests and class struggle, all of which cannot adequately serve the ends of a program of action" (p. 166). Finally, and perhaps most interesting, Corey claimed that "the value of Veblen's analysis is not destroyed by the fact that he is unaware of the pressure capitalist production exerts through the fetishism of commodities, on the recreation of irrationalism"(p. 167). This charge was a strange one for a Marxist to make, for the convergence between Veblen and Marx was perhaps most complete at this particular point in their theories. If emulatory consumption is not a form of commodity fetishism leading to the reproduction of still more irrationalism, then what is it? Corey did not say.

When Corey's critique of Veblen is contrasted with that of John Hobson, the variety and diversity of radical opinion becomes dramatically evident. Hobson (1858–1940), the left-leaning English economist, was both a personal acquaintance and a contemporary of Veblen. His book on Veblen, published in 1936, was essentially sympathetic toward its subject and contained only a few criticisms. One was that Veblen's rejection of hedonism was too extreme because "the element of conscious satisfaction in all human achievement" which plays such an important role in his work is actually compatible with hedonism.[80] Also, Hobson commented negatively on Veblen's failure to take adequate account in *The Nature of Peace* of the economic forces underlying imperialism, although he praised Veblen's efforts to go beyond economic causation into the psychology of patriotism in explaining both war and imperialism.[81]

Hobson believed that Veblen was prone to exaggerate the prevalence of industrial sabotage by the captains of industry. As he put it, "though there are industrial situations where it may pay to restrict production and earn high profits on a limited sale, this is not a normal case."[82] More consistent with radical doctrine and Hobson's own thesis of underconsumption was his complaint that

> Veblen nowhere directly tackled the real problem of maldistribution of income which periodically upsets the changing balance between spending and saving, between new investment and increased consumption, that lies at the root of the failure of current capitalism to function as well as it used to do.[83]

Finally, Hobson argued that "Veblen was in one sense a disorderly thinker and writer, which means that he left his mind free to develop all sorts of aberrations and surface inconsistencies."[84] Hobson, was appreciative of Veblen's critique of capitalism, but unlike the Marxists he was indifferent regarding Veblen's rejection of Marxism. However, like other radicals, he complained of Veblen's sometimes convoluted style, which made it difficult to decipher his intent.

Chapter Twelve

THE IDEOLOGICAL USE AND ABUSE
OF THORSTEIN VEBLEN

> but his memorial remains
> riveted into the language:
> the sharp clear prism of his mind
> (John Dos Passos, *U.S.A. The Big Money*)

THOMAS SOWELL argued that political economists and social philosophers are divisible into two camps. There are those whose vision is "constrained," such as Adam Smith, Edmund Burke, and, more recently, Friedrich Von Hayek and Milton Friedman; and those whose vision is unconstrained: Tom Paine, William Godwin, Jean-Jacques Rousseau, Karl Marx, and, of course, Thorstein Veblen.[1] To Sowell, a vision was a "pre-analytic cognitive act" and

> The unconstrained vision promotes pursuit of the highest ideals and the best solutions. By contrast, the constrained vision sees the best as the enemy of the good—a vain attempt to reach the unattainable being seen as not only futile but often counterproductive, while the same efforts could have produced a viable and beneficial trade-off.[2]

Conservatives, with their constrained vision of what was achievable, believed that Veblen's ideals and optimal solutions were unrealizable without sacrificing both equity and efficiency, not to mention personal freedoms, including free consumer choice and the right of private property. Liberals divided in these respects between those who had constrained vision and those whose view was less constrained, the majority sharing the constrained perspective with conservatives and the minority converging at times with those further left in the spectrum. Radicals, of course, varied from those like C. Wright Mills, who largely shared Veblen's ideals, to those like Theodor Adorno and Paul Baran who believed that Veblen's vision of both self-actualized humanity and the good society were unduly constricted and puritanical.[3]

It is evident from an analysis of Veblen's critics from left to right that his radical opponents had visions not only of present human nature but of its ultimate potential that equaled or exceeded even Veblen's vision of man in the industrial republic. Veblen's liberal critics, often under the guise of "scientific objectivity," saw the potential of man for both good and evil. His conservative critics, with predictable cynicism, set drastic limits to the potential moral and social growth of mankind and sought not so much to achieve good as to avoid evil.[4]

THE CONSERVATIVE CRITICS

There is a remarkable degree of consistency in the ideological structure of conservative criticisms of Thorstein Veblen over the span of three generations. The continuity and coherence of the conservative critique reveals much about the durability of both conservative paradigmatic assumptions and the political predilections of conservatives.

To further illustrate, conservatism supports the continued ideological dominance of existing elites. In the case of Veblen's conservative critics, this even legitimizes attacks on his functional theory of aesthetics because it casts aspersions on the invidious nature of painting, literature, and craftsmanship that cater to a leisure class. Indeed, in our analysis of the five most important conservative critics of Veblen, we discovered no aspects of his thought that they all regarded as praiseworthy. In the final analysis, their differences were rooted in fundamentally different approaches to social value and opposed views of the good society.

The common attitudes and assumptions shared by Veblen's conservative critics thus made their analyses of his work predictable in certain respects. For example, although nearly sixty years in time separated John Cummings from Abram Harris, there is a marked degree of convergence in the tenets that underlay their views of what political economy is and ought to be. Conservatism of this ilk, consciously or not, affirms the inevitability and desirability of structural differentiation and class rule, the permanence of social hierarchy meaning inequalities of power in the chain of command, and the permanent political ineptitude of the masses. It also holds to a pessimistic view of human nature that emphasizes human laziness, selfishness, and irrationality as enduring qualities of humankind.

In varying degrees all these assumptions clearly underlay the attack of Veblen's conservative critics on him, and their critique of his theoretical work cannot be adequately understood without alluding to them. Indeed, the predictability of the conservative assault is more deeply rooted in the doctrinal structure of the critic's thought than in an idiosyncratic reading of Veblen's works.

Why is it that the politically conservative neoclassical economists who played a prominent role in this study saw so little merit in Veblen's work? This query needs further investigation. To illustrate, Irving

Fisher attempted to ground the taking of interest on principles accepted by all right-thinking and moral men, meaning, of course, conventional men. Frank Knight wanted to do the same thing for profit. Fisher's work was an apology for interest, a pro-usury tract for the edification of ignorant workmen and farmers. Knight's work was similar in that it was an apology for profit grounded on principles accepted by all men with normal moral faculties. But they failed to adequately respond to Veblen, who articulated what was also expressed by the Okie Woody Guthrie at a more rudimentary level. In his eulogy for Pretty Boyd Floyd, another Okie, Guthrie sang "As in this world I've hoboed, I've seen lots of funny men. Some rob you with a six gun, some with a fountain pen."[5] Veblen explained how the fountain pen men did it. How the fountain pen men did it and continued to do it is central to Veblen but is legitimized by his conservative opponents. However, what the conservatives have succeeded in doing is confusing Woody with their graphs, equations, and apologetics. Veblen's greatest sin, in their eyes is to point this out.

THE LIBERAL CRITICS

The ambivalence of American liberals toward a radical analysis such as Veblen's is revealing of the bifurcation, indeed, ideological schizophrenia found in the roots of their doctrinal pedigree, the conflicting tenets of which derived from both classical and modern collectivist liberalism. It is evident that much liberal criticism of Veblen emanates from the contradictory structure of a doctrinal position that has neither abandoned the tenets of classical liberalism nor sanctioned advanced collectivism.

What distinguishes Veblen's social conflict theory from that of his liberal critics is that his is rooted in a class analysis while theirs vacillates between viewing conflict as rooted in class and perceiving it as individual in nature. The newer, more advanced form of collectivist liberalism sees conflict as emanating from the class structure, while the older, classical kinds of liberalism view it as occurring primarily among individuals with different interests and aims. Ideologically, then, twentieth-century liberalism can thus be characterized generically as an uneasy and unstable mixture of classical liberal and collectivist liberal tenets with no apparent resolution of its incongruent doctrines and policies in sight. Several generations of liberal scholarship on Veblen is thus riddled with these tensions.

Historically, liberal doctrine advocated the non-intervention of the state because of its desire to reduce the role of government in all areas of life, from regulation of conscience within to regulation of trade without. Thus, ideas necessitating a greater degree of social and economic equality through wealth and income redistribution had to be grafted onto the liberal creed and, in terms of shifts in public policy, were essentially New Deal and post–New Deal developments. It is evident that American liberalism in the post–World War II era was unable to adequately equilibrate the divergent elements in its ideological underpinnings. It could not reconcile the doctrinal bifurcation between its roots in classical liberalism and modern collectivism because it had no criterion of value or method by which to accomplish this. Much of the liberal criticism of Veblen emanates from critics whose thought amply displays this doctrinal contradiction and it is the single most pervasive sourse of their ambiguity toward him. In any case, no firm commitment exists in liberal ideology or programs to substantive equality of income and wealth. Modern liberals have often postulated a link between the growth of equality and that of fraternity and community, but liberal policy has accomplished little by way of unifying the two. This clearly effected the liberal interpretation of Veblen, for his Darwinian evolutionary views of institutional adaptation demanded a degree of human solidarity and other-regardingness that exceeded the parameters of liberalism.

The ideological structure of liberalism will not permit many of its proponents to advance aggressively in the direction of a social determinist view of human nature. Deficiencies in human behavior induced by the system of power and property relations must, instead, be attributed to human nature, because otherwise, the system's renovation would require drastic changes in the capitalist order. Changes in that order, would, in turn, threaten vested interests that liberals hold dear, such as the right to acquire large-scale property holdings and make contractual agreements to dispose of it largely on the basis of self-interest. In the final analysis, much of the liberal criticism of Veblen is ultimately rooted in the conviction that his view of human nature errs in its stress on plasticity and malleability. Liberals were unwilling to pay the costs to make essential change in the institutional fabric of society that would, in turn, reduce emulatory and other invidious distinctions. Indeed, many of Veblen's liberal critics believed that any systematic or rigorous attempt to reduce emulatory waste through public policy would ultimately destroy individual freedom and initiative. Much of the liberal assault on Veblen rested on such convictions.

Liberals have usually reacted to Veblen in one of four ways. The first was to view him primarily as a social satirist whose wit made him perhaps the most important comic writer of the day. But those who portrayed Veblen in this fashion tended not to take him very seriously as a social scientist, since they found him amusing rather than enlightening. More often, however, liberals have either viewed Veblen as a utopian radical who was politically irrelevant, or as one of their own because of his evolutionary reformism. But, in addition to these three fundamental interpretations of him, there were important liberals, such as Robert Merton, who used his ideas in selective, apolitical ways that have had the effect of deradicalizing them by severing structure from function. In short, the liberal critiques of Veblen's ideas can be categorized as (1) the satirization thesis followed by laughter, (2) utopianization followed by dismissal, (3) co-optation followed by ideological usage for legitimation of reformism, and (4) separation of structure from function and thus deradicalization.

Indeed, some of the most skilled and learned social scientists of liberal political persuasion displayed their biases in at least one of these four ways without adequate recognition of the effects their ideological blinders have had on their treatment of Veblen. However, it is important to understand why and how this occurred not only for the sake of understanding Veblen better, but also in anticipation of a more acute understanding of ideological trends in vogue among liberal intellectuals from about 1890 to the mid-1960s.

To illustrate, liberal historians, through a selective reading of Veblen, stripped his work of much of its potential for political and moral enlightenment, at times, without intending to do so. Thus the anarchist-socialist Veblen vanishes only to return as a Wilsonian reformer, New Deal Democrat, or, more recently, as a Kennedy-type New Frontiersman, idiosyncratic and iconoclastic to be sure, but an advocate of reform capitalism nevertheless. He is transformed from a radical critic of capitalism into a "progressive" or "liberal" advocate of welfare and regulatory state collectivism. The liberal political agenda is thus able to accommodate Veblen, although at times the fit is an obviously uncomfortable one; nevertheless the co-optation process has occurred and is successful in making him conform, at least superficially, to the liberal perspective.[6] But, where this is not the case, the deradicalization, utopianization, and satirization strategies have appeal.

So, if Veblen is portrayed as a liberal reformer, his ideas can be stripped of their radical thrust by narrowing their use to the legitimation of selective policy objectives. Or he can be interpreted as a visionary whose doctrines have no roots in political and social reality. Finally, he can simply be laughed away as a comic writer with no serious political import whose main intent was to induce hilarity in his readers. Plainly, these liberal reactions to Veblen are an outgrowth of the structure of liberal doctrine and are not simply due to an eccentric reading of his texts.

THE RADICAL CRITICS

The importance of the radical critique is evident both in its anticipation and reinforcement of many subsequent analyses of Veblen's ideas. Radical interpreters of Veblen often suggest that there were two Veblens. One was the disinterested liberal, reluctant to take sides, while the other, the revolutionary Veblen, emerged more clearly during and after the First World War. While there were themes in his later work that Veblen did not deal with earlier, his later writings did tend to take the form of concrete application and propaganda, thus moving away from the abstraction, detachment, and greater impartiality of his earlier work.

A charge made against Veblen by liberals and radicals alike was that he was deficient in the realm of specific policy prescription and programmatics. Although it has been shown elsewhere that these claims were occasionally exaggerated or irrelevant, it is true that he never outlined a set of legislative reform proposals like those implemented during the Progressive era. Nor did he adequately anticipate the regulatory and welfare state collectivist reforms of the New Deal. Many liberals under his influence claimed they found doctrinal inspiration for the Roosevelt era in his writing, but radicals, instead, noted his failure to suggest or endorse specific policy measures of an egalitarian nature. The latter were thus disappointed at Veblen's refusal to endorse specific forms of property, tax systems, and measures for redistribution. They were also perplexed at his refusal to devise or prescribe new welfare and regulatory policies and wondered what he thought should be done to remedy social injustice. His ambiguity or silence on such issues led some radicals to the conclusion that he was merely a liberal who used radical rhetoric. However, his failure to make specific policy recommendations was logically consistent with his evolutionary, Darwinian perspective that saw the instrumentally adaptive efforts of the community always falling short of what was needed, since institutional reforms would be obsolete by the time they could be implemented.

INTERNATIONAL RELATIONS

Criticisms of Veblen's work on international relations played but a small part in this study, with the exception of the American philosopher and social theorist George H. Mead's review of *The Nature of Peace*. Nevertheless, in order to understand both Veblen's political economy and social theory and its critics, it is essential to comment on his view of politics among nations. Briefly, although Veblen did not condemn all use of force in settling international disputes, he did have pacifist leanings that sometimes took him a long way toward renunciation of military solutions to international conflict. However, in the immediate post–World War I period he proposed a collective security pact among the English- and French-speaking nations to ward off aggression by predators and to enforce peace with military force if necessary. This scheme was advanced to cope with the possible resurgence of German and Japanese militarism. Also, he advocated limiting Western property rights and investment in underdeveloped countries because he believed this would serve as a tension-reduction mechanism between the major powers. Veblen strongly disliked the arms race that produced the Great War, was an acidic critic of the predatory war aims of the bellicose nations, and a principled opponent of patriotism as chauvinistic nationalism.

Veblen's *An Inquiry into the Nature of Peace* attracted attention from critics, but most of the criticism it received did not focus on his analysis of politics among nations or on his prescriptions in the book for policy change after World War I. Instead, the focus of criticism was his analysis of patriotism. Liberals like Mead believed Veblen had distorted the real meaning and significance of patriotism. To both Mead and the conservative Dobriansky, Veblen ignored the mostly positive attributes of the patriot in his eagerness to undermine the ruling class and the support it received for its war aims and duel for empire. Had he perceived patriotism more objectively, he might have observed that it was motivated by altruism and other-regardingness, which was a main source of sustenance for whatever degree of human solidarity and community that existed. Veblen's focus on the hatred, bigotry, and irrationalism of the patriot was misguided in that it made him ignore the positive qualities of patriotism that was the ultimate social bonding agent holding the nation together.

Radicals were more sympathetic to Veblen's perspective because he put in sophisticated conceptual form what many had already come to believe; namely, that patriotism was a form of false consciousness that made the common man susceptible to manipulation for warlike aims and imperialistic aggrandizement. However, it is interesting to note that Veblen was criticized by radicals for his failure to understand the liberating force of patriotism as a component of nationalism after World War I. This interpretation of Veblen thus indicted him for ignoring the emancipatory impact of nationalism when it becomes a fulcrum of anti-imperialist radicalism.

The pros and cons of Veblen's work on patriotism are revealing of the politico-ideological bias of his critics, whether written during the two world wars or later, during the Cold War. Mead, clearly the most important opponent of Veblen's teachings on patriotism at the end of the 1914–1918 conflict, was himself a staunch advocate of American participation in the war, so it was not surprising that he would take issue with Veblen's challenge to patriotism. Dobriansky, another critic, was a doctrinaire anticommunist who found sustenance in American patriotism for Cold War policies he personally favored.

Typically, both liberals and conservatives in the English-speaking world in the first half of the twentieth century viewed balance-of-power politics as necessary and inevitable, although they sometimes disagreed over the means to be employed in the pursuit of these ends. But radicals, particularly the pacifist left, stressed the moral and political imperatives of international disarmament and the need for a flattened or leveled order to replace the present, highly stratified, one. The radical critique pointed toward a "powerless" international environment where countries would no longer have the will or the means to impose their values on less powerful nations; this critique probably converged with Veblen's own long-run perspective, although not always with his short-term prescriptions.

The moral significance of political action, that is, the tension between moral principle and the requirements of successful political action, did not escape the attention of the three politico-ideological groupings. All were moralistic in deploring the often profound divergence between their own moral ideals on the one hand and the intent of foreign policymakers and the consequences of their acts on the other hand. Such major issue-areas as the rights of corporate property holders in foreign countries, human rights violations, freedom of entry and exit, and disarmament, all of which interested Veblen, compelled moralization then as now. In twentieth-century America, conservatives, liberals, and radicals have all, at times, identified the moral and political aspirations of a particular nation with the moral laws that govern the universe. Characteristically, however, the left in the United States has attacked liberals and conservatives alike for their unreflective support of American foreign policy. Indeed, some of Veblen's last and most polemical writing aimed at rousing the acquiescent from their patriotic torpor.

What also separated the left from the right was the question of the extent to which, if any, politics is autonomous from economics. Specifically, were foreign policy maker's options constrained by class power and economic interests or were they independent in varying degrees from such constraints? Generally, radicals have claimed, and Veblen certainly agreed, that liberals and conservatives alike were not cognizant of the degree to which their own values and attitudes were shaped by the dominant classes. Consequently, the radical critique viewed foreign policy options as bound by the dominant class's interests. Much of Veblen's work on politics among nations can best be interpreted as an appeal to his readers, however satirical or subtle, to rid themselves of the hegemonic preconceptions of the ruling classes and their statesmen.

TECHNICAL ELITISM

Much has been said pro and con regarding Veblen's alleged technical elitism. A summation of the political axes ground by his critics in portraying him as a technical elitist in the two generations following publication of *The Engineers and the Price System* (1921) is thus in order.

It is clear that those most interested in this facet of Veblen's work used it to discredit his theories as a whole. They sought to achieve this by portraying him as a technical elitist whose extremism finally culminated in a proposal for rule of the social order through a "soviet" of engineers and technicians. There were "hard" and "soft" versions of this, ranging from Daniel Bell's claims that parallels existed between Veblen's proposal and a technocratic fascism with "scientistic" and "inhuman" proclivities to a softer view of Veblen as motivated largely by a desire to avoid waste and idleness through better economic planning. It was likely, however, that liberals and conservatives alike were fighting both the Second World War and the Cold War by opposing what they perceived as totalitarian or authoritarian propensities in his thought. Or did they seize upon war frenzy to associate him with sinister creeds and leaders whose evil machinations put them in disrepute? However outdated assertions are regarding motives, it is undeniable that the politically and emotionally charged environment of the 1940s and 1950s made it difficult for thinkers like Veblen to get a fair hearing in certain quarters. Those who made allegations against him of autocratic doctrinal and political intent can hardly have been unaware of this.

Another common argument advanced by conservatives ranging from Lev Dobriansky to Abram Harris concerned the problem of efficiency in a planned economy, where there was no price system to allocate resources or measure efficiency, and no effective way for enterprises to know what to produce, since the consumer was not sovereign.

Neoclassical economists, both political liberals and conservatives, claimed that Veblen intended to introduce technological and mechanical criteria of value instead of using the price system to satisfy the subjective preferences of consumers. The moral agnosticism that is so pervasive in neoclassicism was thus inconsistently applied in indicting Veblen; if there are no standards or criteria by which to evaluate tastes or preferences, and if it is impossible to make convincing interpersonal comparisons of utility, why is it wrong to substitute mechanical or technological criteria for consumer judgments, whatever they may be? Neoclassicists had difficulty responding to this query since they lacked evaluative criteria, and thus were crippled in their efforts to undermine what they mistakenly took to be Veblen's analysis.

Conservatives and liberals as proponents of a "catallactic" economics view economics primarily as a science of exchange that studies the most efficient means by which to allocate scarce resources to achieve ends ultimately designated by consumers. Obviously, any view of economics that deviates very much from this paradigm can only be interpreted by them as a likely source of inequity and inefficiency. Any scheme for large-scale social control of industry must be opposed on fundamental doctrinal grounds because, by definition, it cannot work efficiently and, in any case, will very likely lead to deprivation of personal freedom.

However, the further removed the critic is from the doctrinal nesting ground of neoclassical economics, the more ambivalent his attitudes toward Veblen's alleged technical elitism become. The more doctrinaire Marxists are exceptions to this generalization, for they find in Veblen's soviet of engineers and technicians a betrayal of the working class and a forfeiture of his right to speak on behalf of a proletarian socialism. Thus the alleged pervasiveness of technocratic elements in Veblen's thought makes a proper class analysis impossible. Veblen becomes simply another bourgeois liberal unable to transcend idealism to dialectics and materialism, or such was the claim of Trotskyite John Wright and Bolshevik Nikolai Bukharin. But radicals like Paul Sweezy and Arthur Davis downplayed the technical elitist aspects of Veblenian analysis and viewed him as an authentic radical who used class analysis more effectively than his American contemporaries.

According to Arthur Schlesinger, Jr., various liberals distilled analytical and conceptual devices from Veblen's technical elitism by which to understand and, ultimately, develop ways to control the business cycle more effectively. New Dealers such as Mordecai Ezekiel, Jerome Frank, Adolf Berle, Gardiner Means, Rexford Tugwell and Henry Wallace thus sought a more effective social control of industry. They believed that while Veblen's doctrines were too radical, they nevertheless provided insights into the nature of the business cycle and a more effective countercyclical policy. Thus left, right, and center all found doctrinal ammunition in *The Engineers and the Price System* for the achievement of their own very different political aims and social agenda.

TECHNOLOGICAL DETERMINISM AND SOCIAL CHANGE

Veblen's conservative and liberal critics often asserted that he assigned primacy to technology in explaining the causality of social change; in short, that he was what is commonly referred to as a "technological determinist." Veblen's conservative critics made the most extreme accusations of technological determinism against Veblen. They believed that he viewed the cumulative growth of technology as the forcing bed of social change by assigning causal primacy to the realm of the machine process. He was thus charged with attributing to the institutional and cultural superstructure a merely reactive and secondary role. Most of the conservatives and several of the liberals featured in this study favored this interpretation of Veblen, although some versions were more extreme than others; so extreme, in fact, as to claim that the only values he really endorsed were technological or mechanical in nature. His values were thus devoid of moral and aesthetic qualities and his ideal society must, therefore, resemble an assembly line set in a harshly ascetic environment.

Left-liberals and radicals were appreciative of Veblen's stress on the institutional and the cultural apparatus as change-retardant features of social evolution. Although the left was inclined to criticize as too reductionistic his emphasis on technology, particularly the impact of the machine process on the psyche of industrial workers, it generally favored the Veblenian materialist perspective. This was also true of his claims regarding those social strata furthest removed from the conditioning impact of the machine process; namely the leisure class, whose parasitism was manifested in conspicuous consumption, waste, and exemption from useful labor.

C. Wright Mills, Arthur Davis, and Paul Sweezy found ammunition with which to wage ideological warfare on conservatives and liberals alike in Veblen's analysis of technology and social change. The more favorable reception given to his theory of social change on the left, however, may also have reflected the tendency of many radicals to favor the primacy of technology or at least to emphasize the class and techno-economic determinants of social change. On the other hand, the negative reception accorded Veblen's "technological determinism" in the center and right may have reflected its bias toward the role of ideational, moral, and religious factors in bringing about social change. Explaining the varying reaction of critics to his theory of social change thus requires paying heed to their political and cultural orientations as the predeterminant of their conceptual and theoretical predispositions.

THE DICHOTOMY BETWEEN BUSINESS AND INDUSTRY

The dichotomy between business and industry, that is, between making money and making socially useful goods, was understood by all three doctrinal groups to be a central feature of Veblen's work. With few exceptions, conservatives strongly disagreed with it, liberals were ambiguous about it, while radicals were often favorably inclined toward it when they believed it converged with the Marxian approach. Analysis of the doctrinal reaction toward Veblen's dichotomy is important because it is very expressive of the standards of valuation employed by the critic, whether they be of the left, right, or center.

The approach often followed by conservatives was to refuse to make the distinction between "exchange" value and "use" value and to claim that the term use value was essentially meaningless. Although one of Veblen's most astute conservative critics Frank Knight was unwilling to go to this extreme, he, too, believed that the concept of use value was potentially subversive of a market economy. Nevertheless, for the other conservatives, economic value was ultimately exchange value and measurable only by price; value is the subjective preference of individuals and nothing more. Thus conservatives and liberals alike influenced by the moral agnosticism of neoclassical economics found the Veblenian distinction between making money and making socially useful goods implausible; for, in his analysis, many commodities that had exchange value had little or no use value. The expression "use value" implies that a commodity may enhance the "generic ends" of existence, leading to "fullness of life," and to Veblen much with only exchange value was destructive of both.

As the political spectrum is traversed from right to left, the moral agnosticism toward consumer preferences so characteristic of neoclassicism gives way to more systematic efforts to develop standards or criteria of value for the appraisal of goods and services. Those social scientists furthest to the left are thus more likely to favor Veblen's dichotomy between making money and making socially useful goods. This is in accord with the attitudes of critical theorists toward the systemic inability of capitalism to produce socially necessary commodities and the waste that results from producing goods for invidious, that is, status-enhancing reasons. However, it is interesting to note that two of Veblen's strongest critics in this regard were Marxists of European origin, namely, Paul Baran and Theodor Adorno. Both were convinced that Veblen was an American puritan committed to an ethic of constant economic quantities that would force the working class to live at or near some social subsistence level that Veblen believed optimal, rather than to enjoy a more affluent life-style. Adorno also believed that Veblen was so fearful of economic waste that it made him aesthetically blind; indeed, so aesthetically insensitive was he that he assaulted all higher culture as leisure class dissipation of scarce resources.

Ironically, the two Marxists, Baran and Adorno, stressed the extremist nature of Veblen's dichotomy between making money and making socially useful goods because, to them, exchange value represented the use value of consumer abundance found in higher cultural pursuits. However, other leftists were more enamored of the dichotomy because, in their view, the price system systematically misallocates resources; thus what is profitable is often not socially useful and what is socially useful is not profitable. Such Veblen critics as Paul Sweezy and Max Lerner, in his radical years, saw considerable value in the dichotomy both as an analytical device and as a method for developing criterion of value, although in this regard they made no real advance over Veblen himself.

SOCIAL PSYCHOLOGY

What might loosely be termed Veblen's "social psychology" attracted negative comments from his critics left and right. His claims regarding the impact of the machine process on the psyche of industrial workers was one of their focal points. Veblen believed, when he wrote *The Theory of Business Enterprise* in 1904, that the interaction of manual workers with machine technology induced iconoclasm and skepticism in them with regard to conventional beliefs, and promoted egalitarianism and an ability to reason in terms of causal relationships. He also suggested that irreverence toward religious belief and practice, distrust of the existing system of property relations, and political and social attitudes ultimately conducive to collectivism, were becoming pervasive. Marxists were of two minds toward these claims. Some thought his analysis was correct as regards the changing mentality and values of the working class, although they believed he exaggerated the role of technology in causing this. Others thought he did not understand the role of class relations in inducing proletarian consciousness and that his stress on technology as the cause of class consciousness was the reason for this.

Liberals and conservatives alike believed that however accurate his description of the values and behavior of workers, his explanation was nevertheless strongly flavored with technological reductionism. They also thought he overlooked the pluralism and diversity of American thought and culture, which lent a variety of outlooks, as well as mixed values, to all groups in American society. In any case, conservatives tended either to negate the importance of class as such or to deny that classes have any particular identifiable traits that set them off from each other. The class nature of Veblen's analysis did not appeal to the right for reasons that were probably related to its desire to ignore or downplay the durability as well as the depth of class divisions in America.

Radicals often criticized Veblen for underestimating the revolutionary potential of the working class; in short, they scolded him for his failure to subscribe to what C. Wright Mills was later to call the "labor metaphysic." However, Paul Sweezy and Arthur Davis, in particular, were aware of the role that status emulation played as a social bonding agent that prevented classes from becoming class conscious and engaging in mass political action. The failure of political socialism to sink its roots deep into the American working class was thus explained in Werner Sombart's claim that socialism foundered on reefs of roast beef and apple pie or, at least, class-shared dreams thereof.

Veblen's sometimes ambiguous distinction between "instincts" and "tropisms" was often lost on his critics, who failed to adequately grasp his differentiation between instinctual and learned behavior.[7] His use of a vocabulary in transition reflected contemporary trends in psychology and biology up to 1914, but confused some critics while providing others with a rationale for rejecting his entire theoretical and conceptual apparatus. For example, Trotskyite John Wright found ample grounds for negating the Veblenian system because he believed it did not allow scope for proper human development through restructuring the institutional environment to change socialization patterns. Occasionally, even conservatives who ordinarily placed little stress on the environmental determinants of human behavior took Veblen to task for his failure to understand the plasticity and malleability of the species!

Another criticism voiced was that Veblen drew too sharp a distinction between self-regarding and other-regarding forms of behavior; that is, that he exaggerated the qualitative differences between the pecuniary and sporting instincts on the one hand and the instincts of workmanship, idle curiosity, and parental bent on the other hand. Indeed, radical Bernard Rosenberg believed that Veblen's other-regarding traits did not have all of the positive attributes he imagined they had. Apparently, in the view of Rosenberg and those like him, it was possible to have too much critical intelligence, altruism, and workmanlike proficiency to serve the public good; what Veblen perceived as virtue, Rosenberg saw as socially negative.

VEBLEN AND ANTHROPOLOGY

Radicals generally did not have much to say about Veblen's views on anthropology either because the subject did not interest them or because they agreed with Veblen's anthropological analysis. At times, their comments indicated a common sympathy toward the pacifistic, egalitarian communalism and simple life that Veblen found so admirable in the savage state of existence. It thus appeared that it was a secularized, technologized version of Rousseau's Noble Savage that some radicals sought to foster as an ideal species type in the modern community; this seems a plausible extrapolation from what little they actually wrote regarding Veblen's use of the literature and data of anthropology.

Liberals and conservatives alike argued strenuously that Veblen's portrayal of primitive men, particularly in *The Theory of the Leisure Class*, is naive in assuming the inherent goodness of man and implausible in its use of the findings of professional anthropologists. Fundamentally, they were at odds with Veblen over two related points: the first had to do with the nature of man; the second explained why the human species behaves as it does in different settings. This is not merely the nature versus nurture controversy, although that is relevant; rather, it also involves assessment of human potential. Both liberals and conservatives charged Veblen with believing that human beings are inherently good, by which they apparently mean intrinsically curious, altruistic, and driven toward proficiency of workmanship— Veblen's own generic ends of life. Often they also seemed to mean egalitarian, pacifistic, and communally-oriented.

At times, it is difficult to tell whether they were simply charging Veblen with misusing the data and literature of anthropology to rationalize his portrait of intrinsic human goodness, or whether they disliked his projection of what humankind could be like because they could not face the implications of this for the future. Conservatives with a pessimistic view of human potential were frightened by the futuristic aspects of the Veblenian outlook. Liberals with a more ambiguous view of humanity did not react as negatively to his use of the data and literature of anthropology. Nevertheless, they saw themselves, their peers, and their families at the center of Veblen's satirization of emulatory consumption, ostentatious display, and invidious distinction; and wondered how "fullness of life" could develop in a world inhabited by non-Veblenian people like themselves?

Veblen's division of social development into schematic stages drew the criticism of liberals and conservatives for several reasons. First, because they believed the stages were arbitrary, meaning that there were no adequate reasons, for example, for his demarcation between savagery and barbarism. Secondly, Veblen's attacks on teleology were now turned against him and he was charged with believing that societies inevitably move through these stages; in short, it was claimed that he was guilty of implicit teleogism in projecting a pre-determined direction for social evolution. Finally, it was argued that Veblen misinterpreted the actual conditions that existed in each stage by exaggerating the positive qualities and ignoring the negative or by doing the opposite.[8]

Also, by relying on the now obsolescent studies produced by anthropologists such as Edward Tylor, James Frazier, and Lewis Henry Morgan and not using the insights of more contemporary scholars, the literature and data of anthropology served only to rationalize Veblen's own political agenda. Of course, his liberal and conservative critics did likewise, only their aims and programmatics were different from his. The use and abuse of anthropology thus played a vital political role in the discourse between Veblen and his critics.

THE NATURE AND ROLE OF THE STATE

The similarities between Veblen's and Marx's view of the state under capitalism are great except that Veblen emphasized its role as a waster of economic resources more than Marx. However, it is interesting to note that radicals like Paul Baran, conservatives such as Lev Dobriansky, and liberals of various stripes all criticized Veblen's view of the state, although for different reasons.

To Baran, Veblen's view of the American state as an exploitive, repressive, and wasteful apparatus was indiscriminate because he failed to understand its positive functions, such as its public works programs and its generation and sale of electric power. Interestingly, a Marxist was now defending the New Deal against another radical critic whom he castigated for failing to appreciate the positive qualities of the state under capitalism. Of course, Veblen often did not distinguish between economics and politics. For him, business interests dominated both industry and politics and that domination resulted in a stagnant economy. On account of his antistatist bias, liberals often criticized Veblen for not realizing that social legislation and government control of business would serve to indefinitely stabilize and improve the system.

To Lev Dobriansky, Veblen's views were unduly narrow in that they failed to focus on the state as the defender of political and civil rights and liberties. In his acidic attacks, Veblen failed to adequately note the differences between authoritarian and constitutional regimes. This was due, in part, to the fact that he misunderstood the nature of the state itself. But it was also because he could not see the origin of human rights in the transcendental moral structure of the universe as expressed in the perennial philosophy of Thomas Aquinas favored by Dobriansky. But the conservatives' main criticism of Veblen was that he served as an important source of doctrinal inspiration to various kinds of collectivists who wished to impose a statist straitjacket on the economy. They believed that Progressives, New Dealers, and radicals of various stripes found a rationale in his thought for the social control of industry. Worse yet, Veblen's attitudes toward private property were negative and his disapproval of state sanctions to enforce corporate property rights clearly dismayed conservatives.

Liberals like Louis Schneider thought that Veblen, due to his dislike of existing authority and restraint, did not appreciate the need for ordering principles and coercive mechanisms to enforce them. While Schneider's criticisms were aimed at Veblen's attitudes toward social institutions rather than at the central government, it is evident that he found Veblen's preference for ordered anarchy wanting, believing it hopelessly visionary. Thus a favorite theme of Veblen's liberal critics was that his quasi-anarchist dislike of established institutions was extremist and utopian in character. David Riesman, too, believed that Veblen had little positive to say about institutions, for his study of the university focused obsessively on top administrators and trustees. His proposal for the abolition of both was viewed by Riesman as institutionally unfeasible since he offered no realistic alternative form of government for the university.

Veblen's major critics paid relatively little attention to his work on Imperial Germany, or to the essays he wrote during and immediately after World War I on the future role of Germany and Japan in world affairs, although they sometimes praised his foresight. For example, in 1940, Vice President Henry Wallace wrote an article on Veblen, whom he had known years before, praising the value of his analysis of Germany's role in world affairs.[9] He also recommended to President Franklin D. Roosevelt that he read Veblen's *The Nature of Peace*.[10]

However, more to the point were the flaws critics found in Veblen's analysis and prophecy regarding Imperial Germany and Japan. The criticisms focused on Veblen's alleged failure to understand the ideological and institutional overlay surrounding Germany's industrial advance in the late Hohenzollern period. Critics also claimed that Veblen's prediction of the resurgence of right-wing authoritarianism and militarism fell short of the fascist totalitarianism and brutal aggression that was actually to occur. Thus Veblen failed to adequately interpret the cultural and institutional matrix of industrialization in Hohenzollern Germany and Meiji Japan; and his predictions regarding the consequence of failure to socially renovate these societies at the end of World War I, while insightful, did not really grasp the qualitative essence of the totalitarianism that was to come.

VALUE, EQUALITY, AND ADAPTATION

Critics of every doctrinal orientation had difficulty understanding Veblen's social value theory, which was ultimately rooted in group survival through instrumental adaptation. However sympathetic Veblen may have been toward the development of a science of labor value, his Darwinian perspective nevertheless oriented him primarily toward the evolution and survival of the human community. But the successful evolution of mankind, in his view, rested on the continuing development of the tool continuum and upon effective community access to the collective legacy that it represented. In the final analysis, the only apparent justification Veblen offered for any system of property relations or distribution of income was that it provide optimal aid to society in achieving better instrumental adaptation. Veblen thus favored equality because he thought it would lead to a more effective adjustment of the community to its environment and to harmonious relations within the community.

Marxists saw the extraction of surplus value from the labor force as the essence of exploitation while classical liberals saw exploitation in the monopoly power of labor unions and taxing power of government. But Veblen located it in the usurpation and dissipation of industrial resources by vested interests, which weakened the adaptive abilities of the community. Because of his evolutionary, relativistic perspective, Veblen distrusted any doctrine that asserted the absolute or eternal right of a class or group to a specific portion of the income stream of the community, whether the doctrine be Marxian or classical liberal. At least some of his more perceptive critics left, right, and center recognized this and responded accordingly. Others simply failed to grasp his argument and could only observe his Darwinian approach to value dissipate into vapory clouds of satire.

Veblen is sometimes portrayed as a "radical apologist for conservatism." In this vein Ernest Dewey argued that Veblen was "philosophically an optimist" and a sound apologist for the "extrinsic value of the conservative's role in society." "Immanent but impermanent absolutes" may be used to describe Veblen's concept of principles and the application of truth he limited to the case or situation at hand. Ultimately Veblen "saw the institution as a functional social instrument which, though retrogressive in many instances, represents the means by which society preserves what it believes to be the best principles of individual and social adaptation."[11] However, Veblen's view of what should be conserved and changed to assure maximum adaptability affronted political conservatives and liberals alike by identifying institutions they supported as vested interests obstructing instrumental adaptation.

PROPERTY—ITS ORIGINS AND USAGES

Veblen believed that property may have developed out of the practice of seizing and owning women. In short, the existing institutions and practices that are now associated with the possession of private property could ultimately be traced to the seizure and possession of females by primitive men. Naturally, his critics raised many objections to this view; classical liberals in particular, found the modern institution of property, instead, rooted in the fact that individuals are the proprietors of their own persons, so that when they mix their labor with land, for example, it becomes theirs because it is an extension of their personality. Veblen's claim that property originated in acts of coercion and exploitation was not appealing because it made it difficult to legitimize existing property forms. However, his evolutionary perspective gave primary value to group survival through instrumental adaptation that clearly suggested that the exercise of property rights is contingent on the needs of the community. This view of property was obviously more acceptable to the liberal-left side of the political spectrum than to conservatives because it made property ownership and control relative to the well-being of the community. Property was thus not an absolute right as in the libertarian perspective; nor was it necessarily essential to the proper development of the individual personality as in the Aristotelian-Thomistic view, a position held by conservatives and moderates alike. Rather, insofar as Veblen expressed a view on property, it was an instrumentalist one requiring a change in property rights whenever the adaptive needs of the community required it.

By 1920 or so, Veblen felt that these needs required the abolition of absentee ownership, a fact that did not go unnoticed by his critics. Conservatives who were cognizant of his prescription were, no doubt, appalled by it; liberals were shaken by it, although some did not take his support of the abolition of absentee ownership too seriously. Only on the far left did his prescription receive much welcome and even there it met with skepticism on the part of those who felt Veblen did not go far enough. This probably reflected the fact that radicals were never sure what his attitudes really were.

Did he favor nationalization of basic industries and their management by a civil service bureaucracy? He never specifically said that he did. Did he favor a kind of guild socialism or anarchosyndicalism that would require a worker-owned, worker-managed industrial system? Or was his main point that private ownership of the means of production keeps the worker from playing any direct role in making industrial policy and is thus deficient in that it thwarts exercise and development of the instinct of workmanship? Some of Veblen's postwar writings in *The Dial* pointed in this latter direction but were ambiguous, so it is not surprising that his critics reacted in such diverse ways regardless of their own views on property rights.

VEBLEN AS CRITIC OF CLASSICAL AND NEOCLASSICAL ECONOMICS

Veblen's interpretation and criticism of the received economic doctrine aroused considerable interest on the part of his critics, but more to the point was the political exploitation of the history of economic thought to which, perhaps, both he and his critics fell prey. Radicals generally conceded much value to his work in this area except for his analysis of Karl Marx, which several thought was fundamentally wrongheaded. Veblen believed Marx to be infected with Hegelian teleology, while utilitarianism was evident in his claims regarding class consciousness. Also, he saw social metaphysics in Marx's view, if such it was, that the worker had an absolute right to the value of his work. Veblen found the virus of romantic utopianism present in Marx, but Marxists believed that Veblen exaggerated all these traits so much that they prevented his own transcendence to materialism and dialectics. In short, Veblen's negative evaluation of key parts of Marx's work resulted in the doctrinal undercutting of proletarian socialism and in an unfortunate personal detachment from radical politics, or so radicals alleged.

Conservatives had their own political axes to grind as they attempted to discredit Veblen's attack on classical and neoclassical economics; they objected to his repudiation of laissez-faire as public policy and marginal utility as the basis for understanding value, production, and distribution theory. The conservative preference for modified laissez-faire and marginal utility theory stemmed from their belief that no public policy was likely to induce more equity and efficiency and no theory was more capable of explaining what was actually occurring in the economic system. Veblen was repeatedly charged with trying to undermine the only "sound" public policy and economic doctrine.

Liberals were as critical of Veblen's use of the history of economic thought as either conservatives or radicals. Yet their reasons were much like those of the conservatives, although less doctrinaire. They, too, found political axes to grind, for they complained of his efforts to discredit the analytical apparatus of neoclassicism and of insensitivity toward the teleology that infected his own thinking. Alvin Johnson, for example, charged that Veblen was a master at locating traces of teleology in the writings of other but fell prey to it himself.[12] Liberals saw more of value in capitalism than did he and believed his attacks on the price system, market mechanism, and absentee ownership were too extreme. They also resented his efforts to discredit their own apologetics on behalf of these institutions and processes when these apologetics formed an integral part of neoclassical economics. Veblen's attacks on orthodox economics were thus regarded by many liberal economists as too radical. A commonly voiced opinion was that Veblen should have improved upon orthodox economics and not called for its abandonment. Other liberals, in assessing Veblen's contribution, charged him with making disguised value judgments while at the same time alleging objectivity. Not surprisingly, the center and right side of the political spectrum came to the defense of neoclassicism by focusing on Veblen's own ideological bias.[13]

RELIGION

Veblen's often caustic attacks on institutional religious belief and practice did not go unnoticed by his critics, particularly those with religious convictions of their own. To illustrate this point, B. W. Wells, in reviewing *The Theory of the Leisure Class*, argued that it contained "a vicious attack on Christian ideals."[14] Veblen's own generic denunciation of "imbecile institutions" surely included the Roman Catholic church, evangelical Protestant sects, and Eastern Orthodoxy at the least; it may also have meant the Reformation Protestant denominations, including the Lutheran, Veblen's own religious heritage. His critics focused their rebuttals on several aspects of his analysis by proclaiming the validity of formal religious belief, that is, the truth of the Christian creed, the stabilizing role that religion plays in the community, and the moral anarchy that must ultimately result from a relativism such as Veblen's.

The critic perhaps most interested in Veblen's views on religion was, of course, the only critic of any real consequence who wrote from an explicitly religious perspective, namely, Lev Dobriansky. His Thomism provided the metaphysical, epistemological, ontological, and ethical fulcrum for his analysis of Veblen's critique of religion. It is evident that the latter's disbelief in God, soul, and afterlife was offensive to Dobriansky as were his satirical comments regarding the institutional church and the intelligence of the clergy. Even more germane to his analysis, however, was his conviction that Veblen's Darwinian relativism could only lead to moral anarchy and, ultimately, to a political despotism unrestrained by the ethical dictates of the natural law.

Interestingly, most radicals had little to say about Veblen's attitudes toward religion, undoubtedly because they largely shared these attitudes and believed, in any case, that they had other more important theoretical issues to debate with him. Rosenberg, however, stressed the system-maintaining qualities of institutional religious belief and practice that he believed Veblen did not adequately understand. The structural-functional mode of analysis popularized by Talcott Parsons and his students influenced Rosenberg to the point that he did not think that a viable social order could exist without the system-maintaining properties of the Church or ersatz religion. He believed Veblen failed to take religion into consideration adequately, since he did not propose any institutions or social processes to take its place. It was thus ironic to find secularized liberals and radicals like Rosenberg criticizing him for his failure to understand the social equilibrating role of the Church in society.

Veblen's Microeconomics

Veblen's views on microeconomics, particularly the issue of consumer sovereignty, are perhaps better known than his views on any other subject. Indeed, his theory of status emulation and the vocabulary he developed to explain it are familiar to parts of the American public who never read a word of *The Theory of the Leisure Class*. Nevertheless, his conservative and liberal critics, while sometimes amused at the satirical qualities of his theory and interested in its implications, ultimately found it an unconvincing explanation of consumer behavior. This is because they attributed more volition and rationality to consumers who are faced with choices between alternatives than Veblen, who, instead, stressed the role of "habits of mind" that induce status-enhancing consumption that provides sustenance to the self-image, particularly the sense of self-worth.

The influence of moral agnosticism in convincing liberals and conservatives alike that it does not matter if consumer tastes and preferences are status-enhancing because the comparison of interpersonal utility functions is impossible anyway, cannot be disregarded either. If "pushpin is as good as poetry," then status gains derived from consumption are just as good or as bad as the satisfaction of biological or functional needs.

However, radicals using other value criterion found more merit in Veblen's theory of status emulation than liberals or conservatives. Most perceived the promotion of invidious distinctions through emulatory consumption destructive of human solidarity and community and viewed the capitalist system as inherently divisive for this reason. Perhaps, what most separated radical from liberal and conservative opinion was the belief that standards exist to distinguish consumption that serves the generic ends of life from that which does not because it is invidious. Much conservative and liberal criticism of Veblen also stressed the exaggerated emphasis he placed on the manipulative role of advertising and salesmanship and the economic waste that it causes. But to further pursue this issue would encroach on the controversy over the neo-Veblenian aspects of J. K. Galbraith's work as to what extent "dependence effects" are induced by advertising and whether his "revised sequence" doctrine successfully neutralizes the doctrine of consumer sovereignty.

Liberal interpreters of Veblen recognized that an important contribution of *The Theory of the Leisure Class* was its emphasis on the role of consumption as a symbol of social status. In their view, however, a main fault of the book was its failure to understand the function of consumption as an expression of basic cultural values. Further, Veblen pinpointed only the invidious aspects of conspicuous consumption and not the positive ones. Thus his theory of consumption was flawed because he failed to adequately appreciate the freedom and variety of choice made possible by market economies.

Although most criticism regarding Veblen's microeconomics focused on emulatory consumption, his views on economies of scale also attracted attention, particularly from economists. The critics generally agreed that he exaggerated the benefits to be derived from them. Lev Dobriansky claimed Veblen believed that cost curves would slope consistently downward if sufficiently large technologies were utilized; in short, that per unit costs of production would continuously decrease the larger the production technologies used. Veblen was thus accused of believing that at no point would diseconomies of scale start to occur.

His analysis in this respect caused critics to conclude that he favored monopoly, for only very large operating units could generate maximum economies of scale and these would be economically feasible only where a large market was secured. Veblen was thus charged with believing that a prima facie argument existed for monopoly wherever production technologies required large size to reap economies of scale. This led to attacks on him by left, right, and center for advocating industrial giantism and ignoring the benefits of competition. To some radicals, who were opposed to a competitive economic order anyway, this interpretation of Veblen's teaching had a certain attraction. To many liberals, both classical and modern, who believed in the virtues of a competitive economic order and thought such an order would disperse and fragment political power, Veblen's doctrine had little appeal.

CONCLUSION

This study began with criticism of Veblen's work during the presidency of Benjamin Harrison.[15] It concluded chronologically with Daniel Bell's attack on him during the Kennedy Administration. It dealt primarily with American intellectual history and comparative social theory and doctrine and broke his critics into three political camps in order to focus on their common elements as they evolved over time. It also attempted through textual exegesis to ascertain whether the critics properly understood Veblen or whether doctrinal blinders of various kinds distorted their vision. The book argued that the debate and dialogue over Veblen's contribution mostly reaffirmed the critics' own ideological and professional commitments. It concluded that most of the basic conflicts in economics and social theory are political and moral in nature and are thus unlikely to be resolved in the calculable future. But to further develop this argument, the varied analytical, conceptual, and valuative elements that are responsible for the different interpretations of Veblen by American social scientists must be juxtaposed once more.

It is important to note that most critics did not focus in isolation on the logical consistency or empirical validity of Veblen's work. Obviously, these had an important bearing on the viability of his theories. But exclusive of other considerations, they did not adequately characterize the main thrust of what is here labeled "criticism" because this criticism was primarily political and moral in dimension. Thus it was the value-laden, that is, political and moral facets of Veblen and his critics' work that are most potently manifested in their texts, not considerations of either a logical or empirical sort.

Conservatism, like its counterparts, liberalism and radicalism, has not remained static in the twentieth century partly because it has reacted to its ideological rivals who have also been in a process of change.

Conservatism can thus be viewed as (1) an issue orientation on policy matters, or (2) partisan political affiliation, or (3) commitment to a set of doctrines and a body of theory. Often, it means all three but this study focuses on category three. Veblen's critics were mostly political intellectuals and social scientists. Although their issue orientations on policy matters and their partisan political affiliations were important and usually linked, they were less relevant than their attachment to a set of doctrines and a body of theory.

Theory ordinarily descibes an attempt to explore reality and the attribution of cause and effect, while *doctrine* is typically employed to mean a statement of a desired or undesired state of affairs. In short *theory* has to do with "is" and *doctrine* has to do with "ought" in conventional social science usage. Veblen's critics failed to consistently or precisely separate assertions or claims with theoretical import from those with doctrinal significance. Consequently, it is often difficult to tell whether Veblen is charged with theoretical errors or with doctrinal deficiencies or both.

Many eminent American social scientists were sufficiently interested in Veblen's work to read and criticize it. That there was no agreement on its merit or validity will surprise only those who perceive of the social sciences as objective, value-neutral enterprises that will ultimately produce theoretical convergence. But doubt still exists in the minds of many as to the value of his legacy, a legacy whose significance was best summarized by Lewis Mumford in these words in 1931:

> Veblen's thought should not be confined to economic circles: it should be filtering through and penetrating every pore of our intellectual life. In that process, its solecisms would be discovered and thrown aside and its great original contributions would become fundamentally commonplace.[16]

As Mumford recognized in articulating his aspirations for Veblen's future influence, he could occupy a more central role in American intellectual life and in the formation of public policy than he presently does. Whether compulsive structural shifts, institutional changes, and reoccurring crises in the capitalist and world order will give his social thought a more prominent position in public life remains to be seen. In any case, Veblen continues to play an important role in American intellectual history and to be a fruitful contemporary source of insight for social scientists, humanists, educators, and aestheticians. It is a full-time task simply to keep abreast of the scholarly literature written about him, not to mention material written in a more popular vein.

However, insofar as Veblen was responsible for the lack of impact of his own theories and doctrines, what criticisms can legitimately be made of his failure to convert or influence many of his scholarly critics between 1891 and 1963? Some of the most penetrating criticisms in this regard came from a sympathetic foreign critic who had much in common with Veblen. The Englishman John Hobson believed that *The Theory of the Leisure Class* "gained many readers but probably suffered loss of serious intellectual attention because of a pervasive tone of irony conveyed in part by linguistic formalities."[17] Although the book gave him a reputation for wit, it nevertheless "postponed and even damaged his legitimate reputation as the keenest social thinker of his time."[18]

Although Veblen remains an important and influential theorist and critic of the capitalist order, his ideas had less impact on public policy and American culture than his more optimistic disciples anticipated. The reasons for this ranged from the opposition in the academy of neoclassical economists and sociologists practicing structural-functionalism, to a powerful business community and a pervasive materialistic, acquisitive culture that did not take radical criticism very seriously most of the time. It made little difference what Veblen said, or how he said it, for, outside academic life, principled opposition to the main drift of American business civilization was deflected, diffused, or harmlessly absorbed. In this vein, William Dugger has argued that

> Thorstein Veblen came to know better than any other social observer how American ambition distorts values and beliefs. Cultural change and value distortion in the United States can be understood best in terms of four invaluation processes—contamination, subordination, emulation, and mystification—which were first sketched out by Veblen. These four power processes change the motives for action and the meanings of action.[19]

It is in a business culture that Veblen is most illuminating because he explains why radical analyses of the system like his own have difficulty in gathering support. In Veblen's analysis, for example, it is evident that craftsmanship, that is, proficiency of workmanship, meaning to take pride in one's work and derive gratification from its performance, is more or less continuously contaminated by pecuniary motives and careerism. Those so influenced do not wish to be informed of the pernicious impact of this contamination by Veblen or anyone else. Closely related to contamination is another way to change or even implant values in those to be controlled; it is the way of subordination. The corporate culture, which became ever more pervasive in America during Veblen's lifetime, has proven most potent in subordinating existing value systems and modes of behavior not congruent with corporate objectives.

In Veblen's analysis, however, emulation is the most powerful invaluation process and in American society has become an effective mechanism of social control. Massive systemic emulatory strain may take the form of Veblen effects, bandwagon effects, snob effects, or countersnobbery,[20] but the result is the same; reinforcement of the existing value system and cultural mores.

Veblen also asserted that mystification occurs through a process of confusion involving the manipulation of symbols in which the individual or group is persuaded to substitute the values of others for its own. "Private property" and "free enterprise" are used to justify predation and exploit, while communal values are stretched or distorted to cover a multitude of actions that are socially destructive, such as air and water pollution.

By 1963, the year this study closes, the hegemony of the corporate culture was already far advanced in its development. Although Veblen explained what was occurring, all the conservatives and many of the liberals, in short, the bulk of his critics, fundamentally sanctioned the four invaluation processes that he exposed and attacked. Contamination, subordination, emulation, and mystification were the processes of which their dreams were apparently made. It is not surprising that the Veblenian corpus had little positive impact on them.

NOTES

CHAPTER ONE
VEBLEN: THE MAN AND HIS CRITICS

1. Joseph Dorfman, *Thorstein Veblen and His America* (New York: Viking Press, 1934).

2. Andrew Veblen to Joseph Dorfman, 28 February 1930, "Correspondence," Andrew Veblen Papers, Minnesota Historical Society, St. Paul, Minnesota.

3. Andrew Veblen to Joseph Dorfman, 18 March 1930, Volume 45 (dismantled, Folder 2), referred to hereafter as M.H.S. Shortly before this letter was written, Andrew Veblen had apparently complained to Alvin Johnson, director of the New School for Social Research, which sponsored Dorfman's work on Veblen, of the inaccuracies in the manuscript. Johnson wrote back to Veblen telling him, "It does not lie in my discretion to prevent Mr. Dorfman from writing your brother's life. It is, I think, possible for me to keep him from publishing anything so bad as the draft you have seen, which had not received my criticism when it was sent to you" (Alvin Johnson to Andrew Veblen, 5 March 1930), M.H.S.

4. Andrew Veblen to Edward Bemis, 4 October 1929, "Family Letters," M.H.S.

5. Ellen Rolfe Veblen to Thorstein Veblen, 16 May 1920, Thorstein Veblen Collection, Wisconsin Historical Society, Madison, Wisconsin. One description of her mental state came from Eugene S. Rolfe, her brother, who wrote in 1928, two years after her death, that

> she had long suffered from an obscure malady which seemed to baffle the doctors, and probably for this reason she directed that her body be turned over to Stanford for dissection. The peculiar religious cult of Halcyon with which she had allied herself, and to which she had conveyed her trifling estate before death, considered this dissection a desecration and appealed to the family to prevent it, but we felt that her wish was proper and should be respected. Except that Jesus Christ is the foundation of that particular sect, I can understand nothing of their propaganda. True it is vague, attenuated and hopelessly involved in a mass of inexplicable statements—but it seems to have brought peace and security to Nell's troubled soul.

A copy of this letter written in Eugene, Oregon, 16 January 1928 is in the Andrew Veblen Papers. For a brief portrait of Ellen Rolfe Veblen, see also Robert Duffus, *Innocents at Cedro* (New York: Macmillan, 1944), 143–49.

6. Wallace Atwood to Thorstein Veblen, 4 August 1919, Wallace Atwood Papers, Clark University Library, Worcester, Massachusetts.

7. David Starr Jordan to Henry Pratt Judson, 6 October 1909, University President's Papers, 1889–1925, Regenstein Library, University of Chicago. Not long after this letter was written, Veblen's British friend Victor Branford,

who had just spent several hours talking to Albion Small, the eminent sociologist, and Vice President Vincent, both of the University of Chicago, wrote: "Bad news about Veblen—Small says there was 'some scandal' about a woman and he had to leave Leland Stanford—which means doubtless any excuse to effect a quick exit from the university—Small was also cursedly glad to get rid of him from Chicago." (Bradford to Patrick Geddes, 17 April 1910, Geddes Papers, National Library of Scotland, Edinburgh, Scotland).

8. See David Starr Jordan to Thorstein Veblen, 22 August 1917, Thorstein Veblen Collection, Wisconsin Historical Society, Madison, Wisconsin.

9. Jacob Warshaw, "A Few Footnotes to Dorfman's Veblen," in Jacob Warshaw, Papers, 1910–1944, Western Historical Manuscript Collection, Columbia, Missouri.

10. Ibid., 3.

11. Ibid.

12. Ibid., 4.

13. Ibid., 5. Those familiar with the corpus of Veblen's writings will recall the importance of "idle curiosity," which apparently had roots in his early biography. As a small boy of eight or nine living with his Norwegian immigrant parents and many siblings on a farm in rural Minnesota, he made snares of horsehair and trapped gophers and squirrels with them, not to destroy the rodents, but so he could study them. He carried them about inside his shirt while he observed them and then released them after satisfying his curiosity. His lifelong interest in botany manifested itself when the children in the Veblen family went picking berries in the woods and fields, for he was likely to immediately detect any plant that he had not seen before and carefully investigate it. Still further evidence of his interest in natural phenomena is found in his failure to return one day to the farm after having been sent on an errand. When he did not return as expected, one of his brothers went looking for him. In the meantime, a powerful storm had arisen and when the brother found him, he was lying on his back beside the road, the family dog curled up next to him, studying the storm with intense interest. Such were the forms that "idle curiosity" took in the boy Veblen, and it is not surprising that he later assigned it a key role in human motivation. These stories and others regarding Veblen are related by Florence Veblen in "Thorstein Veblen: Reminiscences of His Brother Orson," *Social Forces* 10 (December 1931): 187–95.

14. Warshaw, "A Few Footnotes to Dorfman's Veblen," 8, 12.

15. Ibid., 10.

16. Ibid., 5.

17. Ibid., 4.

18. Madge Jenison, *Sunwise Turn: A Human Comedy of Bookselling* (New York: E. P. Dutton, 1923), 125–26.

19. Andrew Veblen to Edward Bemis, 4 October 1929, M.H.S.

20. Frank Knight, "The Limitations of Scientific Method in Economics," in *The Trend of Economics*, ed. Rexford G. Tugwell (New York: Alfred A. Knopf, 1924), 249–50.

21. John M. Clark, "The Socializing of Theoretical Economics," in *The Trend of Economics*, 86.

22. Wesley C. Mitchell, "The Prospects of Economics," in *The Trend of Economics*, 32.

23. Paul Douglas, "The Reality of Non-Commercial Incentives in Economic Life," in *The Trend of Economics*, 155.

24. Max Lerner, "Veblen, Thorstein Bunde," in *Dictionary of American Biography*, vol. 19 (New York: Charles Scribner's Sons, 1936), 244.

25. Arnold Rogow, "Veblen and the Society of Consent," *Nation* 185 (31 August 1957): 96.

26. Kenneth Boulding, "A New Look at Institutionalism," *American Economic Review: Papers and Proceedings* 47 (May 1957): 10.

27. Allan Gruchy, "Discussion," *American Economic Review: Papers and Proceedings* 47 (May 1957): 16.

28. A. W. Coats, "The Influence of Veblen's Methodology," *Journal of Political Economy* 62 (December 1954): 529.

29. Clair Wilcox, review of *Contemporary Economic Thought* by Paul T. Homan, *Annals of the American Academy of Social and Political Science* 139 (Spring 1928): 215.

30. Leon Ardzrooni, Intro. to Thorstein Veblen's, *Essays in Our Changing Order* (New York: Viking Press, 1934), viii.

31. Donald Walker, "Thorstein Veblen's Economic System" *Economic Inquiry* 15 (April 1977): 236.

32. H. F. Cruise, "The Economic Historian and the Growth Debate," *Australian Economic History Review* 15 (September 1975): 88.

33. Thomas Sowell, "Veblen, Thorstein," *The New Palgrave, A Dictionary of Economics*, vol. 4, ed. John Eatwell et al. (New York: The Stockton Press, 1987), 800.

34. Joseph Dorfman, "New Light on Veblen," in *Essays, Reviews and Reports* (New York: Augustus M. Kelley, 1973), 596.

35. Kenneth J. Arrow, "Thorstein Veblen as an Economic Theorist," *American Economist* 19 (Spring 1975): 5.

CHAPTER TWO
CONSERVATIVE CRITICS: THE EARLY PERIOD

1. The best single statement of Cummings's political philosophy at this time was his review of *The Theory of the Leisure Class*, *Journal of Political Economy* 7 (September 1899): 425–55.

2. The following material is from Joseph Dorfman's *Thorstein Veblen and His America* (New York: Viking Press, 1934), 252, 507–8. It provides further illumination of Cummings's attitudes toward Veblen.

It was hard for me to accept him or his philosophy. It went against my grain. I was eager to find it lop-sided and unreal. . . . My review gives good evidence that I did not at the time fairly appreciate the contribution Veblen was making to our economic and social philosophy. I have often wondered how I could have been so blind. In the years since we have all seen the accumulating evidence of widespread influence of Veblen's analysis of social and economic behaviour, as set forth in his *Theory of the leisure Class*. . . . I know that I should write a very different review . . . today.

I was a product of the gay nineties. My economic thinking was in conventional terms of academic training and of the classical economists and it was difficult off-hand for me to think at all in any other terms. With Veblen one really had to learn the alphabet all over again. It is difficult for me today to appreciate how strange his new alphabet was at that time. . . . Veblen was cubistic and for the time incomprehensible." Looking back to that time, Cummings doubted "if Veblen took my review of his book very seriously. . . . In my academic conventionalism I was just another interesting specimen for observation and analysis—and probably kindly commiseration."

3. Thorstein Veblen, "Mr. Cummings' Strictures on *The Theory of the Leisure Class*," *Journal of Political Economy* 8 (December 1899): 106–17.

4. Veblen, "Mr. Cummings' Strictures on *The Theory of the Leisure Class*," in *Essays in Our Changing Order*, ed. Leon Ardzrooni (New York: Augustus M. Kelly, 1964), 16.

5. Ibid., 23.

6. Ibid., 31.

7. Cummings, "The Theory of the Leisure Class," 454.

8. Ibid., p. 455. In summing up his own review, Cummings claimed that Veblen's writings in *The Theory of the Leisure Class* were filled with a strong personal and ideological bias. Later in life, however, after Veblen was gone, Cummings changed his mind. In 1931 he wrote that

there was . . . no personal equation whatever in his thinking. . . . His scientific work was purely objective, which is all the more extraordinary because of its purely theoretical and philosophical character. . . . His sweeping generalizations and deductive analyses were fundamentally inductions from observed facts of everyday experience. (As quoted in Dorfman, *Thorstein Veblen and His America*, 508.)

9. Veblen, "Mr. Cummings' Strictures," 19.

10. Cummings, "The Theory of the Leisure Class," 428.

11. Ibid.

12. Ibid., 429.

13. Ibid. 445.

14. Ibid., 444.

15. Ibid.

16. Veblen, "Mr. Cummings' Strictures," 29.

17. Ibid., 26.

18. Ibid., 25.

19. Ibid., 23.

20. Ibid., 24.

21. Cummings, "The Theory of the Leisure Class," 441. Cummings believed Veblen's emphasis on the predatory and parasitic role of the "captain of industry" was totally unjustified. He complained that

The quintessence of such socialism is clear-labor alone produces; ergo, to labor alone the product belongs. But the truth is labor alone does not produce. The obvious inference is that since it does not it cannot, and if labor cannot produce alone, that something required to make it productive should have—at least it can legitimately demand and take—its reward, even as it does. (Ibid., 451–52 [Following quotations from this source are cited in text.])

22. Veblen, "Mr. Cummings' Strictures," 24.

23. See the short biography of Fisher by John Perry Miller in *Ten Economic Studies in the Tradition of Irving Fisher* (New York: John Wiley & Sons, 1967), 1–9. A lengthier study of Fisher's life and work is by his son Irving N. Fisher, titled *My Father Irving Fisher* (New York: Comet Press, 1956).

24. Sumner and Fisher admired each other greatly but, in the final analysis, there were significant differences in their ideological perspectives as illustrated by the latter's speech on socialism given before the Yale Socialist Club in 1911. See Irving N. Fisher, *My Father Irving Fisher*, 44. Four of Veblen's letters to Sumner have been preserved in the W. G. Sumner Collection, Yale University Library, New Haven. Written in 1889 and 1891, they contain requests by Veblen for letters of recommendation from Sumner. There is little in them of personal or ideological interest except Veblen's explanation that he has been unable to work in recent years because of bad health.

25. See Fisher, "Why Has the Doctrine of Laissez-Faire Been Abandoned?" *Science* 25 (4 January 1907): 18–27.

26. Fisher once wrote that the four chief causes to which he and his wife had committed themselves were "the abolition of war, disease, degeneracy, and instability in money." While visiting Dresden, Germany, for an exposition, he was disappointed at the fact that brewers of beer were permitted to display and sell their wares. He attended a performance of the can-can, but found it "revolting." He supported prohibition, demanded the suppression of vice at every turn, and attacked the use of tobacco, caffeine, and drugs. Fisher spent much of his time and energy promoting the value of fresh air, exercise, vegetarianism, and other dietary novelties. Not surprisingly, his subscription of various fads to the point of crankishness was linked with elitist attitudes toward social reform. For example, he expressed a strong commitment to eugenics, which arose from his belief that society could only stave off collapse if the excessive reproduction of the intellectually inferior and the trend toward the physical deterioration of the mentally superior were checked. On these points, see Irving N. Fisher, *My Father Irving Fisher*, 105–80. But also see Mark Aldrich, "Capital Theory and Racism: From Laissez-Faire to the Eugenics Movement in the Career of Irving Fisher," *Review of Radical Political Economics* 7 (Fall 1975): 33–42.

27. See Thorstein Veblen, "Fisher's Rate of Interest," *Political Science Quarterly* 24 (June 1909): 296–303. Veblen attacked Irving Fisher's *The Rate of Interest: Its Nature, Determination and Relation to Economic Phenomena* (New York: Macmillan, 1907): Also, see Veblen, "Fisher's Capital and In-

292 NOTES TO CHAPTER 2

come," *Political Science Quarterly* 23 (March 1908): 112–18 in which he criticized Irving Fisher's *The Nature of Capital and Income*, (New York: Macmillan, 1906). Cf. John R. Commons, "Political Economy and Business Economy: Comments on Fisher's Capital and Income," *Quarterly Journal of Economics* 22 (November 1907): 120–25.

28. See the account by Joseph Dorfman in his *Thorstein Veblen: Essays, Reviews and Reports* (Clifton, N.J.: Augustus M. Kelly, 1973), 232–35.

29. Irving Fisher, "Capital and Interest," *Political Science Quarterly* 24 (September 1909): 513.

30. Ibid., 504. In his own defense Fisher wrote: "As early as 1892 I wrote: '"Utility" is the heritage of Bentham and his theory of pleasure and pains. For us his *word* is the more acceptable, the less it is entangled with his theory'" (ibid., 512–13).

31. Ibid., 506. However, Veblen wrote that "this shortsightedness of the taxonomic economist is a logical consequence of the hedonistic postulates of the school, not a personal peculiarity of the present or any other author" (Veblen, "Fisher's Capital and Income," 156–57). Fisher believed that Veblen badly misinterpreted him in claiming that he retained the essentials of psychological hedonism and utilitarianism. However, see Irving Fisher's *The Nature of Capital and Income* (New York: Macmillan, 1906), 3, 19, 42–44, 47, 88. Also see Irving Fisher, *The Rate of Interest* (New York and London: Garland Publishing, 1982), 337–43.

32. Fisher, "Capital and Interest," 512.

33. Thorstein Veblen, "Fisher's Capital and Income," in *Essays in Our Changing Order*, 161.

> In the hedonistically normal scheme of life wasteful, disserviceable, or futile acts have no place. The current competitive, capitalistic business scheme of life is normal, when rightly seen in the hedonistic light. There is not (normally) present in it anything of a wasteful, disserviceable, or futile character. Whatever phenomena do not fit into the scheme of normal economic life, as tested by the hedonistic postulate, are to be taken account of by way of exception. If there are discrepancies, in the way of waste, disserviceability, or futility, e.g., they are not inherent in the normal scheme and they do not call for incorporation in the theory of the situation in which they occur, except for interpretative elimination and correction. In this course the hedonistic economics, with its undoubting faith that whatever (normally) is right, simply follows the rule of all authentic taxonomic science. (Veblen, "Fisher's Capital and Income," 164)

34. Ibid., 164–65.

35. It is doubtful whether Fisher abandoned the tenets of hedonism as he claimed, and Veblen was astute in asserting that his work was still tainted by it. Substituting *satisfaction* for *pleasure* did not remove the Benthamite stigma from Fisher's work. On balance, Fisher used a modified Benthamite vocabulary and an explanation of human psychic processes that kept his economic analysis within the doctrinal parameters of what was once known as Philosophic Radicalism.

36. Ibid., 46–47. But, see Joseph Schumpeter's view as quoted in Irving N. Fisher, *My Father Irving Fisher*, 51. Also see Miller, *Ten Economic Studies*, 7.

37. John R. Commons, *Institutional Economics*, vol. 2 (Madison: University of Wisconsin Press, 1961), 677. Another contemporary of Commons, Veblen, and Fisher, Wesley Mitchell wrote that "Fisher's rejection of hedonism seems merely ephemeral to Veblen. He avoids the terminology of Bentham, but works with Bentham's ideas under new labels" (W. C. Mitchell, "The Rationality of Economic Activity," *Journal of Political Economy*" 28 [July-December 1910]: 109).

38. Paul T. Homan, "Issues in Economic Theory," *Quarterly Journal of Economics* 42 (May 1928): 345. Also, see J. M. Clark, "Recent Development in Economics," in *Recent Developments in the Social Sciences*, ed. Edward C. Hayes (Philadelphia and London: Lippincott, 1927), 243.

39. Veblen, "Fisher's Capital and Income," 149.

40. Fisher, "Capital and Interest," 508. Elsewhere Fisher wrote:

Classification, as I have always insisted, has of itself no power to solve scientific problems. It plays a very subordinate role in all that I have written. Nothing has surprised me more than the opinion expressed by one of my critics that *The Nature of Capital and Income* was a study of classification or taxonomy; but I reserve answer to this criticism for a separate article elsewhere. . . . How malapropos Professor Veblen's characterizations are may be seen by comparing them with my views on economic method as expressed in "Economics as a Science." (Irving Fisher, "A Reply to Critics," *Quarterly Journal of Economics* 23 [May 1909]: 541).

41. Fisher, "Capital and Interest," 508.

42. Ibid., 506–7.

43. Ibid., 510.

44. Ibid., 511.

45. Ibid., 511–12.

46. Veblen, "Fisher's Capital and Income," 160.

47. Ibid., 157. Veblen also commented sardonically that "one writer even goes so far in the endeavor to bring the facts within the scope of the staple concepts of theory at this point as to rate the persons concerned in such a case as 'capital' after having satisfied himself that such income-streams are traceable to a personal source. See Fisher *Nature of Capital and Income*, Chap. V" (Veblen, "On the Nature of Capital: Investment, Intangible Assets, and the Pecuniary Magnate," *Quarterly Journal of Economics* 23 [November 1908]: 125).

48. Veblen, "Fisher's Rate of Interest," 141.

49. Ibid., 138.

50. See Veblen, *The Instinct of Workmanship*, 103–4. Also see Baldwin Ranson, "The Unrecognized Revolution in the Theory of Capital Formation," *Journal of Economic Issues* 17 (December 1983): 901–15 and "The Institutionalist Theory of Capital Formation," *Journal of Economic Issues* 21 (September 1987): 1265–78.

51. Fisher, "Why Has the Doctrine of Laissez-Faire Been Abandoned?" 21.

52. Ibid., 26.

53. Despite Fisher's criticism of emulatory consumption, he lived on a grand scale as long as he could afford it. The following is his son's description of a dinner party in Fisher's large home in New Haven, Connecticut:

> When the guest entered the dining room, the severity of the highbacked carved oak chairs, with their black leather upholstery surmounted by fearsome dragons, was softened by a cheerful hearth fire. The table was set for eight with the gleaming white damask, branched silver candelabra and finely cut crystal goblets. . . . There were wine glasses at each place, since the host's conviction on the subject of total abstinence had not yet eliminated alcohol from the four-sixty menu. While servants glided noiselessly around the heavily-carpeted room, offering unpretentious but delectable viands, the only jarring note was an occasional rumble from the dumbwaiter as it hoisted the next course from the basement kitchen. (Irving N. Fisher, *My Father Irving Fisher*, 92–93).

It is difficult to imagine Veblen hosting such a party in a similar setting even if he had the money.

54. Veblen, "Fisher's Capital and Income," 148. (Following quotations from this source are cited in text.)

55. Fisher, "Capital and Interest," 506.

56. Veblen, "Fisher's Rate of Interest," 140–41.

57. Veblen, "Fisher's Capital and Income," 160.

58. Fisher, "Capital and Interest," 515. (Following quotations from this source are cited in text.)

59. Veblen, "Fisher's Rate of Interest," 141.

60. Fisher, "Capital and Interest," 543.

61. Veblen, "Fisher's Rate of Interest," 143.

62. Ibid., 147.

63. Fisher, "Capital and Interest," 506.

64. Ibid., 516.

65. Friedrich Von Hayek, *Profits, Interest and Investment* (London: Routledge, 1939), 149.

66. In a presumably "authoritative" statement concerning Fisher's role in American economics, Maurice Allais wrote that the "remarkable characteristic of Fisher's work is that it contains no basic error. Taken as a whole . . . it offers only valid ideas. . . . Schumpeter described him as American's greatest scientific economist. The future will certainly confirm this judgement" (Maurice Allais, "Irving Fisher," *International Encyclopedia of the Social Sciences*, vol. 5 (New York: Macmillan/Free Press, 1968), 476, 484). Veblen's exposure of the ideological structure and value-laden nature of Fisher's work apparently escaped the recent Nobel Laureate's notice.

67. Irving N. Fisher, *My Father Irving Fisher*, 201.

68. Ibid., 76.

69. Fisher, "Capital and Interest," 516.

70. However, one interesting similarity between Veblen and Fisher exists. Joseph Dorfman wrote that:

Professor Mitchell found that Irving Fisher much later developed a some-what similar theory of crises which he called the debt-deflation theory of depression. As I wrote elsewhere, "[in] *Booms and Depressions* (1932) he [Fisher] explained that the critical factor in determining the swing of the cycle was the expansion or liquidation of debts. . . . After Wesley C. Mitchell called Fisher's attention to Veblen's view in *The Theory of Business Enter-prise*, Fisher generously acknowledged that Veblen came nearest to his posi-tion." (As quoted in Dorfman, editor *Essays, Reviews and Reports*, 74)

71. Richard V. Teggart, *Thorstein Veblen: A Chapter in American Eco-nomic Thought* (Berkeley: University of California Publications, 1932). Teg-gart received his doctorate in economics from the University of California, Berkeley in 1931 and wrote his dissertation on Veblen. He was employed on the Berkeley campus in the Bancroft Library and never again published in the field of economics. Leon Ardzrooni, Veblen's student and long-time friend, once wrote that Teggart's study of him was

an ungracious and unwarranted attack on Veblen, consisting for the most part of gross misrepresentation and wanton abuse of the man. Under the guise of making a study of Veblen, the main purpose of the author seems rather to have been to achieve some monetary notoriety—all of which is, of course, perfectly good and legitimate American business procedure. Inci-dentally, also, this is one of the most flagrant instances of stultification by an American university appearing in the role of godfather to such an undertak-ing. (Leon Ardzrooni, ed., *Essays in Our Changing Order* (New York: Au-gustus M. Kelley, 1964), x. (Following quotations from this source are cited in text.)

72. Lewis H. Haney (1882–1969), professor of economics at New York Uni-versity, was an early and vitriolic conservative critic of both Veblen and institu-tional economics, the two of which he tended to conflate. Several of the early editions of his widely used *History of Economic Thought*, originally published in 1911, largely ignore Veblen, since Haney apparently did not want to write about him while he was still living. Occasionally, Haney alluded to him, but there was no systematic treatment of Veblen's ideas or ideological confron-tation with him until the 1936 edition of the book. Haney's view of Veblen was not fundamentally different than that held by the other conservatives, al-though it was expressed in more vituperative language. See Lewis H. Haney, *History of Economic Thought* (New York: Macmillan, 1936).

CHAPTER THREE
CONSERVATIVE CRITICS: THE CHICAGOITES

1. That Knight was critical of radical versions of laissez-faire is evident in his statement that "[Ludwig] von Mises would hardly be generally accepted as 'the leader of Contemporary Economic Liberalism' unless this means the aca-demic opponent of socialism most conspicuous for the extremism of his posi-tion" (Frank Knight, *On the History and Method of Economics* [Chicago: Uni-

versity of Chicago Press, 1956], 170). On the other hand, Knight believed that organized labor and the farm bloc imposed greater social costs on the public than corporate monopoly from the time of the New Deal on. For a relatively late statement of his position on this issue, see Frank Knight, *Intelligence and Democratic Action* (Cambridge: Harvard University Press, 1960), 92, 99. Also see J. Patrick Raines, "Frank H. Knight's Contributions to Social Economics," *Review of Social Economy* 47 (Fall 1989): 280–92.

2. Although the New Deal caused Knight to intensify his attack on interventionist policies and to look with a jaundiced eye on such possible doctrinal origins as Veblen's theories, there was no marked change in the opinions Knight expressed of Veblen. Indeed, if the dates of his comments on Veblen were not known, it would be difficult to tell if he wrote them before, during, or after the New Deal. However, his most candid views on the latter are found in his personal correspondence:

> The New Deal represents, not a peculiar American movement, but simply the American expression of a worldwide social development. That development is best characterized, in accordance with its original denomination, as Fascism. It has two essential features. (1) Structurally it consists in the organic partnership of the State and industry. It amounts to an effort by capitalistic industry to find protection and succor under the wing of an older and more respected institution: the State. (2) Functionally it consists in the utilization of propaganda, i.e., an appeal to mass emotions, for the ordering and administration of industry. Class conflicts are sought to be repressed and a certain unity and positive activism achieved through patriotic, nationalistic fervor. These characteristics are no less clearly exhibited under the New Deal, in my judgment, than in the Third Reich under Hitler and in Fascist Italy under Mussolini. (Frank Knight to Ralph Watkins, 3 November 1933, Frank Knight Papers, Regenstein Library, University of Chicago)

Also, see Knight to F. A. von Hayek, 9 May 1934, and Knight, "The New Deal and Liberalism" in *Report of Midwest Conference on Industrial Relations,* School of Business, University of Chicago, October 1934, pp. 35–44.

3. Knight, "Institutionalism" (unpublished manuscript in Knight Papers), 1. Also, see R. A. Gonce, "Frank H. Knight on Social Control and the Scope and Method of Economics," *Southern Economic Journal* 38 (April 1972): 555. Clarence Ayres once wrote to Knight that

> I have always found Veblen's controversial articles quite unsatisfactory. They attack; they stigmatize; they express impatience with the whole conceptual system of economic orthodoxy; but they give little or no clue to what other concepts Veblen would lay down as fundamental, let alone how he would build up from them a systematic understanding of industrial society. (Clarence Ayres to Frank Knight, 23 February 1937, Knight Papers)

4. Frank Knight, "Historical and Theoretical Issues in the Problem of Modern Capitalism," *Journal of Economic and Business History* 1 (January 1928): 120.

5. Frank Knight, *Intelligence and Democratic Action*, 82.

6. Ibid., 76.

7. Frank Knight, "Review of Veblenism: A New Critique," by Lev Dobriansky, *Annals of the American Academy of Political and Social Science* 321 (January 1959): 196–97.

8. Frank Knight, "Homan's Contemporary Economic Thought," *Quarterly Journal of Economics* 43 (November 1928): 132–33. Also see Frank Knight, "Economic Psychology and the Value Problem," *Quarterly Journal of Economics* 39 (May 1925): 372–409, and Morris Copeland, "Professor Knight on Psychology," *Quarterly Journal of Economics* 40 (November 1925): 134–51.

9. Frank Knight and Thornton W. Merriam, *The Economic Order and Religion* (Westport, N.Y.: Greenwood Press, 1979), 75.

10. Frank Knight, *On the History and Method of Economics* (Chicago: University of Chicago Press, 1956), 18. Some of Knight's irritation with Veblen, Ayres, and the institutionalists probably stemmed from what he perceived as their hortatory pronouncements and their moralistic stance on what should more properly be construed as technical economic questions.

11. Knight, *On the History and Method of Economics*, 18.

12. Frank Knight, *Freedom and Reform* (Port Washington, N.Y.: Kennikat Press, 1969), 226.

13. Knight and Merriam, *The Economic Order and Religion*, 62.

14. Frank Knight, *Ethics of Competition and Other Essays* (Newport, N.Y.: Books for Libraries Press, 1969) 285.

15. Ibid., 242.

16. Knight and Merriam, *The Economic Order and Religion*, 73.

17. Frank Knight, *Risk, Uncertainty and Profit* (New York: Houghton-Mifflin, 1921), 28.

18. Ibid.

19. Ibid., 189.

20. See I. H. Rima, *Development of Economic Analysis* (Homewood, Ill.: Richard Irwin, 1972), 294.

21. Knight, *Ethics of Competition*, 43.

22. On this issue see Rick Tilman, "Veblen's Ideal Political Economy and Its Critics," *American Journal of Economics and Sociology* 31 (July 1972): 307–17.

23. Frank Knight, review of *The Place of Science in Modern Civilization*, by Thorstein Veblen, *Journal of Political Economy* 28 (June 1920): 519. Veblen's dichotomy between business and industry came under severe attack from Knight, particularly as it was applied to the realm of values. In 1935 Knight wrote:

A confusion essentially the same as that of Spencer seems to underlie the contrast between industrial and pecuniary values developed by Veblen and Davenport. There is no mechanical measure of values which will bear examination, and we cannot compare values or kinds of value without having something to say about value—standards for reducing to common terms magnitudes infinitely various in kind. (Knight, *Ethics of Competition*, 29)

24. Knight, review of *The Place of Science in Modern Civilization*, 519.

25. Ibid., 519–20. Knight also took Veblen to task for his use of the data and literature of anthropology. First, he suggested that Veblen posed as an anthropological specialist when he really was not. Secondly, the anthropologist Melville Herskovitz, following Veblen, was castigated for treating "all interests and activities above the purely animal level as wasteful and as expressing an immoral struggle for domination and display." See Frank Knight, "Anthropology and Economics," *Journal of Political Economy* 49 (April 1941): 259, 266.

26. Knight, *Risk, Uncertainty and Profit*, 334.

27. Ibid., 182. Also, see Frank Knight, *The Economic Organization* (New York: Augustus M. Kelly, 1951), 130.

28. Ibid.

29. Ibid., 45–46.

30. Ibid., 45.

31. Knight, *Ethics of Competition*, 56.

32. Ibid., 9.

33. Ibid.

34. Ibid., 59.

35. Knight, *Freedom and Reform*, 316–17.

36. Knight, *The Ethics of Competition*, 22.

37. Ibid. Also, see pp. 43–45. Knight comments that

Marx, and Veblen following him, seem to have in mind some metaphysical "principle" of life, a concept belonging to the intuitive thought realms above such requirements as definition of measurement—and in the writer's opinion not devoid of significance if its "unscientific" character is recognized instead of asserting the contrary. (Ibid., 99–100)

However, Veblen's values at times were clearly articulated, although an overburden of satire sometimes must be scraped away to expose them. As for the problem of measurement, using a price system alone to solve it only raises serious questions regarding the efficacy of quantification.

38. Ibid., 22.

39. Ibid., 51–52.

40. As quoted in William Breit and Roger Ransom, *The Academic Scribblers: American Economists in Collision* (New York: Holt, Rinehart & Winston), 201.

41. See Knight, *Ethics of Competition*, 99–100.

42. See I. H. Rima, *Development of Economic Analysis*, 294–95.

43. Knight, "Institutionalism and Empiricism in Economics," *American Economic Review* 42 (May 1952): 52.

44. Knight, *Freedom and Reform*, 258.

45. Regarding the influence of Darwin on Veblen, see Stephen Edgell and Rick Tilman, "The Intellectual Antecedents of Thorstein Veblen: A Reappraisal," *Journal of Economic Issues* 23 (December 1989): 1003–26. Knight believed that there was insufficient ethical justification for the existing distribution of income under capitalism, but he doubted that much could be done about it without making the situation worse. He believed some amelioration of

the human condition had occurred under the capitalist order, but, unlike Veblen, he accepted gross inequality as a more or less permanent part of the social order.

46. Interestingly, free trade was viewed by Knight as hostile to war and colonialism. Of course, Veblen did not share Knight's views on the relationship; nor his enthusiasm for the other Knight-acclaimed virtues of the classical liberal era, such as that commercialism induced tolerance and humanity, friendliness and good humor, and a belief in basic human equality. See Knight's *Economic Order and Religion*, 92, *Ethics of Competition*, 326; and compare with Veblen's *Inquiry Into the Nature of Peace* (New York: Macmillan, 1917) and his review of John Hobson's *Imperialism: A Study in the Journal of Political Economy* 11 (March 1903): 311–19. An important recent study of liberalism, both classical and contemporary, is Anthony Arblaster's *The Rise and Decline of Western Liberalism* (Oxford: Basil Blackwell, 1984), which strongly disagrees with the Knight portrayal of classical liberalism.

47. Myron Watkins, "Veblen's View of Cultural Evolution," in *Thorstein Veblen: A Critical Reappraisal*, ed. Douglas Dowd (Ithaca: Cornell University Press, 1958), 259.

48. Lawrence Nabers, "Veblen's Critique of the Orthodox Economic Tradition" in *Thorstein Veblen: A Critical Reappraisal*, 99.

49. Knight, *Intelligence and Democratic Action*, 74.

50. Thorstein Veblen, *Essays in Our Changing Order*, 100. Contrast this with Knight's belief that "in a social order based on individual liberty, the ultimate consumer must be, will be, and ought to be given what he wants." But also see his discussion of fundamental issues that follows. Knight, "The Newer Economics and the Control of Economic Activity," *Journal of Political Economy* 40 (August 1932): 444. As to the meaning of economics itself, Knight wrote that "On the central issue, I am sure that [Lionel] Robbins is right, that economic theory is a purely rational science of maximizing results through allocation of means among alternative fields of use" (Frank Knight to Talcott Parsons, 7 December 1934, Knight Papers)

51. Abram L. Harris received the B.S. in 1922 from Virginia Union University, the M.A. from Pittsburgh in 1924, and the doctorate from Columbia in 1931. The early years of his academic career were spent at Howard, the rest at Chicago. See the biographical sketch by William Darity, Jr. in *Race, Radicalism and Reform: Selected Papers of Abram L. Harris* (New Brunswick, N.J.: Transaction Publishers, 1989), 1–40. His publications on Veblen include the following: "Types of Institutionalism," *Journal of Political Economy* 40 (December 1932): 721–49; "Economic Evolution: Dialectical and Darwinian," *Journal of Political Economy* 42 (February 1934): 34–49; "Veblen and the Social Phenomenon of Capitalism," *American Economic Review: Papers and Proceedings* 41 (May 1951): 66–77; "Veblen as Social Philosopher:" A Reappraisal," *Ethics* 63 (April 1953): 1–32; *Economics and Social Reform* (New York: Harper & Brothers, 1958), 156–213; and review of *The Values of Veblen: A Critical Reappraisal* by Bernard Rosenberg, *Journal of Political Economy* 67 (August 1959): 422–24.

52. Harris's articles on Veblen in the 1930s tended on the whole, insofar as

they are judgmental, to reflect favorable attitudes toward him. Although Harris did not publish anything on Veblen between 1934 and 1951, by 1953 a dramatic shift in his ideological position had occurred and he found little of value in Veblen's work thereafter. That Harris possessed an inquiring and skeptical mind that led him away from conventional collectivist schemes for social transformation is evident in his correspondence with Frank Knight in the 1930s. However, these qualities of mind were to disappear in the late 1950s and their place taken by the certitudes of Chicago-type economics. Their correspondence illustrated Harris's frame of mind in the 1930s:

> I remember your reference to the necessity of the economist remaining aloof to political controversy. . . . Here of late I have been having considerable difficulty reconciling the so-called objectivity of social science with questions of social policy. I am wondering if by virtue of the nature of economics the so-called scientific economists can actually be objective. (Abram L. Harris to Frank Knight, 3 July 1934, Frank Knight Papers)

53. Harris, *Economics and Social Reform*, xi.
54. Ibid., vii.
55. Ibid., 208–9.
56. Ibid., 208.
57. Ibid., xiv–xv. Harris also commented that

> in their theories, as in those of Marx and Veblen, capitalism is pictured as a system of power. Also, as in the case of Marx and Veblen, the theories of these writers support policies and programs of social action which aim to bring about greater "effective" freedom, security, and welfare for the masses whether by abolishing capitalism or by redistributing power by means of various forms of collective action, all calling for or leading to increasing regulation of economic life by the state.

(Following quotations from this source are cited in text.)
58. Harris, "Veblen as Social Philosopher—a Reappraisal," 29.
59. Harris, *Economics and Social Reform*, 20. (Following quotations from this source are cited in text.)
60. Abram Harris to Frank Knight, 19 July 1932, Knight Papers.
61. Harris, *Economics and Social Reform*, 117.
62. See Thorstein Veblen, *The Instinct of Workmanship* (New York: B. W. Huebsch, 1918), 1–37 and Thorstein Veblen, *Imperial Germany and the Industrial Revolution* (New York: Augustus M. Kelly, 1964), 1–12.
63. Harris, *Economics and Social Reform*, 117.
64. Ibid., 152.
65. Ibid.
66. Ibid., 154.
67. Ibid., 344–45.
68. Ibid., 338.
69. See Darity, *Race, Radicalism and Reform*, 1–40, for analysis of both the change in Harris's views on political economy and his involvement in the civil rights movement.

CHAPTER FOUR
CONSERVATIVE CRITICS: THE RELIGIOUS ASSAULT

1. Lev Dobriansky, *Veblenism: A New Critique* (Washington, D.C.: Public Affairs Press, 1956).

2. The only other Roman Catholic interpretation of Veblen in English is the brief analysis by Henry William Spiegel, *The Growth of Economic Thought* (Durham: Duke University Press, 1971). On page 633, Spiegel summarized his case against Veblen:

> Defects that were many—such as Veblen's disdain for all firm rules guiding human behavior, be they derived from the natural law tradition or from utilitarianism; his elitist claim to superior insight, enabling him to discover ubiquitous make-believe; his false disjunction between the captains of industry and the productive technicians; his insipid hope that the latter might save the world; his apparent belief that in the United States manual labor is considered unworthy and that a leisure class flourishes there; his advocacy of increased output as the only true test of economic well-being; his mercantilist notion that one man's gain is another man's loss, a notion entirely inappropriate in an environment where increasing productivity is the rule. But in spite of these and many other defects, Veblen's work had a profoundly disturbing effect on many American economists, who may have taken it more seriously than did Veblen himself.

Spiegel's criticisms of Veblen closely paralleled those of Dobriansky.

3. Lev Dobriansky, "The Social Philosophical System of Thorstein Veblen" (Ph.D. diss., New York University, 1950). "It is an urbane and dignified book in which the author obviously bends over backwards in the effort to be fair. This was no easy task for him, since his background and assumptions are those of a devout Catholic scholar, and no modern writer on economics could be more challenging and exasperating to a Catholic economic philosopher than Veblen" (Harry Elmer Barnes, "A New Assessment of Veblenian Economics," *Southern Economic Journal* 25 (July 1958): 92–93).

4. Dobriansky, *Veblenism: A New Critique*, 385.

> While Professor Dobriansky surely proves that Veblen's knowledge and handling of some philosophical and psychological, biological and anthropological material was not in accord with the best knowledge in these fields in the mid twentieth century, it may be countered that even Veblen's treatment of instincts is up-to-date science incarnate when compared to the doctrines of natural law, natural rights, transcendental moral norms, and the like, to which Professor Dobriansky firmly adheres." (Barnes, "A New Assessment of Veblenian Economics," 92–94)

5. Dobriansky, *Veblenism: A New Critique*, 374–375.

6. Ibid., viii, ix.

7. Ibid., 309. Interestingly, Dobriansky charged Veblen with adherence to the leadership principle. Although he did not mention Hitler or Mussolini, he did name Lenin. Ibid., 366.

8. Veblen's use of "abstracted elements" and "dichotomous" concepts was criticized by Dobriansky more or less continuously throughout *Veblenism: A New Critique*. (Following quotations from this source are cited in text.)

9. This is not to suggest, however, that Veblen's ideas converged with, or paralleled, other aspects of the "revolt against reason" ideological syndrome. See H. Stuart Hughes, *Consciousness and Society* (New York: Vintage Books, 1977) for portraits of these thinkers and analysis of the commonalities in the ideological structure of their thought. Also, see Andrea Fontana and Rick Tilman, "Rationality, Ideology and Utopia in Vilfredo Pareto and Thorstein Veblen," *Revue Europeenne des Sciences Sociales* 26 (1988): 43–57.

10. Dobriansky, *Veblenism: A New Critique*, 299. (Following quotations from this source are cited in text.)

11. Ibid., 274. "It is an intriguing paradox that both Marx and Veblen violently attack his principle of property. Yet in the former's theory of surplus value is an implicit defense of it as concerns labor's right to a withheld product. And the latter's advocacy of what apparently amounts to an industrial guild organization is a silent support of it."

12. See, for example, Thorstein Veblen's, *The Vested Interests and the Common Man* (New York: Capricorn Books, 1969) for illustrations of the ambiguity of Veblen's views on property.

13. Dobriansky, *Veblenism: A New Critique*, 324.

14. Ibid., 340–42.

15. Ibid., 351. See George H. Mead's review of *The Nature of Peace* in *Journal of Political Economy* 26 (June 1918): 752–62.

16. Dobriansky, *Veblenism: A New Critique*, 351. (Following quotations from this source are cited in text.)

17. Dobriansky, *Veblenism: A New Critique*, 302–3. Dobriansky also comments in this vein that

> Veblen's radical separation of the pecuniary aspect of capital and the concrete recognizes the technical superiority of the current system as against preceding ones; it is almost unbelievable that he should assign little or no weight of fundamental institutional importance to the basic organizational contribution of business enterprise for providing the highest expression of technologic ingenuity and performance. (Following quotations from this source are cited in text.)

18. Veblen's attitudes toward the medieval church were well summarized in his own words:

> The subsequent share of Holy Church and its clerics in the ulterior degradation of the Scandinavian people, including Iceland, was something incredibly shameful and shabby; and the share which the State had in that unholy job was scarcely less so. But these things come into the case of the Icelandic community only at a later date, and cannot be pursued here. The medieval Church in Iceland stands out on the current of events as a corporation of bigoted adventures for the capitalizing of graft and blackmail and the profitable compounding of felonious crimes and vices. It is of course not intended

to question that this medieval Church all this while remained a faithful daughter of Rome and doubtless holy as usual; nor is it to be questioned that more genial traits and more humane persons and motives entered into the case in a sporadic way. It is only that the visible net gain was substantially as set forth. In abatement it should also be noted, of course, that there is no telling what else and possibly shabbier things might have come to pass under the given circumstances in the conceivable absence of Holy Church and its clerics. . . . while for the Norwegian community at home the *Heimskringla*, together with certain detached sagas of the later kings of Norway, will show how the fortunes of the people, from the advent of Christianity onward, swiftly tapered off into a twilight-zone of squalor, malice and servility, with benefit of Clergy. (Thorstein Veblen, intro. to *The Laxdaela Saga* (New York: B. W. Huebsch, 1925), x–xii)

Veblen's attitudes toward the modern Roman Catholic church and contemporary evangelical Christianity were satirically expressed in Thorstein Veblen, *Absentee Ownership and Business Enterprise in Recent Times* (Boston: Beacon Press, 1967), 301, 310, 318–325. Veblen's attitudes toward Lutheranism, his own religious background, were negatively displayed in "An Experiment in Eugenics" in Leon Ardzrooni, ed., *Essays in Our Changing Order* (New York: Augustus M. Kelley, 1964), 232–44.

19. Ibid., 350.
20. See Rick Tilman, "Thorstein Veblen and the New Deal: A Reappraisal," *The Historian* 51 (February 1988): 155–72.
21. Dobriansky, *Veblenism: A New Critique*, 227. Dobriansky succinctly described Veblen's concept of material serviceability as follows: "Its formulation is based on the instinct of workmanship as it expresses itself in brute mechanical efficiency directed to the basic material usefulness of the product. The composition of the product is not adulterated and all superfluities which lead to conspicuous consumption are eliminated." Veblen's own satirical attacks on the role of intangible assets were inverted by Dobriansky to demonstrate the existence of intangible serviceability. The very institutions, practices, and processes that Veblen attacked were defended by Dobriansky. See *Veblenism: A New Critique*, 304–5 and 317.
22. Ibid., 326.
23. Ibid., 316.
24. Ibid., 309.
25. Ibid., 341.
26. Thorstein Veblen, *The Instinct of Workmanship*, 199.

CHAPTER FIVE
LIBERAL CRITICS: THE PROGRESSIVES

1. Roland Stromberg, *Redemption by War: The Intellectuals and 1914* (Lawrence: University of Kansas Press, 1982), 5. British attitudes from 1914 to 1918 are dealt with by Paul Fussell, *The Great War and Modern Memory* (New York and London: Oxford University Press, 1975).

2. "Practically everything in the pasts of Croly, Weyl, and Lippman made them sympathize instinctively with the British and French." Charles Forcey, *The Crossroads of Liberalism: Croly, Weyl, Lippman, and the Progressive Era 1900–1925* (New York: Oxford University Press, 1961), 228–29.

3. Also, see Charles F. Howlett, *Troubled Philosopher: John Dewey and the Struggle for World Peace* (Port Washington, N.Y.: Kennikat Press, 1977), 20–42, and Sidney Kaplan, "Social Engineers as Saviors: Effects of World War I on Some American Liberals," *Journal of the History of Ideas* 17 (June 1956): 347–69.

4. Daniel Aaron, *Writers on the Left* (New York: Harcourt, Brace and World, 1961), 45–49. Also, see Bruce Clayton, *Forgotten Prophet: The Life of Randolph Bourne* (Baton Rouge: Louisiana State University Press, 1984), chaps. 11, 12.

5. See James, "The Moral Equivalent of War" in *Essays on Faith and Morals*, select. by R. B. Perry (New York: Cleveland World Publishing Company, 1967), 311–28.

6. It is generally conceded that both bear an important if ambiguous relationship to the pragmatic movement in philosophy and the social sciences and are eminent figures in the history of American thought. However, no systematic effort has been made to compare any facet of their lives or work, including their attitudes toward the War. This is surprising in view of the fact that they were colleagues at the University of Chicago, knew each other personally, and were mutually acquainted with John Dewey and other leading Chicago scholars of the day. Evidently Mead and Veblen had a personal and intellectual relationship while they were at Chicago but it was not a close one. There is no indication of any relationship after Veblen left Chicago in 1906 for Stanford. Veblen, who was managing editor of the *Journal of Political Economy*, once asked Mead to review *The Theory of the Leisure Class*. Mead's papers clearly indicate that he wrote the review but it was never published in the *Journal*. Instead, an article by John Cummings attacking the book appeared.

7. Veblen never mentioned Mead in his correspondence or cited his work in his published writings. Mead, however, was impressed with Veblen's intellect and his literary style. He once wrote to his daughter-in-law:

"coercive machinery and submissive loyalty." "Defensive rapacity of the power." "Subordination of collective responsibility." "Sacred Rights of Ownership." "Liberal or Nightwatchman State." "The common citizen's 'psychic income.'" "The immaterial category of prestige value." "Retaliate on presumptive enemies for prospective grievances." "The national honor, in short, moves in the realm of magic, and touches the frontiers of religion." "The emulative spirit that comes under the head of patriotism commonly, if not invariably, seeks differential advantage by injury of the rival rather than by an increase of homebred well-being." "The virtuous impulse must be deep seated and indefeasible that drives men incontinently to do good that evil may come of it." One guess allowed you in respect of the author of the above sententious propositions and phrases. (George H. Mead to Irene Tufts Mead, 23 March 1918, G. H. Mead Collection, Regenstein Library, University of Chicago)

8. Shortly after the presidential election of 1916, Mead complained that "Wilson's progressivism seems to me rather vague and occasionally sentimental and lacking in philosophical bottom, but beyond a question he is the one man to formulate the ideas of today and tomorrow. I doubt if he will have the backing in Congress to carry them out, but he can formulate them" (G. H. Mead to Irene Tufts Mead, 19 November 1916). Still more evidence of this is found in his favorable comments on the radical program adopted by the British Labour party in 1918. See G. H. Mead to Henry Mead, 3 March 1918.

9. See Thorstein Veblen, *An Inquiry into the Nature of Peace and the Terms of Its Perpetuation* (New York: Ben Huebsch, 1917), and George H. Mead, review of *An Inquiry into the Nature of Peace*, by Thorstein Veblen, *Journal of Political Economy* 26 (June 1918): 752–62. Mead was more positive in his private appraisals of Veblen's book than he was in print. Indeed, while he was in the process of writing the review, he commented that "the book is great reading" (G. H. Mead to Irene Mead, 23 March 1918). Two days earlier, after reading the first fifty-six pages of Veblen's book, he had written that "it is exciting and exhilarating to get into a book of Veblen's again. With so much one can cry yea and amen." Yet he also made the same complaints he later articulated in his review to the effect that Veblen had a fundamentally deficient understanding of patriotism:

I think the only ground for dissent and it is a fundamental one, is that for him patriotism is the only characteristic of man that is entirely irrational, not only in the losses and costs involved in its exercise, but also in its psychology. It never seems to occur to him to connect patriotism with the process by which personality of the individual has been gained in the consciousness of the group, and to see in this but the further growth of the same consciousness in the larger society. This personality has had an unquestioned function in social behavior. The more highly organized personality of a larger society will not lack—does not lack its function. Patriotism as Veblen sketches it is of course only that phase of the growth which appears at the points of inhibition, and checked development. (G. H. Mead to Irene Mead, 21 March 1918)

10. Veblen, *An Inquiry into the Nature of Peace*, 31. For an analysis of Veblen's view of international relations, see Sondra Herman, *Eleven Against War: Studies in American Internationalist Thought, 1898–1921* (Stanford, Calif.: Hoover Institution Press, 1969), 150–78. Also, of interest in this regard are Carl H. Friedrich, *Inevitable Peace* (New York: Greenwood Press, 1969), 219–25; Michael Howard, *The Causes of War and Other Issues* (London: Unwin Paperbacks, 1983), 66–67, Irving Louis Horowitz, *War and Peace in Contemporary Social and Philosophical Theory*, 2d ed. (New York: Humanities Press, 1973), 10–11. Mead's views are interpreted by John S. Burger and Mary Jo Deegan, "George Herbert Mead on Internationalism, Democracy and War," *The Wisconsin Sociologist* 18 (Spring-Summer 1981): 72–83, and Hans Joas, *G. H. Mead: A Contemporary Re-Examination of His Thought* (Cambridge, Mass.: MIT Press, 1985).

11. Mead, review of *An Inquiry into the Nature of Peace*, 754.

12. Ibid., 753.

13. Veblen, *An Inquiry into the Nature of Peace*, 57. David Starr Jordan, president of Stanford University, who was instrumental in forcing Veblen to resign for "womanizing," wrote to him in a more positive vein that

> I am just reading your book on the *Nature of Peace*. I agree practically with all its statements, except those regarding prehistoric man, none of whom I have ever met, at least not under that guise. [Jordan wrote on the margins of the letter "and so I *know* nothing about him."] I also feel an unholy joy at the subtle and inimitable satire with which you describe the enthusiasms of that group of men which Gelett Burgess recognized as "Bromides." It is a real pleasure once in a while to find a Sulphite—a man who can go around "without any mark or brand on him," as Lincoln put it, and occasionally break out in a new spot. (Jordan to Veblen, 22 August 1917, Thorstein Veblen Collection, Wisconsin State Historical Society, Madison, Wisconsin)

14. Veblen, *An Inquiry into the Nature of Peace*, 33.

15. Mead, *Selected Writings*, ed. with intro. by Andrew Reck (Indianapolis: Bobbs-Merrill, 1964), 230. "Warfare is not the only way in which that has been achieved in the past, but it is one of the most common ways. It seems to be the easiest way in which people can recognize themselves as belonging to the same community, the same group. This they achieve in that attitude of defense against a common enemy" (Mead, *Movements of Thought in the Nineteenth Century* [Chicago and London: University of Chicago Press, 1972], 8).

16. Mead, review of *An Inquiry into the Nature of Peace*, 758.

17. G. W. Mead to Henry Mead, 3 March 1916.

18. Joseph Dorfman, *Thorstein Veblen and His America* (New York: Augustus M. Kelly, 1966), 371–72. Also, see p. 335. Compare Carol S. Gruber, *Mars and Minerva: World War I and the Uses of the Higher Learning in America* (Baton Rouge: Louisiana State University Press, 1975), 60 with Isador Lubin, "Recollections of Veblen" in Carlton C. Qualey, ed., *Thorstein Veblen* (New York: Columbia University Press, 1968), 142–43. Bruce Clayton writes that "nearly everyone but Veblen . . . had been engaged in war propaganda." See his *Forgotten Prophet: The Life of Randolph Bourne*, 246.

19. George H. Mead, *The Conscientious Objector* (New York: National Security League, Patriotism Through Education series, no. 33, 1918), n.p. The National Security League was founded in 1914 by S. Stanwood Menken, a New York corporation lawyer who wished to promote U.S. "military preparedness," which meant large-scale armaments and compulsory military training for American youth. The organization received large sums of money from the Carnegie Corporation and from John D. Rockefeller, and its list of contributors constituted a roster of leaders in Northern financial and industrial circles. The League soon moved beyond military preparedness to the establishment of its own version of "Americanism." See Robert D. Ward, "The Origin and Activities of the National Security League, 1914–1919," *Mississippi Valley Historical Review* 47 (June 1960): 51–65. Also see George T. Blakey, *Historians on the Home Front: American Propagandists for the Great War* (Lexington: University of Kentucky Press, 1970), 26–47. Mead's willingness to write propaganda for the League for mass circulation raises the question as to what extent he was

aware of the larger motives and program of the backers of the League, or whether he was so committed to the American war effort that he no longer cared.

20. Mead, *The Conscientious Objector*, n.p.

21. See, "Dementia Praecox," in *Essays in Our Changing Order* (New York: Augustus Kelley, 1964), 423–36.

22. G. H. Mead to Irene Tufts Mead, 29 May 1917.

23. Mead, *Selected Writings*, 359.

24. On this point, see Rick Tilman, *C. Wright Mills: A Native Radical and His American Intellectual Roots* (University Park: Penn State Press, 1984), chap. 6.

25. Mead, *Selected Writings*, 359.

26. Ibid., 760.

27. Ibid.

28. Henry Steele Commager, *The American Mind* (New Haven: Yale University Press, 1950), 239.

29. Mead, review of *An Inquiry into the Nature of Peace*, 761.

30. Ibid., 762.

31. Mead, *Selected Writings*, 360. But also see Veblen, *Absentee Ownership* (Boston: Beacon Press, 1967), 26.

32. Veblen, *An Inquiry into the Nature of Peace*, 40. In this same vein, he wrote that "national frontiers are industrial barriers" (ibid., 264).

33. Mead, *Selected Writings*, 355.

34. John P. Diggins, *The Bard of Savagery*, 209.

35. Ibid.

36. Ibid.

37. C. T. Gillin, "Freedom and the Limits of Social Behaviorism: A Comparison of Selected Themes from the Works of G. H. Mead and Martin Buber," *Sociology* 9 (January 1975): 32.

38. On this point, see Sondra Herman, *Eleven Against War*, 223–24.

39. Veblen, *The Instinct of Workmanship*, 25.

40. G. M. Mead, *The Individual and the Social Self*, ed. with intro. by David Miller (Chicago: University of Chicago Press, 1982), 19.

41. Veblen, *The Theory of Business Enterprise* (New York: Mentor Books, 1958), 188–89. The eminent physiologist Jacques Loeb, a friend and former colleague of Veblen at Chicago, wrote to him in praise of *The Nature of Peace* that

it is perfectly splendid and I might almost say better than any book you have written before if this were possible. But how sad it all is! I fully agree with you that the abolition of the governments of the central empires is the necessary condition of peace but how truly you picture the nature of the peace which is to follow this war. What you have not emphasized and what has impressed itself most deeply on me—and perhaps Easterners in general—is the suspicion gained from the taxpayers that the movement of preparedness involved by the war has after all as its main aim permanent militarism and compulsory military service for the sole purpose of crushing the labor movement completely and continuing the munition profits. The war spirit is confined in this country mainly to Wall Street and the University constituency. (Loeb to Veblen, 25 April 1917, Jacques Loeb Collection, Library of Congress)

It is doubtful that Loeb would have written such a letter to his old friend if Veblen were not sympathetic to such views; indeed, the fact that Loeb analyzed the forces behind the American entry in such radical tones may indicate that Veblen also held them.

42. Mead, review of *An Inquiry into the Nature of Peace*, 759.

43. Veblen's focus on superstructural phenomena,if not his acuity in analyzing them,is perhaps derived from German Idealism particularly the philosophy of Hegel and Kant. Kant had a pervasive influence on Veblen's *The Nature of Peace*, which owes much to his essay *Perpetual Peace*, vii–viii. Kant's influence is evident in Veblen's analysis of international relations, in which his adoption of the categorical imperative became an essential part of the moral standard he used for evaluating politics among nations.

44. The correspondence between Ely and Veblen shed little light on their intellectual relationship although it is illuminating as regards their professional interaction. On 26 May 1897, Veblen wrote to Ely to recommend a student of his by the name of Hagerty who was an applicant for a scholarship. Veblen commented that Hagerty, who took the History and Scope and Method of Political Economy from him, had "shown both capacity and spirit in scientific work" and slyly commended him for having "fewer preconceptions than most graduate students" at Chicago. On 1 November 1897, Veblen, in his capacity as managing editor of the *Journal of Political Economy*, wrote to Ely asking Ely to "undertake a notice" [write a eulogy] of Henry George, who had just died in New York City. On 19 April 1900, Ely told Veblen that his paper would be read at the Detroit meeting of the American Economic Association. He also asked Veblen to examine the tentative program for the meeting and make suggestions for improving it. This correspondence is in the Richard T. Ely Papers, Wisconsin State Historical Society, Madison, Wisconsin.

45. The other student was Burr J. Ramage who "went south and died there many years ago," according to Ely in his *Ground Under Our Feet: An Autobiography* (New York: Macmillan, 1938), 112.

46. In his eleven-year stay in Baltimore, probably no economist in the country trained so many future leaders in the social sciences as did Ely. In addition to Veblen, Davis R. Dewey, John R. Commons, Edward A. Ross, Albion Small, Albert Shaw, Edward H. Bemis, Thomas Nixon Carver, and Frederic C. Howe did their major work under Ely; and Frederick Jackson Turner, Charles Haskins, W. W. and W. F. Willoughby, Woodrow Wilson, and John Franklin Jameson took a minor under him. See Benjamin Rader, *The Academic Mind and Reform: The Influence of Richard T. Ely in American Life* (Lexington: University of Kentucky Press, 1966) 26–27. Jameson, later an eminent American historian who was instrumental in founding the National Achives, and a friend of Veblen thought Ely no improvement as a teacher over Henry C. Adams, his former instructor. According to Jameson, Ely was difficult to take notes from, repetitious, temperamental, and infatuated with the German Historical School. After one term, his friend Veblen left for Yale, and Jameson felt

that Veblen had "undoubtedly" chosen a better place to study economics. Veblen indicated, however, that he would return to Hopkins if offered a fellowship and, further, that he appreciated Ely's encouragement to publish a paper that he had prepared for Ely's class. The Veblen-Jameson correspondence is reproduced in Joseph Dorfman, *Thorstein Veblen and His America* (New York: Viking Press, 1966), 542–46.

47. See Donald Walker, "William Jaffe, Officer de Liaison Intellectuel," in *Research in the History of Economic Thought and Methodology*, vol. 1 (Greenwich, Conn.: Jal Press, 1983), 26.

48. Ibid., 27.

49. See Grace M. Jaffe's autobiography, *Years of Grace* (Sunspot, N.M.: Sunshine Press, 1978), 113.

50. Ibid. The Ely Papers contain no explanation of why he still intended to use the material on Veblen after his violent disagreement with it, nor is there any evidence of why "The Story of Economics in the United States" was never published. Ely's large correspondence during the 1930s and early 1940s offers no clues to the answer of either question.

51. Richard Ely, "The Story of Economics in the United States." Since drafts of the manuscript are not paginated consistently, it will not be referred to by page numbers.

52. In most of Ely's published writings, Veblen does not play an important role. However, see Richard Ely, *Studies in the Evolution of Industrial Society* (Port Washington, N.Y.: Kennikat Press, 1971), 80, and Richard Ely and Frank Bohn, *The Great Change* (New York: T. Nelson, 1935), 138.

53. William Jaffe, *The Economic and Social Thought of Thorstein Veblen* (Paris: Marcel Grand, 1924), see chaps. 2, 4.

54. Ely, *Ground Under Our Feet*, 271.

55. Thorstein Veblen, *The Vested Interests and the Common Man* (New York: 1969), 100.

56. Ely and Jaffe, "The Story of Economics in the United States."

57. However, Ely's ambivalent attitudes toward the New Deal were expressed in a letter he wrote to the eminent labor economist Selig Perlman. Ely commented: "I am not sure whether or not we would agree with respect to the New Deal legislation. I sympathize with a great deal of it, but I think it fails in very significant points and goes at a good many right things in the wrong way. I wonder if you would agree with this?" (Ely to Perlman, Richard T. Ely Papers, 23 September 1935).

58. Ely, *Ground Under Our Feet*, 263–64.

59. Ibid., 285.

60. On this last point, see Upton Sinclair, *The Goose-Step: A Study of American Education* (Pasadena, Calif., Pub. by author, 1923), 163–64.

61. See Rader, *The Academic Mind and Reform*, 18. Also, see John R. Everett, *Religion in Economics: A Study of John B. Clark, Richard T. Ely, Simmon N. Patten* (New York: Macmillan, 1946), 75–98.

62. Richard Ely to Edward C. Marsh, 26 January 1919. As regards Veblen's views on patriotism, see his *An Inquiry into the Nature of Peace and the Terms of its Perpetuation*, chaps. 1–3.

63. Richard Ely to George Roberts, undated letter. Roberts had written to Ely earlier on 22 January 1919, and Ely was responding to him.

64. The Wisconsin Loyalty Legion's platform and Ely's own signed pledge card are in the Ely Papers. Analysis of the views of Veblen and Ely regarding World War I are found in Carol S. Gruber, *Mars and Minerva*, 54ff.

65. Ely and Jaffe, "The Story of Economics in the United States."

66. Ibid. In this same vein, Veblen once wrote, "You will pardon a bit of conceited garrulity. One of the surprises, and not the least flattering, that has come to me in connection with the 'Leisure Class' is the fact that several of the men in the natural sciences here speak of it as an example of true scientific method! It should be added that there is plenty of comment to the contrary effect" (Thorstein Veblen to E. A. Ross, 7 December 1899, E. A. Ross Collection, Wisconsin State Historical Society, Madison, Wisconsin).

67. Ely and Jaffe, "The Story of Economics in the United States."

68. Ibid.

69. Ibid.

70. Ibid.

71. Ibid.

72. For example, cf. John Hobson, *Veblen* (London: Chapman Hall, 1936), 23–52, and Allan Gruchy, *Modern Economic Thought: The American Contribution* (New York: Prentice Hall, 1947), 35–58.

73. Ely and Jaffe, "The Story of Economics in the United States." (Following quotations from this source are cited in text.)

74. Ibid. Ely and Jaffe also revealingly commented that "for a fuller statement of this point see William Jaffe, *Les Theories Economiques et Sociales de Thorstein Veblen* (Paris, 1924), chap. 1."

75. As quoted in Ely and Jaffe, "The Story of Economics in the United States."

76. Ibid.

77. For Veblen's criticisms of the German Historical School as well as his agreements with it, particularly the work of Gustav Schmoller, see his review of Schmoller's *Uber einige Grundfragen der Socialpolitik und der Volkswirtschaftslehre*, *Journal of Political Economy* 6 (June 1898): 416–19 and his "Gustav Schmoller's Economics" in *The Place of Science in Modern Civilization* (New York: Viking Press, 1930), 252–78. Ely's views on the German Historical School and his relationship with Karl Knies, who was Ely's major professor at Heidelberg, are dealt with by Benjamin Rader in *The Academic Mind and Reform: The Influence of Richard T. Ely in American Life*, 12 ff. Also see Ely's autobiography, *Ground Under Our Feet*, and Jurgen Herbst, *The German Historical School in American Scholarship* (Ithaca, N.Y.: Cornell University Press, 1965) esp. chap. 6.

78. Ely and Jaffe, "The Story of Economics in the United States."

79. Veblen, *The Theory of Business Enterprise*, 108.

80. Grace Jaffe to Richard Ely, November 3, 1931, Ely Collection.

81. Cf. Veblen, *The Theory of Business Enterprise*, 351.

82. Ibid., chap. 10.

83. Ely and Jaffe, "The Story of Economics in the United States."

84. Ibid.

85. Ibid.
86. Veblen, *The Theory of Business Enterprise*, 210.
87. Ibid., 54.
88. Ibid.
89. Ibid.
90. See Veblen, *The Vested Interests and the Common Man* (New York: Capricorn Books, 1969), 73, 91, and *The Engineers and the Price System* (New York: Augustus Kelley, 1965), 62.
91. As Paul Homan argued, Veblen criticisms of neoclassical economists were (1) that their view of normality involves a perspective on economic life and institutions that conflicts with reality, (2) that they uncritically adhere to the philosophy of Natural Rights and Natural Law, (3) that they hold to a diluted belief in teleological purpose and an ameliorative social trend, (4) that they identify acquisition and production, and (5) that they cling to an outmoded hedonistic psychology. In their treatment of Veblen in "The Story of Economics in the United States," Jaffe and Ely analyzed parts of each of these aspects of his attack on conventional economics. It is evident that they did not fully agree with any of his claims, although they found valuable insights in several. See Paul Homan, "Thorstein Veblen," in *Contemporary Economic Thought* (New York: Harper & Row, 1928), 105–92. Also see Richard V. Teggart, *Thorstein Veblen: A Chapter in American Economic Thought* (Berkeley: University of California, 1932).
92. See John Cummings, "The Theory of the Leisure Class," *Journal of Political Economy* 7 (September 1899): 425–55; John M. Clark, "Recent Developments in Economics," in *Recent Developments in the Social Sciences*, ed. Edward C. Hayes (Philadelphia: J. B. Lippincott, 1927), 213–306; and Abram Harris, "Types of Institutionalism," *Journal of Political Economy*, 40 (December 1932): 721–49.
93. It is interesting to note that the authors mentioned Veblen's interest in the process of soil erosion and his concern for the environment. They commented: "It was a far cry from the prairie homestead to the world of pecuniary transactions, of roundabout, capitalistic methods of production, of 'conspicuous consumption,' and of 'conspicuous waste.' . . . But even the economics of the homestead did not escape his caustic pen, for, in one of his essays, Veblen ruthlessly exposes the methods of 'earthbutchery' practiced by the settlers." Ely and Jaffe, "The Story of Economics in the United States."
94. By comparison, see the analysis of radical views of Veblen in Rick Tilman, et al., "Thorstein Veblen and His Marxist Critics: An Interpretive Review," *History of Political Economy* 14 (Fall 1982): 323–41.
95. Ely and Jaffe, "The Story of Economics in the United States."
96. See Rick Tilman, "Thorstein Veblen and the New Deal: A Reappraisal," *The Historian* 50 (February 1988): 155–72.
97. On 8 December 1935, just prior to the publication of *The General Theory*, Keynes wrote to Ely:

In reply to your letter of November 22nd, I am sorry to say that my theories have not yet reached a sufficiently stable and crystalized form for me to write a summary of them. I believe it could be better done by a third party. I suggest, however, that you should await my forthcoming book which will appear early next year. It is this which really represents what is probably my substantive and characteristic contribution to the subject. I will send you a copy of it as soon as one is available, and you will easily find someone, I think, who can, on the basis of this book, put together what you want. (J. M. Keynes to Richard Ely, 8 December 1935)

In spite of the references in the text to the similarities between Keynes and Veblen, this letter indicates Ely's ignorance of Keynes's work.

98. On the problem of liberal illusions in interpreting Veblen, see Rick Tilman, "John Dewey's Liberalism versus Thorstein Veblen's Radicalism: A Reappraisal of the Unity of Progressive Social Thought," *Journal of Economic Issues* 18 (September 1984): 745–69.

99. Richard Ely to Grace Jaffe, 3 November 1931.

100. See esp. Veblen's "Economic Theory in the Calculable Future," *American Economic Review* (supp.) 15 (March 1925): 48–55.

CHAPTER SIX
LIBERAL CRITICS: THE INSTITUTIONALISTS

1. Lucy Sprague Mitchell wrote revealingly of their relationship with Veblen.

While Veblen lived in New York, he came often to our house. I think ours was one of the few homes where he felt thoroughly at ease. Veblen was helpless in getting himself around the city and was usually brought and called for by some admirer. But once there, he relaxed. Veblen, the silent, the shy, talked freely with Robin [Mitchell] not minding me silently sewing on the sofa. He even came to Thanksgiving and Christmas dinners sometimes. He enjoyed the outgoing informality of our children even to having a youngster climb up on his lap. That is my most vivid image of Veblen—slouched down in Robin's big red chair in the 12th Street study, talking to children—an image I fancy that few people share with me. (Lucy S. Mitchell, "A Personal Sketch," in *Wesley Clair Mitchell: The Economic Scientist*, ed. Arthur F. Burns [New York: National Bureau of Economic Research, 1952], 91)

2. Ibid., 90.
3. Ibid.
4. Joseph A. Schumpeter, "The General Economist" in *Wesley Clair Mitchell: The Economic Scientist*, 222.
5. Thorstein Veblen to Wesley Mitchell, 30 September 1909, Wesley C. Mitchell Collection, Butler Library, Columbia University, New York City.
6. Thorstein Veblen to Wesley Mitchell, 1 December 1909.
7. Thorstein Veblen to Wesley Mitchell, 6 September 1908.
8. Wesley Mitchell to Leon Ardzrooni, 9 December 1924.
9. Wesley C. Mitchell, "Human Behavior and Economics: A Survey of Recent Literature," *Quarterly Journal of Economics* 29 (November 1914): 38.
10. Wesley C. Mitchell, *Lecture Notes on Types of Economic Theory*, vol. 2 (New York: Augustus M. Kelley, 1949), 237. According to J. M. Gould and

A. M. Kelley, these are stenographic transcriptions of Mitchell's classroom lectures. Since the views expressed in them are compatible with those articulated elsewhere, I see no reason to treat them differently than if Mitchell himself had written them. However, in an editorial note Gould and Kelley commented that

> it is fortunate then, that the lectures were taken down stenographically by John Myers, a student attending the course delivered at Columbia in the fall of 1935 and the spring of 1935. . . . During his lifetime Professor Mitchell always disclaimed responsibility for the accuracy of the transcript. In fact in a letter to the present publisher written shortly before his death he denied ever having read the *Notes*. (Wesley C. Mitchell, *Lecture Notes on Types of Economic Theory*, vol. I [New York: Augustus M. Kelley, 1949])

11. Wesley C. Mitchell, *The Backward Art of Spending Money and Other Essays* (New York: Augustus M. Kelley, 1950), 339.

12. Wesley C. Mitchell, ed., *What Veblen Taught* (New York: Viking Press, 1945), xix.

13. Wesley C. Mitchell, *Lecture Notes on Types of Economic Theory*, 251.

14. Ibid., 228.

15. Ibid., 251.

16. Ibid., 251–52.

17. In this vein Mitchell also wrote:

> Great as was the service that Veblen rendered by studying the evolution of institutions, it is clear that this theme does not constitute the whole of economics. The problems treated by orthodox theory are genuine problems, and the two sets of discussions should be put into such form that everyone can see how they supplement each other. For example, Veblen's analysis of the cultural incidence of the machine process and of business traffic takes for granted knowledge of how prices are fixed and of the bearing of prices upon the distribution of income. Every scheme of institutions has an implicit logic of its own, and it is not less important to know what that logic is than to know how the institutions came into being and what they are becoming. (Mitchell, *The Backward Art of Spending Money*, 338–39)

> Rarely does he undertake a factual survey. Many of his propositions are not of the type that can be tested objectively with the means now at our disposal. His work as a whole is like Darwin's—a speculative system uniting a vast range of observations into a thoroughly consistent whole, extraordinarily stimulating both to the layman and to the investigator, but waiting for its ultimate validation upon more intensive and tamer inquiries. (Mitchell, *What Veblen Taught*, xxxv–xxxvi)

18. Mitchell, *Lecture Notes on Types of Economic Theory*, 241.

19. Ibid., 240.

20. Mitchell, "Human Behavior and Economics: A Survey of Recent Literature," 22.

21. That Mitchell remained a staunch admirer of Veblen and personally concerned with his well-being and eager to see that he would be fairly treated

by future scholars is evident in his own correspondence. On 6 January 1926 Mitchell wrote to Oswald Veblen, Veblen's nephew, who was an eminent mathematician at Princeton, endorsing Joseph Dorfman as Veblen's biographer. However, Mitchell's view of Dorfman's qualifications for doing a study of Veblen may not have coincided with Veblen's views on the subject. To illustrate the point, Ruthemary Pentinck, archivist at Carleton College, interviewed Becky Mayer and Ann Sims, who were the daughters of Ann Fessenden Bradley, Thorstein Veblen's second wife. Becky Mayer, Veblen's stepdaughter, who knew him well and took care of him in his last years, commented:

> Oh yes, well, I liked Dorfman, its just that Veblen didn't think he was the kind of a person who would know what was significant in Veblen's background. He felt that way that most biographers were not. He didn't want him to do this—he felt there were more important things he could be doing with his bull-headed going after things. But he had been sending lots of books, uh, uh, letters asking him to fill out these and these questions [incoherent] then when Thorstein Veblen died, he started writing to Andrew Veblen and other members of the family. (Taped interview, Ruthemary Pentinck with Becky Mayer, Menlo Park, California, Spring 1979)

In any case, Mitchell soon developed misgivings about Dorfman. See Wesley Mitchell to Oswald Veblen 11 February 1928, Oswald Veblen Collection, Manuscript Division, Library of Congress.

22. "Beyond this, however, Mitchell's approach was *very* different from Veblen's. Despite his skepticism as to the value of much orthodox theory, he nonetheless used those parts of it which seemed appropriate. For example, although Mitchell's conception of the business cycle problem may have been taken from Veblen, it can be argued that the details of his theoretical account of the business cycle in which the interdependence of all prices and quantities played an important role, owed as much to Walras as to Veblen." (Roger Backhouse, *A History of Modern Economic Analysis* [Oxford: Basil Blackwell, 1985], 228).

23. A. B. Wolfe, "Views on the Scope and Method of Economics," in *Wesley Clair Mitchell: The Economic Scientist*, ed. Arthur F. Burns (New York: National Bureau of Economic Research, 1952), 212.

24. Paul T. Homan, "Place in Contemporary Economic Thought," in *Wesley Clair Mitchell: The Economic Scientist*, 186.

25. After teaching at Cornell from 1929 to 1947, Homan served as a staff member to the Council of Economic Advisors from 1947 to 1950, and on the faculty at UCLA and Southern Methodist University. Also, he edited the *American Economic Review* from 1941 to 1952.

26. To a conservative like Frank Knight, Homan's views on Veblen appeared to be dangerously liberal and much too sympathetic. See Frank Knight, review of *Contemporary Economic Trends*, by Paul T. Homan, *Quarterly Journal of Economics* 43 (November 1928): 133. Homan's writings on Veblen include the following: "Thorstein Veblen" in *American Masters of Social Science*, ed. Howard W. Odum (New York: Henry Holt & Company, 1927), 231–70; "Issues in Economic Theory: An Attempt to Clarify," *Quarterly Journal of Eco-*

nomics 42 (May 1928): 333–65; "An Appraisal of Institutional Economics," *American Economic Review* 22 (March 1932): 10–18; but see the rebuttal by D. R. Scott, "Veblen Not an Institutional Economist," *American Economic Review* 23 (June 1933): 274–77; review of *Thorstein Veblen: A Chapter in American Economic Thought*, by R. V. Teggart, *American Economic Review* 23 (September 1933): 480–81; "The Institutional School," in *Encyclopedia of the Social Sciences*, ed. E. R. A. Seligman, vol. 5 (New York: Macmillan, 1938), 387–95; "Nemesis of the Leisure Class," *Saturday Review of Literature* 28 November 1953, 26.

27. Homan, review of Teggart's *Thorstein Veblen*, 480–81.
28. Homan, "Thorstein Veblen," 265.
29. Ibid., 259.
30. Clarence Ayres complained to Addison Cutler of Fisk University that

for Homan to dismiss Veblen's work as a "few thin essays . . ." is only to advertise his own lack of understanding . . . as I understand it, Veblen is not disparaging Adam Smith as a critic of mercantilism nor Ricardo as a opponent of the landed gentry; but he is pointing out that the system of ideas elaborated by those men for those purposes contain a lot of hum-bug, and that the same hum-bug has been in circulation ever since. Of course, this is only the negative side of the picture." (Ayres to Cutler, 19 December 1938, Clarence E. Ayres Collection, Barker Texas History Archive, University of Texas, Austin)

31. Homan, "Thorstein Veblen," 262.
32. Ibid., 259.
33. Homan, "Issues in Economic Theory: An Attempt to Clarify," 351.
34. Ibid.
35. Homan, "Thorstein Veblen," 248. (Following quotations from this source are cited in text.)
36. Ibid., 260. Homan wrote to Clarence Ayres regarding Ayres's pro-Veblen tract *The Problem of Economic Order*, which had just been published. In polite but argumentative tones he commented as follows:

My first impression is that you leave the subject about where Veblen left it. What I wonder is whether that position is worth repeating, running as it does in strictly negative terms of the deficit, of the price denominator as a guide to the just and efficient use of economic resources. If one is writing for elementary students, one has to say those things, but I should say that you, like Veblen, do far too thorough a job of derationalizing the price system. When one exercises the basis of rational economic behavior, one has left a lot of interesting anthropological data, but nothing with which to construct improved operative structures of economic life. (Homan to Ayres, Clarence E. Ayres Collection, 8 February 1938)

37. Homan, "Nemesis of the Leisure Class," 26.
38. Ibid.
39. Homan, "Thorstein Veblen," 239–40.
40. Ibid.

41. A contemporary of Paul Homan who was familiar with his work on Veblen was Karl Anderson (b. 1905). In 1932 Anderson completed a doctoral dissertation at Harvard entitled "Thorstein Veblen's Economics." The next year he wrote an important article based on it entitled "The Unity of Veblen's Theoretical System." Anderson believed Veblen's importance lay in the fact that he was a "deranger" of orthodox economics and he discussed at some length the latter's criticism of its psychological assumptions and static character. He claimed that there was a system or unity to Veblen's thought that had been overlooked by social scientists. Anderson believed that critics have focused on Veblen's role as a social satirist, as a critic of neoclassical theory, as a philosopher of history, and as an opponent of capitalism, but that none of these are really important! Much more significant is the fact that he was the originator of a new theoretical system. However, Anderson was not impressed with the Veblenian system. As he put it, "the integrated system of theory put forward by this irritating iconoclast is a very rickety affair." See Karl Anderson, "The Unity of Veblen's Theoretical System," *Quarterly Journal of Economics* 47 (August 1933): 598–626.

42. The John R. Commons Collection in the archives of the Wisconsin State Historical Society in Madison contains no correspondence between Commons and Veblen; nor is there any in the archives containing Veblen's unpublished papers. Most of their communication was probably transmitted through intermediaries or mutual friends such as Wesley C. Mitchell. For example, on 30 October 1922 Commons wrote to Mitchell:

> I am taking the liberty of sending you by express the manuscript of my latest revision of my chapters on value theories, based on court decision. This year I am working on Veblen's theories and on wage theories which will about complete the circuit of application, so that I probably have a couple of years ahead of me before the manuscript can be ready for publication. On this account there is no need to hurrying yourself in looking over the chapters. (Wesley C. Mitchell Collection, Butler Library, Columbia University, New York City)

Interestingly, Commons wrote to Davis Rich Dewey, editor of the *American Economic Review*, asking him to have Mitchell review *The Legal Foundations of Capitalism*. It appears that then, as now, authors attempted to influence editors of journals as to who should review their books. (See Commons to Dewey, 27 November 1923, Records of the American Economic Association, Northwestern University Library, Evanston, Illinois.)

43. At the turn of the century Commons wrote:

> In an original and discerning discussion on "The Beginnings of Ownership," in the *American Journal of Sociology, 1898*, Dr. Veblen makes the distinction between "economic" property and that "quasi-personal" fringe of material things which the primitive man conceived as accompanying his own personality, and which had not yet come to have economic value to him. (John R. Commons, *A Sociological View of Sovereignty*, intro. by Joseph Dorfman [1899–1900; New York: Augustus M. Kelley, 1965], 63)

Also, see John Commons, *The Economics of Collective Action*, ed. Kenneth Parsons (Madison: University of Wisconsin Press, 1970), 29.

44. Relevant studies include A. M. Endres, "Veblen and Commons on Goodwill: A Case of Theoretical Divergence," *History of Political Economy* 17 (Winter 1985): 637–50. Endres stressed the contrast between Veblen's conception of goodwill as exploitation and Commons's view of it as capitalizable reputation for good service. A broad-gauged comparison of Commons and Veblen is contained in David Hamilton, "Veblen and Commons: A Case of Theoretical Convergence," *Southwestern Social Science Quarterly* 34 (September 1953): 43–50. Hamilton skillfully shows the theoretical convergence between Veblen and Commons, but he largely ignores their basic doctrinal differences. Also, see Leona Spilman, *A Comparison of Veblen's and Commons' Institutionalism* (Ph.D. diss., University of Wisconsin, 1940); and Ervin K. Zingler, "Veblen vs. Commons: A Comparative Evaluation," *Kyklos* 27, no. 2 (1974): 322–34; Grant L. Harter's, *John R. Commons: His Assault on Laissez-Faire* (Corvallis: Oregon State Press, 1962) is the most comprehensive study of Commons and contains many references to Veblen also.

45. See Jeff E. Biddle, "The Ideas of the Past as Tools for the Present: The Instrumental Presentism of John R. Commons" (Department of Economics, Michigan State University, 1988).

46. John Commons, *Institutional Economics*, vol. 2 (Madison: University of Wisconsin Press, 1961), 673.

47. Ibid., 650.

48. John Commons, *Institutional Economics*, vol. 1 (Madison: University of Wisconsin Press, 1961), 4.

49. Commons, *Institutional Economics* 2:658.

50. Ibid.

51. Commons, *Institutional Economics* 1:5.

52. Commons, *Institutional Economics* 2:667.

53. Ibid., 651.

54. For example, Commons wrote of Veblen's "gay comment" that the hedonic man never existed, referred to him as a "distinguished exponent [of Darwin] in economics," and praised "Veblen's characterization of the faulty concepts of human nature of the Austrian economists." See Commons, *Institutional Economics* 1:228–29; *Legal Foundations of Capitalism* (Madison: University of Wisconsin Press, 1968), 376; *Institutional Economics* 2:656.

55. Commons, *Institutional Economics* 2:665.

56. Ibid., 663.

57. Ibid., 677.

58. Ibid., 673.

59. On this point, see Ron Phillips, "Veblen and the 'Wobblies': A Note," *Review of Radical Political Economics* 192, no. 1 (1987): 98–103.

60. Commons, *Institutional Economics* 2:653. Also, see Wesley Mitchell, *The Backward Art of Spending Money* (New York: McGraw-Hill, 1937), 340, and Joel B. Dirlam, "The Place of Corporation Finance in Veblen's Economics," in *Thorstein Veblen: A Critical Reappraisal*, ed. Douglas Dowd (Ithaca: Cornell University Press, 1958), 203.

61. Veblen, *The Place of Science in Modern Civilization, and Other Essays* (New York: Viking Press, 1930), 27. Veblen also considered training in law "alien . . . to the scientific spirit and subversive of it" (ibid., 20).

62. Commons, *Institutional Economics* 2:651. Also, see pp. 653–54, and Mitchell, *The Backward Art of Spending Money*, 333.

63. Commons, *Institutional Economics*, 2:656.

64. Ibid.

65. Ibid., 679. Also, see p. 659.

66. Ibid., 675.

67. Ibid., 675–76.

68. Ibid., 674–75.

69. Ibid., 659.

70. Michael Starr, "The Political Economy of American Institutionalism" (Ph.D. diss., University of Wisconsin, Madison, 1983), 192.

71. Most recently, see Donald Stabile, *Prophets of Order: The Rise of the New Class, Technocracy and Socialism in America* (Boston: South End Press, 1984); "Veblen and the Political Economy of Technocracy: The Critic Developed a Collectivist Ideology," *American Journal of Economics and Sociology* 46 (January 1987): 35–48; "Veblen and Political Economy of the Engineers," *American Journal of Economics and Sociology* 45 (January 1986): 41–52. Also, see Donald Stabile, "Veblen's Analysis of Social Movements: Bellamyites, Workers, and Engineers," *Journal of Economic Issues* 22 (March 1988): 211–12, 216. Stabile was critical of Tilman's "Veblen's Ideal Political Economy and Its Critics," *American Journal of Economics and Sociology* 31 (July 1972): 307–17 and "Review of *Prophets of Order*," *Journal of Economic Issues* 20 (September 1986): 906–9.

72. Malcolm Rutherford, "John R. Commons' Institutional Economics," *Journal of Economic Issues* 17 (September, 1983): 724.

73. Commons, *Institutional Economics* 2:844–45.

74. In this regard, Clarence Ayres wrote to Frank Knight:

> In discussing this question you and I might use your interest in "legal philosophy and legal history" as a point of departure. I presume you mean the study of the evolution of institutions and their ideology. That seems to have been Commons' ruling interest, and it certainly is one aspect of Veblen's thought. But whereas Commons' interest is motivated by an avowed reformism of an immediate and "pragmatic" type (in the bad sense of action first and thought afterwards if at all), Veblen's is theoretical. That is, his picture of institutional evolution is important only as a part, and (as I think) derivative part, of a larger picture. Commons gets closest to this when he cuts out Veblen's prescience with respect to capital. (The old boy, Commons, is occasionally quite intuitive. But then he slips back into reformism: the administrative challenge of the changed functions of capital, losing interest in the theoretical significance of Veblen's critique of capital.) (Ayres to Knight, 23 February 1937, Frank Knight Papers)

75. See Walter C. Neale, "Institutions," *Journal of Economic Issues* 21 (September 1987): 1200. To illustrate, Veblen was highly critical of neoclassi-

cal economics in part because it was a manifestation of cultural lag, but according to one of Commons's students and friends, "He [Commons] never spoke disparagingly of the orthodox economics of his day" (Kenneth H. Parsons, "The Veblen-Commons Award," *Journal of Economic Issues* 20 [June 1986]: 283).

76. Veblen's influence on the New Deal is dealt with by Rick Tilman, "Thorstein Veblen and the New Deal: A Reappraisal," *The Historian* 50 (February 1988): 155–72. In an interesting, indeed, theoretically intriguing statement, Commons described the state as "not an ideal super-imposed on society, but . . . an accumulated series of compromises between social classes, each seeking to secure for itself control over the coercive elements which exist implicitly in society with the institution of private property" (Commons, *A Sociological View of Sovereignty*, 762).

77. Commons's views in this respect were very similar to those of John Maynard Keynes, who apparently paid little attention to Veblen's work. Indeed, the multivolume edition of his collected works did not even index Veblen's name. On the other hand, one of Veblen's most penetrating political essays, written in 1920, was a critical review of Keynes's *The Economic Consequences of the Peace*. See Veblen, *Essays in Our Changing Order*, 462–70. However, Keynes's political realism and his moderate reformist propensities were closer to Commons's liberal Progressivism than to Veblen's postwar radicalism. Interestingly, in 1927 Keynes wrote from Bloomsbury in London to Commons in Madison that he was "entirely in sympathy" with an article by Commons in the *Analyst*, which the latter had sent him. Keynes also commented: "I should very much like to have some conversations with you on this and other matters. Judging from limited evidence and at great distance, *there seems to me to be no other economist with whose general way of thinking I feel myself in such genuine accord* [author's emphasis]" (J. M. Keynes to John R. Commons, 26 April 1927, John R. Commons Collection).

78. See Thorstein Veblen, "Professor Clark's Economics," *Quarterly Journal of Economics* 22 (February 1908): 147–95. On 28 June 1903, E. R. A. Seligman received a letter from John Bates Clark in which the latter commented that: "Veblen and Cummings have attended my lectures [at the University of Chicago] and I have greatly enjoyed their society. Veblen is, if I can judge, the ablest of the six economists here . . . though, of course [J. Laurence] Laughlin is the best known. Veblen is a quiet mouse-like man who has such a gift of reticence that one has to force things out of him in order to get any impression of what he is capable of" (Joseph Dorfman, "The Seligman Correspondence, I," *Political Science Quarterly*, 61 (March 1941): 116).

79. See Allan G. Gruchy, *Modern Economic Thought: The American Contribution* (New York: Prentice-Hall, 1947), chap. 5 for a brief biographical sketch of Clark and summation of his work. Also see the articles on Clark in the *Review of Social Economy* 39 (December 1981). Clark went to his father's alma mater, Amherst College, in 1901 for his early academic training. After completing his undergraduate work, he moved on to Columbia University for graduate study in the field of economics. Clark began his teaching career in 1908 as an instructor in economics and sociology at Colorado College. After two years at that institution, he returned to Amherst College, where he was appointed asso-

ciate professor of economics. In 1915 Clark became a member of the economics faculty at the University of Chicago. After doing important work at that institution, he accepted a position as professor of economics in 1926 at Columbia University, at which time J. B. Clark had the pleasure of seeing his son fill the position from which he had retired. Clark remained at Columbia until his death in 1963.

80. C. Addison Hickman, *J. M. Clark* (New York: Columbia University Press, 1975), 26. Also, see Laurence Shute, "J. M. Clark on Corporate Concentration and Control," *Journal of Economic Issues*, 19 (June 1985): 409–18.

81. John M. Clark, "Recent Developments in Economics," in Edward C. Hayes, ed., *Recent Developments in the Social Sciences* (Philadelphia and London: J. B. Lippincott, 1927), 248.

82. Ibid., 249.

83. Ibid., 248.

84. Ibid., 285.

85. Clark, "Thorstein Bunde Veblen, 1857–1929," in Dorfman, *Essays Reviews and Reports*, 598–99.

86. Clark, "Recent Developments in Economics," 259. (Following quotations from this source are cited in text.)

87. John M. Clark, "The Socializing of Theoretical Economics," in *The Trend of Economics*, ed. Rexford G. Tugwell (New York: Alfred A. Knopf, 1924), 85.

88. Ibid.

89. Ibid.

90. Clark, "Recent Developments in Economics," 271.

91. Ibid., 263.

92. Ibid., 245.

93. Ibid., 246.

94. Clark, review of *Thorstein Veblen: A Critical Appraisal*, by Douglas Dowd, *Political Science Quarterly* 74 (September 1959): 128.

95. Clark, review of *Absentee Ownership*, by Thorstein Veblen, *American Economic Review* 14 (June 1924): 29.

96. Clark, "Recent Developments in Economics," 245–46.

97. Ibid., 250.

By way of contrast, Thorstein Veblen combined a merciless deflation of the pretensions of the business system with an Olympian detachment from questions of what to do about it. His critique had much more a Marxian thought in it than Veblen himself would have willingly recognized, and it centered largely on failures in serviceability to the "material" interests of the common man. He appears to have taken democratic values as seriously as he took anything; but his final suggestion of a "soviet of technicians"—the germ of "technocracy"—was hardly a democratic proposal. His whole bent was against making purposive recommendations. (John M. Clark, *Economic Institutions and Human Welfare* [New York: Alfred A. Knopf, 1957], 57).

98. John M. Clark, *Preface to Social Economics* (New York: Augustus M. Kelley, 1967), 323.

99. Clark, "The Socializing of Theoretical Economics," 86.

100. John M. Clark, "The Concept of Value," *Quarterly Journal of Economics* 29 (August 1915): 722.

101. Clark, *The Social Control of Business*, 227–28.

102. Clark, in Dorfman, "Thorstein Bunde Veblen, 1857–1929," 599–600.

103. Ibid.

CHAPTER SEVEN
LIBERAL CRITICS: THE NEOINSTITUTIONALISTS

1. On Ayres's life and work, see Rick Tilman, "New Light on John Dewey, Clarence Ayres and the Development of Evolutionary Economics," *Journal of Economic Issues* 25 (December 1990): 963–79, and Rick Tilman, "Value Theory, Planning, and Reform: Ayres as Incrementalist and Utopian," *Journal of Economic Issues* 8 (December 1974): 689–706. On Gruchy, see Dudley Dillard, "Allan G. Gruchy 1906–1990: A Scholar's Life," *Journal of Economic Issues* 24 (September 1990): 663–72.

2. Allan G. Gruchy, *Modern Economic Thought: The American Contribution* (New York: Prentice-Hall, 1947), 127. Gruchy's last commentary on Veblen is dispersed throughout his *The Reconstruction of Economics* (Westport, Conn.: Greenwood Press, 1987).

3. Gruchy, *Modern Economic Thought*, 58. (Following quotations from this source are cited in text.)

4. See Clarence Ayres, "Veblen's Theory of Instincts Reconsidered," in *Thorstein Veblen: A Critical Reappraisal*, ed. Douglas Dowd (Ithaca: Cornell University Press, 1958), 29. Also see p. 36.

5. Clarence Ayres, *The Industrial Economy* (Cambridge: Houghton Mifflin, 1952), 163.

6. Clarence Ayres to John Dewey, Clarence Ayres Collection, Barker Texas History Archive, University of Texas, Austin, 9 February 1928.

7. Ayres, *The Industrial Economy*, 402.

8. Clarence Ayres, *The Divine Right of Capital* (Boston: Houghton Mifflin, 1946), 149.

9. Clarence Ayres, *The Theory of Economic Progress* (Chapel Hill: University of North Carolina Press, 1944), 163.

10. Ibid., 278.

11. Ayres, *The Industrial Economy*, 25.

12. Ibid., 24.

13. That Ayres was still trying to develop an adequate approach to value was evident as late as 1961. In a reference to what became *Toward a Reasonable Society*, he wrote, "I have been conducting a seminar in recent years in which I have been trying to go back to price theory to the underlying problem of value, and this has led to the writing of a book on the operational conception of value and an operational assessment of the values of industrial society" (Clarence Ayres to Joan Robinson, Clarence Ayres Collection, 25 September 1961).

14. Clarence Ayres to John Dewey, Clarence Ayres Collection, 11 October 1949.

CHAPTER EIGHT
LIBERAL CRITICS: HARVARD AND COLUMBIA STYLE

1. The institutional process of separating advocacy from objectivity in order to develop a "value-free" science was a device during Veblen's day for dissuading powerful, hostile groups both inside and outside the university from interfering with "academic freedom." See Mary Furner, *Advocacy and Objectivity: A Crisis in the Professionalization of American Social Science, 1865–1905* (Lexington: University of Kentucky Press, 1975) esp. chaps. 8–13.

2. David Riesman, *Thorstein Veblen: A Critical Interpretation* (New York: Charles Scribner's Sons, 1960), 51.

3. Ibid., 1–2.

4. David Riesman, "The Social and Psychological Setting of Veblen's Economic Theory," *Journal of Economic History* 13 (1953): 453.

5. Riesman, *Thorstein Veblen: A Critical Interpretation*, 69.

6. Ibid., 13.

7. Ibid., 6–7.

8. David Riesman and Staughton Lynd, "The Relevance of Thorstein Veblen," *The American Scholar* 29 (Autumn 1960): 547.

9. Riesman, *Thorstein Veblen: A Critical Interpretation*, 96–97.

10. Ibid., 98.

11. Ibid., 65–66.

12. See Parsons, "Clarence Ayres's Economics and Sociology" in *Science and Ceremony: The Institutional Economics of E. E. Ayres*, ed. William Breit and William P. Culbertson, Jr. (Austin and London: University of Texas Press, 1976), 175–80. Clarence Ayres also introduced C. Wright Mills, and Marion Levy to Veblen's social theory. Parsons was a student of Ayres at Amherst in the early 1920s, Mills worked under him at Texas from 1937 to 1939; while Levy was also Ayres's student at the same institution in 1939–40.

13. See esp. Parsons, "Sociological Elements in Economic Thought, I," *Quarterly Journal of Economics* 49 (May 1935): 414–53.

14. See Alvin Gouldner, *The Coming Crisis of Western Sociology* (New York: Basic Books, 1970), and William Buxton, *Talcott Parsons and the Capitalist Nation State* (Toronto: University of Toronto Press, 1985). Also, critical interpretations of Parsons's use and abuse of the history of social theory, excluding Veblen, are found in Anthony Giddens, "Classical Social Theory and the Origins of Modern Sociology," *American Journal of Sociology* 81 (January 1976): 703–29; Charles Camic, "The Utilitarians Revisited," *American Journal of Sociology* 85 (November 1979): 516–550; Whitney Pope et al., "On the Divergence of Weber and Durkheim: A Critique of Parsons's Convergence Thesis," *American Sociological Review* 40 (August 1975): 417–27.

15. Buxton, *Talcott Parsons and the Capitalist Nation-State*, 17.

16. Ibid.

17. Talcott Parsons, "The Problem of Controlled Institutional Change," *Psychiatry* 8 (1945): 79–101. In addition, Parsons also employed Veblen's distinction between self-regarding and other-regarding traits. Like Veblen, he recommended reducing, if not eliminating, the structural role of the hierarchical,

authoritarian, and formalistic elements in postwar Germany. By this he meant the conservative parts of the German institutional structure, particularly those in the army, higher civil service, and corporations. Like Veblen, he also recommended systematically fostering those social values and propensities most congruent with industrialism.

18. On these points, see Buxton, *Talcott Parsons and the Capitalist Nation-State*, 29:

> Like most Americans growing up in the social sciences since the war, my starting-point has been what may broadly be called the "positivistic" movement in those fields—the tendency to imitate the physical sciences and to make physical science the measuring rod of all things. I quite early reached a conviction of the inadequacy of these current views. . . . In particular, "institutionalist" economics and behaviorism. (Talcott Parsons, "The Place of Ultimate Values in Sociological Theory," *Ethics* 45 (April, 1935): 313)

Also, see Talcott Parsons, *The Structure of Social Action*, (New York: The Free Press, 1961), 122; and *The Integration of Economic and Sociological Theory: The Marshall Lectures, 1953*, intro. Richard Swedberg (Uppsala University, Department of Sociology, 1986), 10, 66, 68; and Charles Camic, "The Making of a Method: A Historical Reinterpretation of the Early Parsons," *American Sociological Review* 52 (August 1987): 429.

19. P. A. Sorokin to Underhill Moore, 24 January 1934, Underhill Moore Papers, Yale University Library, New Haven, Connecticut.

20. See P. A. Sorokin, *Sociological Theories of Today* (New York and London: Harper & Row, 1966), 118–19, 289–301, 509–10.

21. Parsons put it this way, introducing his translation of Weber:

> It would be interesting to compare Weber's analysis of the capabilities of the modern capitalistic economy with that of a common Anglo-Saxon type of "heterodox" economics in the United States, particularly Veblen. Veblen undoubtedly lays his finger on *some* of the factors of instability in the modern "business" economy, in his analysis of business relationships as a process of jockeying for strategic position, etc. In so doing, he with considerable success, pricks the bubble of the utopian optimism of the existing order so common among orthodox exconomists, especially of the past generation. But as compared with Weber his analysis even of elements of instability is exceedingly narrow. Quite adequate comprehension of all Veblen's real contributions can be found in Weber's work—many of them he took for granted as too obvious to need demonstration. Weber, however, was able to understand the positive functional significance of the modern price system, more broadly the business economy, in a way which was entirely inaccessible to Veblen. Furthermore, though he is at least as affective in deflating "individualistic" utopianism, he is singularly free from anything corresponding to the counter-utopianism of Veblen, his idealization of "technology." The conclusion seems inescapable that Veblen was a highly unsophisticated person who demonstrates the typical reaction of a disillusioned idealist in his scientific work. Weber, who it should be remembered was a close contemporary, was on a

totally different level of scientific and cultural sophistication. The fact that a Veblen rather than a Weber gathers a school of ardent disciples around him bears witness to the great importance of factors other than the sheer weight of evidence and analysis in the formation of "schools" of social thought. (Talcott Parsons, intro. to Max Weber's *The Theory of Social and Economic Organization*, trans. A. M. Henderson and Talcott Parsons [New York: Free Press, 1969], 40)

Parsons's invidious comparison of Weber and Veblen is due to his idiosyncratic reading of Veblen's social theory. John Diggins was closer to the truth than Parsons when he wrote that

no two social theorists could be more intellectually and temperamentally opposed than Thorstein Veblen and Max Weber. Between the radical empiricism of the American and the conservative humanism of the German ran an ideological fault that was as wide as it was deep. Neither scholar had any influence on the other, and in tone and thesis their works are so widely different as to invite little basis for comparison. (John Diggins, *The Bard of Savagery: Thorstein Veblen and Modern Social Theory* [New York: Seabury Press, 1978], 70, 113)

Also, see Parsons, *The Structure of Social Action*, 529.

22. Talcott Parsons, "Distribution of Power in American Society," in *C. Wright Mills and the Power Elite*, ed. G. W. Domhoff and Hoyt Ballard (Boston: Beacon Press, 1968), 84.

23. Ibid.

24. Ibid.

25. Talcott Parsons, *Politics and Social Structure* (New York: The Free Press, 1969), 87.

26. Ibid., 87–88.

27. Parsons, *The Structure of Social Action*, 125. Also see Talcott Parsons and Neil J. Smelser, *Economy and Society* (Glencoe, N.Y.: Free Press, 1956), 5–6.

28. Parsons and Smelser, *Economy and Society*, xviii.

29. Talcott Parsons, "General Theory in Sociology," in *Sociology Today*, vol. 1, ed. Robert Merton, et al. (New York: Harper & Row, 1965), 12–13.

30. Talcott Parsons, *Social Systems and the Evolution of Action Theory* (New York: Free Press, 1977).

31. Ibid., 364.

32. Ibid.

33. Talcott Parsons, *The Social System* (New York: Free Press, 1963) 244–45.

34. Talcott Parsons, *Essays in Sociological Theory* (New York: Free Press, 1963), 80.

35. Ibid., 431.

36. Janice Harris, "Thorstein Veblen's Social Theory: A Reappraisal" (Ph.D. diss., New School for Social Research, New York, 1956), 25. In this regard Parsons wrote:

But Veblen, underneath his empiricism, shared the positivistic bias of the thought of his time. When he went beyond merely pointing to the facts to fit them into a theoretical scheme, he took over the vague psychological concept of habit and then, conscious that it is impossible to derive a particular institutional structure from a general psychological mechanism alone, he resorted to very complicated combinations of his four "instincts" with each other and with particular environmental conditions and stages of social evolution to give some specific content to the concept. All this is within the circle of positivistic factors with which we have dealt. Veblen may be held up as the primary example of "positivistic institutionalism." (Parsons, "Institutionalism (1934)," 3, Talcott Parsons Collection)

37. Ibid. The only positive comments Parsons made regarding any specific part of Veblen's social theory was in a draft of "Sociological Elements of Economic Thought," this portion of which was not included in the published version. Parsons wrote that

Veblen has some very important and clear insights into social phenomena. Above all, he saw and emphasized the historical relativity of economic activities. He also saw that they were related to a framework of factors, a "social structure," the main outline of which was independent of the individual ad hoc actions. From the point of view of freedom of adaptation to environmental exigencies it was a restraining framework.

38. Buxton, *Talcott Parsons and the Capitalist Nation-State*, 5.

39. Robert K. Merton, *Social Theory and Social Structure* (New York: Free Press, 1956), 309.

40. Buxton, *Talcott Parsons and the Capitalist Nation-State*, 5–6.

41. Parsons and Smelser, *Economy and Society*, 309.

42. Ibid.

43. See Robert Merton, *Science, Technology and Society in Seventeenth Century England* (New York: Howard Fertig, 1970), 158.

44. Merton, *Science, Technology and Society in Seventeenth Century England*, 158.

45. Merton, *Social Theory and Social Structure*, 69.

46. Ibid., 70. Merton drew upon Veblen as well as on a long line of previous theorists when he formulated the notions of latent and manifest functions. Merton also pointed out that Veblen's gift for seeing paradoxical, ironic, and satiric aspects of social life predisposed him to pay attention to latent functions. His student Louis Schneider was to further develop this insight in his own work on Veblen.

47. Merton also referred to J. J. Spengler's painstaking examination of [Arthur] Lovejoy's claim that Mandeville's *Fable of the Bees* (1714) had anticipated all of Veblen's principal ideas advanced in *The Theory of the Leisure Class*. Rather than taking superficial resemblance as evidence enough, Spengler subjected the two sets of ideas to thoroughgoing analysis, thus exhibiting the profound differences as well as the occasional similarities between them. In so doing, he showed how "initially small but functionally consequen-

tial differences of formulation eventuate in different theoretical implications which are then followed up and developed by successors." The Spengler article was published in *Weltwirtschaftliches Archiv: Zeitschrift des Institus fue Weltwirtschaft and der Universitat Kiel* 82, no. 1 (1959): 35–67. I concur in Merton's estimate of the value of the Spengler article. Based on Merton's and Spengler's analysis, it can be argued that critics of Veblen such as Riesman and Parsons have failed to appreciate the originality of his contributions.

48. Cf. the biographical sketch of Schneider by Robert Merton in *The Grammar of Social Relations: The Major Essays of Louis Schneider*, ed. Jay Weinstein (New Brunswick, N.J.: Transaction Publishers, 1984). Also, see Weinstein's introduction.

49. However, also cf. Schneider, *The Sociological Way of Looking at the World* (New York: McGraw-Hill, 1975), 253.

50. Louis Schneider, "review of *The Theory of the Leisure Class*, by Thorstein Veblen," *Social Science Quarterly* 57 (June 1976): 220.

51. Louis Schneider, *The Freudian Psychology and Veblen's Social Theory* (Morningside Heights, N.Y.: King's Crown Press, 1948), 120.

52. Ibid., 135–36.

53. Ibid., 128–34.

54. Ibid., 115.

55. Ibid., 136. Schneider pointed perhaps correctly to Veblen's efforts to use both William McDougall's "upward thrust" toward "consciousness" or "intelligence" or "will" and Jacques Loeb's efforts "downward" to "reduce the data of physiology and even of psychology to the terms of physics or physical chemistry." Veblen's use of the former's idealism and the latter's "metaphysics of mechanism" resulted in "a fumbling biological hand that puts norms into the sphere of instincts" (ibid., 88–89). Schneider justifiably complained of Veblen's "biological flourishes and much vague talk about selection," the vagueness of the category of instinct and the attendant confusions and . . . failure to solve the problem of how instincts mesh with cultural growth (ibid., 70, 80).

56. Ibid., 119. Karl Mannheim, himself, cited Veblen's *The Vested Interests and the Common Man* "for an exposition of a divergent interpretation of the influence of industrialization on the possibilities of substantial rationality." See C. Wright Mills, *Images of Man* (New York: George Braziller, 1970), 512.

57. Schneider, *The Freudian Psychology and Veblen's Social Theory*, 119. (Following quotations from this source are cited in text.)

58. Schneider, "review," 219–20. Like many of Veblen's liberal critics, Schneider found his use of the data and literature of anthropology to be deficient. He charged Veblen with claiming

rather unqualifiedly that "magical" and "religious" usages cohering around technological expedients necessarily had an inhibitive or impairing effect on technology itself. He made these magical and religious usages analogous in their inhibitive effect to encrustation of conventional usage that had a technologically inhibitive effect in the case of expedients used in modern cultures. The "functionalists" in anthropology have certainly cast doubt on such a view, especially when it is stated in the more or less unqualified form in which Veblen stated it. According to their evidence, magical and "animistic" techniques come in at the point where scientific control ends, and are neither substitutes for nor derangements of practical technological applications of knowledge where such exist. (Schneider, *The Freudian Psychology and Veblen's Social Theory*, 79)

Schneider overlooked examples of religious teaching inhibiting the introduction of new technologies, such as anesthetics, contraception, and photography.

59. Veblen, *The Place of Science in Modern Civilization*, 306.

60. Schneider, *The Freudian Psychology and Veblen's Social Theory*, 219.

61. Ibid., 135.

62. See Louis Schneider, "Some Psychiatric Views on 'Freedom' and the Theory of Social Systems," *Psychiatry* 12 (1949): 251–64. Although this article does not focus on either Veblen or Freud, it is a penetrating statement of the author's conviction that there is no way for humankind to be free of all social restraints, since all behavior is constrained or channeled in one way or another.

63. Schneider apparently came to regret having written *The Freudian Psychology and Veblen's Social Theory*. Indeed, not long before his death he wrote that he would "probably omit reference to this book more and more since I now disagree with it so basically." In 1973, in reflecting on the changes in his own thinking that occurred since 1948 on the subject of Veblen, he wrote that "there are statements here with which I would certainly disagree and others with which I would be acutely uncomfortable. . . . Veblen himself has limitations I would have done well to recognize more clearly and fully." Schneider clearly had regrets about his study of Veblen (and Freud), but this does not mean that he came to view Veblen in a more favorable light than he did in 1948. On these points, cf. Weinstein, *The Grammar of Social Relations*, 3, and Louis Schneider, *The Freudian Psychology and Veblen's Social Theory* (Westport, N.Y.: Greenwood Press, 1973), pref.

64. Three recent studies in which Bell played an important role are Peter Steinfels, *The Neoconservatives* (New York: Simon & Schuster, 1979), 161–87, Richard H. Pells, *The Liberal Mind in a Conservative Age* (New York: Harper & Row, 1985), and Alexander Bloom, *Prodigal Sons: The New York Intellectuals and Their World* (New York: Oxford University Press, 1986). Also, see Benjamin S. Kleinberg, *American Society in the Postindustrial Age* (Columbus, Ohio: Charles E. Merrill, 1973), Nathan Liebowitz, *Daniel Bell and the Agony of Modern Liberalism* (Westport, N.Y.: Greenwood Press, 1985), Job L. Dittberner, *The End of Ideology and American Social Thought: 1930–1960* (Ann Arbor: University Research Press, 1979). Howard Brick has analyzed Bell's use of Veblen's ideas in the 1940s, including Veblen's critique of business restrictionism, that is, industrial "sabotage," the "instinct of workmanship," and his social satire. See Howard Brick, *Daniel Bell and the Decline of Intellectual Radicalism* (Madison: University of Wisconsin Press, 1986), 71, 73, 74, 75, 171.

65. As quoted in *The End of Ideology Debate*, ed. Chaim I. Waxman (New York: Simon & Schuster, 1969), 261.

66. Daniel Bell, *The End of Ideology* (New York: Collier Books, 1961), 397.

67. Ibid., 399–400.

68. See Daniel Bell, *The Coming of Post-Industrial Society* (New York: Basic Books, 1973), 279.

69. Daniel Bell, "Veblen and the New Class," *American Scholar* 32 (Autumn 1963): 638.

70. Ibid., 634.

71. Several of Veblen's ideas on status emulation and conspicuous consumption can be traced directly to John Rae, the Scottish-Canadian political economist (1796–1872). See Stephen Edgell and Rick Tilman, "John Rae and Thorstein Veblen on Conspicuous Consumption: A Neglected Relationship," *History of Political Economy* 23 (Winter 1991).

72. See Bell's new afterword to *The End of Ideology* (Cambridge: Harvard University Press, 1988), 409–47.

CHAPTER NINE
RADICAL CRITICS: THE FRANKFURT SCHOOL

1. See esp., T. W. Adorno, "Veblen's Attack on Culture," *Studies in Philosophy and Social Science* 9, no. 3 (1941): 389–413. Also, see the articles by Herbert Marcuse, "Some Social Implications of Modern Technology," and Max Horkheimer, "The End of Reason," in the same issue. More recently, Adorno returned to the analysis of Veblen when he wrote an introduction to Peter von Haselberg's *Functionalismus und Irrationalitat: Studien uber Thorstein Veblen's "Theory of the Leisure Class"* (Mannheim: Europaische Verlagsanstalt, 1962). This provided him with an opportunity to focus on familiar themes regarding Veblen and to state them even more baldly than in his earlier writings. However, it should not be assumed that the members of the Frankfurt School were of one mind concerning Veblen. By the 1960s it became apparent that Horkheimer and Adorno had become rather conservative in important aspects of their work, whereas Marcuse had become even more radical than in the past. Was this politico-ideological shift anticipated in their earlier analysis of Veblen? It is difficult to say.

2. See, for example, Max Horkheimer, *Eclipse of Reason* (New York: Oxford University Press, 1947), 41–57, in which he criticized Dewey, James, and Pierce; and Herbert Marcuse's review of *Theory of Valuation*, by John Dewey in *Studies in Philosophy and Social Science* 9 (April 1941): 144–48. For a summation of critical theory's difference with pragmatism, see Phil Slater, *Origin and Significance of the Frankfurt School* (London: Routledge & Keegan Paul, 1977), 29–30. C. Wright Mills, who knew well the work of the pragmatists and Veblen and was personally acquainted with several members of the Frankfurt School, once complained that Horkheimer did not understand pragmatism. He had been asked by Oxford University Press to evaluate the manuscript of Horkheimer's *Eclipse of Reason*, and although he recommended publication, he asked that parts of it be rewritten. Mills argued that Horkheimer

goes too far . . . in stating the negative implications of the subjective view of reason. For example . . . he uses the phrase "completely meaningless," etc. This is just not so. Pragmatism's whole effort has been to give *new* meaning to this view of reason; he must at least come to explicit grips with these attempts either here (which I should favor) or by cross reference acknowledge this duty and delay its execution. . . . *But* frankly, I don't see any evidence that Horkheimer has really gotten hold of pragmatism except (1) in a rather vulgar form and (2) in the later pronouncements of the Partisan Review writers whom he belatedly attacks. Shouldn't he dignify the view enough to make evident his knowledge of more of its literature than such minor essays by followers? . . . His remarks . . . certainly do not give one confidence that he knows the pragmatists whom he is attacking. (As quoted in Rick Tilman, *et al.*, "Critical Theory and Institutional Economics: Frankfurt's Encounter with Veblen," *Journal of Economic Issues* 14 (September 1980): 647)

3. Adorno, "Veblen's Attack on Culture," 411.

4. Ibid., 412.

5. Ibid., 411.

6. Ibid., 408.

7. Thorstein Veblen, *The Theory of the Leisure Class* (New York: Modern Library, 1934), 191.

8. Thorstein Veblen, "The Economics of Karl Marx: II," in *Veblen on Marx, Race, Science and Economics* (New York: Capricorn Books, 1969), 436.

9. Ibid., 442.

10. See Thorstein Veblen, *Absentee Ownership and Business Enterprise in Recent Times*, intro. by Robert Lekachman (Boston: Beacon Press, 1967), esp. chaps. 2, 3, and 7.

11. Horkheimer also made this allegation against the other pragmatists; see his *Eclipse of Reason*, 41–57.

12. Adorno, "Veblen's Attack on Culture," 401.

13. Ibid.

14. Ibid., 402.

15. Ibid., 389.

16. Langdon Winner, *Autonomous Technology* (Cambridge, Mass.: MIT Press, 1977), 31.

17. Adorno, "Veblen's Attack on Culture," 389.

18. Ibid., 407.

19. Ibid.

20. Ibid.

21. In this regard, Adorno made a revealing comment: "Beneath the outer armor of this rebellious arch-enemy of the theological tradition of New England hides the asceticism of the Lutheran peasant, not only as a psychological force but as a pervasive element of theory" (ibid., 398–99). Veblen's insights into the cultural and social background of Jewish intellectuals were revealed in "The Intellectual Pre-eminence of Jews in Modern Europe," reprinted in Max Lerner, ed. *The Portable Veblen* (New York: The Viking Press, 1961), 467–79.

22. Ibid., 393.

23. Ibid., 394.

24. John Diggins, *The Bard of Savagery: Thorstein Veblen and Modern Social Theory* (New York: Seabury Press, 1978), 81.

25. Adorno, "Veblen's Attack on Culture," 404.

26. Ibid., 405.

27. Veblen's last book, *Absentee Ownership*, is susceptible to either interpretation.

28. Adorno, "Veblen's Attack on Culture," p. 404.

29. Veblen, *The Theory of the Leisure Class*, 260.

30. Ibid., 261. See the analysis of Veblen and the Frankfurt School on the subject of sport in John M. Hoberman, *Sport and Political Ideology* (Austin: University of Texas Press, 1984), 87–88, 241–48.

31. Adorno, "Veblen's Attack on Culture," 394–95.

32. Ibid., 395.

33. Marcuse, "Some Social Implications of Modern Technology," p. 418.

34. Ibid.

35. Veblen's optimistic early view of the socialist potential of the working class is found in *The Theory of Business Enterprise*. It should be contrasted with the pessimism manifest in *Absentee Ownership* and *The Engineers and the Price System*.

36. See Veblen, *Theory of Business Enterprise*, chap. 9.

37. Adorno, "Veblen's Attack on Culture," 410.

38. Marcuse, "Some Social Implications of Modern Technology," 414. (Following quotations from this source are cited in text.)

39. Horkheimer, preface, 365.

40. Horkheimer, "The End of Reason," 378.

41. Ibid., 378–79.

42. While the Frankfurt School was preparing an issue of their theoretical journal, which was largely devoted to an analysis of Veblen, they were also corresponding about him. On 3 November 1941, Horkheimer who had just received and read a draft of Adorno's article on Veblen, wrote to Adorno:

> You distinguish Veblen from nationalism most decisively, from such notions as the identity of thinking and being, as the category of totality, of freedom. These are the very ideas with which I am now grappling as I begin this work. Strangely enough, I myself feel that we are being forced into a confrontation with a rationalism that no longer exists; I am consequently thinking that the main focus of my paper will be the limitations of rationality! But I must confess that I'm having a hard time. The separation immediately shifts into a movement from quantity into quality.

This correspondence is in the Max Horkheimer-Archiv, Staat-Und Universitats-Bibliothek, Goethe University, Frankfurt, Federal Republic of Germany.

CHAPTER TEN
RADICAL CRITICS: *THE MONTHLY REVIEW*

1. Paul Marlor Sweezy was born in New York City in 1910. He received all of his academic degrees from Harvard, including his doctorate in economics in 1937. He taught at Harvard from 1934 to 1946, an experience that he found disillusioning. Apparently, Sweezy left Harvard because he believed that his

political and intellectual views made it unlikely that he would receive tenure. See the biographical sketch of Sweezy in Stephen Resnick and Richard Wolff, eds., *Rethinking Marxism: Struggles in Marxist Theory: Essays for Harry Magdoff and Paul Sweezy* (Brooklyn: Autonomedia, 1985), 400–3. Sweezy's own writings on Veblen include "Thorstein Veblen: Strengths and Weaknesses," in Paul Sweezy, *The Present as History* (New York: Monthly Review Press, 1953), 295–301, "The Influence of Marxism on Thorstein Veblen," in *Socialism and American Life*, vol. 1, ed. Donald Drew Egbert and Stow Persons (Princeton: Princeton University Press, 1952), 473–77; Paul Sweezy and Leo Huberman, "Thorstein Bunde Veblen," 1857–1957," *Monthly Review* 9 (July-August 1957): 65–75; Paul Sweezy, "The Theory of Business Enterprise and Absentee Ownership," *Monthly Review* 9 (July-August 1957): 105–12; "Veblen on American Capitalism," in *Thorstein Veblen: A Critical Reappraisal*, ed. Douglas F. Dowd (Ithaca: Cornell University Press, 1958), 177–97; "Veblen's Critique of the American Economy," *American Economic Review: Papers and Proceedings* 48 (May 1958): 21–29.

2. In planning the publication of this issue to celebrate the centennial of Veblen's birth, Sweezy had written to Veblen's nephew, the eminent Princeton mathematician, Oswald Veblen, Albert Einstein's friend and colleague. Sweezy was particularly interested in persuading him to write some personal remembrances of his famous uncle, but while Veblen thanked Sweezy for inviting him to participate, he declined to do so because of lack of time. See Paul M. Sweezy to Oswald Veblen, 22 December 1956 and Oswald Veblen to Paul M. Sweezy, 7 January 1957, Oswald Veblen Collection, Manuscript Division, Library of Congress, Washington, D.C.

3. Paul Sweezy and Leo Huberman, "Thorstein Bunde Veblen, 1857–1957," 66. Sweezy has also written:

Here we have the key, I think, to one of the most quizzing things about Veblen, namely, that the so-called "institutionalist" school which he inspired disintegrated rapidly and never produced anything of lasting value. He was a great man, and he attracted followers because of it. But he was greater than his own theories; and unfortunately greatness cannot be passed on, while theories can. (Paul Sweezy, "Veblen: A Cautionary View," *New Republic* 114 [25 February 1946]: 288)

Even in the 1940s and 1950s, the weakness of institutional economics was exaggerated; witness the work of John Gambs, Allan Gruchy, Clarence Ayres, Wesley Mitchell, and J. K. Galbraith. Since the creation of the Association for Evolutionary Economics, the publication of the *Journal of Economic Issues* (1966), and the more recent organization of the Association for Institutional Thought (1979), and European Association for Evolutionary Political Economy (1987), criticisms like Sweezy's are even less convincing.

4. Sweezy and Huberman, "Thorstein Bunde Veblen, 1857–1957," 72.

5. Ibid., 74.

Veblen's isolation had grave consequences. It deprived him of the priceless benefits of genuine intellectual collaboration and criticism. It accounted for many, and accentuated all, of his weaknesses: his shyness, his indirectness, his repetitiousness, at times what it is no exaggeration to call his "half-baked-ness." The amazing thing, perhaps, is not that this should be so but that in spite of it his insights should have been so sure and his vision should have remained so clear. Veblen, of all American intellectuals, was most nearly "the bough that might have grown full straight." (Ibid., 75)

6. Sweezy, "Veblen's Critique of the American Economy," 27.

7. Sweezy, "Veblen on American Capitalism," 188.

8. Solomon Adler, "Imperial Germany and the Industrial Revolution," *Monthly Review* 9 (July-August 1957): 82.

9. See Sweezy, "The Illusion of the 'Managerial Revolution,'" *Science and Society* 21 (Winter 1957): 75.

10. Davis, "Thorstein Veblen Reconsidered," 75.

11. Sweezy, "The Theory of Business Enterprise and Absentee Ownership," 106.

12. Sweezy, *The Present as History*, 299.

13. Ibid.

14. Sweezy, "Thorstein Veblen: Strengths and Weaknesses," 300.

15. Ibid.

16. Ibid., 195. The claim that Veblen subscribed to any aspect of the application of Say's Law may strike the reader as bizarre. Sweezy erred on this point.

17. Sweezy, "Veblen's Critique of the American Economy," 28.

18. Ibid.

19. Ibid.

20. Sweezy, "The Theory of Business Enterprise and Absentee Ownership," 111.

21. Ibid., 110.

22. Ibid., 110–11.

23. Sweezy, "Veblen on American Capitalism," 195.

24. Ibid.

25. Ibid.

26. Sweezy, *The Present as History*, 300.

27. Ibid.

28. Sweezy, "Veblen's Critique of the American Economy," 25.

29. Sweezy, "Thorstein Veblen: Strengths and Weaknesses," 297–98.

30. Ibid., 298. Sweezy stated that Veblen also ignored the role of national-ism in the bourgeois revolutions of the past.

31. Sweezy, "Thorstein Veblen: Strengths and Weaknesses," 287.

32. Ibid., 287–88.

33. Sweezy, "The Influence of Marxism on Thorstein Veblen," 475.

34. Solomon Adler, "Imperial Germany and the Industrial Revolution," 79–80.

35. Sweezy, "The Theory of Business Enterprise and Absentee Ownership," 105.

36. Ibid., 110.

37. Solomon Adler, "Imperial Germany and the Industrial Revolution," 79.

38. Ibid.

39. Sweezy's political radicalism was apparent while he was still a graduate student at Harvard. To illustrate the point, he wrote to Frank Knight when he was twenty-three years old to let him know that capitalism was finished, although he was uncertain as to what would take its place (Paul Sweezy to Frank Knight, 1 February 1934, Knight Papers). The question of whether Sweezy's "radicalization" was ultimately traceable to Veblen or Marx or both cannot be easily answered through textual exegesis of his published work. What is evident, however, is that when he wrote about Veblen, Marx was the yardstick by which he measured Veblen's performance.

40. A biographical sketch of Baran is found in Paul Sweezy and Leo Huberman, eds., *Paul A. Baran: A Collective Portrait* (New York: Monthly Review Press, 1965). Baran (1910–1964) was born in czarist Russia and was educated in Poland, Germany, the Soviet Union, and the United States. He received a doctorate from Berlin in 1932 and an M.A. from Harvard in 1941. In 1948 Baran went to Palo Alto, California as a visiting lecturer for the Hoover Institute and the Stanford University Department of Economics. He became an associate professor at Stanford, beginning in 1949 and he was promoted to the rank of professor in 1951, a position which he held until he died in 1964. Baran joined Communist youth and student organizations while in Germany and continued with these activities until 1930, at which time he cut all ties with Communist organizations and joined the German Social Democratic party; he remained a Social Democrat until he left Germany in 1933. Baran never again joined, or was associated with, any political party or organized political group. It is important to recognize that, like his cohort Paul Sweezy, he was a nonparty Marxist with a strong streak of political independence as a basic component in his social philosophy. Cf. Paul Althoff, "Paul A. Baran: American Marxist Political Economist" (Ph.D. diss., University of Iowa, 1970), and Peter Clecak, *Radical Paradoxes: Dilemmas of the American Left: 1945–1970* (New York: Harper & Row, 1973) for sensitive treatments of Baran and Sweezy.

41. Paul Baran, "The Theory of the Leisure Class," *Monthly Review* 9 (July-August 1957): 85. (Following quotations from this source are cited in text.)

42. Ibid., 89–90. Baran's criticism of Veblen's "undialectical" approach warrants comparison with T. W. Adorno's similar charge. See T. W. Adorno, "Veblen's Attack on Culture," *Studies in Philosophy and Social Science* 9 (1941): 389–413.

43. But Douglas Dowd suggested that Veblen's writings "point squarely—if with different theoretical overtones"—to the same major tendencies of American capitalism as Baran's *The Political Economy of Growth*. See Douglas Dowd, "Social Commitment and Social Analysis: The Contribution of Paul Baran," *Politics and Society* 5, no. 2 (1975): 231.

44. Davis's writings on Veblen from 1941 to 1948 were basically liberal in tone and included "Thorstein Veblen's Social Theory" (Ph.D. diss., Harvard University, 1941); "Veblen on the Decline of the Protestant Ethic," *Social Forces* 22 (March 1944): 282–86; "Veblen's Study of Modern Germany," *American Sociological Review* 9 (December 1944): 603–9; "Sociological Ele-

ments in Veblen's Economic Theory," *Journal of Political Economy* 53 (June 1945): 132–49; review of *The Freudian Psychology and Veblen Social Theory*, by Louis Schneider, *Social Forces* 27 (October 1948): 94–95. His later works on Veblen, produced in the mid-1950s, show strong evidence of his political radicalization. See "The Postwar Essays," *Monthly Review* 9 (July-August 1957): 91–98; and "Thorstein Veblen and the Culture of Capitalism" in *American Radicals: Some Problems and Personalities*, ed. Harvey Goldberg (New York: Monthly Review Press, 1957), 279–93. Also, see "Veblen, Thorstein" in *International Encyclopedia of the Social Sciences*, vol. 16, ed. David L. Sills, (New York: Macmillan and Free Press, 1968), 303–8.

45. Davis's radicalization, however, apparently had its beginnings not in the 1950s but in the 1930s. The depression weighed heavily on him and so did the Spanish Civil War. Indeed, he seriously considered going to Spain to join the International Brigades. Although his experiences at Harvard and during World War II temporarily diverted him from a radical path, the impact of the Cold War and the Chinese Revolution "reradicalized" him. See Arthur Davis, "Veblen Once More: A View From 1979," in *Thorstein Veblen's Social Theory* (New York: Arno Press, 1980). Davis held academic posts at Harvard, Union College, and Vermont before becoming a Canadian expatriate at the University of Calgary.

46. Davis, "Thorstein Veblen and the Culture of Capitalism," 291.

47. See Davis, "Thorstein Veblen Reconsidered," 52.

48. Ibid.

49. Ibid.

50. Davis, "The Postwar Essays," 92, 98.

51. Davis, "Sociological Elements in Veblen's Economic Theory," 145; "Thorstein Veblen Reconsidered," 59; "Thorstein Veblen and the Culture of Capitalism," 282.

52. Davis, "Veblen on the Decline of the Protestant Ethic," 285.

53. Davis, "Veblen's Study of Modern Germany," 606.

54. Ibid.

55. Davis, "Sociological Elements in Veblen's Economic Theory," 145.

56. Davis, "review of *The Freudian Psychology*," 94.

57. Davis, "Thorstein Veblen Reconsidered," 62.

58. Ibid., 59.

59. Davis, "Veblen on the Decline of the Protestant Ethic," 283.

60. Davis, "Sociological Elements in Veblen's Economic Theory," 142.

61. Davis, "Veblen on the Decline of the Protestant Ethic," 284.

62. Davis, "Veblen's Study of Modern Germany," 603.

63. Davis, "Thorstein Veblen Reconsidered," 71.

64. Ibid.

65. Davis, "Veblen on the Decline of the Protestant Ethic," 283.

66. Ibid., 285.

67. Ibid.

68. Davis, "Thorstein Veblen Reconsidered," 61.

69. Davis, "The Postwar Essays," 93.

70. Davis, "Veblen, Thorstein," *International Encyclopedia of the Social Sciences*, 305.

71. Davis, "Thorstein Veblen and the Culture of Capitalism," 289.
72. Ibid., 285.
73. Davis, "Veblen on the Decline of the Protestant Ethic," 284.
74. Davis, "Veblen's Study of Modern Germany," 605.
75. Ibid., 604. Also, see p. 608.
76. See Davis, "Sociological Elements in Veblen's Economic Theory," 146.
77. Ibid.
78. Ibid.
79. Davis, "Veblen's Study of Modern Germany," 604.
80. Davis, "Sociological Elements in Veblen's Economic Theory," 146.
81. Ibid., 144.
82. Ibid., 133.
83. Ibid., 137.
84. Ibid., 143.
85. Ibid., 147.
86. Ibid., 148.
87. Ibid., 49.
88. Ibid., 148.
89. Ibid., 136.
90. Davis, "Veblen on the Decline of the Protestant Ethic," 286.
91. Cf. Karl Mannheim, *Man and Society in an Age of Reconstruction* (New York: Harcourt, Brace, 1940), 51–60, 117–20, 124–26, 128–43.
92. Davis, "Sociological Elements in Veblen's Economic Theory," 143. Also, see "Veblen, Thorstein," *International Encyclopedia of the Social Sciences*, 304.
93. Davis, "Sociological Elements in Veblen's Economic Theory," 143.
94. Davis, "Thorstein Veblen Reconsidered," 76–77. Also, see Davis, "Veblen, Thorstein," *International Encyclopedia of the Social Sciences*, 305.
95. Davis, "Thorstein Veblen Reconsidered," 61.
96. Davis, "Veblen, Thorstein," *International Encyclopedia of the Social Sciences*, 303.
97. Davis, "The Postwar Essays," 96.
98. Davis, "Thorstein Veblen Reconsidered," 80–81.
99. Davis, "Veblen Once More: A View From 1979," n.p.
100. Davis, "Thorstein Veblen and the Culture of Capitalism," 288.
101. Davis, "Thorstein Veblen Reconsidered," 54.
102. Davis, "Sociological Elements in Veblen's Economic Theory," 134, 149.
103. Davis, "Thorstein Veblen Reconsidered," 85.
104. Ibid., 79, 85.

CHAPTER ELEVEN
RADICAL CRITICS: MARXISM, TROTSKYISM, AND SOCIAL DEMOCRACY

1. See Addison T. Cutler, "The Ebb of Institutional Economics," *Science and Society* 2 (Fall 1938): 448–70, and Randolph Landsman, "The Philosophy of Veblen's Economics," *Science and Society* (Fall 1957): 333–45. Also, see the

exchange between Cutler and Joseph Dorfman in *Science and Society* 3 (Fall 1939): 509–18.

2. Cutler, "The Ebb of Institutional Economics, 451.

3. Clarence E. Ayres to Addison T. Cutler, 19 December 1938, Clarence Ayres Collection, Barker Texas History Archive, University of Texas, Austin. Although Cutler and Ayres were apparently on good terms personally, the political and ideological differences between them were significant. Indeed, the doctrinal tone of Ayres's letter was much like that of Veblen's other liberal critics. These differences were also evident in the radical Cutler's response to Ayres. See Addison Cutler to Clarence Ayres, 6 January 1939, Ayres Collection.

4. Ibid.

5. Ibid.

6. Cutler, "The Ebb of Institutional Economics," 452.

7. See Leonard Dente, *Veblen's Theory of Social Change* (New York: Arno Press, 1977), and Clarence Ayres, *The Theory of Economic Progress* (Chapel Hill: University of North Carolina Press, 1944).

8. Lewis Corey, "Veblen and Marx," *Nation*, 139 (26 December 1934): 745. Corey was one of the first Marxists to recognize the value of Veblen's superstructural analysis as anticipating later theories of cultural hegemony such as Gramsci's. For a masterly treatment of Veblen on the issue of the hegemony of ideas, see John P. Diggins, *The Bard of Savagery*, chap. 6.

9. Ibid.

10. Cutler, "The Ebb of Institutional Economics," 451.

11. V. J. McGill, "The Main Trend of Social Philosophy in America," in *Philosophic Thought in France and the United States*, ed. Marvin Farber (Albany, N.Y.: State University of New York Press, 1968), 686. McGill originally made these comments in 1950 while an editor of *Science and Society*.

12. Randolph H. Landsman, "The Philosophy of Veblen's Economics," 336. Corey, "Veblen and Marx," *Nation* 139 (26 December 1934): 745–46, and "Veblen and Marxism," *Marxist Quarterly*, 1 (January-March 1937): 162–68. Corey faulted Veblen for neglecting the factors of consciousness and purposeful struggle. From Corey's standpoint, the chief problem in Veblen's theory was his reliance upon the limited Darwinian theory of evolution with its emphasis upon natural selection, variation, and survival. Hence Veblen's theory could not adequately explain "how men, habituated to the older order, may avoid habituation to a declining civilization and revolt to create the new" (Corey, "Veblen and Marx," 745). Moreover, Corey felt that Veblen's attachment to the conception of "immutably given human nature" and its fixed biological basis was at odds with the Marxian notion that man through labor changes the outer world as well as his own nature" ("Veblen and Marxism," 165). However, as Veblen himself was fond of pointing out, there is no evidence that man's biological makeup has changed significantly since the start of the New Stone Age. The Italian Franco Ferrarotti, otherwise, sympathetic, likewise faulted Veblen's method for its undialectical positivism and biological character. See "La Sociologia di Thorstein Veblen," *Rivista di Filosofia* 41 (October-December, 1950): 402–19.

13. Ibid., 338.

14. Compare Landsman's position in this regard with that of T. W. Adorno: "The pragmatist is conscious of the perennial limits put upon men's attempts to go beyond the existent limits set to both thought and action" (T. W. Adorno, "Veblen's Attack on Culture," *Studies in Philosophy and Social Science* 9 [1941]: 441).

15. Randolph Landsman, "The Philosophy of Veblen's Economics," 336.

16. Ibid.

17. Ibid., 345.

18. Ibid.

19. Ibid.

20. John G. Wright, "Thorstein Veblen, Sociologist," *The New International* 2 (January 1936): 21–23. John G. Wright (real name Joseph Vanzler) was the main writer on theoretical questions for the Socialist Workers party in the United States. He had translated many of Trotsky's works and was widely respected in the Party for his learning. See Christopher Z. Hobson and Ronald D. Tabor, *Trotskyism and the Dilemma of Socialism* (Westport, Conn.: Greenwood Press, 1988), 360.

21. Ibid., 22.

22. Ibid. "Since the laws Veblen speaks of are nothing but habits of thought; and since he defines institutions also as habits of thought, this complex sentence merely sums up to the assertion that habits of thought are engendered, controlled, selectively conserved and so forth by habits of thought" (ibid., 23).

23. Ibid., 22.

24. Ibid.

25. See Edyth Miller, "Veblen and Womens' Lib: A Parallel," *Journal of Economic Issues* 6 (September, 1972): 75–86.

26. Wright, "Thorstein Veblen, Sociologist," 22.

27. Ibid.

28. Ibid.

29. See Thorstein Veblen, "The Socialist Economics of Karl Marx," 1 and 2, in *The Place of Science in Modern Civilization* (New York: Viking Press, 1930), 409–56.

30. Wright, "Thorstein Veblen, Sociologist," 23.

31. Wright believed Veblen badly misunderstood Charles Darwin's theory of evolution and misapplied his teaching in the realm of sociology. He wrote that

Veblen likewise confounded the development of the organic species with the development of society. He wrote that "the life of man in society, just like the life of other species, is a struggle for existence, and therefore it is a process of selective adaptation. The evolution of social structure has been a process of natural selection of institutions. (Ibid., 22)

On recent controversy concerning the relationship between evolutionary theory and economics, cf. Rick Tilman, "Darwinism and Economics: Recent Criticisms of Veblen and Ayres," *Journal of Economic Issues* 24 (March 1990): 263–67.

32. Ibid., 21.

33. Ibid.

34. Ibid. Wright also commented that "they are as fraudulent (in a non-invidious sense) as his Instinct of Workmanship." He also complained that "many of his views are novel only in so far as they are far-fetched. Many of his seemingly iconoclastic postulates are in reality conformist" (Ibid., 22).

35. Wright also commented that "he derives the development of institutions from human nature. In his definition he merely repeats what Plato said, to wit, that "the states are as the men are, they grow out of human characters"; a dictum which was rehashed by Spencer to read: "the forms of social organization are determined by men's natures" (ibid., 22). Wright's position was that Veblen was on the side of nature in the nature versus nurture controversy despite the stress placed by Veblen on the malleability and plasticity of the human species, and the role played by man's institutional environment in determining his behavior.

36. Peter Clecak, *Radical Paradoxes: Dilemmas of the American Left 1945–1970* (New York: Harper & Row, 1973), 17. C. Wright Mills occasionally wrote for both *Monthly Review* and *Dissent*, but was too much an intellectual maverick to be included in either of these groups.

37. See Bernard Rosenberg, "Veblen and Marx," *Social Research* 15 (March 1948): 88–117, "Thorstein Veblen: Portrait of the Intellectual as a Marginal Man," *Social Problems* 2 (January 1955): 181–87, *The Values of Veblen: A Critical Appraisal* (Washington, D.C.: Public Affairs Press, 1956), intro. to *Thorstein Veblen* (New York: Thomas Y. Crowell, 1963), 1–14.

38. Rosenberg wrote that

as a man, as a scholar, and as a stylist, he was an original, always incomparably himself. This uniqueness makes it all the more ironic that Veblen should so often be put down as a derivative thinker. Talcott Parsons, the eminent but often indecipherable sociologist, has clearly stated, "quite adequate comprehension of all Veblen's real contributions can be found in Weber's works." We shall have to inspect some of Veblen's "real contributions"; it will then become apparent that they cannot be found in Weber's works—which were probably more important, but different. A less eccentric, if equally indefensible, opinion was expressed in the 1930's by Lewis Corey, then a radical activist, when he wrote, "All that is vital in Thorstein Veblen may fulfill itself in Marxism and socialism." This of Veblen, as if he had not, at Harvard University in 1906, discussed and dismissed "The Socialist Economics of Karl Marx and His Followers" in a special series of subsequently published lectures. (Rosenberg, intro. to *Thorstein Veblen*, 1)

39. Rosenberg, *The Values of Veblen*, 117.

40. Ibid.

41. Rosenberg, intro. to *Thorstein Veblen*, 3.

42. Rosenberg, *The Values of Veblen*, 10.

43. Ibid., 33.

44. Rosenberg, "Veblen and Marx," 105.

45. Rosenberg, *The Values of Veblen*, 114.

46. Rosenberg, intro. to *Thorstein Veblen*, 13–14.
47. Rosenberg, "Veblen and Marx," 115.
48. Rosenberg, *The Values of Veblen*, 113.
49. See Rick Tilman, *C. Wright Mills: A Native Radical and His American Intellectual Roots* (University Park: Penn State Press, 1984), chaps. 4, 5, 9 for a detailed comparison of the two men.
50. See esp. Rosenberg, intro. to *Thorstein Veblen*, 13.
51. Rosenberg, *The Values of Veblen*, 114.
52. Ibid., 76.
53. Ibid., 49.
54. Ibid.
55. Ibid.
56. Rosenberg, "Veblen and Marx," 110.
57. Ibid.
58. Rosenberg, *The Values of Veblen*, 106.
59. Ibid.
60. Ibid., 104
61. Rosenberg, "Veblen and Marx," 101, 108; also see *The Values of Veblen*, 46, and "A Clarification of Some Veblenian Concepts," 182.
62. Rosenberg, *The Values of Veblen*, 45.
63. Ibid.
64. Ibid., 46.
65. Rosenberg, "A Clarification of Some Veblenian Concepts," 183.
66. Ibid.
67. Rosenberg, *The Values of Veblen*, 47.
68. Ibid., 48.
69. Ibid., 71.
70. Ibid.
71. Veblen, *The Theory of the Leisure Class*, 261.
72. Rosenberg, *The Values of Veblen*, 76.
73. Rosenberg, intro. to *Thorstein Veblen*, 11.
74. Ibid., 12.
75. Rosenberg, *The Values of Veblen*, 100.
76. Ibid., 65.
77. Ibid., 106.
78. Rosenberg, intro. to *Thorstein Veblen*, 2.
79. Lewis Corey (Fraina), "Veblen and Marxism," *Marxist Quarterly*, 1 (January, March, 1937): 168. (Following quotations from this source are cited in text.)
80. John Hobson, *Veblen* (New York: Augustus M. Kelly, 1971), 37. Hobson also commented on p. 50 that

to many psychologists and sociologists Veblen will appear to drive to an extreme his anti-hedonism, when he makes it a ground for repudiating the whole utilitarian calculus or method of valuation. For the most primitive urges to activity in a human being, or any animal, cannot be explained except as desired escapes from some static condition, some action conducive to personal safety. Nor can it be denied that such activities, once established as methods of escape, begin to carry elements of conscious satisfaction in their performance. Such biological utility is always touched with conscious satisfaction, and the practices of the activity carries an immediate pleasure. The denial of such conscious satisfaction as a motive must lead to a doctrine of "behaviourism," which is not really held by Veblen, and which his economic determinism does not require.

81. Ibid., 138–39. Hobson appears to have forgotten Veblen's own favorable review of *Imperialism* (1902) in which Hobson articulated the economic taproot of capitalism doctrine. On the relationship between the two men, see Stephen Edgell and Rick Tilman, "Thorstein Veblen and John Hobson: Friends and Critics" in *John A. Hobson,* ed. John Pheby (London: Macmillan, 1992). Shortly after Veblen's death on 3 August 1929, his friend British sociologist Victor Branford wrote, "I am afraid the [sociological] review will be late again, as I had to keep the proofs back in order to insert a memoir of Veblen, which, after considerable correspondence, I got Hobson to write. He said that he has seen no appreciation of Veblen anywhere either in American or English papers, except an article in the *New Republic*" (Branford to Patrick Geddes, 21 September 1929, Geddes Papers, National Library of Scotland, Edinburgh, Scotland).

82. John Hobson, "The Economics of Thorstein Veblen," *Political Science Quarterly* 52 (March 1937): 143.

83. Ibid.

84. Ibid., 144.

CHAPTER TWELVE
THE IDEOLOGICAL USE AND ABUSE OF THORSTEIN VEBLEN

1. This is the central thesis in Thomas Sowell, *A Conflict of Visions* (New York: William Morrow, 1987).

2. Ibid., 33.

3. On these and related figures, see Rick Tilman, *C. Wright Mills: A Native Radical and His American Intellectual Roots* (University Park: Penn State Press, 1984); Tilman et al., "Critical Theory and Institutional Economics: Frankfurt's Encounter with Veblen," *Journal of Economic Issues* 14 (September 1980): 631–47; and Peter Clecak, *Radical Paradoxes: Dilemmas of the American Left, 1945–1970* (New York: Harper & Row, 1973), chaps. 3 & 4.

4. See Sowell, *A Conflict of Visions,* 38, where, in summation, he argued that "despite necessary caveats, it remains an important and remarkable phenomenon that how human nature is conceived at the outset is highly correlated with the whole conception of knowledge, morality, power, time, rationality, war, freedom, and law which defines a social vision."

5. The Woody Guthrie quotation comes from a song recorded by Alan Lomax at the U.S. Department of the Interior studio in Washington, D.C., 22 March 1940. It is from a song entitled "Pretty Boy Floyd." I am indebted to another Okie, Bill Dugger, for this information.

6. On these points, see Rick Tilman, "Thorstein Veblen and the New Deal: A Reappraisal," *The Historian* 50 (February 1988): 155–72. An issue-oriented liberalism in the United States is often perceived as a pragmatic, nonideological response to problems demanding political action for their amelioration. Such, at least, were the claims of some New Dealers, Fair Dealers, and New Frontiersmen who were critical of Veblen because of what they perceived as his ideological rigidity and doctrinal absolutism. Their perception of him as a utopian visionary thus made it difficult for them to distill from his theories any specific policy orientation that promised to have an immediate, ameliorative effect on pressing social problems. Yet this was by no means the interpretation of Veblen arrived at by all liberal scholars and politicians in the period from 1930 to 1965. Indeed, it was just as commonplace for them to find doctrinal inspiration for welfare and regulatory state collectivism in his writings.

7. See Charles T. Rasmussen and Rick Tilman, "Mechanistic Physiology and Institutional Economics: Jacques Loeb and Thorstein Veblen," *International Journal of Social Economy*, 18 (Spring 1991).

8. See Colin Loader, Jeff Waddoups, Rick Tilman, "Thorstein Veblen, Werner Sombart and the Periodization of History," *Journal of Economic Issues* 25 (June 1991).

9. Henry A. Wallace, "Veblen's Imperial Germany and the Industrial Revolution," *Political Science Quarterly* 55 (October 1940): 435–45. The question of the relationship between the ideas of theorists and their translation into public policy by politicians was rarely more important than in 1940. While war raged in Europe, Africa, and Asia, the United States remained officially neutral. President Franklin Roosevelt's advisers jockeyed for position around him, some urging a more aggressive posture toward fascism than others. Vice President Wallace, an acquaintance and admirer of Veblen and a Veblen scholar, urged Roosevelt to familiarize himself with *Imperial Germany* and *The Nature of Peace*. On 30 March 1940 Wallace wrote these words to Roosevelt:

> Sometime ago Isador Lubin, who, as you know, is one of Madame Secretary's [Frances Perkins] right hand men, requested me to write for an economic journal a review of Thorstein Veblen's "Imperial Germany," a book which I read at that time but which I re-read recently. While most of this book was written before the great war broke out in 1914, Veblen's understanding of the German institutions was such that he foresaw in essence almost all of that which has taken place between 1915 and 1940. Those who think that getting rid of Hitler will clear up the situation simply don't know what they are talking about.
>
> I would not ask you on your vacation to go to the labor of reading all of Veblen's "Imperial Germany." You can perhaps get sufficient of the drift by reading my review. However, I would suggest that at your earliest opportunity you get from the Congressional Library Veblen's book "The Nature of Peace" which he completed in late 1916 or early 1917 just before we entered the war. His full appreciation of what it is that produces the bandit character of Germany and Japan, and what is required to offset their destructiveness is more amazing. Mind you, he foresaw in 1917 that at the next turn of the wheel Germany and Japan were almost certain to be working together.

10. On 1 April 1940 Wallace again urged Veblen's case on Roosevelt and this time mentioned his efforts to influence the secretary of state, also. I

> forgot to mention to you when sending you my review of Veblen's book "Imperial Germany" that I sent a copy of this review to Secretary [Cordell] Hull. He had it carefully read independently by two of his best men. The suggestions which they made have been incorporated.
>
> The postscript, however, referring to Veblen's book, "The Nature of Peace" has not been passed on by the State Department.
>
> No one can read Veblen's book "The Nature of Peace" without being gravely concerned with what will eventually happen if England and France make a premature peace with Germany. Veblen, writing in late 1916 and early 1917 before we entered the World War, feared what ultimately came to pass, He feared that premature peace would be made with Germany and that eventually she would again break the peace.

This correspondence is in P.S.F. File, Box 73, Franklin D. Roosevelt Collection, F.D.R. Memorial Library, Hyde Park, New York.

11. Ernest W. Dewey, "Thorstein Veblen: Radical Apologist for Conservatism," *American Journal of Economics and Sociology* 18 (January, 1959): 171–80.

12. Alvin S. Johnson, review of *The Instinct of Workmanship*, by Thorstein Veblen, *Political Science Quarterly* 21 (December 1916): 631–33.

13. Veblen might well have responded to these critics with the same words he used to deflate the scientific pretensions of the eminent neoclassicist John Bates Clark:

> What would be the scientific rating of the work of a botanist who should spend his energy in devising ways and means to neutralize the ecological variability of plants, or of a physiologist who conceived it the end of his scientific endeavors to rehabilitate the vermiform appendix of the pineal eye, or to denounce and penalize the imitative coloring of the viceroy butterfly? What scientific interest would attach to the matter if Mr. Loeb, e.g., should devote a few score pages to canvassing the moral responsibilities incurred by him in his parental relation to his parthenogenetically developed sea-urchin eggs? Those phenomena which Mr. Clark characterizes as "positive perversions" may be distasteful and troublesome, perhaps, but "the economic necessity of doing what is legally difficult" is not of the "essentials of theory." (Veblen, "Professor Clark's Economics," in *The Place of Science in Modern Civilization*, 189).

14. B. W. Wells, review of *The Theory of the Leisure Class*, by Thorstein Veblen, *Sewanee Review* 7 (July 1899): 373.

15. See George Gunton, review of "Some Neglected Points in the Theory of Socialism," by Thorstein Veblen, *Social Economist* [Gunton's Magazine] 2 (November, 1891): 61–62.

16. Lewis Mumford, "Thorstein Veblen," *New Republic* 67 (5 August 1931): 315.

17. Hobson, *Veblen*, 220.

18. Ibid.

19. William Dugger, *Corporate Hegemony* (Westport, Conn.: Greenwood Press, 1989), 39.

20. See Harvey Leibenstein, "Bandwagon, Snob, and Veblen Effects in the Theory of Consumer's Demand," *Quarterly Journal of Economics* 64 (May 1950): 183–207; and Robert L. Steiner and Joseph Weiss, "Veblen Revised in the Light of Counter-Snobbery," *Journal of Aesthetics and Art Criticism* 9 (March 1951): 263–68.

ARCHIVES CONSULTED

Rather than list the bibliography in the conventional manner the reader is referred to Rick Tilman et al. *Thorstein Veblen: A Reference Guide* (Boston: G. K. Hall, 1985), which has a comprehensive listing and abstracting of literature concerning Veblen in various languages from 1891 to 1982. Below is a list of archival materials used by the author and their location.

Collection	*Location*
Theodor Adorno	Stadt-Und Universitats Bibliothek, Frankfurt, Federal Republic of Germany
Records of the American Economic Association	Northwestern University Library, Evanston, Illinois
Arts & Science Dean's Papers (1908–1965)	Joint Collection, University of Missouri Western Historical Manuscript Collection, State Historical Society of Missouri Manuscripts, Columbia, Missouri
Wallace Atwood	Clark University, Worcester, Massachusetts
Clarence Ayres	Barker Texas History Archive, University of Texas, Austin, Texas
Franz Boas	American Philosophical Society, Philadelphia, Pennsylvania
Victor Branford	University of Keele, Keele, England
Earnest Dewitt Burton	Regenstein Library, University of Chicago, Chicago, Illinois
John B. Clark	Butler Library, Columbia University, New York City
John M. Clark	Butler Library, Columbia University, New York City
John R. Commons	Wisconsin State Historical Society, Madison, Wisconsin
Morris L. Cooke	Franklin D. Roosevelt Memorial Library, Hyde Park, New York

Winterton C. Curtis	Joint Collection, University of Missouri Western Historical Manuscript Collection, State Historical Society of Missouri Manuscripts, Columbia, Missouri
Paul Douglas	Chicago Historical Society, Chicago, Illinois
Richard Ely	Wisconsin State Historical Society, Madison, Wisconsin
Irving Fisher	Yale University Library, New Haven, Connecticut
Patrick Geddes	National Library of Scotland, Edinburgh, Scotland University of Strathclyde, Glasgow, Scotland
J. C. M. Hanson	Regenstein Library, University of Chicago, Chicago, Illinois
William Rainey Harper	Regenstein Library, University of Chicago, Chicago, Illinois
Albert Ross Hill	Joint Collection, University of Missouri Western Historical Manuscript Collection, State Historical Society of Missouri Manuscripts, Columbia, Missouri
John Hobson	University of Hull, Hull, England University of Reading, Reading, England
Max Horkheimer	Stadt-Und Universitats Bibliothek, Frankfurt, Federal Republic of Germany
"House" Inquiry	National Archives, Washington, D.C.
Manley Ottmer Hudson	Law Library, Harvard University, Cambridge, Massachusetts
B. W. Huebsch	Library of Congress, Washington, D.C.
Charles H. Hull	Cornell University Libraries, Ithaca, New York
David S. Jordan	Stanford University Archives, Cecil H. Green Library, Stanford, California

Frank H. Knight	Regenstein Library, University of Chicago, Chicago, Illinois
Jacques Loeb	Library of Congress, Washington, D.C.
Isador Lubin	Franklin D. Roosevelt Memorial Library, Hyde Park, New York
Macmillan Publishing Co.	New York Public Library, New York City
Herbert Marcuse	Stadt-Und Universitats Bibliothek, Frankfurt, Federal Republic of Germany
Alfred Marshall	Alfred Marshall Library, Cambridge University, England
Guido Marx	Stanford University Archives, Cecil H. Green Library, Stanford, California
George H. Mead	Regenstein Library, University of Chicago, Chicago, Illinois
C. Wright Mills	Barker Texas History Archive, University of Texas, Austin, Texas
Wesley C. Mitchell	Butler Library, Columbia University, New York City
Underhill Moore	Yale University Library, New Haven, Connecticut
C. Lloyd Morgan	University of Bristol Library, Bristol, England
Hubert Newton	Yale University Library, New Haven, Connecticut
Talcott Parsons	Nathan Pusey Library, Harvard University, Cambridge, Massachusetts
Matthew White Paxton	Joint Collection, University of Missouri Western Historical Manuscript Collection, State Historical Society of Missouri Manuscripts, Columbia, Missouri
Selig Perlman	Wisconsin State Historical Society, Madison, Wisconsin

Noah Porter

Yale University Library,
New Haven, Connecticut

Presidential Papers (F.D.R.)

Franklin D. Roosevelt Memorial
Library, Hyde Park, New York

President's Office Papers
(1892–1966)

Joint Collection,
University of Missouri Western
Historical Manuscript Collection,
State Historical Society of Missouri
Manuscripts, Columbia, Missouri

James Harvey Rogers

Yale University Library,
New Haven, Connecticut

E. A. Ross

Wisconsin State Historical Society,
Madison, Wisconsin

Stanford University Archives,
Cecil H. Green Library,
Stanford, California

Albion Small

Regenstein Library,
University of Chicago,
Chicago, Illinois

Pitirim Sorokin

Nathan Pusey Library,
Harvard University,
Cambridge, Massachusetts

W. G. Sumner

Yale University Library,
New Haven, Connecticut

Marion Talbot

Regenstein Library,
University of Chicago,
Chicago, Illinois

Rexford G. Tugwell

Franklin D. Roosevelt Memorial
Library, Hyde Park, New York

Frank Taussig

Nathan Pusey Library,
Harvard University,
Cambridge, Massachusetts

Andrew Veblen

Minnesota State Historical Society,
St. Paul, Minnesota
Norwegian-American Historical
Association Archives,
St. Olaf College,
Northfield, Minnesota

Oswald Veblen

Library of Congress,
Washington, D.C.

Thorstein Veblen

Wisconsin State Historical Society,
  Madison, Wisconsin
Carleton College,
  Northfield, Minnesota

War Labor Policies Board

National Archives, Washington, D.C.

Jacob Warshaw

Joint Collection,
  University of Missouri Western
  Historical Manuscript Collection,
  State Historical Society of Missouri
  Manuscripts, Columbia, Missouri

Raymond L. Weeks

Joint Collection,
  University of Missouri Western
  Historical Manuscript Collection,
  State Historical Society of Missouri
  Manuscripts, Columbia, Missouri

INDEX